...siness and
Marketing Environment
Second edition

...an Palmer
and
Bob Hartley

THE McGRAW-HILL COMPANIES

London · New York · St Louis · San Francisco · Auckland · Bogotá · Caracas
Lisbon · Madrid · Mexico · Milan · Montreal · New Delhi · Panama · Paris
San Juan · São Paulo · Singapore · Sydney · Tokyo · Toronto

Published by
McGRAW-HILL Publishing Company
Shoppenhangers Road, Maidenhead, Berkshire, SL6 2QL, England
Telephone 01628 23432
Facsimile 01628 770224

British Library Cataloguing in Publication Data
Palmer, Adrian (Adrian James)
  The business and marketing environment. – 2nd ed.
  1. Business 2. Marketing
  I. Title II. Hartley, Bob
  658

ISBN 0077092627

Library of Congress Cataloging-in-publication Data
Palmer, Adrian
  The business and marketing environment/Adrian Palmer and Bob Hartley. – 2nd ed.
  p. cm.
  Includes index.
  ISBN 0–07–709262–7 (pbk: alk. paper)
  1. Marketing. 2. Export marketing. 3. Organizational effectiveness.
  4. Market research. I. Hartley, Bob.
  II. Title.
  HF5415.P234 1996
  658.8 – dc20   96–19556
                                                      CIP

McGraw-Hill

A Division of The McGraw-Hill Companies

12345 BP 99876

Typesetting and artwork origination by David Gregson Associates, Beccles, Suffolk
Printed and bound in Great Britain by The Bath Press, Bath

Printed on permanent paper in compliance with ISO Standard 9706

CONTENTS

PREFACE

Marketing describes the processes by which firms seek to meet the needs of customers in a market place, so that customers go away happy and the organization stays in business. As customers become more discerning and competitors emerge from sometimes unlikely sources, the need for marketing has never been greater. Successful market-led organizations are those that have continually monitored their changing business environment and responded appropriately. In this way, the firm in its business environment is similar to any living organism in the natural environment—survival and prosperity comes to those best able to adapt to their environment.

The principles of marketing represent the tools by which firms respond to the needs of their environment. These are introduced briefly in Chapter 1, but most of the remainder of this book is concerned with analysing the organization's operating environment. This environment can be viewed from a number of perspectives, for example, the environment as it affects finance or personnel decisions may be crucial to some. The focus of this book is the marketing environment. All issues are analysed in the context of the question 'what does change mean for the ways in which we can profitably meet our customers' needs?'. The division of the environment into elements labelled economic, social, political, legal and technological is somewhat arbitrary and it must be remembered that only by seeing the linkages between them can a holistic analysis of an organization's marketing environment be made. In addition, marketing is just one function within an organization, and the way in which marketing is able to respond to customers' needs may be constrained by other internal functions such as production and personnel management. With increasing recognition of the importance of marketing as an inter-functional co-ordinator, the crucial nature of these internal relationships is examined.

This book introduces a marketing reality which is often lacking in general analysis of an organization and its environment. It is a recommended text for the Chartered Institute of Marketing's recently introduced Marketing Environment module and has been widely used on HND, undergraduate and MBA programmes. It is particularly appropriate for students who need to know about the context of marketing without necessarily being familiar with the techniques associated with the discipline.

Finally, this second edition has responded to changes in the marketing environment with strengthened coverage of topics of contemporary concern. A new chapter is devoted to socially responsible marketing at a time when the responsibilities of business organizations to their 'stakeholders' are being increasingly asserted by society. In the analysis of the economic environment, more attention is given to the problem of spotting turning points in the business cycle and the implications of 'rational expectations theory' which holds that firms learn to be sceptical about government management of the economy. Finally, the analysis of relationships between firms in an organization's business environment is addressed with extended coverage of what has come to be known as 'relationship marketing'.

Adrian Palmer
Bob Hartley

AUTHORS' PROFILES

Adrian Palmer is Principal Lecturer in Marketing at Leicester Business School, De Montfort University.

Bob Hartley is Principal Lecturer in Marketing at Leicester Business School, De Montfort University.

Specialist contributor to the Legal Environment, **Mary Mulholland** is Senior Lecturer in Law at the School of Law, De Montfort University.

ONE

MARKETING: AN OVERVIEW

OBJECTIVES

After reading this chapter, you should understand:

- The importance of marketing as a fundamental business philosophy in competitive business environments
- The nature of needs, wants and exchanges in market based distribution systems
- The relationship between businesses and their operating environment
- The tools by which marketing management responds to environmental change

1.1   INTRODUCTION

Marketing as a business discipline is becoming all embracing in Western economies, being adopted by large sections of both the private and public sectors. There are many definitions of marketing and two typical definitions are presented here:

> The management process which identifies, anticipates and supplies customer requirements efficiently and profitably (Chartered Institute of Marketing).

> Marketing consists of individual organisational activities that facilitate and expedite satisfying exchange relationships in a dynamic environment through the creation, distribution, promotion and pricing of goods, services and ideas (Dibb, Simkin, Pride and Ferrell, 1994).

Most definitions of marketing revolve around the primacy of customers as part of an exchange process. Customers' needs are seen as the starting point for all marketing activity—marketing managers try to identify these needs and then develop products that will satisfy customers' needs through an exchange process. While customers may drive the activities of a marketing oriented-organization, organizational factors constrain the extent to which it is actually able to cater to identified customer needs. Most private sector organizations operate under some kind of profit-related objectives, and if an adequate level of profits cannot be earned from a particular group of customers, a firm will not normally wish to meet those needs. In general, though, the closer an organization comes to meeting customers' needs, the greater its ability to gain an advantage over its competitors, thereby allowing it to sell a higher volume and/or at a higher price than its competitors. It is consequently also more likely to be able to meet its profit objectives.

Within the public/not-for-profit sectors, financial objectives are often qualified by non-financial social objectives. An organization's desire to meet individual customer's needs must be further constrained by its requirement to meet these wider social objectives. In this way, a public library may set an objective of providing the public with a range of materials that help to develop the knowledge and skills of the population that it serves. Therefore the 'quality press' may be the only newspapers purchased, although customers actually request popular tabloid newspapers. This apparently centrally planned approach is not incompatible with a marketing philosophy—the library may work within its objectives of developing knowledge and skills by seeking to maximize the number of people reading its quality newspapers. Marketing strategies that might be employed to achieve this could include a promotional campaign, convenient hours and a staff with a friendly welcoming attitude.

Marketing management is essentially about marshalling the resources of an organization so that they meet the changing needs of internal and external publics on whom the organization depends. Changes in customers' needs are clearly very important for a market-oriented organization to monitor and respond to if the organization is to survive. If customers' buying behaviour has shifted and the company has not shifted with them, it may end up with no business. However, for most organizations, it is not just customers who are crucial to their continuing success. The availability of finance and labour inputs may be quite critical, and in times of shortage of either, an organization must adapt its production processes if it is to be able to continue meeting customers' needs. In addition, a whole range of internal and external pressures can affect an organization's ability to profitably meet customers' needs, such as changes in legislation or new emerging technologies. In each case, organizations must adapt if they are to survive and prosper.

The greater part of this text looks at the world outside an organization. The sum total of the types of pressures, constraints and opportunities described above is commonly referred to as a firm's marketing environment. By and large, things occurring in this marketing environment are beyond the control of an individual organization. The emphasis of this book is on looking at just what these forces are and how they can affect the marketing activities of an organization. Chapter 2 provides a holistic overview of the complexity of an organization's marketing environment, while subsequent chapters break the environment down into a number of elements for more detailed analysis. The marketing environment comprises many interrelated elements, so it must be remembered that the division of the marketing environment adopted in this book is to some extent arbitrary and linkages between one part of the marketing environment and others must be borne in mind.

The purpose of this initial chapter is to look inwardly at an organization's marketing function by briefly reviewing the methods open to firms to respond to a changing environment. Many substantial texts have been written on the principles of marketing and this brief overview cannot hope to go into such depth on the basic principles. This chapter will review the basic principles within the context of a firm's need to respond to environmental change.

1.2 THE DOMINANT BUSINESS ENVIRONMENT

As the example of the public library above illustrates, it can sometimes be difficult to define the circumstances in which marketing is considered to be either desirable or feasible. This is particularly true in the case of many services provided by the government that are being exposed to increasing levels of competition. Before examining the philosophies and practices of marketing in more detail, it is useful to examine some alternative philosophies by which goods and services have been delivered to consumers, both from the private and the not-for-profit sectors. Despite its increasing importance as a business discipline, marketing is neither universal, nor has it been with us at all times.

Today, the needs of consumers assume primary importance in the provision of most services. However, in some circumstances, organizations have been driven more by a desire to reduce costs than to maximize the benefit received by consumers of their output—organizations providing services on this basis are said to be operating in a production-oriented environment. At other times, the business

AIMS   EMPHASIS

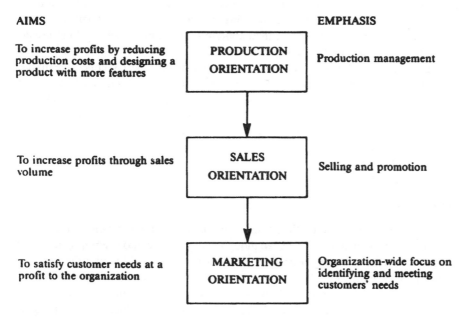

To increase profits by reducing
production costs and designing a   **PRODUCTION**   Production management
product with more features   **ORIENTATION**

To increase profits through sales   **SALES**
volume   **ORIENTATION**   Selling and promotion

To satisfy customer needs at a   **MARKETING**   Organization-wide focus on
profit to the organization   **ORIENTATION**   identifying and meeting
                                                                  customers' needs

Figure 1.1   The development of the dominant business environment

environment has been dominated by the need for aggressive selling of an organization's output. This
has been described as a philosophy of sales orientation (see Figure 1.1).

1.2.1   Production orientation

Marketing as a business discipline has much less significance where goods or services are scarce and
considerable unsatisfied demand exists. If an organization is operating in a stable environment in
which it can sell all that it can produce, why bother spending time and money trying to understand
precisely what benefit a customer seeks from buying a product? If the market is stable, why take time
trying to anticipate future requirements? Furthermore, if a company has significant monopoly power,
it may have little interest in being more efficient in meeting customer requirements. The former state
monopolies of Eastern Europe are frequently cited as examples of organizations that produced what
they imagined consumers wanted. Planning for full utilization of capital equipment was often seen as
more important than ensuring that the equipment was used to provide goods and services that people
actually wanted. Production-oriented firms generally aim for efficiency in production rather than effectiveness in meeting customers' needs.

   In the developed countries of America and Europe, it has been argued that production orientation
was common until the 1920s when a general shortage of goods relative to demand for them, and a lack
of competition, resulted in a sellers' market. In many goods markets, the world depression of the 1920s
and 1930s had the effect of tilting the balance of supply and demand more in favour of buyers, resulting
in sellers having to address the needs of increasingly selective customers more seriously. Services
markets in most countries have tended to retain a production orientation longer than most goods
markets. This has reflected the fact that many key services—such as postal services, telecommunications, electricity, gas and water supply—have been dominated by state or private monopolies which
gave consumers very little—if any—choice of supplier. If the consumer did not like the service they
received from their electricity supplier, they could not switch their business to another electricity

company. Management in these circumstances would have greater freedom to satisfy their own interests rather than those of the consumer, and could increase financial returns to their organization more effectively by keeping production costs down rather than applying effort and possibly taking greater risk through developing new services based on consumers' needs.

Production orientation sometimes returns to industries operating in an otherwise competitive market during periods of shortage. The shortage could come about through supply limitations caused by strikes or bad weather or it could be the result of a sudden increase in demand relative to supply. For example, during a public transport strike, taxi operators may realize that there is a temporary massive excess of demand relative to supply and so may be tempted to lower their standards of service to casual customers (e.g. by allowing longer waiting times and overlooking many of the operational courtesies that would have been provided at other times).

1.2.2   Sales orientation

Faced with an increasingly competitive market, the natural reaction of some organizations has been to shout louder to attract customers to buy its products. No thought had yet gone into examining precisely what benefits customers sought from buying a product. Product policy was driven by the desire to produce those products which the company felt it was good at producing. However, in order to increase throughput, the focal point of the business moved away from the production manager to the sales manager. The company sought to increase effective demand by the use of various sales techniques. Advertising, sales promotion and personal selling were increasingly used to emphasize product differentiation and branding.

A sales orientation was a move away from a strict product orientation, but it still did not focus on satisfying customer needs. Little effort was made to research customer needs and devise new offerings which were customer led rather than production led.

A sales orientation has been evident in a number of business sectors. Supermarkets have often grown by heavy advertising of their competitive price advantage, supported by aggressive sales promotion techniques within their stores. There are signs that this sales-led approach is now being replaced in the UK by a greater analysis of the diverse needs that customers seek to satisfy in a supermarket visit, such as the range of goods available, the atmosphere of the store, speed of check-outs, quality of after-sales service, etc.

If a company had accurately identified consumers' needs and provided a product offering that satisfied these needs, then consumers should want to buy the product, rather than the company having to rely on intensive sales techniques. In the words of Peter Drucker:

> The aim of marketing is to make selling superfluous. The aim of marketing is to know and understand the customer so well that the product or service fits him and sells itself. Ideally, marketing should result in a customer who is ready to buy. All that should be needed is to make the product or service available ... (Drucker, 1973).

1.2.3   Marketing orientation

Marketing orientation as the dominant business discipline came about as increasingly competitive markets turned to favour buyers. It was no longer good enough for a company to simply produce what it was good at or to sell its products more aggressively than its competitors.

Some of the elements of marketing orientation can be traced far back to ancient Greece, the Phoenicians and the Venetian traders. In modern times, a marketing orientation became important in the relatively affluent countries, among products where competition between suppliers had emerged most strongly. It became an important discipline in the United States from the 1950s and has since become dominant around the world. In a marketing-oriented business environment, an organization will only survive in the long term if it ascertains the needs of clearly defined groups in society and produces goods and services that satisfy their requirements. The emphasis is put on the customer wanting to buy rather than the producer needing to sell.

Many people have tried to define just what is meant by marketing orientation. Recent work by Narver and Slater (1990) has sought to define and measure the extent of a company's marketing orientation (Figure 1.2). Their analysis identifies three important components:

- *Customer orientation*, meaning that an organization has a sufficient understanding of its target buyers that allows it to create superior value for them. This comes about through increasing the benefits to the buyer in relation to the buyer's costs or by decreasing the buyer's costs in relation to the buyer's benefits. A customer orientation requires that the organization understands value to the customer not only as it is today, but also as it will evolve over time.
- *Competitor orientation*, defined as an organization's understanding of the short-term strengths and weaknesses and long-term capabilities and strategies of current and potential competitors.
- *Interfunctional co-ordination*, referring to the manner in which an organization uses its resources in creating superior value for target customers. Many individuals within an organization have responsibility for creating value, not just marketing staff, and a marketing orientation requires that the organization draws upon and integrates its human and physical resources effectively and adapts them to meet customers' needs.

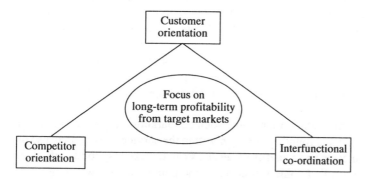

Figure 1.2   Elements of a firm's marketing orientation
Source: based on J. C. Narver and S. F. Slater (1990) 'The Effect of a Market Orientation on Business Profitability', *Journal of Marketing*, October, pp. 20–35.

Marketing orientation is used to describe both the basic philosophy of an organization as well as the techniques that it uses. As a *business philosophy*, marketing puts the customer at the centre of all the organization's considerations. Basic values such as the requirement to understand and respond to customer needs and the necessity to constantly search for new market opportunities are instilled in all members of a truly marketing oriented organization. For a fast food retailer, the training of serving staff would emphasize those items—such as the standard of dress and speed of service—which research had found to be particularly valued by existing and potential customers. The personnel manager would have a selection policy that sought to recruit staff who could fulfil the needs of customers rather than simply minimizing the wage bill. The accountant would investigate the effects on customers before deciding to save money by cutting stock-holding levels, thereby possibly reducing customer choice. It is not sufficient for an organization to merely appoint a marketing manager or set up a marketing department—viewed as a philosophy, marketing is an attitude that pervades the whole organization.

A marketing orientation is associated with a range of *techniques*. As an example, market research is a technique for finding out about customers' needs and advertising is a technique to communicate the service offered to potential customers. However, these techniques lose much of their value if they are conducted by an organization that has not fully embraced the philosophy of marketing. The techniques of marketing also include—among other things—pricing, the design of channels of distribution and new product development. Within the services sector, it is now widely accepted that the motivation and control of front-line personnel are important issues to be considered by marketing managers.

1.2.4 Towards societal marketing orientation?

The idea that the overriding purpose of marketing is to satisfy individuals' needs profitably is increasingly being challenged. Many have argued that when a consumer buys a product, he or she is today inclined to think not just of the benefit that it will bring to him or her directly, but also the benefit that it will bring to society more widely. Societal considerations can be manifested in two important ways—in the evaluation of an individual product's acceptability to society at large and in terms of the overall societal credentials of the supplier. Initial interest in societal marketing concepts has focused on the manufactured goods sector, with environmentalism emerging as a major factor affecting consumer purchases during the 1980s. Much of the promotion of environmentally friendly aerosols, timber products and packaging has been dismissed by many as excessively hyped and showing a concern by their manufacturers, not so much for the environment but a unique positioning strategy which will increase product awareness. However, a significant segment of the market for many products has expressed a need to buy products that they believe benefit people other than themselves. Similarly, many consumers have been selective in who they make their purchases from, buying not from the organization that is best able to satisfy their own narrowly defined personal needs but from one that does more for society in general. For example, preference may be given to products of an organization that supports environmental or child welfare charities, or refuses to purchase supplies from countries with oppressive governments.

As with the development of a general marketing orientation, societal marketing ideas first achieved prominence in the goods sector but have since found application within the services sector. Because of the intangible nature of services, social costs and benefits of services can be less easy to identify than for goods. Nevertheless, there is evidence that some segments of the population are widening their evaluatory criteria to include the benefits that they bring to society (or the social cost that they avoid). Within the financial services sector, there is now a wide range of fund management services available to investors who are concerned about the ethics of their investments. Within the travel and tourism sector, it is now recognized that intensive tourism development can create significant environmental problems, for example the threat to the breeding habits of the Loggerhead turtle on the Greek island of Zakynthos which has resulted from the intensive development of beaches for recreational purposes. Some purchasers of package holidays—admittedly a small niche group at the moment—choose their vacation destination on the basis of tourism's environmental impact at a resort and choose their service provider—the tour operator—on the basis of their policies towards environmentally benign development of resorts.

WE'RE NOT DELTA—BUT WE'RE TRYING TO FLY!

Amidst the chaos of the former Soviet Union, the Chief Executive of the Russian airline Aeroflot proclaimed that his mission was to make his airline as good as America's Delta Airlines. That's quite an easy thing to say, but poses such an enormous challenge for an airline that is only just coming to terms with marketing. Delta has grown steadily from its 1920s origins as a small crop-spraying company to be the USA's number 3 airline and a member of an alliance of quality airlines which includes Britain's Virgin Airlines and Swissair. By all accounts, Delta is popular with its customers and it has to be, for most of its routes are operated in competition with other airlines. Aeroflot, by contrast, has been associated with everything that is anathema to the management of Delta. Travel on Aeroflot has been so dire that the airline, disparagingly referred to as 'Aeroflop', has often been described as 'the world's worst airline'.

The contrast between Delta and Aeroflot can be explained in terms of the extent to which the two airlines have adopted a marketing orientation in response to the challenges of their environments. Delta has had to fully embrace the principles and practices of marketing because, if it didn't, competitors who did would soon win over customers. Aeroflot, on the other hand, has had little need for marketing. It operated in a centrally planned economy where consumer sovereignty had little meaning. If a passenger wanted to fly somewhere, they usually had no choice but to fly with Aeroflot. Aeroflot's managers were not really concerned with attracting more passengers or making life better for their existing passengers—they saw themselves just like any other government bureaucrat who was charged with implementing a centrally planned economic programme. So long as they met very loosely defined targets, they were OK. The targets themselves weren't marketing targets at all but operational targets referring to the number of flights operated or the fuel consumption of aircraft; there was little concern for whether, for example, the flights were going to the right places at the right times or with the right level of facilities before, during and after the flight.

In a communist centrally planned economy, it was not surprising to find Aeroflot adopting a production orientation to its business. Operational considerations came first, customers came second. Stories abound about what this actually meant for passengers. Planes were known to leave late because members of the crew were drunk, baggage was routinely stolen by ground staff and ticketing and reservations systems were corrupt and inefficient. It was commonplace for passengers to bribe flight attendants to be allowed on an aircraft, even though all seats were full. As for in-flight

services, there weren't any, unless warm water in plastic cups was counted.

The breakup of the former Soviet Union and the rapid disintegration of the centrally planned economy propelled Aeroflot into a new era in which marketing took on significance for the first time. The spur to marketing was the withdrawal of the heavy subsidies that the airline received from the government—the airline now had to earn all of its income from fares paid by passengers. Those passengers were able to exercise increasing choice as the domestic civil aviation market was opened to competition for the first time.

The first thing the new management did was to repaint its fleet of aircraft with a new name—Aeroflot Russian International Airlines. That was a skin deep change—to achieve a true marketing orientation, the airline had to embark on a much more fundamental change. Part of that fundamental change was to impress upon staff that passengers were important people whose needs had to be satisfied, rather than being brushed aside as nuisances. Staff had to be made aware that over 70 new regional airlines had appeared on the scene, many of them competing with Aeroflot for passengers' business. Already one of these carriers—Uzbekistan Air—had acquired modern Western-built aircraft and put its crews through a customer care programme which even Delta might have been proud of. The management structure also had to change from a monolithic, authoritarian structure to one that was able to integrate operational and marketing functions, in order to allow new opportunities to be profitably exploited.

Despite the enormity of the airline's task, some changes have already been put in place. The aircraft fleet is being modernized, including the lease of five European Airbuses. This should go some way to allay potential customers' fears over the safety record of Aeroflot's primitive Tupolev and Illuyshin aircraft, many of which will be scrapped. Locally prepared in-flight meals have been replaced with Western made products. Flight attendants have been attending politeness seminars, often run in conjunction with Western consultants. A number of key executives have been enrolled on Western-run marketing and management courses. Fares are now determined with due regard to market considerations, rather than being set according to a central plan. Marketing research is now taken very seriously to monitor customers' reactions to the airlines service levels. In short, 'passengers' have become 'customers' whose business can no longer be taken for granted.

Is Delta worried by the regeneration of Aeroflot? At the moment, there is very little direct competition between the two airlines, but, over the longer term, Aeroflot has expressed its desire to become a global airline. It has already signed an agreement with British Airways which will help it to expand beyond its Russian base. Global success would have seemed preposterous to an observer of Delta back in 1924. However, by putting customers first and adopting the principles and practices of marketing, Delta has achieved its current enviable position. With the same attitude and determination, Aeroflot could just do the same.

QUESTIONS

1. What do you consider to be Aeroflot's principal problems in its attempts to introduce a marketing orientation to its business?
2. Discuss how airlines have segmented the air travel market. Compare the marketing efforts of Delta Airlines and a low-cost charter airline operator in reaching these different segments.
3. How should Aeroflot go about analysing the needs of its potential customers? How could Aeroflot make effective use of market segmentation and other marketing techniques in the light of increasing competition in the Russian air travel market?

1.3   KEY MARKETING CONCEPTS

Marketing activity in any organization has no beginning or end—marketing-oriented organizations continually monitor their operating environments and respond by adapting their output to meet changing needs. Some of the key elements of the marketing process are presented here. These will be returned to in more detail in later chapters.

1.3.1   Needs

The starting point for all marketing activity is the complex set of needs that consumers seek to satisfy. We no longer live in a society in which the main motivation of individuals is to satisfy the basic needs for food and drink. Maslow (1943) recognized that once individuals have satisfied these basic physiological needs, they may seek to satisfy social needs (e.g. the need to have fruitful interaction with peers). More complex still, Western cultures see increasing numbers of people seeking to satisfy essentially internal needs for self-fulfilment. Goods and services therefore satisfy increasingly complex needs. Food is no longer seen as a basic necessity to be purchased and cooked for self-consumption. With growing prosperity, people have sought to satisfy social needs by eating out with friends or family. With further prosperity still, the need to simply eat out with friends becomes satisfied and a higher order need emerges to experience different types of meals. Thus the great growth in eating out which occurred during the 1970s and 1980s has been followed by a growing diversity of restaurants which cater to peoples' need for variety and curiosity—hence the emergence in many towns of restaurant styles as diverse as Spanish, Japanese, Malaysian and Australian. With the fulfilment of basic needs, consumers develop higher expectations of services. Figure 1.3 shows a hypothetical application to the drinks market, indicating how we might understand the emergence of specialized, higher value drinks as a reflection of the changing needs of members of a society.

Maslow's hierarchy of needs is no more than a conceptual model—it is difficult to measure the nature of the needs motivating an individual and even more difficult when the motivations of societies as a whole are being analysed. Nevertheless, the marketer must recognize that consumers in Western countries are likely to be seeking to satisfy a much wider range of needs than those in a developing country.

Figure 1.3   Maslow hierarchy of needs—an application to the drinks sector

Need refers to something which is deep rooted in an individual's personality. How the individual seeks to satisfy a need will be conditioned by the society of which they are a member. Thus the need for team-based competitive physical exercise may express itself in the United States in a desire to play basketball, whereas in Britain it is more likely to be met by playing football. The latter are referred to as expressed *wants* rather than needs. Wants are culturally conditioned by the society in which an individual lives. Wants subsequently become effective demand for a product where there is both a willingness and an ability to pay for the product (see Figure 1.4).

While the above analysis reflects the needs likely to be felt by private buyers of services, it must not be forgotten that commercial buyers of services also have complex needs that they seek to satisfy. Greater complexity occurs where the economic needs of the organization may not be entirely the same as the personal needs of individuals within the organization.

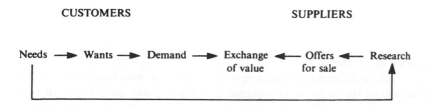

Figure 1.4   Needs, wants, demand and exchange

1.3.2 Exchange

Goods and services can be acquired in a number of ways. One primitive way is by hunting for food or, for some people in some societies, by begging. In socialist economies—and for many public services in Western economies—goods and services are acquired as a result of centrally planned decisions. For organizations operating in a marketing environment, goods are acquired—and needs satisfied —on the basis of exchange. Exchange implies that each party gives something of value to the other party. There is a presumption that each party can decide whether or not to enter into an exchange with the other party and can choose between a number of alternative potential partners. Exchange usually takes the form of a product being exchanged for money, although the bartering of goods and services is commonly used in some trading systems. In some cases, the value that potential customers place on a product will be below the cost to an organization of producing it. Therefore, in the case of profit-motivated organizations, no exchange of value would normally take place over the longer term.

There has been debate among marketers as to whether exchange is an essential element of marketing. The restricted view that marketing is based on a series of discrete exchanges has been refined, adapted and extended by many writers to try and incorporate the concept of external benefits which are provided by some producers (usually in the not-for-profit sector) but where it is neither possible nor desirable to charge the recipient for the benefits received. In this sense, it has been argued that the payment of taxes to the government in return for the provision of social services is a form of social marketing exchange, although it is difficult to identify what sovereignty consumers of government services have in determining the manner or source of their delivery (Bagozzi, 1975). Others have sought to move the defining characteristic of marketing away from the concept of exchange to one of matching (Alderson, 1982). More recently, marketers have sought to move analysis of exchange transactions away from a series of discrete exchanges towards ongoing relationships (see Chapter 2).

1.3.3 Value

In an exchange between an organization and its customers, one party generally expects to receive something that they value from the other party, in return for which they give something that the other party values. For the supplier, value may be represented by payment received or, in the case of some not-for-profit services, more qualitative factors such as the 'A' level grades of incoming students to a university. For customers, value is represented by the ratio of perceived benefits to price paid. Customers will evaluate benefits according to the extent to which a product allows their needs to be satisfied. Customers also evaluate how well the product benefits add to their own well-being as compared to the benefits provided by competitors' offerings.

The value that consumers place on an offer might be quite different from the value perceived by the producer. Business organizations succeed by adding value at a faster rate than they add to their own production costs. Value can be added by specifying the service offer in accordance with customers' expectations of its attributes, for example by providing easy access to the service or the reassurance of after-sales service.

1.3.4 Customers

Customers provide payment to an organization in return for the delivery of goods and services and therefore form a focal point for an organization's marketing activity. The customer is generally understood to be the person who makes the decision to purchase a product and/or pays for it. In fact, products are often bought by one person for consumption by another; therefore the customer and consumer need not be the same person. For example, colleges must not only market themselves to prospective students but also to their parents, career counsellors and employers. In these circumstances it can indeed be difficult to identify who an organization's marketing effort should be focused upon. Society as a whole benefits from the consumption of many public services, and not just the immediate customer. In the case of education, society as a whole can be regarded as the customer, because we all benefit from having a more highly trained and literate work-force.

Suppliers of services are often put in a position of trust in relation to their customers, and this is reflected in the titles often used to describe them. The term 'patient' implies a caring relationship, 'passenger' implies an ongoing responsibility for the safety of the customer and 'client' implies that the relationship is governed by a code of ethics (formal or informal).

1.3.5 Markets

The term 'market' has traditionally referred to a place where buyers and sellers gather to exchange goods and services. Economists refined this definition to include the abstract concept of the interaction of buyers and sellers, so that we can talk about the insurance market as referring to the aggregate level of transactions between all buyers and sellers of insurance, regardless of the existence of a formal market-place. For marketers, the term 'market' is more commonly confined to describing characteristics of consumers rather than producers. The hotel market is defined in terms of those people who have the need and want for hotel accommodation and have the willingness and ability to pay for it.

1.4 SEGMENTATION, TARGETING AND POSITIONING

Different customers within a market have different needs that they seek to satisfy. To be fully marketing oriented, a company would have to adapt its offering to meet the needs of each individual. In fact, very few firms can justify aiming to meet the needs of each specific individual—instead, they target their product at a clearly defined group in society and position their product so that it meets the needs of that group. These subgroups are often referred to as 'segments'.

1.4.1 Segmentation

A segment represents a subsection of a market where people share similar needs, to which a company responds with a product designed to meet these specific needs. People or firms within a market can be segmented according to a number of criteria, including socioeconomic, geodemographic, life-style and behavioural factors (see Table 1.1).

An example of how a market can be broken down into segments is shown in Figure 1.5, where a three-dimensional criteria for segmenting a market in terms of gender, income level and environmental awareness results in 27 different segments, only some of which are likely to be of interest to an organization.

A target market is the segment towards which a business directs its strategies. The development of segmentation and target marketing reflects the movement away from production orientation towards marketing orientation. When the supply of goods and services is scarce relative to supply, organizations may seek to minimize production costs by producing one homogeneous product that satisfies the needs of the whole population. In the early days of mass production of cars, the emphasis was on keeping costs down through economies of scale. Production capacity was initially limited and people were only too happy to buy a uniform black car, something which until recent times would have been no more than a dream for most people. Over time, increasing affluence has increased customers' expectations. Affluent customers are no longer satisfied with a basic car, but instead are able to demand one that satisfies an increasingly wide range of needs—not just for transport, but for security, comfort and status associations. Furthermore, society has become much

Table 1.1 Bases for segmenting consumer markets

Bases for segmentation	Comments
Age	Widely used (e.g. holidays—Sandals and Saga)
Gender	Many obvious examples such as clothing—often also used more subtly as a basis for segmentation (e.g. cars, alcoholic drinks)
Household structure	Size and structure of a household (e.g. economy size packages aimed at the young couple with a family; convenience meals for single adult households)
Socio-economic groups	A widely used basis which takes account of a person's occupation, arguably an important influence on spending power and consumption pattern (see Chapter 8)
Geodemographic	Where a person lives can be correlated with their spending patterns; e.g. postcodes are used to define ACORN classifications. Each classification represents a particular life-style
Education	Very important for newspapers (e.g. *Sun* versus *Guardian*)
Benefits sought	Different segments can buy the same product but seek different benefits (e.g. fashion as against time-keeping as a primary benefit from watch buying)
Rate of usage	Frequent users of a product such as rail customers will require a different marketing programme compared to non-users—reliability and price discounts against the need for timetable and fare information
Loyalty status	Groups that remain loyal to one specific brand as against those who are prepared to switch brands

more fragmented—the 'average' consumer has become much more of a myth, as incomes, attitudes and life-styles have diverged.

This fragmentation can be related to changes in the basic levels of need which are being satisfied at different stages of a society's development. A society that is surviving at the most basic level of existence will be in a position to demand no more than basic commodities which satisfy the need for food and shelter. As these basic needs are satisfied, individuals seek to satisfy higher order needs (Section 1.3.1).

Alongside the greater fragmentation of society, technology is increasingly allowing specially tailored products to be produced for ever smaller segments. Initially, Henry Ford did not have the technology to offer anything more than one basic model of car in one colour—black. To have produced variations on the basic model would have meant stopping the production line and expensive re-tooling. Today, computer-controlled production methods allow Ford to produce many variants of the same

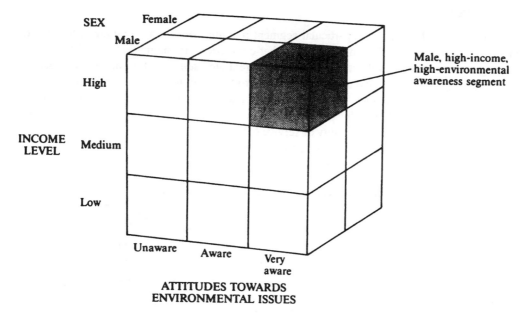

Figure 1.5   Hypothetical segmentation of a population by income, sex and attitudes towards environmental issues

basic model. Therefore the 'Popular' version of the Ford Escort is aimed at the budget-conscious company buyer or the household seeking a cheap run-around. The 'XR3' model is aimed at the needs of a younger, more affluent segment which seeks excitement and status from a car. The 'Ghia' is a more refined car aimed at the needs of the affluent, elderly male segment. Some short-run models are aimed at quite specific segments—the 'Cosmopolitan' was aimed at the needs of career-minded women, for example. In addition to these basic model types, Ford is able to offer a range of engine sizes and colours to meet the needs of very small segments.

1.4.2   Selection of target market

Defining segments of the market is only a preliminary to deciding which specific segments to aim to satisfy. Large companies with adequate resources may choose to address a large number of segments—for example Ford provides a number of variants of each car to satisfy a large number of different segments. Smaller companies may choose to target only one or two segments at a time—Aston Martin and Morgan are examples of companies that offer a much more limited product range to a small number of segments.

The choice of a target segment will involve the company looking inwardly at its strengths and weaknesses and outwardly at the opportunities and threats in its environment. For each segment, the company will examine whether it is growing or declining. This in turn may involve having to read the demographic environment (to predict what will happen to the size of that particular age group), the economic environment (will this group be getting richer or poorer than the average?) or possibly the political environment (will government actions affect this group with legislation?).

This book addresses the question of how a company can analyse an increasingly turbulent business environment in order to select the groups of customers it should aim to serve and how it should adapt the products it offers to meet their changing needs.

1.4.3 Positioning

A company can address the needs of a particular segment in a number of ways that are acceptable to that segment. The company could simply copy the other competitors in the market by imitating their marketing programmes. Alternatively, it could seek to differentiate itself from the competition slightly. A company producing breakfast cereal may try to give its product a slightly different flavour and build up a 'fun' image which may position it away from other cereals focusing on value for money. British supermarkets are typically evaluated by potential customers by two principal sets of criteria—the perceived price levels charged and the quality of service offered in terms of range of goods, quality of merchandise, opening hours, store environment, etc. The relative positions of some of the main UK competitors are plotted schematically in Figure 1.6.

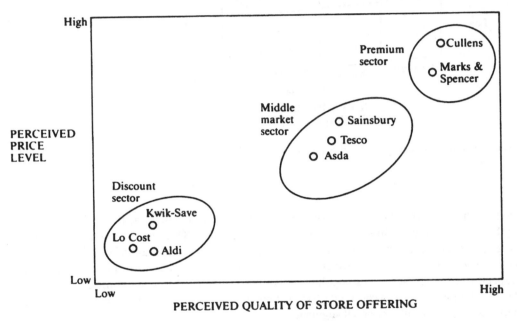

Figure 1.6   A hypothetical product positioning map for UK supermarkets

Product positioning in its fullest sense involves a number of tools that an organization uses to address its market and to differentiate its products from those of its competitors. These tools are known as the marketing mix.

1.5   THE MARKETING MIX

Marketing managers need tools that they can use to configure the goods and services they produce so that they continue to meet customers' changing needs. These tools have often been described as the marketing mix. The marketing mix is not a theory of management that has been derived from scientific analysis, but a conceptual framework that highlights the principal decisions marketing managers must make in tailoring their output to customers' needs. The tools can be used both to develop long-term strategies and short-term tactical programmes.

A marketing manager can be seen as somebody who mixes a set of ingredients to achieve a desired outcome in much the same way as a cook mixes ingredients for a cake. At the end of the day, two cooks can meet a common objective of baking an edible cake, but use very different sets of ingredients to achieve their objective. Marketing managers can similarly be seen as mixers of a number of ingredients which may differ in content but achieve similar objectives. Just as the nation's changing tastes result in bakers producing new types of cake, so too the changing marketing environment results in marketing managers producing new goods and services to offer to their markets. The mixing of ingredients in both cases is a combination of a science—learning by a logical process from what has proved effective in the past—and an art form, in that both the cook and marketing manager frequently encounter situations where there is no direct experience to draw upon and a creative decision must be made.

The concept of the marketing mix was given prominence by Borden, who described the marketing executive as

> ... a mixer of ingredients, one who is constantly engaged in fashioning creatively a mix of marketing procedures and policies in his efforts to produce a profitable enterprise (Borden, 1965).

Identifying the ingredients of the marketing mix has led to some debate. Borden initially identified 12 elements of the marketing mix of manufacturers, although these were later simplified by a number of authors. The framework that has endured reduced the marketing mix to four elements—the familiar four 'Ps' of Product, Price, Promotion and Place. Each of these elements would in turn have its own mix of ingredients. Thus the promotion element involves the mixing of various combinations of advertising, sales promotion, personal selling and public relations (Figure 1.7).

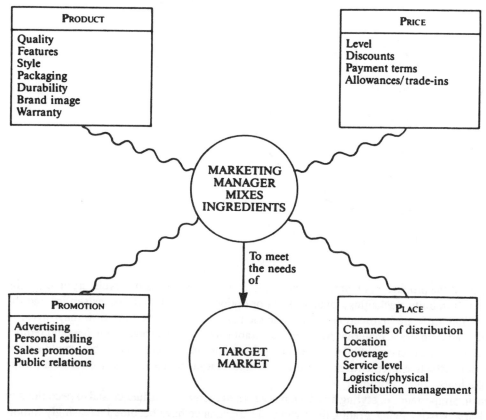

Figure 1.7 The marketing mix

1.5.1 Products

Products are the means by which organizations seek to satisfy consumers' needs. A product in this sense is anything that an organization offers to potential customers that might satisfy a need, whether it be tangible or intangible. After initial hesitation, most marketing managers are now happy to talk about an intangible service as a product.

A manufactured product can be viewed at a number of levels. At the most basic level, the product may comprise a plain generic item, such as a radio. However, customers would normally expect to buy more than this basic offering—they would, for instance, expect it to be made locally available and to have a suitable after-sales service. The product offering is added to by the inclusion of local delivery and a guarantee of performance. At a higher level still, marketers talk about a product being augmented with specific brand attributes. Although technically very similar and equally available, the image of a Sony radio may be perceived as being quite different to that of a Phillips radio—image has become an integral part of the total product offering (Figure 1.8).

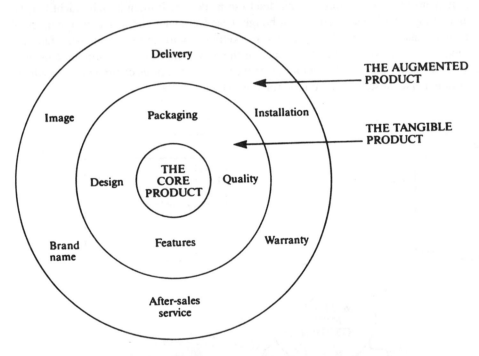

Figure 1.8 The total product offering

The elements of the product mix that the marketer can control include quality levels, styling, special design features, durability, packaging, range of sizes or options, warranty, after-sales service and the brand image. Trade-offs are involved between these elements. For example, one firm may invest in quality control and high-grade materials to provide a durable, top-quality product which would require a low level of after-sales service, while another company might offer lower quality but would ensure that a much more effective after-sales service did not make their customers any worse off than if they had bought the higher quality product.

The increasing importance of styling and design is a sign of increasing affluence and expectations of consumers. For a person buying a radio, the styling and appearance have become increasingly important compared to the quality of sound reproduction—people look increasingly for a design that suits their life-style. Similarly, the retail scene in most Western countries underwent considerable change during the 1980s, with stores spending large amounts of money on refurbishment programmes. With increasing wealth, shopping became an area where consumers were prepared to pay more in return for enjoying a more pleasant environment in which to buy goods.

Brands are used by companies to help differentiate their product from those of their competitors. A brand is a name, term, symbol or combination of these which is intended to differentiate the goods of one seller from all other sellers. Having established a product with unique attributes and maintained consistent quality standards, a product acquires a 'brand equity', representing the difference between what a buyer would be prepared to pay for an unbranded product and a basically similar branded product.

With increased wealth, consumers have looked increasingly to products that carry a brand image, especially for items of conspicuous consumption where the image may be more important than the tangible product itself. Perfumes and training shoes are often selected for their life-style associations rather than the tangible qualities of the product and do much to convey a message about the life-style of the purchaser.

The fragmentation of society referred to earlier means that companies must offer a wider range of product options. For example, a brewery can no longer produce just a couple of bitters and lagers; it has to additionally meet the needs of groups who want high-strength lagers, non-alcoholic lager, low calorie drinks, traditional cask-conditioned 'real ale' and lagers with exciting life-style associations.

A firm's product mix may need to be altered to reflect changing social and cultural values. As an example, cosmetics have traditionally been considered to be a product aimed solely at a female market. However, as with fashion clothing some years earlier, it is now being seen as acceptable for males to buy cosmetics for themselves. Although many of these cosmetics are essentially the same as those that have traditionally been purchased by women, manufacturers have repackaged and reformulated the product to appeal to the new male market.

Sometimes changes in the legal environment require the product mix to be altered. For example, new homes are not typically sold on their thermal efficiency, but a gradual tightening of Building Regulations over time has forced house builders to improve insulation levels.

Within the product mix of firms in general, recent years have seen a growing emphasis on short-life, high-fashion designs. Clothing, home furnishings and electrical equipment are instances where products have been selected to fulfil fluctuating life-style requirements. It can be argued that short-term fashionability represents needs felt by the relatively young segments in society—older segments tend to value durability rather than fashionability. The changing age structure of most west European countries, with increasing proportions of elderly people, may bring about a general shift in emphasis from fashionability to durability as the cultural norm.

1.5.2 Pricing

Of all the elements of the marketing mix, only price brings in revenue to a company—the others result in expenditure. If the selling price of a product is set too high, a company may not achieve its sales volume targets. If it is set too low, volume targets may be achieved, but no profit earned. Setting prices is a difficult part of the marketing mix. In theory, prices are determined by the interaction of market forces (the underlying principles of price determination are considered in Chapter 5).

There are three basic approaches to the practical task of setting prices for products (see Figure 1.9):

1. What it costs to produce
2. What the competition is charging
3. What customers are prepared to pay

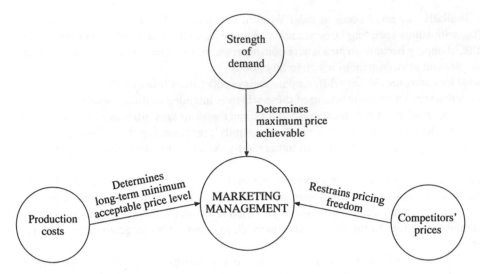

Figure 1.9 The influence of the marketing environment on pricing

Production costs set a minimum limit on the price that a company will charge, at least over the longer term. In fact, determining just what a product's costs are can sometimes be quite difficult for multiproduct firms where there are high levels of interdependency between products. A bank, for example, may find it very difficult to calculate the cost of carrying out a foreign currency exchange transaction when the cost of staff and buildings involved are shared between many other types of banking activities.

A further problem of using costs as a basis for pricing is that it can be difficult to predict how much it will actually cost to make a product at some time in the future. Where inputs are bought in turbulent resource markets, companies take a number of measures to hedge themselves against fluctuating costs:

- One solution is for a company to organize itself so that price changes can be made very rapidly in response to cost fluctuations. Oil companies have developed an ability to adjust the forecourt price of petrol at very short notice in response to movements in the cost of oil.
- At other times, companies minimize risk by buying 'future' contracts for materials at a given price.
- Companies may reserve the right to change the price charged to customers on the basis of cost fluctuations (a practice commonly employed by tour operators).

What customers are actually willing to pay sets the maximum price that a company can charge. A profit-maximizing company seeks to discover the maximum price that a particular consumer is prepared to pay for a product. The haggling that takes place in many Arab and Far Eastern markets is part of the process whereby the seller tries to find out the highest price that each potential purchaser is prepared to pay. Haggling of this kind is not typical of a Western approach to business. Instead, companies define a number of segments of the population which represent different groups who respond in different ways to a particular price. A high-income group may be prepared to pay slightly more for a basically similar product than a segment composed of students or the unemployed. The extent to which a company can discriminate its pricing between different segments will depend on a number of factors:

1. The extent to which product differentiation is possible (while commodity products such as milk and salt cannot be easily differentiated, there is much greater scope for differentiation and price discrimination for manufactured goods such as cars and clothing).

2. The extent to which potential customers can be segmented (e.g. railway operators can discriminate between students and other passengers and charge different prices for a basically similar service).
3. The ease or difficulty with which customers buying in a low-price segment can resell to a higher price segment (services provided on a personal basis cannot easily be resold, but major price differences for goods can lead to goods being bought in a low-price market and sold in a high-price one).

Price discrimination often involves charging different amounts for different times of the day, month or year (e.g. off-peak pricing for airlines, telephone companies and railways) and between different points of consumption (hotels usually charge more for hotels located in prime tourism and business locations and less for those located away from main attractions).

The nature of competition facing a firm limits its ability to determine its own selling prices. At one extreme, in a perfectly competitive market, the firm will have to take its prices from the market. A company selling basic commodities such as fruit and vegetables from a market stall will find it very difficult to charge anything other than the going rate. At anything less than the going rate there will be no profit margin left to make it worth their while selling—anything more and they will be unlikely to sell any. In an undifferentiated commodity market, it is very difficult to persuade a customer to pay more than the going rate. The price must be taken from what the competitors are charging or the firm must seek to differentiate its product in some way. The methods by which market equilibrium prices are determined are examined in more detail in Chapter 5.

In some markets where there are relatively few companies, it is common for one of them to become the acknowledged price leader, while others act as price followers. The followers wait for the leader to make a price adjustment and then generally follow to a varying degree in terms of amount and timing. In the United Kingdom new car market, Ford has been acknowledged as the traditional price leader—other car manufacturers wait to see what action Ford takes before adjusting their prices.

In addition to the three factors of costs, strength of demand and competitive pressure, many companies face a fourth environmental influence on their prices—regulation. As nationalized industries throughout the world are privatized, many newly privatized companies have effective monopolies over the services they provide. To prevent the abuse of monopoly power, government regulatory agencies have often been given power to set limits on the prices charged by such companies and to ensure that they do not discriminate unfairly between groups of customers.

Marketing managers use pricing policy to achieve three basic objectives:

1. To get a product accepted by a market
2. To maintain market share against competition
3. To earn profits

As the relative emphasis placed on each of these objectives is likely to change during the life of a product, the price charged is itself likely to change. Relatively undifferentiated new product launches may require a relatively low price at first to tempt people to try the product. Once customers have developed a liking for it, the company will try and increase the selling price in real terms, capitalizing on the brand loyalty that it has built up. New confectionery and magazine launches frequently follow this price pattern. Marketers refer to this as a *saturation* or *penetration* pricing strategy. Alternatively, where a new innovative product is launched, a firm may start with a relatively high price to capitalize on the product's uniqueness and novelty value. As more competitors move into the market, price is gradually reduced to protect market share and allow access to more price sensitive segments of its market. This type of pricing strategy (known as *prestige* pricing or *skimming*) is often used for new high-technology products—fax machines, home computers and video cassette recorders have all followed this pattern.

The pricing of a firm's products will depend on the stage in the life cycle for the market as a whole.

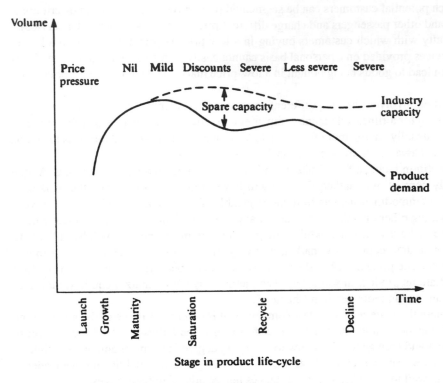

Figure 1.10   Product life cycle and its effects on pricing

If the market is new and growing, there will be relatively less pressure on prices than when the market becomes mature or saturated—the level of competition will impose a strong downward pressure on price levels. Figure 1.10 shows a typical product life cycle and the pressure that is placed on pricing decisions by the extent of competition in the company's business environment.

1.5.3   Promotion

Promotion is a means by which companies communicate the benefits of their products to their target markets. Promotional tools include advertising, personal selling, public relations, sales promotion, sponsorship and—increasingly—direct marketing methods. Just as product ranges need to be kept up to date to reflect changing customer needs, so too promotional methods need to be responsive to environmental change. A number of aspects of a firm's promotional activities can be identified (see Figure 1.11):

1. *Developing the message* As customers' needs change, so the unique selling proposition of a product used in promotion needs to change. Car adverts reflect this trend by increasingly emphasizing safety rather than speed. The language and imagery of the advert also need to change to reflect changing attitudes. A couple of decades ago, many advertisers would have been happy to promote household products in which the housewife was portrayed as a subservient member of the household, but today this would be considered by most to be politically incorrect. Messages that work well in one culture may fail abysmally in another. Imagery that works successfully in one culture may not work in others—cuddly dogs may produce positive association in the United Kingdom but revulsion in others.

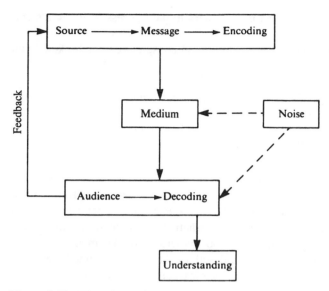

Figure 1.11   The communication process

2. *Developing the medium* Promotion is only effective if it reaches its target audience and has some effect on it. A company seeks to minimize the cost of getting its message through to a specified target market and this target market must be matched with the audience of the available media. Audience habits have been changing and the range of media available to promote products has been growing. In some instances, the choice of advertising medium may be influenced by legislation or voluntary codes of conduct. In the United Kingdom, for example, the Independent Television Commission's Code of Advertising Practice does not allow cigarette advertising on television, forcing the bulk of advertising expenditure for cigarettes into press and poster advertising.

3. *Eliminating 'noise'* Promotion involves sending out a coded message to customers who then decode it. The original intentions of the communicator could become distorted in the minds of the receiver by a misleading message, a poor medium or interference from other sources. An example of this interference is provided by editorial comments in newspapers which might contradict the claims of a company's advertising.

4. *Developing a campaign* A campaign brings together the various elements of a company's promotional effort. The proliferation of media brought about by developments in satellite and cable television, direct mail and telemarketing is leading promotion planners to carefully plan a campaign so that they hit their target audience and do not waste money communicating with people who are not likely sales prospects. The increasing fragmentation of society is matched by increasingly focused media which are able to target specialized market segments. Mounting a promotional campaign demands a number of specialist skills, such as media planning, copywriting and the production of material. Many of these skills are not to be found in most companies, so the task of promotion is often subcontracted to an agency with a clear set of promotional objectives. Many client companies benefit from having access to an independent and creative culture which might be difficult to achieve in their own structure.

1.5.4   Place

Firms usually make their goods and services in places that are convenient for production, but customers usually prefer to buy them where the purchase process is easiest. Place decisions involve determining how easy a company wishes to make it for customers to gain access to its goods and services.

The question of how to get a product from the producer to the final consumer can be broken down into two separate issues:

1. Which intermediaries to use in the process of transferring the product from the manufacturer to the final consumer. This is referred to as the design of 'channels of distribution'.
2. How to physically move and handle the product as it moves from manufacturer to final consumer. This is referred to as 'logistics' or 'physical distribution management'.

Channels of distribution comprise all those people and organizations involved in the process of transferring title to a product from the producer to the final consumer. Sometimes, products will be transferred directly from manufacturer to final consumer—a factory selling specialized kitchen units directly to the public would fit into this category. Alternatively, the manufacturer could sell its output through retailers or, if these are considered too numerous for the manufacturer to handle, it could deal with a wholesaler who in turn would sell to the retailer. Sometimes more than one wholesaler is involved in the process. The relationships between members of a distribution channel (or 'value channel') are undergoing significant changes and these are discussed in Chapter 2.

1.5.5   An extended marketing mix

More recently, the four Ps of the marketing mix have been found to be too limited to explain the decisions marketing managers must make in relation to their marketing environment. Consider the following shortcomings of the traditional four Ps for providing an adequate framework for managing the marketing of services in particular:

- Customers are increasingly differentiating between goods and services on the basis of their quality, yet quality as a marketing management response is not explicitly a heading of the traditional marketing mix.
- Many services organizations rely heavily on the efforts of their employees. Traditionally, the management of employees has not been seen as primarily a marketing function, although it is now being recognized that appropriate recruitment, training, motivation and control of employees can significantly affect marketing success.
- The price element overlooks the fact that many services are provided by the not-for-profit sectors without a price being charged to the final consumer.
- The intangibility of many services results in tangible outcomes being less important in customers' eyes as the *process* of production and the level of reassurance they receive from tangible evidence of the service process.

These weaknesses have resulted in a number of analysts redefining and adding elements to the marketing mix. The expansions by Booms and Bitner (1981) and Christopher, Payne and Ballantyne (1991) provide useful frameworks for an extended marketing mix. In addition to the four traditional elements of the marketing mix, both frameworks add the additional elements of People and Production Processes. In addition, Booms and Bitner talk about Physical Evidence making up a seventh 'P', while the latter adds Customer Service as an additional element.

Decisions on one element of the mix can only be made by reference to other elements of the mix in order to give a sustainable product positioning. The importance attached to each element of the extended marketing mix will vary between products. In a highly automated service such as vending machine dispensing, the people element will be a less important element of the mix than a people-intensive business such as a restaurant.

A brief overview of these extended marketing mix elements is given below.

People   For services in particular, people can be a vital element of the marketing mix. Where production can be separated from consumption—as is the case with most manufactured goods—management can usually take measures to reduce the direct effect of people on the final output as received by customers. Therefore, how a car is made is usually of relatively minor interest to the person who buys it—he or she is not concerned with whether a production worker dresses untidily, uses bad language at work or turns up for work late, so long as there are quality control measures that reject the results of lax behaviour before they reach the customer. However, in service industries, people planning assumes much greater importance where staff have a high level of contact with customers. Marketing effectiveness is likely to be critically affected by the actions of front-line employees who interact with customers. The car worker may be unseen by customers, but a restaurant waiter could make or break a visit to a restaurant.

Process   Services are best defined in terms of their production processes rather than their tangible outcomes. Whereas the process of production is usually of little concern to the consumer of manufactured goods, it is often of critical concern to the consumer of 'high contact' services. Customers of a restaurant are deeply affected by the manner in which staff serve them. For busy customers, the speed at which a restaurant processes its customers may be just as important as the meal itself.

Customer service/quality   The meaning of customer service varies from one organization to another, but can be roughly interpreted as the quality level that a firm offers. Quality can be a very subjective concept and can essentially only be defined in the eyes of customers. A wide body of knowledge now recognizes that quality is associated with customers' expectations prior to a purchase being met by their perceptions after purchase (Parasuraman, Zeithaml and Berry, 1985). Although firms have in general been producing 'better', more reliable products, customers' expectations have often moved on too. If firms' standards of delivery have not kept up with customers' rising expectations, customers may perceive a deterioration in quality standards (Figure 1.12).

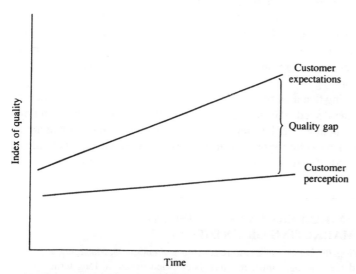

Figure 1.12   The changing 'quality gap'

The growing importance of quality is reflected in many firms' decision to include explicit internal and external quality targets in their marketing plans. These have taken a number of forms, from purely internal targets to performance targets that are stressed in advertising (e.g. parcel companies that *guarantee* next day delivery, failing which they give compensation to customers). There are now a number of widely recognized quality standards that are shared by many firms, such as British Standard BS 5750 (and its international equivalent, ISO 9002), which indicate the consistency of a firm's production processes, if not necessarily their output. Public sector services are increasingly adopting quality standards (or having them imposed), in the form of 'Customer Charters' (for example, British Rail and UK hospitals have adopted a 'Passengers' Charter' and 'Patients' Charter' respectively). In the case of public sector customer charters, their existence has given guidance to staff who may previously have had little focus on the needs of the customers they seek to serve. However, critics have pointed out that their main effect is to raise customers' expectations, without any matching increase in resources that would allow those expectations to be met.

Physical evidence   The intangible nature of most services means that potential customers are unable to judge a service before it is consumed, increasing the riskiness inherent in a purchase decision. An important part of marketing mix strategy is therefore to reduce this level of risk by offering tangible evidence about the nature of the service. This evidence can take a number of forms. At its simplest, a brochure can describe and give pictures of important elements of the service product—a vacation brochure gives pictorial evidence of hotels and resorts for this purpose. The appearance of staff can give evidence about the nature of a service—a tidily dressed ticket clerk for an airline gives some evidence that the airline operation as a whole is run with care and attention. Buildings are frequently used to give evidence of service nature. A clean, bright environment used in a service outlet can help reassure potential customers at the point where they make a service purchase decision. For this reason, fast food and photo processing outlets often use red and yellow colour schemes to convey an image of speedy service.

1.5.6   Alternatives to the marketing mix

The definition of the elements of the marketing mix is not scientific—it is largely intuitive and semantic. For some years, the four 'Ps' have been considered to be the framework within which marketing management makes decisions in response to the needs of its environment. As the discussion above indicates, these have been found to be too limited to explain the nature of the decisions that marketing managers must make—hence the use of additional 'Ps'. More fundamentally, dividing management responses into apparently discrete areas may lead to the interaction between elements being overlooked. Promotion mix decisions, for example, cannot be considered in isolation from decisions about product characteristics or pricing.

   A growing body of opinion is suggesting that a more holistic approach should be taken by marketing managers in responding to their customers' needs (Gronroos, 1994). This view sees the marketing mix as a production-led approach to marketing in which the agenda for action is set by the seller and not by the customer. An alternative relationship marketing approach starts by asking what customers need and developing a response that integrates all the functions of a business in a manner that evolves in response to customers' changing needs.

VICTORIA AND ALBERT MUSEUM DISPLAYS
NEW MARKETING ORIENTATION

Museums in Britain have traditionally been seen as guardians of culture and the role of their curator as one who preserves the history of a culture for future generations. Managing a museum has been viewed as a long-term mission founded on educational objectives and the idea of basing exhibitions on short-term popularity with visitors has often been met with resistance from curators.

The days of dull exhibits being displayed in dusty glass cases is rapidly disappearing as public sector museums take on board a much greater marketing orientation, reflecting changes in the museums' environment. Visitors' expectations of a museum have changed with the emergence of a wide range of private sector theme museums offering elaborate displays. The relatively high prices charged by museums such as the Jorvick Viking Centre in York indicated that a significant segment of the population was prepared to pay for a museum offering a higher standard of presentation. At the same time, the political environment has changed with government trying to move as many public services as possible towards a business-like orientation.

Against this background, the Victoria and Albert Museum (V&A) in London appointed its first Marketing Manager in 1988. After considerable research, a marketing plan was developed to achieve the museum's aim of doubling the number of visitors from 500 000 in 1990 to 1 million in 1995 and then on to 5 million by 2000. A strategic plan sought to target specific groups by creating highly visible, highly segmented events which would attract new audiences as well as building repeat audiences. One result of this strategy was the creation of the Tsui Gallery of Chinese Art. Market research carried out by NOP (National Opinion Poll) into visitor expectations had revealed that visitors were interested in thematic displays rather than the traditional chronological shows. Carrying marketing practices further, the exhibition earned sponsorship of £1.25m from Hong Kong businessman T. T. Sui and was supported by a £30 000 poster campaign and the distribution of leaflets in Chinese restaurants throughout London. By adopting these marketing techniques, the V&A succeeded in attracting a segment of the population that may not otherwise have visited the museum, as well as generating additional revenue that will contribute towards the long-term cost of maintaining existing collections and acquiring new ones of national importance.

The new-found marketing orientation of the Victoria and Albert Museum has found critics among traditionalists who have often taken the view that the museum's scholarly aims had been compromised and lowered by its adoption of a marketing orientation. During the early 1990s, one particular advertising campaign irritated the traditionalists. The strap line described the V&A as 'an ace cafe with a museum attached', reflecting the improved facilities for visitors to the museum. To traditionalists, this was the ultimate sign that scholarly quality had been sacrificed for profit-led business objectives. Reformers pointed out, however, that museums had to keep up with the times in terms of visitor facilities and that additional numbers of visitors—however generated—would give the museum more money with which to pursue its scholarly objectives.

QUESTIONS

1. In a marketing environment, who are the competitors of the Victoria and Albert Museum?
2. Summarize the main problems facing museums seeking to introduce admission charges for the first time.
3. Can the marketing and scholarly objectives of museums such as the Victoria and Albert be reconciled?

REVIEW QUESTIONS

1. Discuss how a car wash business might operate if management embraced a production orientation? a sales orientation? a marketing orientation? a societal marketing orientation?
2. Of what relevance is marketing to the public sector?
3. Of what value is the concept of an expanded marketing mix (as opposed to the traditional four 'Ps')?

4. Why is it important for companies to segment their markets? Should providers of public services (e.g. police forces) segment their markets?
5. Analyse the nature of the needs that may be satisfied by a household mortgage.
6. What is the difference between selling and marketing?

REFERENCES

Alderson, W. (1982) *Marketing Behaviour and Executive Action*, Irwin, Homewood, Illinois.

Bagozzi, R. P. (1975) 'Marketing as Exchange', *Journal of Marketing*, vol. 39 (October), pp. 32–9.

Booms, B. H. and Bitner, M. J. (1981) 'Marketing Strategies and Organisation Structures for Service Firms', in *Marketing of Services*, eds J. Donnelly and W. R. George, American Marketing Association, Chicago, Ill., pp. 51–67.

Borden, N. H. (1965) 'The Concept of the Marketing Mix', in *Science in Marketing*, ed. G. Schwartz, pp. 386–97, John Wiley, New York.

Christopher, M., Payne, A. and Ballantyne, D. (1991) *Relationship Marketing*, Heinemann, London.

Dibb, S.,Simkin, L., Pride, W. M. and Ferrell, O. C. (1994), *Marketing: Concepts and Strategies*, Houghton-Mifflin, London.

Drucker P. F. (1973) *Management: Tasks, Responsibilities and Practices*, Harper & Row, New York.

Gronroos, C. (1994) 'From Marketing Mix to Relationship Marketing', *Management Decision*, vol. 32, no. 1, pp. 4–20.

Maslow, A. (1943) 'A Theory of Human Motivation', *Psychological Review*, vol. 50 (July).

Narver, J. C. and Slater, S. F. (1990) 'The Effect of a Market Orientation on Business Profitability', *Journal of Marketing*, October, pp. 20–35.

Parasuraman, A., Zeithaml, V. A. and Berry, L. (1985) 'A Conceptual Model of Service Quality and Its Implications for Future Research', *Journal of Marketing*, vol. 49 (Fall), pp. 41–50.

FURTHER READING

Collier, David A. (1991) 'New Marketing Mix Stresses Service', *The Journal of Business Strategy*, March/April, pp. 42–5.

Gronroos, C. (1989) 'Defining Marketing: A Market-Oriented Approach', *European Journal of Marketing*, vol. 23, no. 1, pp. 52–60.

Gronroos, C. (1991) 'The Marketing Strategy Continuum: Towards a Marketing Concept for the 1990s', *Management Decision*, vol. 29, no. 1, pp. 7–13.

Gummesson, E. (1991) 'Marketing-Orientation Revisited: The Crucial Role of the Part-Time Marketer', *European Journal of Marketing*, vol. 25, no. 2, pp. 60–75.

Houston, Franklin S. (1986) 'The Marketing Concept: What It Is and What It Is Not', *Journal of Marketing*, vol. 50 (April), pp. 81–7.

Kent, R. A. (1986) 'Faith in the Four Ps: An Alternative', *Journal of Marketing Management*, vol. 2, no. 2, pp. 145–54.

Kohli, A. K. and Jaworski, B. J. (1990) 'Market Orientation: The Construct, Research Propositions and Management Implications', *Journal of Marketing*, vol. 54 (April), pp. 1–18.

Kotler, P. (1994) *Marketing Management: Analysis, Planning, Implementation and Control*, 8th edn, Prentice-Hall, Englewood Cliffs, N.J.

Kotler, P. and Armstrong, G. (1996) *Principles of Marketing*, 7th edn, Prentice-Hall, Englewood Cliffs, N.J.

THE NATURE OF THE MARKETING ENVIRONMENT

OBJECTIVES

After you have read this chapter, you should understand:

- The nature of an organization's marketing environment and the consequences for it of environmental change
- The elements that make up an organization's micro-, macro- and internal environments
- The changing relationships between members of an organization's 'environmental set'
- The concept of a value chain
- The importance attached to the development of ongoing buyer–seller relationships
- The role of information in assisting managers to understand and respond to changes in their marketing environment

2.1 THE MARKETING ENVIRONMENT DEFINED

In the previous chapter, marketing orientation was distinguished from production orientation. One of the key differences between the two is the tendency for production-oriented organizations to focus attention inwardly when planning for the future, whereas marketing-oriented organizations focus their attention outwardly. A marketing orientation requires an organization to monitor its environment and to adjust its offering so that customers' needs are fulfilled. In fulfilling customers' needs, the task of meeting an organization's business objectives is thereby facilitated.

The focus of an outward-looking marketing department's attention is often referred to as its marketing environment (Figure 2.1). An organization's marketing environment can be defined as:

> ... the actors and forces external to the marketing management function of the firm that impinge on the marketing management's ability to develop and maintain successful transactions with its customers (Kotler, 1994).

The external environment comprises all of those forces and events outside the organization that impinge on its activities. Some of these events impinge directly on the firm's activities—these can be described as forming an organization's *microenvironment*. Other events that are beyond the immediate environment nevertheless affect the organization and can be described as the *macroenvironment*.

As well as looking to the outside world, marketing managers must also take account of factors within other functions of their own firm. This is referred to as the *internal marketing environment*.

The microenvironment of an organization includes suppliers and distributors. It may deal directly with some of these, while others exist with whom there is currently no direct contact, but could

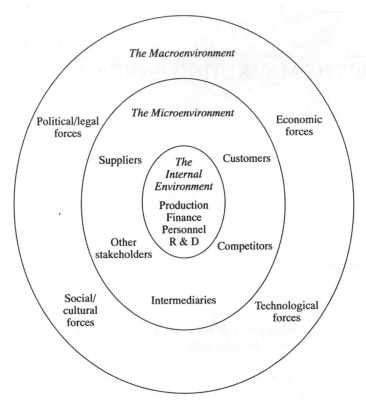

Figure 2.1   The organization's marketing environment

nevertheless influence its policies. Similarly, an organization's competitors could have a direct effect on its market position and form part of its microenvironment.

Beyond this immediate microenvironment is the macroenvironment which comprises a whole set of factors that can indirectly affect an organization's relationship to its markets. The organization may have no direct relationships with legislators as it does with suppliers, yet their actions in passing new legislation may have profound effects on the markets that the organization seeks to serve, as well as affecting its production costs. The macroenvironmental factors cover a wide range of nebulous phenomena. They represent general forces and pressures rather than institutions with which the organization relates.

2.2   THE MICROENVIRONMENT

The microenvironment of an organization can best be understood as comprising all those other organizations and individuals who directly or indirectly affect the activities of the organization. The following key groups can be identified:

1. *Customers* are a crucial part of an organization's microenvironment. In a competitive environment, no customers means no business. An organization should be concerned about the changing requirements of its customers and should keep in touch with these changing needs by using an appropriate information gathering system. In an ideal world, an organization should know its customers so well that it is able to predict what they will require next, rather than wait until it is possibly too late and then follow.

2. *Suppliers* provide an organization with goods and services that are transformed by the organization into value-added products for customers. Very often, suppliers are crucial to an organization's marketing success. This is particularly true where factors of production are in short supply and the main constraint on an organization selling more of its product is the shortage of production resources. For example, following the Kobe earthquake in 1995, supplies of some types of computer chips became scarce, affecting computer assemblers' production schedules and consequently the range and prices of computers sold to the public. For companies operating in highly competitive markets where differentiation between products is minimal, obtaining supplies at the best possible price may be vital in order to be able to pass on cost savings in the form of lower prices charged to customers. Where reliability of delivery to customers is crucial, unreliable suppliers may thwart a manufacturer's marketing efforts.

3. *Intermediaries* often provide a valuable link between an organization and its customers. Large-scale manufacturing firms usually find it difficult to deal with each one of their final customers individually, so they choose instead to sell their products through intermediaries. The advantages of using intermediaries are discussed below. In some business sectors, access to effective intermediaries can be crucial for marketing success. For example, food manufacturers who do not get shelf space in the major supermarkets may find it difficult to achieve large volume sales.

4. *Other stakeholders* form an increasingly important part of an organization's microenvironment. In the case of customers, suppliers and intermediaries, an organization has some form of contractual relationship (or may conceivably have, if it targets new customers, or changes suppliers or intermediaries). However, there is a wide range of other organizations and individuals in a firm's microenvironment which can directly affect its marketing effectiveness. These are sometimes referred to as the 'publics' of an organization and include pressure groups, government agencies and the local community. Society at large has rising expectations of organizations that are increasingly having to act in a socially responsible manner. A factory may, for example, be able to emit lawful amounts of pollution from its factory and doing so may have no direct consequence for the dealings it has with its customers, suppliers or intermediaries. However, the support of the affected publics may be crucial in the future, if, for example, the firm seeks planning permission to extend its plant. The social responsibility of organizations is an increasingly important subject which is considered in Chapter 9.

2.2.1   Relationships between members of an organization's microenvironment

A firm's microenvironment is distinguished from its macroenvironment by being comprised of actual individuals and organizations with whom the firm does business, or at least may potentially do business. The relationship between these 'environmental set' members (see Figure 2.2) is likely to be constantly changing. Change can take the form of shifts in the balance of power between members of the environment (e.g. retailers becoming more dominant relative to manufacturers), the emergence of new groups of potential customers and fringe pressure groups becoming mainstream in response to changes in social attitudes. Understanding the relationship between members of an organization's environmental set is a crucial part of environmental analysis. Later in this chapter, shifts in relationships between buyers and sellers in a value chain will be reviewed. In later chapters, economic, political, social and technological forces will be reviewed in terms of their likely impacts on a firm's relationships with members of its environmental set.

2.3   THE MACROENVIRONMENT

While the microenvironment comprises individuals and organizations with whom a company interacts, the macroenvironment is more nebulous. It comprises general trends and forces that may not

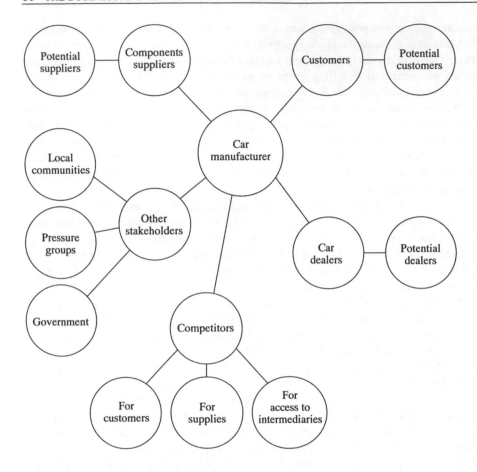

Figure 2.2   The 'environmental set' of a car manufacturer

immediately affect the relationships that a company has with its customers, suppliers and intermediaries, but, sooner or later, macroenvironmental change will alter the nature of these relationships. As an example, change in the population structure of a country does not immediately affect the way in which a company does business with its customers, but, over time, it may affect the numbers of young or elderly people who it is able to do business with.

Most analyses of the macroenvironment divide the environment into a number of areas. The principle headings, which form the basis for chapters of this text, are described below. It must, however, be remembered that the division of the macroenvironment into subject areas does not result in watertight compartments. The macroenvironment is complex and interdependent and these interdependencies will be brought out in later chapters. These are the headings for macroenvironmental analysis which are commonly used:

2.3.1   The Economic environment

Businesses need to keep an eye on indications of a nation's prosperity. There are many indicators of a nation's economic health, of which two of the most common are measures of gross domestic product (GDP) and household disposable income. Many of these indicators tend to follow cyclical patterns related to a general economic cycle of expansion followed by contraction.

Throughout the economic cycle, the consumption of most goods and services tends to increase during the boom period and to decline during recessionary periods. The difficulty in forecasting the level of demand for a firm's products is therefore often quite closely linked to the difficulty of forecasting future economic prosperity. This difficulty is compounded by the problem of understanding the relationship between economic factors and the state of demand—most goods and services are positively related to total available income, but some, such as bus services and insolvency practitioners, are negatively related. Furthermore, while aggregate changes in spending power may indicate a likely increase for goods and services in general, the actual distribution of spending power among the population will influence the pattern of demand for specific products. In addition to measurable economic prosperity, the level of perceived wealth and confidence in the future can be an important determinant of demand for some high-value services.

An analysis of the economic environment will also indicate the level of competitor activity—an oversupply of products in a market sector normally results in a downward pressure on prices and profitability. Competition for resources could also affect the production costs of an organization, which in turn will affect its production possibilities and pricing decisions. Rising unemployment may put downward pressure on wage rates, favouring companies who offer a labour-intensive service.

2.3.2   The political environment

Politicians are instrumental in shaping the general nature of the external environment as well as being responsible for passing legislation that affects specific types of organization. At a national level, government is responsible for the nature of the economic environment (through its monetary and fiscal policy), the distribution of income and wealth between the public sector, the company sector and individuals and also between different groups of individuals. As the legislator, government passes laws that can affect market and production possibilities for individual firms, including the competitive framework within which firms operate.

The political environment includes supranational organizations that can directly or indirectly affect companies. These can be highly specific in their effects on an industry (e.g. the International Civil Aviation Organization is an international quasi-governmental body concerned with setting international standards in civil aviation) or they can be general multilateral agreements between governments (e.g. the General Agreement on Tariffs and Trade affects access to overseas markets for a number of industries).

2.3.3   The social and cultural environment

Attitudes to specific products change through time and at any one time between different groups. As an example, attitudes towards healthy living have changed from representing values held by a small fanatical minority to those that now represent mainstream cultural values. Marketers who monitored this emerging value system have been able to respond with a wide range of goods and services, such as fitness clubs and residential health breaks. The dominant cultural attitude towards the role of women has similarly changed, presenting many new challenges for marketers. The increased acceptability for young mothers to continue working has given rise to a large child and home care service sector. New challenges for marketing are posed by the diverse cultural traditions of ethnic minorities, as seen by the growth of travel agencies catering for families wishing to visit relatives or to go on religious pilgrimages.

2.3.4   The demographic environment

Changes in the size and age structure of the population are critical to many organizations, for predicting both the demand for its products and the availability of personnel required for production.

Analysis of the demographic environment raises a number of important issues. Although the total population of most Western countries is stable, their composition is changing. Most countries are experiencing an increase in the proportion of elderly people. Organizations have monitored this growth and responded with the development of residential homes, cruise holidays and financial portfolio management services aimed at meeting the needs of this growing group. At the other end of the age spectrum, the birth rate of most countries is cyclical. The decline in the birth rate in the United Kingdom in the late 1970s initially had a profound effect on those manufacturing and services companies providing for the very young, such as maternity wards in hospitals and kindergartens. Organizations that monitored the progress of this diminished cohort were prepared for the early 1990s when there were fewer teenagers requiring high schools or wanting to buy music from record shops. Companies who had relied on the early 1980s over the supply of teenage labour to provide a cheap input to their production process would have been prepared for the downturn in numbers by substituting the quantity of staff with quality and by mechanizing many jobs previously performed by this group.

Other aspects of the demographic environment that organizations need to monitor include the changing geographical distribution of the population (between different regions of the country and between urban and rural areas) and the changing composition of households (especially the growing number of single person households).

2.3.5   The technological environment

Marketing managers need to monitor technological developments and to understand their possible impact on four related business areas:

1. Technological development allows new goods and services to be offered to consumers—mobile telecommunications, kar-a-oke bars and multimedia computers for example.
2. New technology can allow existing products to be made more cheaply, thereby lowering their price and widening their markets. In this way, more efficient aircraft have allowed new markets for air travel to develop.
3. Technological development allows for new methods of distributing goods and services. Bank ATM machines allow many banking services to be made available at times and places that were previously not economically possible, while modern technology-based control systems allow home shopping services to be made more widely available than hitherto.
4. New opportunities for companies to communicate with their target customers have emerged. Many financial services organizations have used information technology to develop databases to target potential customers and to maintain a dialogue with established customers.

2.4   VALUE CHAINS

The purpose of organizations is to transform inputs bought from suppliers into outputs sold to customers. In carrying out such a transformation, organizations add value to resources. In fact, the buyer of one firm's output may be another firm who treats the products purchased as inputs to its own production process. It in turn will add value to the resources and sell on its outputs to customers. This process can continue as goods and services pass though several organizations, gaining added value as they change hands. This is the basis of a value chain.

An illustration of the principles of a value chain can be made by considering the value-added transformation processes that occur in the process of making ice cream available to consumers. Table 2.1 shows who may be involved in the value-adding process and the value that is added at each stage.

Table 2.1 A value chain for ice cream

Value chain member	Functions performed
Farmer	Produces a basic commodity product—milk
Milk merchant	Adds value to the milk by arranging for it to be collected from the farm, checked for purity and made available to milk processors
Ice cream manufacturer	By processing the milk and adding other ingredients, turns raw milk into ice cream. Through promotion, creates a brand image
Wholesaler	Buys bulk stocks of ice creams and stores in warehouses close to customers
Retailer	Provides a facility for customers to buy ice cream at a place and a time that is convenient to them, rather than the manufacturer

The value of the raw milk contained in a block of ice cream may be no more than a couple of pennies, but the final product may be sold for one pound. Customers are happy to pay one pound for a few pennies worth of milk because it is transformed into a product that they value and it is made available at a time and place where they want it. In fact, on a hot sunny day at the beach, many buyers would be prepared to pay even more to a vendor who brings cold ice cream to them on the beach. Value—as defined by customers—has been added at each stage of the transformation process.

Who should be in the value chain? The ice cream manufacturer might decide that it can add value at the preceding and subsequent stages better than other people are capable of doing. It may, for example, decide to operate its own farms and produce its own milk, or sell its ice cream direct to the public. The crucial question to be asked is whether the company can add value more cost-effectively than other suppliers and intermediaries. In a value chain, it is only value in the eyes of customers that matters. If high value is attached to having ice cream easily available, then distributing it through a limited number of company-owned shops will not add much value to the product.

The process of expanding a firm's activities through the value chain is often referred to as *vertical integration* where ownership is established. Backward vertical integration occurs where a manufacturer buys back into its suppliers. Forward vertical integration occurs where it buys into its outlets. Many firms expand in both directions.

From a marketing perspective, particular attention needs to be paid to the selection of intermediaries who distribute a firm's output to its final customers. These are referred to as channels of distribution.

2.4.1 Channels of distribution

Channels of distribution comprise all those people and organizations involved in the process of transferring title to a product from the producer to the consumer. These are referred to as intermediaries. Sometimes, products will be transferred directly from producer to final consumer—a factory selling specialized kitchen units directly to the public would fit into this category. Alternatively, the producer could sell its output through retailers or, if these are considered too numerous for the manufacturer to handle, it could deal with a wholesaler who in turn would sell to the retailer. Sometimes more than one wholesaler is involved in the process.

Intermediaries perform a number of functions:

1. They make products locally available to consumers. Instead of customers having to travel to a central point of production, intermediaries assist in the task of making goods and services locally available at a time and a place that customers value.
2. They break down volumes from the very large quantities produced by the manufacturer to the small volumes required by the final customer.
3. In breaking down volume, intermediaries assist in the task of transferring ownership of goods and services. If the chocolate manufacturer Cadburys had to deal with each buyer of its products, its administrative and financial systems would be overwhelmed. It is much easier for it to deal with a small number of wholesalers who in turn deal with a larger number of retailers who sell the chocolate to millions of final customers.
4. Intermediaries provide valuable sales support at a local level, especially at the point of purchase. While manufacturers can advertise their products to the public nationally through the media, intermediaries can supplement this with valuable local promotional support.
5. Where a manufacturer is seeking to enter a market with which it is unfamiliar (e.g. a new overseas market), an intermediary can provide valuable insights into the proposed market.
6. Sometimes, intermediaries process goods and services as well as making them available to customers. Timber merchants, for example, cut timber to size for customers and car distributors carry out pre-delivery inspection of cars.
7. Customers often prefer to buy goods and services from intermediaries who offer a choice of competing products. Sometimes, customers may show greater loyalty to the intermediary than to the producer (e.g. many buyers of financial services may trust their broker of long standing to choose between competing policies on their behalf).
8. Goods and services often require after-sales support, such as carrying out warranty repairs on manufactured goods. Manufacturers often find this easier to undertake through intermediaries than doing it themselves.
9. Intermediaries often share part of the risk of new products by agreeing to buy stock on a no-return basis before the product is launched.

These functions are of varying levels of importance in different markets. In some cases the manufacturer will be able to manage quite adequately without intermediaries and sell direct to its final consumers. The design of a channel of distribution is influenced by a number of factors:

1. *The type of product.* For fast-moving consumer goods, customers will generally be unwilling to travel far to obtain a particular brand—an extensive network of outlets will be necessary. On the other hand, customers may be prepared to travel further to seek out higher value consumer durables.
2. *The nature of the product.* Bulky and perishable products will be generally less capable of being handled by large numbers of intermediaries.
3. *The abilities of intermediaries.* If the product is very specialized, it may be difficult to obtain intermediaries who can handle the product effectively. Ski tour operators have often sold their holidays direct to the public, claiming that travel agents have insufficient knowledge and training to effectively sell their holidays.
4. *The expectations of consumers.* For some products, consumers expect to buy from an intermediary who offers a choice of products from a number of producers, as in the case of books and holidays. This could make direct selling of one company's products direct to the public more difficult. Consumers may, furthermore, have expectations about what constitutes an acceptable channel through which to buy a product. Attempts to sell cars and houses through supermarkets have failed partly for this reason.

In many markets, different channel structures can exist side by side. Commemorative porcelain products are frequently sold direct to the public by means of advertisements in magazines. Manufacturers of the same type of product can also be found selling them direct to retailers and indirectly to retailers through wholesalers. In this case, the company selling direct may find a niche product to sell direct or may present the offer to appeal to a particular segment that is more responsive to the idea of ordering by mail. Where multiple channels are used simultaneously, companies must avoid alienating channel members who feel that they are facing unfair competition from other channels. For this reason, insurance brokers are often hostile to insurance companies who they act for when those companies choose to additionally sell their policies direct to the public.

Channel design is constantly adapting to changes in the business environment. A major change during the past two decades has occurred in the size of intermediaries. In many market sectors, multiple retail outlets have become dominant, often at the expense of the smaller unit. Grocery retailing and DIY retailing are two areas where this has been particularly significant. The diversity of organizations involved in retailing can be appreciated by considering the following:

- In 1992, a total of 219 132 retailers were recorded in the United Kingdom. Of these, 196 104 (or 89.5 per cent of the total) were single-outlet retailers.
- Large multiple retailers accounted for just 3.6 per cent of all retail business organizations.
- Despite their small numbers, large multiples have accounted for a growing proportion of total retail turnover (46 per cent in 1992).
- The greater efficiency of large multiples is evident from a comparison of the annual sales value per employee (£49 628 for single-outlet retailers compared to £65 561 for large multiples).

Economies of scale in purchasing and promotion have been important causes of the increase in concentration. Where retailers have become more concentrated and individually more powerful, there has been a tendency for them to deal directly with manufacturers, rather than to deal through wholesalers. The turnover of a large grocery supermarket can be more than that of a large wholesaler, leaving the latter to cater for the small and medium sized retailer.

2.4.2   Push and pull channels of distribution

Before the advent of strong branding, a manufacturer would aggressively sell a product to a wholesaler who would buy and stock the product on what it considered to be the merits of the product. The wholesaler would in turn aggressively sell the product to retailers, who would buy on the basis of his or her experience and what he or she thought could be profitably sold to customers. This is known as a 'push' strategy of distribution. With the advent of branding, the manufacturer was able to cut out the uncertainty associated with the intermediaries by appealing to the final consumer directly through the medium of advertising. The final consumer would then go to a retailer and demand a specific brand rather than accept the generic brand that the retailer tried to push. Having demanded a specific brand from the retailer, the retailer will in turn order that brand from the wholesaler, who in turn will order from the manufacturer. This is known as a 'pull' strategy. In this situation, the intermediaries had become merely dispensers of pre-sold goods. The two strategies are compared in Figure 2.3.

More recently, the growing strength of retailers has put them at the focal point of the channel of distribution. By building up their own strong brands, large retailers are increasingly able to exert pressure on manufacturers in terms of product specification, price and the level of promotional support to be given to the retailer. It is estimated that, in Britain, the four largest grocery retailers may account for over half of the sales of a typical manufacturer of fast-moving consumer goods. The dependency is not reciprocated, with very few retailers relying on one single supplier for more than 1 per cent of their supplies.

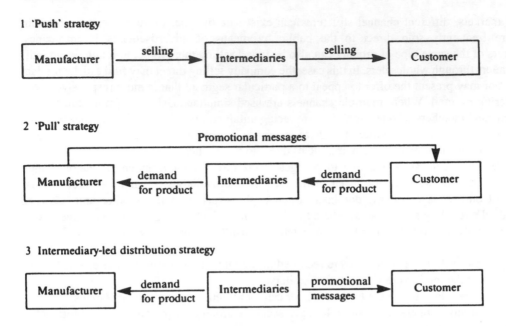

1 'Push' strategy

2 'Pull' strategy

3 Intermediary-led distribution strategy

Figure 2.3 'Push' and 'pull' strategies of distribution

2.4.3 Developments in channel structures

While large retailers have been consolidating their position, the 1980s and 1990s have seen the development of small specialist niche retailers. These have concentrated on such specialist niches as ties, fine cheeses, sportswear and bags. A number of factors contributed towards the development of these niche outlets. Greater affluence has resulted in consumers being able to express a desire for individualism which may be incompatible with a purchase from a large mainstream retailer. Although large retailers have often tried to enter niche markets, they have often not had the flexibility of movement open to the smaller company.

Movement towards integrating the different stages of a channel of distribution has occurred in a number of ways. In its most simple form, integration can occur through agreement over operational matters—standardization of pallet sizes and packaging methods to suit the needs of manufacturer, wholesaler and retailer is one example. More recently, bar coding of products allows all intermediaries to process goods by a common standard much more efficiently. Sometimes, the agreement takes the form of a voluntary buying chain set up to act as a wholesaler on behalf of a group of retailers. Londis and Nisa are examples.

Channel integration could occur through common ownership of different stages in the channel of distribution—a manufacturer, for instance, buying its own retail outlets. Although this has occurred on a number of occasions during the past decade (e.g. the Corah textile group established a chain of shops under the Harcourt name to sell its products), the more common trend has been for companies to concentrate on the point of the value chain that they are best at doing. The Burton group, for example, decided that it was better at selling clothes rather than making them and, similarly, Asda—originally founded as a dairy to which retailing was later added—decided that its capital could be better employed in exploiting economies of scale in retailing rather than in operating dairies.

A very significant source of channel integration has come about through the development of franchising, which is discussed in more detail in Chapter 3.

Formats for intermediaries go through life cycles, just like any normal product. Forms of retailing are born and eventually die in response to changes in the business environment. Thus full service retailing went into decline with increasing real wage levels, to be replaced by the self-service store. With increasing car ownership and rising aspirations of consumers for greater choice, the supermarket may be approaching the end of its life cycle, being superseded by the larger out-of-town hypermarket. The concept of the department store appears to be at a point of maturity, being overshadowed by the emergence of small niche outlets. Catalogue shops are a relatively recent innovation in the United Kingdom, resulting from the increasing cost of city centre floor space and rapidly gaining social acceptability as a method of shopping. Developments in technology may allow further developments in the home shopping sector, allowing it to exploit the growing number of money-rich, time-poor households. There are signs that in areas such as financial services, insurance companies are able to use information technology to target specific groups with sales offerings and achieve a sale with good after-sales service, without the need to deal through the traditional intermediary of the insurance broker.

2.4.4 Physical distribution management

Aside from considerations of which intermediaries are to be involved in transferring goods from a manufacturer to final consumers is the question of how they are to be physically handled. It is very easy to overlook the importance of this aspect of marketing management, and many companies have run into difficulties on account of poor physical distribution management. For example, the retail chain Laura Ashley achieved notable success during the 1980s on account of its product designs and the life-style images that they convey. However, the fortunes of the company turned for the worse during the early 1990s and part of the downturn was attributed to poor physical distribution management. Stores found themselves with excessive stocks of items that were not selling, while highly sought products were 'lost' in a fragmented distribution system which involved too many warehouses and incompatible computer systems. The distribution system was unable to satisfy the needs of customers for goods at a time and a place where they wanted them and resolving these problems was a key element in the company's recovery strategy.

The design of a physical distribution system has to reflect changing environmental pressures, such as customers' increasing expectations for immediate availability of goods and the changing speed and cost of competing modes of transport. Distribution management should begin by considering the needs of the customers that a company seeks to serve. These needs can be specified in terms of parameters such as reliability of delivery, time taken to deliver from the placing of an order and the condition in which goods are delivered. Physical distribution management involves balancing the need to maximize these benefits to consumers against the need to minimize costs.

The basic elements of a physical distribution system are shown in Figure 2.4 and comprise six elements that are used in designing an optimum system: suppliers, outlets, stocks, warehouses, transport and information. Companies often give the task of distributing their goods to specialist distribution companies.

Suppliers   A marketing-orientated system will have to balance the need for suppliers to be close to customers against economies of scale which may be obtained from having one central point of supply. Technology is increasingly allowing multiple supply points to produce goods close to the market. In the case of bread baking, the supermarket has itself often become the point of production, meeting the requirements of customers for freshly baked bread.

Where markets are turbulent, the distribution system may incorporate suppliers who are closest to the customer rather than necessarily the cheapest sources of production. High fashion clothing sold in Western Europe is likely to be sourced from within Europe, allowing rapid delivery to a changing market, whereas basic items such as plain standard shirts or trousers may be sourced from lower cost but more remote areas such as the Far East or Eastern Europe.

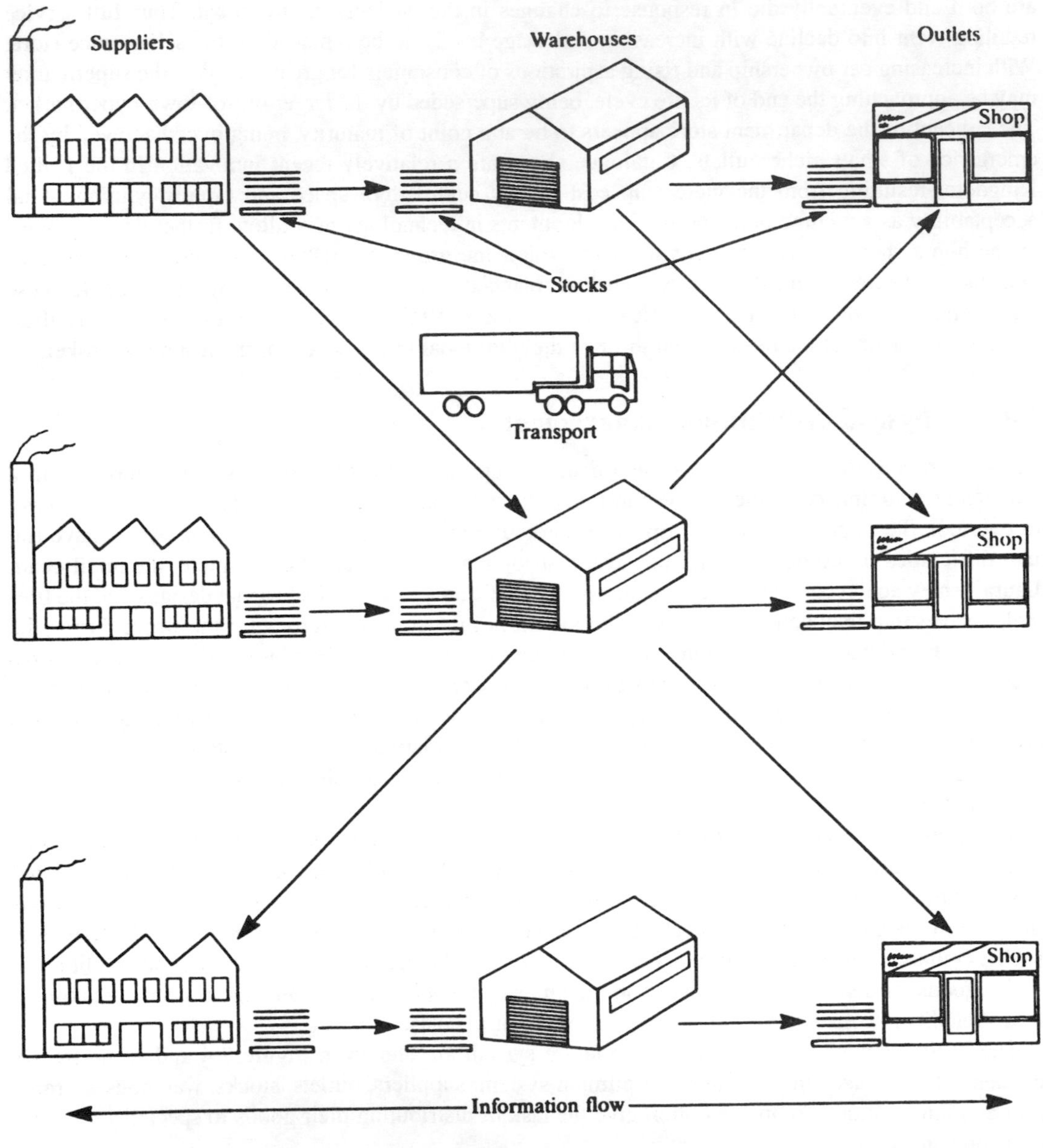

Figure 2.4 Elements of a physical distribution system

Outlets These can range from the individual household through to the largest hypermarket. With the development of direct marketing, consumer goods are increasingly being delivered to an individual customer's house. There is much debate about whether this trend will continue, with proponents of 'electronic shopping' arguing that increasingly wide ranges of goods, including routine grocery items, will be delivered in this way. Against this argument, home delivery of goods is labour intensive and expensive and recent trends have been away from home delivery towards cheaper sources of consumer goods in large retail outlets. In the United Kingdom, home delivery of milk, bread, vegetables and meat have all declined over the past two decades.

Stocks   Stocks are held by various organizations in a channel of distribution for a number of reasons:

- To balance seasonal patterns of production and consumption
- To provide rapid availability of goods to customers
- To provide contingencies against disruptions of production

A physical distribution system has to balance the need to hold large stocks in order to be able to fulfil customer orders against the cost of excessive stockholding. The tendency towards specialized products aimed at small segments of the market has meant that much higher stocks have to be held if the company is going to be able to rapidly satisfy an order for each variant. At times of high interest rates and capital shortage, there is pressure to keep stockholding to a minimum. In rapidly changing markets, such as fashion clothing, there is a tendency to keep stock levels at a minimum level to guard against large stocks of goods suddenly becoming obsolete because of a change in tastes.

Warehouses   These are incorporated into a system to provide a break of bulk point and to hold stocks. A company must decide on the number and nature of the warehouses that are incorporated into its system, in particular the balance between the need for local warehouses as against the need for efficiency savings which favour large warehouses. Automation of warehouses with the development of computerized picking systems is increasingly favouring larger warehouses. A typical national supermarket would now include just half a dozen strategically located warehouses in its distribution system to serve a national chain of outlets.

Transport   This moves the stocks from manufacturer to retail outlet and sometimes, as in the case of mail order or home delivery of milk, to the final consumer. Transport is becoming an increasingly important element of the distribution system, with goods tending to travel for longer average distances within the system. Road haulage has become the dominant form of goods transport within Britain, accounting in 1993 for 81 per cent of all tonnage carried (or 64 per cent of all tonne-miles) (*Transport Statistics*, 1995). The strength of road transport has been helped by the increasing size and efficiency of lorries and the progressive development of the motorway network. Very few distribution systems include rail as an important element of their physical distribution system, being mainly confined to relatively low-value, high-volume products such as aggregates and coal. The opening of the Channel Tunnel may increase the opportunities for UK rail transport by eliminating the need for goods to or from Continental Europe to be transhipped at the port.

Information flow   The requirement to respond to customer requirements rapidly, while at the same time keeping down stockholding levels, demands a very effective flow of information. The development of 'just-in-time' (JIT) systems has only been possible with the improvement of data flow. The development of bar codes has achieved notable results in this respect. A supermarket can now know minute by minute the state of stocks for all of its products and can order replacement stocks—by a computerized data link—for delivery from a regional distribution centre the following day. The regional distribution centres can similarly rapidly reorder stocks from their suppliers. The development of just-in-time systems has not only allowed a more reliable level of availability of goods to the final consumer but it has also allowed retailers to reduce warehouse space provided within shops. Because it is no longer necessary to hold large stocks locally, warehouse space can be turned over to more valuable sales floor space and cash invested in stocks turned to more profitable use.

Specialized distribution firms   Physical distribution is a specialized activity that can often be carried out more efficiently by a company that is independent of manufacturers or intermediaries. The last two decades have seen many manufacturers identifying their core business activities and concentrating their management and financial resources on these. Physical distribution management has often been seen as a relatively peripheral activity with the result that many companies have hived the activity off to a specialist organization such as TNT or subsidiaries of the National Freight Corporation. Cash has often been raised for investment in the core business by selling vehicle fleets and warehouses to the distribution company. Because specialist distribution companies usually work on behalf of a large number of companies, they can achieve significant economies of scale compared to the free-standing operation of a single manufacturer. Warehouses can be built to a more efficient scale and peaks and troughs in demand can be reconciled more easily within a larger and more broadly based operator. The company also benefits by being able to use staff with a level of specialist knowledge which may not be achievable within a manufacturing company.

2.5   BUYER–SELLER RELATIONSHIPS

The discussion of value chains earlier indicated that members of an organization's marketing environment are often being brought closer together to act co-operatively rather than in confrontation with each other. The process of turning casual, one-off transactions between buyers and sellers into ongoing relationships has often been described as 'relationship marketing'. This topic has received a lot of attention recently.

There is nothing new in the way that firms have sought to develop ongoing relationships with their customers. In simple economies where production of goods and services took place on a small scale, it was possible for the owners of businesses to know each customer personally and to come to understand their individual characteristics. They could therefore adapt service delivery to the needs of individuals on the basis of knowledge gained during previous transactions and could suggest appropriate new product offers. They would also be able to form an opinion about customers' credit worthiness. Networks of relationships between buyers and sellers are still the norm in many Far Eastern countries and many Western exporters have found it difficult to break into these long-standing, closed networks.

With the growth in size of Western organizations, the personal contact that an organization can have with its customers has been diluted. Instead of being able to reassure customers on the basis of close relationships, organizations in many cases sought to provide this reassurance through the development of strong brands. Recent resurgence of interest in relationship marketing has occurred for a number of reasons:

1. In increasingly competitive markets, good products alone are insufficient to differentiate an organization's products from that of its competitors. For example, in the car sector, manufacturers traditionally differentiated their cars on the basis of superior design features such as styling, speed and reliability. Once most companies had reached a common standard of design, attention switched to differentiation through superior added-service facilities, such as warranties and finance. Once these service standards became the norm for the sector, many car manufacturers have sought to differentiate their cars on the basis of superior relationships. Therefore most major car manufacturers now offer customers complete packages which keep a car financed, insured, maintained and renewed after a specified period. Instead of a three-yearly one-off purchase of a new car, many customers enter an ongoing relationship with a car manufacturer and its dealers which gives the customer the support they need to keep their car on the road and to have it renewed when this falls due.
2. Developments in information technology have had dramatic effects in developing relationship marketing schemes. The development of powerful user-friendly databases has allowed organizations to recreate in a computer what the individual small business owner knew in his or her head. Large businesses are therefore now able to tell very quickly the status of a particular customer, for example their previous ordering pattern, product preferences and profitability. Developments in information technology have also allowed companies to enter individual dialogues with their

customers through direct mail and increasingly through electronic means. Increased production flexibility based on improved technology allows many manufacturers and service organizations to design unique products that meet the needs of individual customers, rather than broad groups of customers.

3. Just-in-time production methods (JIT) have become very widespread in Western countries, thanks to the lead given by Japanese manufacturing companies. It often makes sense for a manufacturer to keep its holdings of component parts down to an absolute minimum. This way, it ties up less capital, needs less storage space and suffers less risk of stocks becoming obsolete. Instead of keeping large stocks of components, manufacturers arrange for them to be delivered 'just in time' for them to be used in their production process. It is not uncommon to find car manufacturers receiving batches of components which within an hour are incorporated into a car. JIT systems demand a lot of co-operation between supplier and customer which cannot easily be achieved if each transaction is to be individually bargained. Some form of ongoing relationship between the two is essential.

A number of attempts have been made to analyse the development of relationships, often using the principles of life cycle theories. A theoretical model of relationship proposed by Dwyer, Schurr and Oh (1987) identifies five stages of relationship development: awareness, exploration, expansion, commitment and dissolution. Their model proposes that a relationship begins to develop significance in the exploration stage when it is characterized by attempts of the seller to attract the attention of the other party. The exploration stage includes attempts by each party to bargain and to understand the nature of the power, norms and expectations held by the other. If this stage is satisfactorily concluded, an expansion phase follows. Exchange outcomes in the exploratory stage provide evidence as to the suitability of long-term exchange relationships. The commitment phase of a relationship implies some degree of exclusivity between the parties and results in an information search for alternatives—if it occurs at all—being much reduced. The dissolution stage marks the point where buyer and seller recognize that they would be better able to achieve their respective aims outside the relationship. A number of studies have validated the existence of a relationship life cycle.

Organizations use a number of strategies to move their customers through the stages of relationship development:

1. The possibility of relationships developing can only occur where the parties are aware of each other and of their mutual desire to enter into exchange transactions. At this stage, the parties may have diverging views about the possibility of forming a long-term relationship. The supplier must be able to offer potential customers reasons why they should show disloyalty to their existing supplier. In some cases, low introductory prices are offered by organizations that provide a sufficient incentive for disloyal customers of other companies to switch supplier. Non-price-related means of gaining attention include advertising and direct mail aimed at the market segments with whom relationships are sought. Over time, the supplier would seek to build value into the relationship so that customers would have little incentive for seeking lower price solutions elsewhere. Inevitably, sellers face risks in adopting this strategy. It may be difficult to identify and exclude from a relationship invitation those segments of the population that are likely to show most disloyalty by withdrawing from the relationship at the point when it is just beginning to become profitable to the supplier.

2. On entering into a relationship, buyers and sellers make a series of promises to each other (Gronroos, 1989). In the early stages of a relationship, suppliers' promises result in expectations being held by buyers as to the standard of goods and services that will actually be delivered. Many studies into service quality have highlighted the way in which the gap between expected performance and actual performance determine customers' perception of quality. Quality in perceived service delivery is a prerequisite for a quality relationship being developed.

3. Many organizations record information about customers that will be useful in assessing their future needs. This can be used to build up a database from which customers are kept in touch with new product developments of specific interest to them.

4. Financial incentives are often given to customers as a reward for maintaining their relationship. These can range from a simple money-off voucher valid for a reduction in the price of a future purchase to a club-type scheme that allows a standard level of discount for club members. Incentives that are purely financially based have a problem in that they can defeat the service supplier's central objective of getting greater value out of a relationship. It is often expensive to initiate a relationship and organizations therefore seek to achieve profits at later stages by raising price levels to reflect the value that customers attach to the relationship. There is a danger of buyers becoming loyal to the financial incentive, rather than the brand that it is designed to promote. Once the financial incentive comes to an end, loyalty may soon disappear. In some cases, greater bonding between customer and supplier can be achieved by selling membership plans to customers which allow subsequent discount, as is the case with a number of store discount cards. Having invested in a membership plan, customers are likely to rationalize their reasons for taking advantage of it, rather than taking their business elsewhere.

5. Rather than offer price discounts, companies can add to the value of a relationship by offering other non-financial incentives, for example many retailers offer special preview evenings for customers who have joined their membership club.

6. A strategy used by some companies is to create relationships by trying to turn discrete service delivery into continuous delivery. In this way, companies offering travel insurance often encourage customers to buy all-year-round coverage rather than purchasing a policy each time that they travel abroad.

7. Information about the preferences of individual customers can be retained in order that future requests for service can be closely tailored to their needs. In this way a travel agent booking accommodation for a corporate client can select hotels on the basis of preferences expressed during previous transactions. By offering a more personalized service, the travel agent is adding value to the relationship, increasing the transaction costs of transferring to another travel agent.

8. A more intensive relationship can develop where customers assign considerable responsibility to another company for identifying their needs. In this way a car repairer may attempt to move away from offering a series of discrete services initiated by customers, to a situation where it takes total responsibility for maintaining a customer's car, including diagnosing problems and initiating routine service appointments.

Although there has been much recent interest in relationship marketing—for goods as well as for services—this has tended to emphasize the producer's perspective on a relationship. It can be argued that, with increasing knowledge and confidence, consumers are increasingly happy to venture outside a long-term relationship with a service provider. This is reflected in the observation that in 1990 43 per cent of a sample of US bank customers had changed banks within the last 5 years (Lewis, 1991), running counter to earlier anecdotal observations that a relationship that individuals have with their bank is more enduring than the relationship with their spouse. With increased knowledge of financial services, consumers are more willing today to venture to another bank that offers the best personal loan for them or the most attractive credit card. Also, a long-term relationship often begins with attractive introductory discounts and a significant segment of many service markets is prepared to move its business regularly to the service provider that is offering the most attractive discount. The motorist who reviews his or her car insurance each year, for example, may not allow an insurance company to develop a long-term profitable relationship. In the case of many business-to-business services contracts, these may be reviewed regularly as a matter of course, as in the competitive tendering that is required for many government purchases of services. In such circumstances, it is often not possible to add value and higher prices to a long-term relationship. Finally, it has been argued that many loyalty schemes offered by companies develop loyalty to the scheme rather than to the company and can become an expensive overhead cost which does not lead to any long-term development of willing commitment from customers (Barnes, 1994).

RELATIONSHIPS SOUGHT TO BOOST AMERICAN EXPRESS' SAGGING PRESTIGE

During the 1980s, the market for charge cards in many Western countries approached saturation as a proliferation of new cards appeared. Visa and Mastercard had dominated the market for some time, bolstered by the growing number of affinity cards launched in collaboration with industrial companies, such as the GM card launched in collaboration with HFC Bank. Among the plethora of cards, American Express had sought to position its card as an exclusive status symbol—a card that could not be compared with the likes of Visa and Mastercard.

By the early 1990s, American Express was facing a tough time in the card market. Since 1989, its arch rival Visa had been targeting AmEx instead of its traditional rival, Mastercard. Banks began adding privileges to their cards, such as free travel accident insurance, which were once considered a privilege of holding an AmEx card. It seemed that the AmEx card was becoming a commodity item undifferentiated from its competitors' offers. By the 1990s, the card had lost much of its prestigious image, not helped by consumers' increasing consciousness of card charges and willingness to shop around for the best card. The outcome of all of these factors was to reduce AmEx's world-wide market share from 20.3 per cent in 1987 to 14.5 per cent in 1991. By contrast, Visa's market share had increased from 44.7 to 51.0 per cent.

Not only was AmEx loosing favour with cardholders, it was becoming increasingly derided by merchants, from whom AmEx obtained about two-thirds of its card income. In 1991, AmEx continued charging its merchants fees of between 3 and 4 per cent of sales value, while Visa had whittled its fee down to an average of just 1.8 per cent. Merchants knew that about 90 per cent of all AmEx cardholders also carried a Visa card and many tried to 'suppress' the use of AmEx by encouraging customers to use Visa instead. Some merchants stopped accepting AmEx completely, a potentially dangerous strategy for any firm relying on business expense customers travelling with corporate cards. There were numerous local rebellions against AmEx's charges, the most notable being the so-called 'Boston fee party' in the United States, where Boston restaurateurs led many other businesses throughout the country in refusing to accept AmEx cards, following the refusal of the company to lower its merchant fees.

AmEx initially underestimated its competition, but eventually sought to regain profitable business through the development of loyal relationships between the company and both its cardholders and merchants. AmEx recognized the limitations of its 1980s strategy of simply acquiring new cardholders and then taking their business for granted. Instead, it realized that it would make more financial sense to sacrifice numbers if it meant having a quality base of loyal customers. Similarly, the company recognized that it wasn't good enough to simply sign up more merchants—it would be better to have a core of merchants who were committed to working with the company to increase use of its cards.

AmEx decided to focus its attention on the 20 per cent of its cardholder base who accounted for 80 per cent of sales volume. For this core group of customers, the company made an effort to tailor its service to meet the specific needs of each individual, for example in the way that it allowed cardholders to receive their monthly statement on any day of their choice. It also refined its customer database so that it could send mailings for goods and services that most accurately reflected its customers' interests and lifestyles. To try and get itself seen as a partner in problem solving, AmEx offered many more services; for example, it offered to reserve tickets at concerts for its gold and platinum card holders. In a bid to encourage a greater proportion of its cardholders' spending to be charged to its AmEx card rather than its competitors' cards, AmEx developed its Membership Miles scheme, a form of frequent flyer loyalty programme which awarded miles on selected airlines in return for charge volume.

More importantly, AmEx sought to develop closer relationships with its merchants. To try and discourage defectors, the company promised to be more attentive to merchant concerns such as discount rates, speedy payment and marketing support. The company reassigned the duties of its merchant service representatives by requiring them to make more frequent visits to existing merchants, rather than spending most of their time looking for new ones. Where a problem had been identified, representatives were also empowered to make deals on the spot in an attempt to resolve it.

In a further attempt to develop loyalty with its merchant members, AmEx agreed to be sensitive in its own direct marketing efforts, which in the past had upset many merchants by directly competing with their own goods and services. Finally, AmEx demonstrated its enthusiasm for working together with its merchants through a series of television advertisements. These focused on a specific business—usually small, rapidly growing businesses with a high level of awareness among cardholders—and promoted the business as much as the AmEx card.

AmEx had determined that in the increasingly fierce charge card market, features and benefits are no longer adequate to give its card a competitive edge. Its strategy was designed to sell much wider, quality relationships through which cardholders and merchants could receive a total service that met their specific needs. Only time will tell if merchants and cardholders are prepared to pay a premium price to reflect the value of such relationships, or indeed if similar emphasis on relationships becomes the norm for all charge cards, again causing AmEx to lose its competitive advantage.

QUESTIONS

1. Summarize the reasons why American Express pursued a strategy of developing closer relationships with its cardholders and merchants.
2. Suggest further strategies that might be appropriate to American Express in its bid to develop relationships with its cardholders and merchants.
3. Review the positioning strategies open to American Express for its card services.

2.6 THE INTERNAL ENVIRONMENT

Internally, the structure and politics of an organization affect the manner in which it responds to environmental change. An organization that assigns marketing responsibilities to a narrow group of people may in fact create tensions within the organization which make it less effective at responding to changing consumer needs than one where marketing responsibilities in their widest sense are disseminated throughout the organization. Such internal relationships are often referred to as an organization's *internal marketing environment*. Marketing plans cannot be developed and implemented without a sound understanding of marketing managers' relationship to other members of their organization.

There are two aspects to a marketing manager's internal environment: firstly, the internal structure and processes of the marketing department itself (where one actually exists) and, secondly, the relationship of the marketing functions to other business functions.

2.6.1 Marketing department organization

Marketing departments allocate responsibilities to individual managers on a number of bases, the most common being functions performed, products managed, customer segments and geographical areas, although, in practice, most marketing departments show more than one approach to structure. Each approach has its own advantages and disadvantages in terms of responsiveness to environmental change (Figure 2.5).

Functional organization   The simplest approach to marketing department organization is to allocate individual responsibilities on the basis of specific marketing functions performed. Typical responsibilities include advertising, market research and sales. The main advantage of this approach is that functional specialists can keep abreast of developments in their area of specialization. For example, a market research manager could become very knowledgable about new methods of automated data collection. Against this, a pure functional organization may result in individual products having nobody to oversee their development in response to external environmental change.

Product management organization   This approach develops a more holistic approach to the management of products. Individual product managers (and group product managers) develop

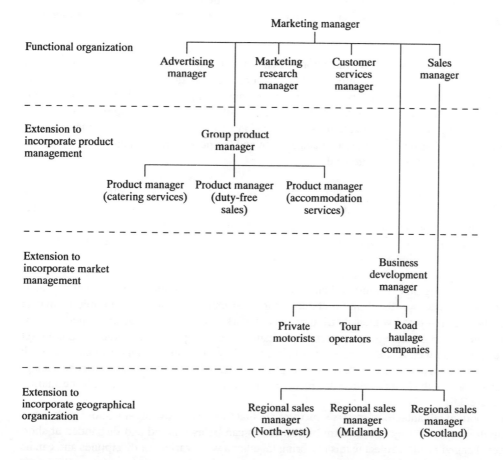

Figure 2.5   Alternative forms of marketing department organization structure, showing typical applications to a ferry operator

marketing plans for individual products and groups of products. By specializing in one product area, an individual can become a specialist in tracking and understanding the marketing environment of that product. Within a confectionery manufacturer, for example, a product manager responsible for a range of chocolates can spend time monitoring trends in household expenditure, observing competitors' activity and commissioning specialized market research. Based on such knowledge, an appropriate marketing response can be developed. Product managers typically work with other functional managers. The main problem associated with product managers is that while they frequently have a lot of responsibility for products, this may not be matched by authority over resources. The chocolate products manager may, for example, seek to promote their product in one way, but is overruled by an advertising manager who seeks to develop an alternative corporate style of advertising for all of the organization's products. The appointment of product managers can add to a company's costs, putting it at a competitive disadvantage.

Market segment management   This follows a similar principle to product managers, except that instead of having product managers responsible for specific products, market managers are responsible for developing specific market segments. For example, a ferry company may appoint market managers to oversee the freight, motorist and group tour markets. In theory, each market manager is able to gain a thorough understanding of their market segment and to develop a response that satisfies customers' needs. However, there is again the problem of market managers having a lot of responsibility for market development, but very little authority over resources that would allow their plans to be implemented.

Geographical area management   Organizations often manage part of their marketing effort on a geographical basis. This is particularly important for functions such as sales where it is important to be close to customers and to be able to respond to environmental change rapidly. Sometimes, responsibilities for promotion and new service development are also allocated on a geographical basis. Most organizations use geographical organization as an extension of centralized marketing management structures. Economies of scale in centralized management and the need to retain a corporate approach limit the use of this approach to management.

Matrix management organization   Organizations that produce many different products for many different markets may experience difficulties if they adopt a purely product- or market-based structure. If a product management structure is adopted, product managers would require detailed knowledge of very diverse markets. Likewise, in a market management structure, market managers would require detailed knowledge of possibly very diverse product ranges. An alternative is to introduce a matrix type of organization that combines market managers with product managers. Product managers concentrate on developing and promoting their own particular product, while market managers focus on meeting consumer needs without any preference for a particular product. An example of matrix structures can be found in many vehicle distributors where market managers can be appointed to identify and formulate a market strategy in respect of the distinct needs of private customers and contract hire customers, etc., as well as being appointed to manage key customers. Market managers work alongside product managers who can develop and promote specialized activities such as servicing, bodywork repairs and vehicle hire which are made available to final customers through the market managers (Figure 2.6).

The most important advantages of matrix structures are that they can allow organizations to respond rapidly to environmental change. Short-term project teams can be assembled and disbanded at short notice to meet changed needs. Project teams can bring together a wide variety of disciplines and can be used to evaluate new services before full-scale development is undertaken. A bank exploring the possibility of developing a banking system linked to personal customers' home computers might bring

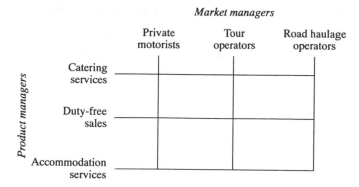

Figure 2.6 Matrix marketing management structure, showing typical application to a ferry operator

together a team drawn from staff involved in marketing to personal customers and those responsible for technology-based research and development. The former may include market researchers and the latter computer development engineers. Matrix structures need not necessarily be confined within the boundaries of a traditional marketing department—indeed matrix organizations would normally embrace all of an organization's functions (see below). In this wider context, the flexibility of matrix structures can be increased by bringing temporary workers into the structure on a contract basis as and when needed. During the 1990s there has been a trend for many organizations to lay off significant numbers of workers—including management—and to buy these back when needed. As well as cutting fixed costs, such organizations have the potential to respond very rapidly to environmental change.

Where matrix structures exist, great motivation can be present in effectively managed teams. Against this, matrix type structures can be associated with problems. Most serious is the confused lines of authority that may result. Staff may not be clear about which superior he or she is responsible to for a particular aspect of their duties, resulting in possible stress and demotivation. Where a matrix structure is introduced into an organization with a history and culture of functional specialization, it can be very difficult to implement effectively. Staff may be reluctant to act outside a role that they have traditionally defined narrowly and guarded jealously. Finally, matrix structures invariably result in more managers being employed within an organization. At best this can result in a costly addition to the salary bill. At worst, the existence of additional managers can also actually slow down decision-making processes where the managers show a reluctance to act outside a narrow functional role.

The great diversity of organizational structures highlights the fact that there is not one unique structure that is appropriate to all firms, even within the same industry sector. Overall, the organization of a marketing department must allow for a flexible and adaptable response to customers' needs within a changing environment, while aiming to reduce the level of confusion, ambiguity and cost inherent in some structures.

2.6.2 The relationship between marketing and other organizational functions

In a production-oriented firm, a marketing department has little role to play, other than merely processing orders. In this way the gas and electricity boards in the United Kingdom before privatization faced relatively stable markets with little effective competition. Marketing assumed less importance than the exploration of new energy sources and more efficient methods of distribution. Even with the advent of privatization, the majority of the new companies' markets remained stable, with marketing assuming most significance in those areas of activity, such as showroom sales of gas and electricity equipment, which faced effective competition.

In a truly marketing oriented-organization, marketing responsibilities cannot be confined to something called a marketing department. In the words of Drucker:

> Marketing is so basic that it cannot be considered to be a separate function. It is the whole business seen from the point of view of its final result, that is, from the customer's point of view (Drucker, 1973).

In marketing-oriented organizations, customers are at the centre of all of the organization's activities. Customers are not simply the concern of the marketing department, but also all of the production and administrative personnel whose actions may directly or indirectly impinge upon the customers' enjoyment of the service. In a typical organization, the activities of a number of functional departments impinge on the service outcome received by customers, for example:

1. Personnel plans can have a crucial bearing on marketing plans. The selection, training motivation and control of staff cannot be considered in isolation from marketing objectives and strategies. Possible conflict between the personnel and marketing functions may arise where, for example, marketing demands highly trained and motivated front-line staff, but the personnel function pursues a policy that places cost reduction above all else.
2. Production managers may have a different outlook compared to marketing managers. A marketing manager may seek to respond as closely as possible to customers' needs, only to find opposition from production managers who argue that output of the required standard cannot be achieved. A marketing manager of a train operating company may seek to segment markets with fares tailored to meet the needs of small groups of customers, only to encounter hostility from operations managers who are responsible for actually issuing and checking travel tickets on a day-to-day basis and who may have misgivings about the confusion that finely segmented fares might cause.
3. The actions of finance managers frequently have a direct or indirect impact on marketing plans. Ultimately, finance managers assume responsibility for the allocation of funds which are needed to implement a marketing plan. At a more operational level, finance managers' actions in respect of the level of credit offered to customers or towards stockholdings, where these are an important element of the service offered, can also significantly affect the quality of service and the volume of customers that the organization is able to serve.

Marketing requires all of these departments to 'think customer' and to work together to satisfy customer needs and expectations. There is argument as to what authority the traditional marketing department should have in bringing about this customer orientation. In a truly mature marketing-oriented company, marketing is an implicit part of everybody's job. In such a scenario, marketing becomes responsible for a narrow range of specialist functions such as advertising and marketing research. Responsibility for the relationship between the organization and its customers is spread more diffusely throughout the organization. Gummesson (1991) uses the term 'part time marketer' to describe staff working in service organizations who may not have any direct line management responsibility for marketing, but whose activities may indirectly impinge on the quality of service received by customers.

It can be argued that the introduction of a traditional marketing department—as described above—to an organization can bring problems as well as benefits. In a survey of 219 executives representing public and private sector service organizations in Sweden, Gronroos (1982) tested the idea that a separate marketing department may widen the gap between marketing and operations staff. This idea was put to a sample drawn from marketing as well as other functional positions using a Likert-type scale with five points ranging from agreeing strongly to disagreeing strongly. The results indicated that respondents in a wide range of service organizations considered there to be dangers in the creation of a marketing department. An average of 66 per cent agreed with the notion, with higher than average agreement being found among non-marketing executives and those working in the hotel, restaurant, professional services and insurance sectors.

2.6.3   Organizational culture

It is common to talk about the 'culture' of an organization as a factor that contributes towards its marketing orientation. Organizational culture can be defined as 'some underlying structure of meaning that persists over time, constraining people's perception, interpretation and behaviour' (Jelinek, Smirich and Hirsch, 1983). Numerous comparative studies into the performance of European, American and Japanese managed organizations have introduced the concept of culture as a possible explanation for differences in competitive effectiveness where few differences in the structural characteristics of organizations are evident (Pascale and Athos, 1981). Within many industry sectors, it has proved difficult to change cultural attitudes when the nature of an organization's operating environment has significantly changed, rendering the established culture a liability in terms of strategic marketing management. As an example, the cultural values of UK clearing banks have continued to be dominated by prudence and caution when in some product areas, such as insurance sales, a more aggressive approach to marketing management may be called for.

In addition to the dominant culture of an organization, it is often possible to identify different subcultures within the same organization. Handy (1989) argues that organizations tend to have elements of different cultures appropriate to the structure and circumstances of different operating units within their structure. He identifies four types of culture:

1. The *power* culture is found mainly in smaller organizations where power and influence stem from a single central source, through which all decisions, communication and control are channelled. Because there is no rigid structure within the organization, it is theoretically capable of adapting to change very rapidly, although its actual success in adapting is dependent on the abilities of the central power source.
2. The *role* culture is characterized by a formal, functional organization structure in which there is relatively little freedom and creativity in decision making. Such organizations are more likely to be production oriented and can have difficulty responding to new market opportunities.
3. The *task* culture is concerned primarily with getting a given task done. Importance is therefore attached to those individuals who have the skill or knowledge to accomplish a particular task. Organizations with a task oriented culture are potentially very flexible, changing constantly as new tasks arise. Innovation and creativity are highly prized for their own sake.
4. The *person* culture is characterized by organizations which are centred around serving the interests of individuals within them. It is a relatively rare form of culture in any market-mediated environment, but can characterize campaigning pressure groups.

2.6.4   The flexible firm

Many organizations face demand for their goods and services that is highly variable, with peaks and troughs that can be daily, weekly, annual, seasonal, cyclical or unpredictable in pattern. While it may be possible for some organizations to influence and change the pattern of demand for their products, producing a more flexible and demand-responsive organization is often critical to marketing success.

As well as being able to achieve short-term flexibility, organizations must also have the flexibility over the longer term to shift their human resources from areas in decline to those where there is a prospect of future growth. For example, in order to retain its profitability, a bank must have the ability to move personnel away from relatively static activities such as cash handling and current account chequeing towards the more profitable growth area of financial services.

Flexibility within an organization can be achieved by segmenting the work-force into core and peripheral components (Figure 2.7). Core workers have greater job security and have defined career opportunities within an internal labour market. In return for this job security core workers may have to accept what Atkinson (1984) terms 'functional flexibility' by becoming responsible for a variety of job tasks. Peripheral employees, on the other hand, have less job security and limited career opportunity. They are 'numerically flexible', and are often employed on short-term contracts or treated as self-employed subcontactors. Increasingly, many management jobs are being 'outsourced' and many organizations retain consultants whose functions would have previously been undertaken by full-time, permanent employees. There is, however, debate about whether excessive use of short-term, flexible labour increases the effectiveness of an organization or reduces commitment of employees, which harms the company's dealings with its customers.

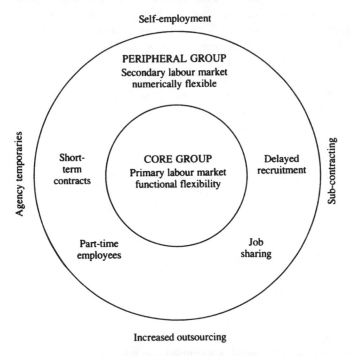

Figure 2.7   Components of a flexible firm

2.6.5   Improving organizational effectiveness for marketing

There has been debate about the relationship between marketing responsiveness and an organization's internal structure. The traditional view is that structures adapt to fit a chosen marketing strategy, although more recent thought has focused on the idea that strategy is very much dependent upon the structure adopted by an organization. An approach suggested by Giles (1988) is a 'structured iterative marketing planning process' which works by creating a cross-functional team of managers for the purpose of designing a marketing plan for a market or market segment selected by top management for attention. The managers' initial view of their target market is challenged and refined through a focused marketing audit, which requires continual iteration, forcing participants to go backwards and forwards through the process. The resulting marketing plan is likely to represent a high degree of commitment and ownership by those involved in creating it. The attraction of this type of approach is that it challenges managers to design better ways of addressing their markets by allowing things to be said that in a conventional planning process may be politically unacceptable. The marketing problem defines the agenda, rather than having it determined by the structure and political ideology of the organization. The process is designed to bring about marketing-led strategic change within the organization (Piercy, 1990).

A number of specific methods have been suggested by which organizations can develop an internal culture which improves marketing orientation:

- The appointment of senior management who have a good understanding of the philosophies and practices of marketing
- The introduction of in-house educational programmes which aim to train non-marketing management to empathize with customers' expectations
- The introduction of outside consultants who can apply their previous experience of introducing a marketing culture to an organization from an impartial perspective
- A commonly used method of making management think in marketing terms is to install a formal market-oriented planning system. This can have the effect of forcing managers to work through a list of market-related headings, such as an analysis of the competitive environment and identification of market opportunities when developing their annual plans.

2.6.6   Internal marketing

The marketing of many goods and services suffers because employees of an organization do not have any great commitment to the organization and this lack of commitment is reflected in their attitudes towards customers and product quality. Many organizations therefore seek to market themselves to an internal audience of employees.

Internal marketing describes the application of marketing techniques to audiences within the organization and has been defined as

> ... the means of applying the philosophy and practices of marketing to people who serve the external customers so that (i) the best possible people can be employed and retained and (ii) they will do the best possible work (Berry, 1980).

Internal marketing has two aspects:

1. All employees operating in their functional areas interact with other functional specialists in a quasi-trading manner. In this way, the personnel department can be seen as providing recruitment expertise for an organization's accounting department, while the latter can be seen as providing payment systems on behalf of the personnel department. Therefore, each functional group within an organization engages in trade with other functional groups as though those functions were external customers.
2. All functional staff must work together in support of an organization's business strategy. All staff must be able to share a common purpose and be able to work alongside rather than against other functional specialists in achieving the organization's aims. The mission of an organization must therefore be communicated to employees in much the same way as brand values are communicated to external customers.

Internal marketing has come to be associated with efforts to sell the message of an organization to its internal audience, using much the same techniques as would be used in the organization's relationships with external audiences. In reality, of course, true internal marketing would encompass all human resource management policies which are designed to attract, select, train, motivate, direct, evaluate and reward personnel. In this way, internal marketing becomes a core business philosophy in the same way as the traditional marketing philosophy involves more than merely using the tools of promotion.

The focal point of the narrower understanding of internal marketing lies in communicating values of an organization to its employees in order to increase their level of consent and moral involvement. The following are commonly observed internal marketing techniques used by companies:

1. The organization's mission statement must be clearly formulated and communicated to employees. It should provide a general statement about the organization's essential purpose.
2. Internal newsletters help to develop a sense of involvement of individuals within a business and can be used to inspire confidence by reporting significant new developments. Newsletters are commonly used to inform the workforce about achievements of individual employees.
3. External advertising should regard the internal labour force as a secondary target market. The appearance of advertisements on television can have the effect of inspiring confidence of employees in their management.
4. Staff uniforms and the physical environment in which they work can be used to inspire staff confidence in the organization and to convey the personality of the organization which it is desired to achieve.

OWNER DRIVERS STEER BUS COMPANIES TO BIGGER PROFITS

Bus companies went through a bad period during the 1980s. Increasing levels of car ownership, legislation deregulating the bus industry and finally the recession at the end of the decade resulted in many business failures. Against this bleak background, research undertaken by Dolan and Brierley (1992) showed how two companies—People's Provincial of Fareham and Derbyshire based Chesterfield Transport—had capitalized on their worker ownership to perform better in their market-places than their more conventionally owned rivals.

Employee ownership of bus companies assumed great importance following the British government's decision to sell off the state-owned National Bus Company and legislation which encouraged local authorities to do the same with their bus fleets. By 1990, nearly a third of bus operating turnover was accounted for by companies where employees owned 30 per cent or more of the shares. People's Provincial and Chesterfield Transport were at that time among the relatively small number where employees—rather than management—were the principal shareholders.

To the employees, a financial investment in the two companies studied proved attractive. Over a period of five years, the value of employees' investments in People's Provincial

doubled, while with Chesterfield Transport, it increased by over fourfold within two years.

To the companies as a whole, the research highlighted four important benefits which had resulted from worker ownership:

- All workers had access to financial information, resulting in a more constructive approach to negotiations on work schedules and pay, for example. Workers felt that information was not being withheld from them in order to give management an advantageous negotiating position.
- Traditional hierarchies were broken down, which gave much greater operational flexibility to the companies. As an example, inspectors and management would accept it as normal to change their duties and drive buses when the need arose. This was particularly important as the uneven pattern of demand required great flexibility.
- Costs were held down because staff recognized that they would benefit directly from the resulting increase in profits. Similarly, staff became more willing to pass on ideas about ways in which services could be improved, or costs saved.
- An indication of the greater commitment to the company was provided by lower levels of absenteeism and a reduced need for

formal disciplinary measures to be taken. Employees could see the reasons for a high level of service performance and were able to share in the resulting benefits.

The authors concluded that employee ownership—by increasing the level of participation—can give companies a competitive marketing advantage in services industries where flexibility in production and commitment to standards of service quality are important.

QUESTIONS

1. What are the marketing advantages to a company of being owned by its employees?
2. Are there potential marketing problems associated with large employee-owned businesses?
3. In which business sectors is employee ownership particularly attractive?

2.7   THE INFORMATION ENVIRONMENT

It has already been noted that information is crucial to organizations in the analysis of their environment. Information about the current state of the environment is used as a starting point for planning future marketing strategy, based on assumptions about how the environment will change. Information is also vital to monitor the implementation of an organization's marketing plans and to note the cause of any deviation from plan. Information therefore has both a planning function and a control function. They are brought together within the framework of a marketing information system.

Marketing information allows management to improve its strategic planning, tactical implementation of programme and its monitoring and control. A practical problem is that information is typically much more difficult to obtain to meet strategic planning needs than it is to meet operational and control needs. There can be a danger of marketing managers focusing too heavily on information which is easily available at the expense of that which is needed.

2.7.1   Marketing information systems

Many analyses of organizations' information collection and dissemination activities take a systems perspective. The collection of marketing information can be seen as one subsystem of a much larger management information system. Other systems typically include production, financial and personnel. In a well-designed management information system, the barriers between these systems should be conceptual rather than real—for example, sales information is of value to all of these subsystems to a greater or lesser extent (see Figure 2.8).

A marketing information system has been defined by Kotler as a system that:

… consists of people, equipment and procedures to gather, sort, analyze, evaluate and distribute needed, timely and accurate information to marketing decision-makers (Kotler, 1994).

Insofar as a marketing information subsystem can be identified, it can conceptually be seen as comprising four principal components, although in practice they are operationally interrelated:

1. Much information is generated internally within organizations, particularly in respect of operational and control functions. By carefully arranging its collection and dissemination, internal data can provide a constant and up to date flow of information at relatively little cost, useful for both planning and control functions.

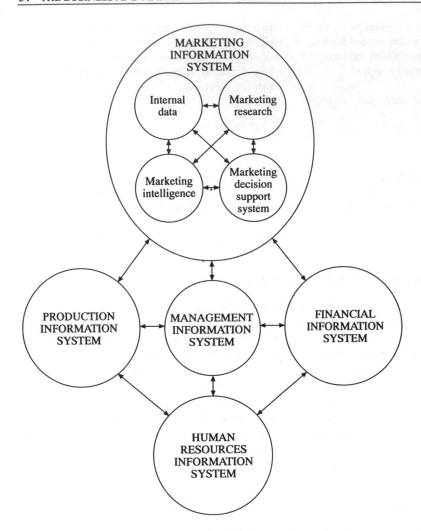

Figure 2.8 A systems approach to managing information

2. Marketing research is that part of the system concerned with the structured collection of marketing information. This can provide both routine information about marketing effectiveness, such as brand awareness levels or delivery performance, and one-off studies, such as a survey of changing attitudes towards diet.
3. Marketing intelligence comprises the procedures and sources used by marketing management to obtain pertinent information about developments in their marketing environment. It complements the marketing research system for, whereas the latter tends to focus on structured and largely quantifiable data-collection procedures, intelligence gathering concentrates on picking up relatively intangible ideas and trends. Marketing management can gather this intelligence from a number of sources, such as newspapers, specialized cutting services, employees who are in regular contact with market developments, intermediaries and suppliers to the company, as well as specialized consultants.

4. Marketing decision support systems comprise a set of models that allow forecasts to be made. Information is both an input to such models, in that data are needed to calibrate a model, and an output, in that models provide information on which decisions can be based. Models are frequently used, for example, in service outlet location decisions, where historical data may have established a relationship between one variable (e.g. the level of sales achieved by a particular service outlet) and other variables (e.g. pedestrian traffic in a street). Predicting the sales level of a proposed new outlet then becomes a matter of measuring pedestrian traffic at a proposed site, feeding this information into the model and calculating the predicted sales level.

For those organizations that have set up marketing information systems, a number of factors will determine their effectiveness:

1. *The accuracy with which the information needs of the organization have been defined* Needs can themselves be difficult to identify and it can be very difficult to identify the boundaries of the firm's environments and to separate relevance from irrelevance. This is a particular problem for large multiproduct firms. The mission statement of an organization may give some indication of the boundaries for its environmental search, for example, many banks have mission statements which talk about becoming a dominant provider of financial services in their domestic market. The information needs therefore include anything related to the broader environment of financial services rather than the narrower field of banking.
2. *The extensiveness of the search for information* A balance has to be struck between the need for information and the cost of collecting it. The most critical elements of the marketing environment must be identified and the cost of collecting relevant information weighed against the cost that would result from an inaccurate forecast.
3. *The speed of communication* The marketing information system will only be effective if information is communicated quickly and to the appropriate people. Deciding what information to withhold from an individual and the concise reporting of relevant information can be as important as deciding what information to include if information overload is to be avoided.

2.7.2   Trends in information analysis

As information collection, processing, transmission and storage technologies improve, information is becoming more accessible not just to one particular organization, but also to its competitors. Attention is therefore moving away from how information is collected to who is best able to make use of the information. It is too simple to say that marketing managers commission data collection by technical experts and make decisions on the basis of these data. There has been recent research interest in the relationship between market researchers and marketing managers, focusing on the role of trust between the two and how its presence helps to reduce risk in decision making (Moorman, Zaltman and Deshpande, 1992).

Recent technological innovations—e.g. electronic point of sale (EPOS) systems—have enabled organizations to greatly enhance the quality of the information they have about their operating environment. Resulting increases in operational efficiency, combined with the additional information which it is now possible to generate, has allowed many organizations to improve other areas of their product offering—such as the development of ongoing customer relationships—as a means of gaining competitive advantages. Many supermarkets are now using loyalty cards to collect information about customers which they can then use to target small segments of customers with offers that very closely fit their needs. At the same time, the increasing ease with which data can be collected and disseminated has made it easier for companies to manage production quality by setting quantifiable objectives that can be effectively monitored.

REVIEW QUESTIONS

1. (a) Explain briefly what you understand by the 'marketing environment' of a business.   (12 marks)
   (b) Prepare a list of recommendations which would aid a business to address change in its technical environment   (8 marks)
   (CIM Marketing Environment Examination, December 1994, Q.3)
2. 'Suppliers and intermediaries are important stakeholders in the micro-environment of the business'.
   (a) Explain the evolving role and functions of these stakeholders in the marketing-orientated business of the 1990s.   (12 marks)
   (b) With examples, comment on the growing importance of relationship marketing in this regard.   (8 marks)
   (CIM Marketing Environment Examination, June 1995, Q.3)
3. Using a company of your choice, produce and justify an environmental set. You should include and rank at least five factors in your set.
   (CIM Marketing Environment Examination, June 1995, Q.10, part ii)

REFERENCES

Atkinson, J. (1984) 'Manpower Strategies for Flexible Organizations', *Personnel Management*, August.

Barnes, J. G. (1994) 'Close to the Customer: But is it Really a Relationship', *Journal of Marketing Management*, vol. 10, no. 7, pp. 561–70.

Berry, L. L. (1980) 'Services Marketing is Different', *Business*, May–June, vol. 30, no. 3, pp. 24–29.

Dolan P. and I. Brierley (1992) 'A Tale of Two Bus Companies', *Partnership Research*, London.

Drucker, P. F. (1973) *Management: Tasks, Responsibilities and Practices*, Harper & Row, New York.

Dwyer, F. R., P. H. Schurr, and S. Oh (1987) 'Developing Buyers and Seller Relationships', *Journal of Marketing*, vol. 51, April, pp. 11–27.

Giles, W. (1988) 'Marketing Planning for Maximum Growth', in *The Marketing Handbook*, ed. M. J. Thomas, Gower Press, London.

Gronroos, C. (1982) 'Strategic Management and Marketing in the Service Sector', *Swedish School of Economics and Business Administration*, Helsingfors, Finland.

Gronroos, C. (1984) *Strategic Management and Marketing in the Service Sector*, Chartwell-Bratt Ltd, Bromley, Kent.

Gronroos, C. (1989) 'Defining Marketing: A Market-Oriented Approach', *European Journal of Marketing*, vol. 23, no. 1, pp. 52–60.

Gummesson, E. (1991) 'Marketing-Orientation Revisited: The Crucial Role of the Part-Time Marketer', *European Journal of Marketing*, vol. 25, no. 2, pp. 60–75.

Handy, Charles B. (1989) *The Age of Unreason*, Harvard Business School Press, Boston, Mass.

Jelinek, M., Smirich, L. and Hirsch, P. (1983) 'Introduction: A Code of Many Colours', *Administrative Science Quarterly*, vol. 28, p. 337.

Kotler, P. (1994) *Marketing Management: Analysis, Planning, Implementation and Control*, Prentice-Hall, Englewood Cliffs, N. J.

Lewis, B. R. (1981) 'Bank Service Quality', *Journal of Marketing Management*, vol. 7, no. 1, pp. 47–62.

Moorman, C., Zaltman, G. and Deshpande, R. (1992) 'Relationships between Providers and Users of Market Research: The Dynamics of Trust within and between Organizations', *Journal of Marketing Research*, vol. 29 (August), pp. 314–28.

Pascale, R. T. and Athos, A. (1981) *The Art of Japanese Management*, Simon and Schuster, New York.

Piercy, N. (1990) 'Marketing Concepts and Actions: Implementing Marketing-led Strategic Change', *European Journal of Marketing*, vol. 24, no. 2, pp. 24–39.

FURTHER READING

Achrol, R. (1991) 'Evolution of the Marketing Organization: New Forms for Turbulent Environments', *Journal of Marketing*, October, pp. 77–93.

Bagozzi, R. P. (1994) *Principles of Marketing Research*, Blackwell, Oxford.

Christopher, M., Payne, A. and Ballantyne, D. (1991) *Relationship Marketing*, Heinemann, London.

Cravens, D. W. and Piercy, N. F. (1994) 'Relationship Marketing and Collaborative Networks in Service Organizations', *International Journal of Services Management*, vol. 5, no. 5, pp. 39–53.

Gummesson, E. (1994) 'Making Relationship Marketing Operational', *International Journal of Services Management*, vol. 5, no. 5, pp. 5–20.

Hofstede, G. (1991) *Culture and Organizations*, McGraw-Hill, London.

O'Brien, Louise and Jones, Charles (1995) 'Do Rewards Really Create Loyalty?', *Harvard Business Review*, May–June, pp. 75–82.

Piercy, N. and Morgan, N. (1990) 'Internal Marketing: The Missing Half of the Marketing Programme', *Long Range Planning*, vol. 8, no. 1, pp. 4–6.

Porter, M. and Millar, V. (1985) 'How Information Gives You Competitive Advantage', *Harvard Business Review*, vol. 85 (July–August), pp. 149–60.

Webster, F. E. (1992) 'The Changing Role of Marketing in the Corporation', *Journal of Marketing*, vol. 56 (October), pp. 1–17.

THREE
BUSINESS ORGANIZATIONS—CLASSIFICATION

OBJECTIVES

After reading this chapter, you should understand:

- The relationship between organizational form and marketing
- The diversity of business organizations, including sole traders, partnerships, limited companies, government and voluntary sector organizations and the marketing strengths and weaknesses of each
- The differing legal frameworks by which organizations are created

3.1 ORGANIZATIONS AND THEIR ENVIRONMENT

Business organizations are extremely diverse in their form and functions, even within a single business sector. It is therefore difficult to define an 'ideal' organization. Instead, all organizational forms have advantages and disadvantages relative to the environment in which they operate and successful organizations capitalize on their advantages while recognizing their disadvantages. In a single business sector, there can be a role for both the one-person owner-managed business and the multinational organization. Both can adapt and find a role.

Analogies can be drawn between business organizations and their environment and the animal kingdom. In a natural habitat, the largest and most powerful animals can coexist with much smaller species. The smaller species can avoid becoming prey for the larger ones by being more agile or developing defences such as safe habitats which are inaccessible to their larger predators. Sometimes, a mutually beneficial symbiotic relationship can develop between the two. In a bid to survive, animals soon learn which sources of food are easily obtainable and abandon those that are either inedible or face competition from more powerful animals. As in the business environment, macroenvironmental change can affect the relationships between species, as for example, has occurred with deforestation and the use of intensive farming methods.

Just as any study of the animal world may begin by examining the characteristics of the participants, so an analysis of the marketing environment could begin by looking at the characteristics of the organizations that make it up. Marketers need to understand the diversity of organizational types for a number of reasons.

1. Different types of organizations will be able to address their potential customers in different ways. Lack of resources could, for example, inhibit the development of expensive new products. Sometimes, the objectives of an organization—either formal or informal—will influence what it is able to offer the public.

2. As sellers of materials to companies involved in further manufacture, marketers should understand how the buying behaviour of different kinds of organizations varies. A small business is likely to buy equipment in a different way to a large public sector organization.
3. Marketers should be interested in the structure of business units at the macroeconomic level. It has been argued by many economists that a thriving small business sector is essential for an expanding economy and that the effect of domination by large organizations may be to reduce competition and innovation. Marketers should therefore be interested in the rate of new business creation and trends in the composition of business units.

3.1.1   Classification of business organizations

There are many approaches to classifying organizations that would satisfy the marketer's interests identified above. Organizations are commonly classified according to their:

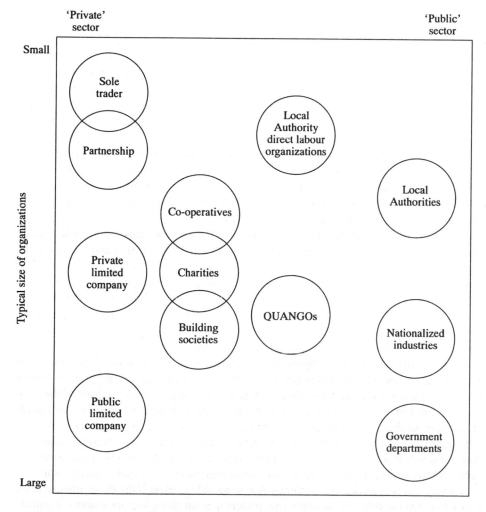

Figure 3.1   A classification of organizational types

- Size (e.g. turnover, assets, employees, geographical coverage)
- Ownership (e.g. public, private, co-operative)
- Legal form (e.g. sole trader, limited company)
- Industry sector

A good starting point for classifying business organizations is to look at their legal form. A business's legal form is often closely related to the level of resources it has available for marketing, its size and objectives (the issues of organizational size and objectives are considered in more detail in the next chapter).

This chapter will firstly consider private sector organizations, which range from the small owner-managed sole trader to the very large public limited company. It will then review the diverse range of publicly owned organizations which operate as businesses. A third, and growing, group of organizations cannot be neatly categorized into private or public sector and include QUANGOs (quasi-autonomous national government organizations) and charities. To put the diversity of organizations into context, Figure 3.1 illustrates the types of organizations that will be described in this chapter.

3.2 THE SOLE TRADER

The most basic level of business organization is provided by the sole trader. In fact, the concept of a separate legal form does not apply to this type of organization, for the business and the individual are considered to be legally indistinguishable. The individual carries on business in his or her own name, with the result that the individual assumes all the rights and duties of the business. Thus, if the business is sued for breach of contract, this amounts to suing the individual and if the business does not have the resources to meet any claim, the claim must be met out of the private resources of the individual.

Becoming a sole trader requires the minimum of formality and for this reason it can be difficult to tell how many are being created or are in existence at any one time. The most commonly used indication is provided by VAT registrations, although this does not give a complete picture as businesses with a turnover of less than £46 000 (1994–5) do not need to register. Maintaining a business as a sole trader requires a minimum of formality—for example, there is no obligation to file annual accounts, other than for the assessment of the individual's personal tax liability.

It has been estimated that about 80 per cent of all businesses in the United Kingdom are sole traders, although they account for only a small proportion of Gross Domestic Product. In some sectors of the economy they are a very popular business form and dominate sectors such as newsagents, window cleaners and hairdressers. Sole traders can grow by taking on additional employees. There is no legal limit on the number of employees that a sole trader may have and there are many examples of sole traders employing over 100 people. At the other extreme, it is sometimes difficult to describe just when a sole trader business unit comes into existence, with many sole traders operating on a part-time basis—some 'moonlighting' without the knowledge of the tax authorities.

Marketers should recognize a number of important characteristics of sole traders. Firstly, they tend to have limited capital resources. Risk capital is generally only provided by the sole proprietor or close personal backers and additional loan capital is often only made available against security of the individual's assets. In the field of new product development, this type of business has very often made discoveries, but has been unable to see new products through to production and launch on account of a lack of funds. If a new product does make it into a competitive market, this type of business may face competition in price, promotional effort or product offering from larger and better resourced firms. The larger firm is likely to have greater resources to mount a campaign to see off a newer competitor.

Being relatively small, the sole trader may suffer by not being able to exploit the economies of scale available to larger firms. On the other hand, many sole traders aim for those sectors where economies of scale are either unimportant or non-existent, for example painting and decorating, hairdressing and outside catering. In many personal services, smallness and the personal touch, plus the fact that many small businesses do not need to charge their customers VAT, can be a strong selling point.

The small sole trader could find that it is too small to justify having its own expertise in many areas. Many do not have specialists to look after the accounting or advertising functions, for example. Furthermore, the goals and policies of the business can become totally dominated by the sole trader. Although goals can be pursued determinedly and single-mindedly, the sole trader presents a narrower view than may be offered by a larger board of directors. The goals of a sole trader may appear very irrational to an outsider, where many individuals may be happy to continue uneconomic ventures on emotional grounds alone. Many very small caterers, for example, may be financially better off drawing unemployment benefit, but being a sole trader may satisfy wider goals of status or the pursuit of a leisure interest.

Many sole traders fail after only a short time, often because of the lack of management skills of an individual who may well be an expert in his or her own field of specialization. Others continue until they reach a point where lack of expertise and financial resources impose a constraint on growth. At this point, many sole traders consider going into partnership with another individual, or setting up a company with limited liability.

3.2.1 Sole trader or employee?

It can sometimes be difficult to decide whether a person is a self-employed sole trader or an employee of another organization. There can be many advantages in classifying an individual as self-employed rather than an employee. For the self-employed, tax advantages could result from being able to claim as legitimate business expenses items (such as travelling expenses and tools) that are denied to the employee. The method of assessing income tax liability in arrears also usually favours the self-employed. For the employer, designation as self-employed could save on National Insurance payments. It also relieves the employer of many duties that are imposed in respect of employees but not subcontractors, such as entitlement to sick pay, notice periods and maternity leave.

The problem of distinction is particularly great in the construction sector and for service sectors (such as market research) which employ large numbers of part-time workers. The courts would decide the matter on the basis of the degree of control that the employer has over the employee—if the employer is able to specify the manner in which a task is to be carried out, then an employment relationship generally exists. If, however, the required end result is specified but the manner in which it is achieved is left up to the individual, then a contract for services will exist, in other words, self employment.

3.3 PARTNERSHIPS

Two or more persons in partnership can combine their resources and expertise to form what could be a more efficient business unit. The Partnership Act 1890 defines a partnership as 'the relation which subsists between persons carrying on a business with a view to profit'. Partnerships can range from two builders joining together to a very large accountancy or solicitors' practice with hundreds of partners. In practice, the maximum number of people who can form a partnership is limited by legislation to 20 (although certain professional partnerships may exceed this number).

Partnerships are generally formed by contract between the parties, although, where this is not done, the Partnership Act 1890 governs relationships between the partners. Among the main items in a Partnership Agreement will be terms specifying:

1. The amount of capital subscribed by each partner
2. The basis on which profits will be determined and allocated between partners and the management

responsibilities of each partner—some partners may join as 'sleeping partners' and take no active part in the management of the business

3. The basis for allocating salaries to each partner and for drawing personal advances against entitlement to profits

4. Procedures for dissolving the partnership and distributing the assets of the business between members

Despite this internal agreement between partners, a partnership in England and Wales does not have its own legal personality. As a consequence, the partners incur unlimited personal liability for the debts of the business. Furthermore, each partner is jointly liable for the debts incurred by all partners in the course of business. An added complication of a partnership is that the withdrawal of any one partner, either voluntarily or upon death or bankruptcy, causes the automatic termination of the partnership. A new partnership will come into being, as it would if an additional partner was admitted to the partnership.

Because of the lack of protection afforded to partners, this form of organization tends to be relatively uncommon, except for some groups of professional people, where business risks are low and for whom professional codes of practice may prevent the formation of limited companies. Partnership is a particularly common form of business organization with accountants, solicitors, dentists and opticians.

3.4   LIMITED COMPANIES

It was recognized in the nineteenth century that industrial development would be impeded if investors in business always ran the risk of losing their personal assets to cover the debts of a business over which very often they had no day-to-day control. At the same time, the size of business units had become larger, causing the idea of a partnership to become strained. The need for a trading company to have a separate legal personality from that of its owners was recognized from the Middle Ages, when companies were incorporated by Royal Charter. From the seventeenth century, organizations could additionally be incorporated by Act of Parliament. Both methods of incorporating a company were expensive and cumbersome, and a simpler method was required to cope with the rapid expansion of business enterprises that were fuelling the Industrial Revolution. The response to this need was the Joint Stock Companies Act 1844, which enabled a company to be incorporated as a separate legal identity by the registration of a Memorandum of Association and payment of certain fees. The present law governing the registration of companies is contained in the Companies Act 1985. Today, the vast majority of trading within the United Kingdom is undertaken by limited companies. The legislation of most countries allows for organizations to be created that have a separate legal personality from their owners. In this way, separate legal identity is signified in the United States by the title 'Incorporated' after a company's name, by 'Societie Anonym' in France, 'Gmbh' in Germany and 'Sdn. Bhd.' in Malaysia.

When a limited company is created under UK legislation, it is required to produce a Memorandum and Articles of Association. The Memorandum regulates the relationships of the company with the outside world while the Articles of Association regulate the internal administration of the company. Most limited companies are registered as private limited companies, indicated in company names by the designation 'Limited'. However, some larger companies choose to register as Public Limited Companies (PLCs) and face tougher regulatory requirements. These are described later in this chapter.

3.4.1   The Memorandum of Association

This statement about the company's relations with the outside world includes a number of important provisions:

1. The first item to be considered is the name of the company. If it is a Private Limited Company, the name must end with the word 'Limited' (or its Welsh equivalent ('Cyf') for companies registered in Wales). A number of restrictions exist on the company's choice of name—for example, the name must not cause confusion with an existing company or suggest a connection with royalty. The trading name will very often be quite different from the registered name, in which case the company is required to display the name and address of its owner at their business premises, on their business stationery and to customers and suppliers on request.

2. The second important element of the memorandum is a statement as to whether the liability of its members is limited, and if so what the limit of liability will be in the event of the company being wound up with unpaid debts. The majority of companies are limited by shares. Members' liability to contribute to the assets of the company is limited to the amount—if any—that is unpaid on their shares. An alternative is for companies to be limited by guarantee. In these companies, the liability of each member to make up for any shortfall in assets in the event of the company being wound up is limited to the value of his or her guarantee. This type of company is comparatively rare, being found mainly among non-profit-making organizations, such as professional and trade associations. A further less common type of company occurs where the Memorandum specifies unlimited liability of members. Because the members of such companies have unlimited liability for the company's debts, they are liable to lose their personal assets—a problem that gave rise to the limited liability company in the first place. There has, however, been an increase in the number of unlimited companies since 1967 because the Companies Act of that year exempts them from filing their accounts with the Registrar of Companies, and hence publicizing their financial affairs.

3. The third important element of the Memorandum is the objects clause. This is particularly important because it specifies the scope within which the company can exercise its separate legal personality. There are two principal consequences of having an objects clause. Firstly, the clause protects investors who can learn from it the purposes for which their money is to be used. Secondly, it protects individuals dealing with the company, who can discover the extent of the company's powers. Any act that the company performs beyond its powers is deemed to be *ultra vires* and therefore void. Thus even where the directors of a company were in agreement with a contract which was beyond its powers, the contract itself would be void. The principal of *ultra vires* was amended by the Companies Act 1985, section 35, so that any person who enters into a contract with a company which is outside its objects, but which is sanctioned by the directors of the company, will be able to enforce it against the company, providing that he or she did not know that the contract was beyond the company's powers. In practice, it is common for companies to contain an objects clause that is drafted in a deliberately broad manner, allowing considerable freedom for the directors to move away from their traditional business area. Nevertheless, marketers within limited companies would be wise to check their Memorandum of Association to ensure that diversification is allowed by their objects clause.

3.4.2   The Articles of Association

While the Memorandum regulates the relationships of the company with the outside world, the Articles of Association regulate the internal administration of the company, the relations between the company and its members and between the members themselves. The articles cover such matters as the issue and transfer of shares, the rights of shareholders, meetings of members, the appointment of directors and procedures for producing and auditing accounts.

Companies seeking to expand by acquiring a company may be held back by the target company's Articles of Association. The Articles may, for instance, restrict ownership of shares by any one person to a fixed percentage of the total, as has been the case in many newly privatized companies. Different shares may attract different voting rights, so that, despite acquiring a majority of shares, the acquiring company is not able to acquire effective control of the company. The Forte Hotel Group has, for example, owned a majority of the shares in the Savoy Hotel Group for some time. However, most of the shares that it held carried no voting rights and it did not hold a majority of the voting shares. It has therefore been unable to exercise control over the Savoy Group.

3.4.3   Company administration

A company acts through its directors who are persons chosen by shareholders to conduct and manage the company's affairs. The number of directors and their powers are detailed in the Articles of Association and, so long as they do not exceed these powers, shareholders cannot normally interfere in their conduct of the company's business. The Articles will normally give one director additional powers to act as managing director, enabling him or her to make decisions without reference to the full board of directors.

Every company must have a secretary on whom Companies Acts have placed a number of duties and responsibilities, such as filing reports and accounts with the Registrar of Companies. The secretary is the chief administrative officer of the company, usually chosen by the directors.

3.4.4   Shareholders

The shareholders own the company, and in theory exercise control over it. A number of factors limit the actual control that shareholders in fact exercise over their companies. It was mentioned earlier that the Articles of a company may discriminate between groups of shareholders by giving differential voting rights. Even where shareholders have full voting rights, the vast majority of shareholders typically are either unable or insufficiently interested to attend company meetings, and are happy to leave company management to the directors, so long as the dividend paid to them is satisfactory. There has been a tendency in recent years for individual shareholders to use their privileged position to raise issues of social concern at companies' annual shareholders' meetings. For example, small shareholders have used meetings of water companies as a platform to protest about poor levels of service and excessive directors' salaries. Shareholders' revolts can have widespread public relations implications for companies.

3.4.5   Company reports and accounts

A company provides information about itself when it is set up through its Memorandum and Articles of Association. To provide further protection for investors and people with whom the company may deal, companies are required to provide subsequent information.

An important document that must be produced annually is the annual report. Every company having a share capital must make a return in the prescribed form to the Registrar of Companies, stating what has happened to its capital during the previous year, for example by describing the number of shares allotted and the cash received for them. The return must be accompanied by a copy of the audited balance sheet in the prescribed form, supported by a profit and loss account that gives a true and fair representation of the year's transactions. Like the Memorandum and Articles of Association, these documents are available for public inspection, with the exception of unlimited companies which do not have to file annual accounts. Also, most small companies need only file an abridged balance sheet and do not need to submit a profit and loss account.

As well as providing the annual report and accounts, the directors of a company are under a duty to keep proper books of account and details of assets and liabilities.

3.4.6 Liquidation and receivership

Most limited companies are created with a view to continuous operation into the foreseeable future (although, sometimes, companies are set up with an expectation that they should cease to exist once their principal objective has been achieved). The process of breaking up a business is referred to as liquidation. Voluntary liquidation may be initiated by members. Alternatively, a limited company may be liquidated (or wound up) by a court under section 122 of the Insolvency Act 1986. The first stage of an involuntary liquidation is generally the appointment of a receiver who has authority which overrides the directors of the company. An individual or company who has an unmet claim against a company can apply to a court for it to be placed in receivership. In the United Kingdom in 1994, 1882 companies went into receivership. Most receivers initially seek to turn round a failing business by consolidating its strengths and cutting out activities that brought about failure in the first place, allowing the company to be sold as a going concern. The proceeds of such a sale are used towards repaying the company's creditors, and, if there is a sufficient surplus, the shareholders of the company. However, many directors who have lost their businesses claim that receivers are too eager to liquidate assets and unwilling to take any risks that may eventually allow both creditors and shareholders to be paid off. The legislation has been revised by the Insolvency Act 1986, section 5.8, which allows a period of 'administration' during which a company can seek to put its finances into order with its creditors. Section 5.8 of the Act defines the circumstances in which an administration order may be made by a court.

Receivership affects organizations small and large and prolonged periods of receivership can leave staff and customers very uncertain about the future. Recent notable receiverships have included the International Leisure Group and the Bank of Credit and Commerce International. An example of a smaller company that went into receivership was the Automagic chain of shoe repair shops which went into receivership in 1995. However, the latter is an example of where a business is sold on by receivers almost intact to a new owner (in this case to the larger Timpson chain).

3.4.7 Public limited companies

The Companies Act 1985 recognized that existing companies legislation did not sufficiently distinguish between the small owner-managed limited company and the large multinational firm. Thus the concept of the public limited company—abbreviated to PLC—came about. The basic principles of separate legal personality are similar for both private and public limited companies, but the Companies Act 1985 confers a number of additional duties and benefits on public limited companies.

The difference is partly one of scale—a PLC must have a minimum share capital of £50 000 compared to the £100 of the private limited company. It must have at least two directors instead of the minimum of one for the private company. Before a public limited company can start trading, or borrow money, it must obtain a 'business certificate' from the Registrar of Companies, confirming that it has met all legal requirements in relation to its share capital.

Against these additional obstacles of the public limited company is the major advantage that it can offer its shares and debentures to the public, something that is illegal for a private company, where shares are more commonly taken up by friends, business associates and family. As a private limited company grows, it may have exhausted all existing sources of equity capital, and 'going public' is one way of attracting capital from a wider audience. During the latter part of the 1980s, many groups of managers bought out their businesses, initially setting up a private limited company with a private placement of shares. In order to attract new capital, and often to allow existing shareholders to sell their holding more easily, these businesses have often been re-registered as public companies.

For the marketer, PLC status has a number of strengths and weaknesses. Many companies highlight PLC status in promotional material in order to give potential customers a greater degree of confidence in the company. Another major strength is the greater potential ability to fund major new product developments (discussed in more detail in Chapter 4). Against this, the PLC is much more open to public examination, especially the financial community. Management may have plans that will achieve a long-term payback, bringing it into conflict with possibly short-term objectives of City financial institutions. Management could end up being influenced unduly by short-term financial market considerations rather than long-term market factors. Indeed, a number of companies have recognized this problem of PLC status and reverted to private status by buying back shares from the public—the Virgin Group was one example in the late 1980s.

Today, although public limited companies are in a numerical minority, they account for a substantial proportion of the equity of the limited company sector and cover a wide range of industries which typically operate at a large scale—for example banking, car manufacture and property development.

3.4.8   Advantages and disadvantages of limited companies

Comparisons between sole traders and partnerships, on the one hand, and limited companies, on the other, can be made at a number of levels. Firstly, formation of a limited company is relatively formal and time consuming—for a sole trader there is the minimum of formality in establishing a business. The added formality continues with the requirement to produce an annual return and set of accounts. On the other hand, limited company status affords much greater protection to the entrepreneur in the event of the business getting into financial difficulty. Raising additional funds would usually be easier for a limited company, although personal guarantees may still be required to cover loans to the company. Additional funding which limited company status makes possible, especially public limited company status, allows organizations to embark on more ambitious marketing plans. While a sole trader may concentrate on small niche markets, a limited company may be in a better position to tackle mainstream mass markets.

3.5   PUBLIC SECTOR ORGANIZATIONS

Government has traditionally been involved in providing goods and services that cannot be sensibly provided by market forces—for example defence, education and basic health services. Government involvement has, however, developed beyond providing these basic public services to providing goods and services that could arguably be provided just as efficiently by private sector organizations.

Public sector organizations take a number of forms, embracing government departments and agencies, local government, nationalized industries and all other undertakings in which central or local government has a controlling interest. This chapter will focus on those public sector organizations that supply goods and services to consumers. Those government organizations that are primarily policy making in nature will be considered in more detail in Chapter 7 dealing with the political environment. In between those branches of government responsible for providing goods and services and those responsible for policy are an increasing number that are involved in both. For example, many public services such as health authorities are increasingly selling services at a profit, although this is not their primary function and represents a small part of their total turnover.

3.5.1   Nationalized industries

Most government goods and services provided on a commercial basis have been provided through nationalized industries. Most countries have a nationalized industry sector and the size of the sector generally reflects the political ideology of a nation. Thus the United States has traditionally had very few government-owned business organizations, France has taken nationalization to sectors such as banking which many would consider a prerogative of the private sector, while Britain has seen a once large nationalized industry sector shrink with changes in political ideology. UK nationalized industries accounted for less than one per cent of GDP in 1994, having fallen from 9 per cent in 1979).

Governments first became involved in industry for largely pragmatic reasons. Thus in 1913, a key shareholding in the Anglo-Iranian Oil Company—the precursor of British Petroleum—was acquired by the British government to ensure oil supplies to the Royal Navy. During the inter-war years, the Central Electricity Generating Board, the British Broadcasting Corporation and the London Passenger Transport Board were created to fill gaps that the private sector had not been capable of filling. Whereas the reasons for the creation of these early nationalized industries were largely pragmatic, the early post-war period saw a large number of nationalized industries created for increasingly ideological reasons. During the Labour government of the early post-war years, the state acquired control of the coal, electricity, gas, iron and steel industries and most inland transport. Some industries returned to the private sector during the Conservative government of the 1950s, while others were added by subsequent Labour governments.

The 1980s and 1990s have seen a great demise in the role of nationalized industry, not just in the United Kingdom but throughout the world. Post-war Europe may have needed centralized planning and allocation of resources to facilitate the reconstruction effort, but the mood had changed by the relatively affluent, consumer-oriented years of the 1980s. The view went around that governments were bad managers of commercial businesses and that private sector organizations were much more capable of giving good value to consumers. In the rush to sell off nationalized industries, privatization was often confused with deregulation. Simply transferring a nationalized industry to the private sector could easily create a private monopoly which was unresponsive to consumers' needs. Consequently, most privatization has been accompanied by measures to deregulate sectors of the economy. Where this has been impractical, government intervention has been retained in the form of regulation of prices and service standards.

Governments have chosen a number of methods to transfer state-owned industries to the private sector. The most common have been:

1. *Sale of shares to the public* Before shares in a state-owned organization can be sold to the public, a private sector limited company with a shareholding must be formed. Initially, all of the new company's shares are owned by the government, and privatization subsequently involves selling these shares to the public. For very large privatizations, shares may be targeted at large international investors in order to secure the substantial amounts of share capital sought. Sale to the general public is often undertaken where it would be considered politically unacceptable to exclude small investors from the benefits of privatization.
2. *Trade sale* Smaller state-owned industries can often be easily sold to other private sector companies as a complete entity. This happened, for example, in the sale of the then state-owned Rover Group to British Aerospace. Sometimes, parts of nationalized industries have been broken away for sale to private buyers (e.g. the shipping and hotel operations of British Rail were separated from the parent organization before sale to private sector organizations). The administrative costs of this method of disposal are relatively low, but governments are open to allegations that they sold off a private sector asset too cheaply to favoured buyers.
3. *Management/employee buy-out* This is often a popular option for people-intensive businesses which financial institutions may have difficulty in deciding on a value, especially in industries with a history of poor industrial relations. It was used as a method of disposing of the National Freight Corporation and parts of the National Bus Company.

Prior to their privatization, many state-owned organizations have been restructured to make them more attractive to potential buyers. This has typically involved writing off large amounts of debt and offering generous redundancy payments to workers who would not therefore become a liability to a new owner. In doing this, Conservative governments have been accused of providing subsidies for private buyers, although, very often, such action has been essential to provide a buyer with a competitive business proposition.

While governments may be ideologically committed to reducing the role of state-owned industries, it has proved difficult to sell many of them for a variety of practical and ideological reasons. Thus the nuclear generating sector of the UK electricity industry was initially omitted from electricity privatization because the private sector was not prepared to underwrite the long-term risks associated with decommissioning nuclear power stations. Privatization of the coal and rail industries was delayed largely because of the underlying unprofitability of the industries, faced with competition from other means of transport in the case of British Rail and from relatively cheap imported coal in the case of British Coal. The coal industry was drastically reduced in size before sale and British Rail has been substantially reorganized into a large number of separate business units, with the intention of selling these units to the private sector. In the case of the Post Office, ideological objections have been raised at the prospect of the Royal Mail letter delivery service being owned by a private sector company. This has not, however, prevented the Post Office from being reorganized along business lines, with private limited companies being formed for the main business units, one of which—Girobank—has been sold off to the Alliance and Leicester Building Society while another—the parcel delivery service—has been restructured to act more like one of the private parcel companies with which it is having to compete in an increasingly competitive market.

Table 3.1 gives a list of recent British privatizations. This is not a complete list. In some cases, the sale of shares was phased over a number of periods.

Table 3.1 Recent UK privatizations

Organization	Date of privatization	Method of privatization
British Aerospace	1981	Public sale of shares
National Freight Corporation	1982	Employee/management buy-out
British Telecom	1984	Public sale of shares
Jaguar	1984	Public sale of shares
Sealink	1984	Trade sale
British Gas	1986	Public sale of shares
British Petroleum	1986	Public sale of shares
BA Helicopters	1986	Trade sale
National Bus Company	1986–91	Trade sales/management buy-outs
British Airports Authority	1987	Public sale of shares
British Airways	1987	Public sale of shares
Rolls-Royce	1987	Public sale of shares
Leyland Bus Company	1987	Trade sale
British Steel	1988	Public sale of shares
Rover Group	1988	Trade sale
Regional Water Companies	1989	Public sale of shares
Regional Electricity Compamies	1990	Public sale of shares
Powergen/National Power	1991	Public sale of shares
Scottish Electricity Companies	1991	Public sale of shares
British Coal	1994	Trade sale

The role of marketing within public corporations has been influenced by the nature of the market in which they operate. Following the late 1940s nationalizations, marketing was seen in many of the nationalized industries as being very secondary to production. The relative unimportance of marketing was often associated with some degree of monopoly power granted to the industry. In these circumstances, public corporations could afford to ignore marketing. However, as production of the basic industries caught up with demand and the economy became more deregulated during the 1980s, consumers increasingly had choice between suppliers offered to them. For example, the deregulation of the coach industry in 1981 and the growth in private car ownership have placed increasing competitive pressure on British Rail, and hence an increasing importance for the organization to become marketing orientated. The latter has increasingly been set profit objectives rather than poorly specified social objectives.

What could be seen as either a strength or a weakness for the nationalized industry marketer has been finance for investment and new product development. Investment comes from government—either directly or through guarantees on loans from the private sector. Profits earned have not necessarily been ploughed back into the business. The public sector has since the 1930s been seen as one instrument for regulating the economy, cutting back or increasing investment to suit the needs of the national economy rather than the needs of the particular market that the corporation is addressing. As well as limiting the amount of investment funds available, government involvement has also been accused of delay caused by the time which it has taken to scrutinize and approve a proposal. By the time approval had been granted, the investment could be too late to meet changed market conditions.

Nationalized industries are perceived as an instrument of government and although theoretically they may have an independent constitution, government is frequently accused of exercising covert pressure in order to achieve political favour. Fuel prices, rail fares and telephone charges have all at some time been subject to these allegations, which make life for the marketer more difficult because of their confused objectives.

Britain is widely credited with having taken the lead in privatizing state-owned industries, and many countries have followed. For example, the state-owned telephone and airline industries of most European countries are being progressively sold off to the private sector, partly to meet European Union competition requirements.

3.5.2 Local authority enterprise

In addition to providing basic services such as roads, education, housing and social services, local authorities have a number of roles in providing marketable goods and services in competitive markets. For a long time, local authorities have operated bus services and leisure facilities, among others. Initially they were set up for a variety of reasons—sometimes to provide a valuable public service, at other times to help stimulate economic development or to earn a profit to supplement the local authority's income. Sometimes, where a project was too large for one authority and benefited many neighbouring authorities, a joint board would be formed between the authorities. This sometimes happened with local authority controlled airports, for example East Midlands Airport.

Increasingly, UK local authorities are being forced to turn their trading activities into business-like units, separately accountable from the rest of the local authority's responsibilities. In the case of local authority bus and airport operations, the government has passed legislation in the form of the Local Government Act 1988, requiring local authorities to create limited companies into which their assets will be placed. Like any limited company, they will be required to appoint a board of directors and to produce an annual profit and loss statement. It was also the government's intention that, by creating a company structure, it would be easier to introduce private capital, or indeed to sell off the business in its entirety to the private sector. This has already occurred in the case of a large number of local authority bus companies and smaller airports.

Even where separate business units have not been created, local authority services are being exposed to increasing levels of competition. Operations in such areas as highway maintenance, refuse collection and street cleaning must now—following the Local Government Act 1988—be put out to compulsory competitive tender (CCT). The scope of CCT is spreading deeper into local authority services and authorities are now required to handle parts of their legal and architectural services in this way, for example. Where a service is put out to competitive tender, the existing local authority work-force very often puts in a bid of its own to provide the services in question. The legislation requires that, in these circumstance, a direct labour organization (DLO) should be created which is separately accountable from the rest of the authority's activities. The management of these direct labour organizations must study the market carefully to judge the likely price at which its competitors will bid. One interesting anomaly of the Act is that while private sector companies can compete for local authority contracts, the local authority's direct labour organization is not allowed to compete for contracts to supply services to the private sector. Where a private sector company takes over the provision of services for a local authority and takes on its employees, the new employer will generally take on responsibilities for accrued rights to redundancy payments, among other things.

In other areas of local authority services, clients are being offered greater choice. With the advent of local management of schools, the governing bodies of schools are adopting—if somewhat grudgingly—a marketing orientation to ensure that the service they are offering is considered better than neighbouring schools that pupils would have the choice of attending. Only by attracting clients can they ensure funding for their school.

3.5.3   Distinctive characteristics of public sector organizations

Although public sector organizations cover a wide range of services operating in diverse environments, a few generalizations can be made about the ways in which their marketing differs from that practised by the private sector:

- The aim of most private sector organizations is to earn profits for the owners of the organization. By contrast to these quantifiable objectives, public sector organizations operate with relatively diverse and unquantified objectives. For example, a museum may have qualitative scholarly objectives in addition to relatively quantifiable objectives, such as maximizing revenue or the number of visitors.
- The private sector is usually able to monitor the results of its marketing activity as the benefits are usually internal to the organization. By contrast, many of the aims that public sector organizations seek to achieve are external and a profit and loss statement cannot be produced in the way that is possible with a private sector organization operating to narrow internal financial goals.
- The degree of discretion given to a private sector marketing manager is usually greater than that given to a counterpart in the public sector. The checks and balances imposed on many of the latter reflects the fact that their organizations are accountable to a wider constituency of interests than the typical private sector organization.
- Many of the marketing mix elements that private sector organizations can tailor to meet the needs of specific groups of users are often not open to the public sector marketer. For non-traded public services, price—if it is used at all—is a reflection of centrally determined social values rather than the value placed on a service by consumers.
- Public sector organizations are frequently involved in supplying publicly beneficial services where it can be difficult to identify just who the customer is. Should the customer of a school be regarded as the student, their parents or society as a whole which is investing in a trained work-force of tomorrow?
- Just as the users of some public services may have no choice in who supplies their service, so too the suppliers may have no choice in who they can provide services to. Within the public sector,

organizations may be constrained by statute from providing services beyond specified groups of users. On the other hand, some public sector organizations may be required by law to supply service to specific groups, even though a market-led decision may lead them not to supply.

3.6   QUANGOS

There are many types of organizations that do not fit neatly into the private or public sectors. QUANGOs, or 'quasi-autonomous governmental organizations' are one step removed from publicly-owned organizations and have increased significantly in importance in recent years. One estimate by the organization Charter 88 put the number of QUANGOs in the United Kingdom in 1994 at over 5500. They are important at both a national level and, increasingly, at a local level.

3.6.1   Characteristics of QUANGOs

QUANGOs generally have a number of characteristics:

1. They provide services that are considered politically inappropriate for private companies to dominate.
2. The assets of the organization are vested in a body whose constitution is determined by government and cannot be changed without its approval.
3. Management of a QUANGO is generally by political appointees rather than directly elected representatives.
4. In theory, QUANGOs operate at 'arms length' from government and are free from day-to-day political interference.
5. QUANGOs have structures and processes that resemble private sector organizations in terms of their speed and flexibility.
6. QUANGOs are generally relatively small organizations compared to the larger bureaucracies which they were separated from. In general, QUANGOs are more accountable than a department within a large government departmental structure.

QUANGOs have been particularly important in providing services that would be impractical or politically inappropriate for private sector organizations to provide. This impracticability or political inappropriateness often derives from the fact that the service provided is considered essential and there are few competing alternatives that could be provided within a competitive marketing environment. Outright competition may be considered undesirable, while some degree of central policy co-ordination is considered important. QUANGOs often replace government departments that were perceived as too bureaucratic and lacking in basic business disciplines.

The following are examples of QUANGOs that have been created recently in Britain:

- National Health Service Trusts, which have been created to run hospitals, ambulance services and community health services (among others) previously run as part of an area structure of the National Health Service. Their creation has been accompanied by a purchaser/provider split, in which an internal market has been developed, allowing fundholders to buy in services on behalf of clients from the best quality and/or lowest cost provider (e.g. general practitioners can choose which hospital to refer a patient to).
- Higher Education Corporations, which were formed to take over polytechnics from local authorities who previously controlled them.
- Urban Development Corporations, which bring together public and private sector organizations in a bid to bring about economic regeneration of an area.

- Schools that have 'opted out' of local authority control and become 'grant maintained' are effectively QUANGOs and have more day-to-day control over their policy and budgets than schools that remain with local authorities.
- In many areas, organizations with the characteristics of QUANGOs have been created to market areas as a tourism destination (see Case Study).

3.6.2   Marketing implications of QUANGOs

The marketing implications of transferring a government-provided service to a QUANGO are potentially considerable. An important argument for their creation is that decisions can be made much more speedily by a self-governing organization compared to a department of a large organization where approval must first be obtained from several layers of a hierarchy. The greater accountability of QUANGOs generally means that they have clearly defined social and financial objectives and these can only be met where they provide needed services as efficiently as possible. The clients of QUANGOs generally have a choice of providers and a QUANGO that does not meet the needs of its clients may lose them to other QUANGOs (or, indeed, to the private sector). Funding, in principle, therefore follows customers, rather than being allocated centrally. In this way, universities and schools compete with each other to attract able students, knowing that resources available to them are dependent on their success in attracting students.

In practice, the marketing activity of QUANGOs is often highly constrained. Many continue to depend upon central or local government for a large part of their income, which is protected from competition. Marketing managers cannot act with as much freedom as their equivalents in the private sector as the public and local media often take a keen interest in vital public services and are ready to voice their opposition about the activities of a non-elected body responsible for essential services. Another issue that has not been significantly put to the test is what happens to a QUANGO if it fails to attract clients and therefore funding. Government would generally not allow a QUANGO to go out of business in a way that a private sector organization can go into receivership. Instead, the tendency has been for the assets of a failed QUANGO to be handed over to another whose management has proved itself to be more capable of meeting clients' needs efficiently and effectively.

MARKETING INWARD TOURISM— AN ORGANIZATIONAL CHALLENGE FOR LOCAL AUTHORITIES

Tourism is becoming increasingly important to the economy of many areas, as traditional employment declines and people have more time and money available to spend on tourism. Private sector organizations have traditionally been good at attracting customers to their own facilities such as hotels and amusement parks. Local authorities have increasingly been taking an active role in promoting inward tourism to their areas, largely on account of their role in local economic development. How can local authorities with a traditional bureaucratic culture match the entrepreneurial skills of the private sector? Moreover, how do they avoid duplicating the efforts of the private sector they are helping to promote? The solution adopted in many tourist-seeking areas is

co-operation between all parties involved in tourism. In many areas, tourism development companies have been created, based on Tourism Development Action Programmes.

The tourism product being marketed is a combination of elements from both the private and public sectors—the former responsible for tourist attractions operating to narrow commercial criteria, while the latter has responsibility for infrastructure and planning policies that affect tourism. In view of the external benefits inherent in area tourism promotion, the local authority also plays a large role in promoting the benefits of its area.

Tourism marketing management poses a number of problems for local authorities. Many of the facilities that impinge on tourists' enjoyment of an area, such as car parking, cleanliness, planning and conservation policies, have traditionally operated in a bureaucratic planning culture rather than a marketing culture. In marketing an area, local authorities are constrained by bureaucratic culture and political pressure to meet the needs of their own residents as well as those of potential visitors. Against this, however, the visitors who the local authority is seeking to attract are becoming increasingly selective in the face of competition from many areas—in short, local authorities have had to become very customer centred in their attempts to attract visitors.

In an attempt to combine the need for centrally administered marketing of an area with the dynamism of the private sector, local collaborative marketing ventures have become common in this field. During the latter part of the 1980s, a new type of collaborative body— the Tourism Development Action Programme (TDAP)—was created in a number of tourism-seeking areas with a view to overcoming some of the problems identified above.

TDAPs are an initiative of the English Tourist Board and involve a partnership between private and public sector organizations. The partners typically comprise district and county councils, urban development corporations, local landowners, hotel owners and operators of tourism attractions. Each partner contributes funds to support items of expenditure, which in their own right might not yield a return but result in more tourist spending across the area as a whole. Most of the later TDAPs have been incorporated as formal limited companies, providing an organizational structure which is separately accountable and is attractive to private sector partners. The first TDAP was established in Bristol in 1984. By 1992, 26 TDAPs had been created, of which 8 had completed their initial 3 year term and have continued in some modified form (Bramwell and Broom, 1989).

The creation of TDAPs has allowed the dynamism of private sector type organizations to allow strategic marketing decisions and action programmes to be developed. The TDAP marketing management culture has been found to filter back to the local authority in the way in which it provides public sector facilities to satisfy tourists' needs. Examples of successful collaboration include the development of conference centres which bring together private sector conference and hotel developers, transport operators and local authorities. The latter can achieve diverse objectives (such as creating employment or eliminating eyesores) more effectively by delivering its services, such as signposting, car park provision and land-use planning, within the framework of a marketing strategy developed jointly with the private sector.

QUESTIONS

1. Contrast the objectives of public and private sector organizations which are involved in tourism.
2. Summarize the benefits of collaboration between public and private sector organizations in the tourism sector.
3. What do you understand by 'external benefits' of tourism promotion?

3.6.3 QUANGOs and policy formulation

This section has concentrated attention on QUANGOs which engage in some kind of trade in an environment that has an element of competitiveness. In recent years, the number of QUANGOs has been swollen by a number which have a policy-making role in addition to a basically operational one. There is growing concern over unelected QUANGOs formulating policy that many would see as the responsibility of elected representatives. These broader issues are considered further in Chapter 7 in the context of an organization's political environment.

3.7 OTHER TYPES OF ORGANIZATION

3.7.1 Co-operative societies

Co-operatives can be divided into two basic types according to who owns them: consumer co-operatives and producer co-operatives.

Consumer co-operative societies date back to the mid-nineteenth century when their aims were to provide cheap, unadulterated food for their members and to share profits among members rather than hand them over to outside shareholders. The number of co-operative societies grew during the latter half of the nineteenth century but has declined during recent years as a result of mergers, so that there were 62 retail societies in 1992. Nevertheless, co-operative societies collectively remain the fifth largest retailer in the United Kingdom.

Each co-operative society is registered under the Industrial and Provident Societies Acts, and not the Companies Acts, and has its own legal personality, very much as a private limited company. The main contrast between the two comes in the form of control of the society—an individual can become a member of a co-operative by buying one share and is entitled to one vote. Further shares can be purchased, but the member still only has one vote, unlike the private limited company where voting power is generally based on the number of shares held. The appeal of a shop owned by customers has declined of late, as customers have been lured by competing companies offering lower prices and/or better service. So the co-operative movement has responded by taking on many of the values of the private sector, for example through the abolition of 'dividend' payments and advertising low prices for all. However, the movement has tried to capitalize on its customer ownership by appealing to customers on the basis of its social responsibility. Marketing of co-operative retail stores have sought to stress their 'green' credentials, while the Co-operative Bank has stressed that it does not lend for unethical purposes.

Producer co-operatives are formed where suppliers feel they can produce and sell their output more effectively by pooling their resources, for example by sharing manufacturing equipment and jointly selling output. Producer co-operatives are popular among groups of farmers, allowing individual farmers to market their produce more effectively than they could achieve individually. A recently created example is Milk Marque, a dairy farmers' co-operative that has taken over many of the functions of the UK government's Milk Marketing Board. For the marketing of a producer co-operative to be successful, members need to share a sense of vision and have clear leadership. Where this is lacking, many producer co-operatives may be successful in buying products for their members at a discount, but less successful at marketing their output.

3.7.2 Charities and voluntary organizations

The aims of this group of organizations can be quite complex. Meeting a good cause, such as famine relief or cancer research, is clearly very important. However, these organizations often also set trading objectives, as where charities run shops to raise funds. Often, the way in which such businesses are run is just as important as the funds generated. For example, Dr Barnados runs coffee shops where providing training for disadvantaged staff is seen to be as important as providing a fast service for customers or maximizing the profits of the outlet.

Charities that are registered with the Registrar of Charities are given numerous benefits by the government, such as tax concessions (although recent changes in legislation have introduced stricter controls over their activities in order to stamp out abuses of their status). They have taken on board many of the practices of marketing, as in their increasingly sophisticated communications strategies and trading activities.

Charities and voluntary organizations can act very differently to private and public sector organizations. Customers may show a loyalty to the cause which goes beyond any rational economic explanation. Employees often work for no monetary reward, providing a dedicated and low-cost work-force which can help the organization achieve its objectives.

3.7.3   Building societies

Building societies are governed by the Building Societies Acts which have evolved over time to reflect their changing role. They were for some time seen as being almost monopoly providers of money for house purchase, with strict regulations on the powers of societies in terms of their sources of funds and the uses for which loans could be advanced. With the liberalization of the home mortgage market, building societies now have wider powers of lending and borrowing and face much greater competition. As a result of this, societies have had to embrace marketing more fully. The Building Societies Act 1986 further allowed building societies the possibility of converting to Public Limited Company Status, eliminating the remaining controls imposed by the Building Society Acts.

3.7.4   Franchise organizations

Franchising refers to trading relationships between companies (see Figure 3.2). In terms of their legal status, the companies themselves could be any one of the types previously described. The franchisor (who owns the franchise brand name) is more likely to be a public or private limited company, while the franchisee (who buys the right to use the franchise from the franchisor) is more likely to be a sole trader, partnership or private limited company. The franchisor and franchisee have legally separate identities, but the nature of the franchise agreement can make them very interdependent.

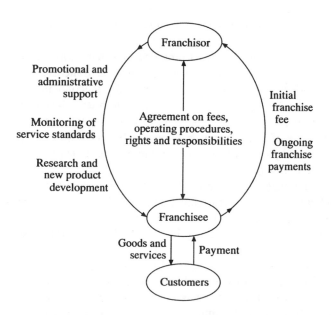

Figure 3.2   The elements of franchising

Franchising is a rapidly growing type of business relationship and the British Franchise Association estimates that by the early 1990s, it accounted for over 20 per cent of retail sales in the United Kingdom. Franchising offers a ready-made business opportunity for the entrepreneur who has capital but does not want the risk associated with setting up a completely new business afresh. A good franchise operation will have a proven business format and would already be well established in its market. The franchisee would be required to pay an initial capital sum for the right to use the name of the franchisor. This may sometimes seem high, but represents a relatively less risky investment than starting a completely new business. It has been estimated that whereas about 90 per cent of all new businesses fail within three years of starting up, 90 per cent of all franchisees survive beyond this period (British Franchise Association 1995).

As well as the initial capital sum, a franchise agreement will usually include provisions for the franchisee to purchase stock from the franchisor and to pass on a percentage of turnover or profit. The franchisor undertakes to provide general marketing back-up for the franchisees.

Public services are increasingly being delivered by franchised organizations in order to capitalize on the motivation of smaller scale franchisees which was described above. Public sector franchises can take a number of forms:

1. The right to operate a vital public service can be sold to a franchisee who in turn has the right to charge users of the facility. The franchisee will normally be required to maintain the facility to a required standard and to obtain government approval of prices to be charged. In the United Kingdom, the government has begun offering private organizations franchisees to operate vital road links, including the Dartford river crossing and Severn Bridge. In the case of the latter, an Anglo-French consortium has acquired the right to collect tolls from users of the bridge and in return must carry out routine maintenance work on it and develop a second river crossing.
2. Government can sell the exclusive right for private organizations to operate a private service which is of public importance. Private sector radio and television broadcasting is operated on a franchise basis where the government invites bids from private companies for exclusive rights to broadcast in specified areas and/or times.
3. Where a socially necessary but economically unviable service is provided in a market-mediated environment, government can subsidize provision of the service by means of a franchise. An example of this can be seen in the way subsidies are paid by local authorities for uneconomic but socially necessary bus services. Following the Transport Act 1985, local authorities wishing to support such services can invite tenders from interested bus operators to provide such services. Successful bidders are awarded a franchise type of contract which allows the bus operator to keep the revenue that it generates from passengers, subject to meeting the minimum requirements of the local authority in terms of timetables and reliability, etc.
4. Even though a public service is not market mediated at the point of delivery, production methods may nevertheless be market mediated and part of the production function may be provided through a franchise agreement. Such an arrangement can have benefits for customers where the franchisee is rewarded partly on the basis of feedback from users. A recent application of this type of franchise can be found in the field of higher education.
5. In the United Kingdom, possibly the longest established public sector franchise is seen in the Post Office. In addition to government-owned 'Crown' post offices, 'sub' post offices have traditionally been operated on a franchise basis in smaller towns. Franchises have been taken up by a variety of small shops and newsagents and generally offer a more limited range of postal office services compared to Crown offices.

HIGHER EDUCATION EXPANDED THROUGH FRANCHISE RELATIONSHIPS

Universities and the former polytechnics in England and Wales faced a challenge in 1989 when the Secretary of State for Education set a target for the proportion of students studying at higher education level to double by the year 2014. One solution to the inevitable pressure which this would place on universities has been the development of a franchised system of delivering Degree and HND programmes through local colleges of further education.

While there had been many long-standing examples of collaboration between the further and higher education sectors in providing specialized courses (e.g. agricultural engineering), the new interest in franchising borrowed many of the practices from private sector service franchising. The new wave of franchising involved a local college of further education delivering all or part of a higher education programme in a manner prescribed by the university. For the latter, franchising offered a number of attractive benefits:

● Franchising allowed the institution to overcome short-term capacity constraints imposed by buildings and staff availability, particularly where spare resources existed within the further education sector.
● Parts of some degree programmes—such as first year foundation courses—may be relatively easy to provide as they require less specialized staff and equipment to deliver them. It becomes possible to deliver these elements of a course more cheaply at colleges of further education which are not burdened with the overhead costs associated with research and specialized library resources. A university may be financially better off by taking a 10 per cent franchise fee and letting somebody else deliver a course, rather than taking the whole of a student's fee income and having to pay the costs of delivery itself.
● On the marketing side, franchising allows higher education to be made locally available, for all or part of a course. This may offer important new opportunities for some segments of the population, for example mature students, who may be put off by the prospect of moving away from home into the uncertain world of higher education.

For local colleges of further education, there were also numerous attractions to taking on a higher education franchise:

● Faced with the prospect of a decline in the number of 16 to 18 year olds on which colleges had traditionally relied, participation in the expanding higher education sector allowed full use of facilities to be maintained.
● The addition of higher education courses added to the status of the college and could become a valuable stimulus to staff.

Many franchised operations grew rapidly during the late 1980s. For example, the former Lancashire Polytechnic scheme started with 11 students in 1984, but by 1991 accounted for 531 students in 9 franchised colleges.

Both the university and the local college become involved in the marketing of franchised courses. The franchised college can appeal to its local population on the basis of being a caring local community facility, while the university can add to this at both a local and national level. If the reputation of the university is itself weak, the task of recruiting students for franchised colleges will be more difficult.

At the heart of an educational franchise is the requirement to maintain consistent standards so that a student studying at a franchised college receives substantially the same education as one studying at the franchising university. Vetting of colleges at the outset is crucial to ensure that they have the staff, accommodation and technical resources capable of delivering the specified course. Once a scheme is running, close monitoring is required from the university on such matters as assessment standards and the quality of teaching materials delivered.

Quality control of franchise colleges was an issue highlighted in an HMI report into higher education provision within the further education sector (HMI, 1991). The report indicated that quality control had failed from the beginning of many franchise operations, for example through poor specification of requirements at the outset and through some of the essential quality requirements not having been met. The importance of clear and unambiguous guidelines for course operation and regular monitoring systems was emphasized. A number of universities that had tried to introduce totally new courses to franchised colleges without having had any experience of delivering the course themselves encountered much the same difficulties as any private sector franchisor would.

A franchise relationship between a university and college will last for as long as it is in both organizations' interests for it to do so. A college could in many cases run a course on its own without reference to a university, but against the saving in franchise fees must be set the greater cost and difficulty of recruiting students who may be unaware of the qualities of the college. Students may perceive a franchised course which is validated by a university as being much more valuable than one validated by a local college in its own name.

QUESTIONS

1. Summarize the advantages to universities of developing franchised networks of colleges.
2. How can the quality of education at a franchised college be monitored and maintained?
3. What factors might limit the growth of franchising in higher education?

REVIEW QUESTIONS

1. (a) Identify the main strengths of two of the following types of business enterprise:
   - Sole trader
   - Partnership
   - Limited company
   - PLC
   and assess the extent to which the strengths of one form are weaknesses of the other.   (12 marks)
   (b) Prepare two slides for a business presentation comparing the ability of the two forms of enterprise to cope with a changing environment.   (8 marks)
   (CIM Marketing Environment Examination, December 1994, Q.3)
2. In what ways are the marketing efforts of a sole trader and a limited company of similar size likely to differ?
3. For what reasons might a manufacturer of fitted kitchens seek PLC status? What are the advantages and disadvantages of this course of action?
4. Why have governments found it difficult to privatize state-owned postal services? Suggest methods by which private sector marketing principles can be applied to state-owned postal services.
5. Critically assess the benefits to the public of turning branches of the National Health Service into self-governing trusts.
6. Why have franchise organizations become so important in the United Kingdom?

REFERENCES

Bramwell, B. and Broom, G. (1989) 'Tourism Development Programmes—An Approach to Local Authority Tourism Initiatives', *Tourism Intelligence Papers*, English Tourist Board.
British Franchise Association (1995) *Business Franchise Directory*, BFA, Henley.
HMI (1991) 'Higher Education in Further Education Colleges', HMI report 228/91/NS, Department of Education and Science, London.

FURTHER READING

Cyert, R. and March, J. (1992) *A Behavioural Theory of the Firm*, 2nd edn, Blackwell, Oxford.

Donnelly, G. (1987) *The Firm in Society*, 2nd edn, Pitman, London.

Handy, C. (1993) *Understanding Organizations*, 4th edn, Penguin, London.

Office of the Minister for the Civil Service (1990) *Public Bodies*, HMSO, London.

Weir, S. and Hall, W. (ed.) (1994) *Ego-trip: Extra-governmental Organizations in the UK and Their Accountability*, Charter 88 Trust, London.

FOUR

ORGANIZATIONAL GROWTH

OBJECTIVES

After reading this chapter, you should understand:

- The diversity of objectives that business organizations seek to achieve
- The reasons for organizational growth
- Patterns of organizational growth
- Sources of finance for expanding businesses
- Limits to growth and the role of small businesses

4.1 INTRODUCTION

Like most living organisms, business organizations have an almost inherent tendency to grow. This can come about for a variety of formal and informal reasons, such as the need to maintain market share in a growing market and the desire of managers to boost their own career prospects. Growth can take several different forms, and the rate and type of growth will have an influence on the marketing function of a business. This chapter will firstly seek to understand the diverse nature of objectives and the effect they may have on patterns of growth. It will then consider the methods by which organizations grow, the implications for marketing of growth patterns and the limits to growth that an organization may face.

4.2 THE OBJECTIVES OF ORGANIZATIONS

All organizations exist to pursue objectives of one description or another. It is important for the marketer to understand the nature of organizational goals as these will affect—among other things—the way the organization makes purchases, sets prices or pursues a market share strategy. Whether somebody is selling to or competing with another organization, a study of the organization's objectives will help to understand how it is likely to act.

Very broadly, organizational goals can be classified into a number of categories:

1. Those that aim to make a profit for their owners
2. Those that aim to maximize benefit to society
3. Those that aim to maximize benefits to their members

Specific objectives of organizations are considered below:

4.2.1   Profit maximization

It is often assumed that business organizations will always try to maximize their profits, through a combination of maximizing revenue and minimizing costs. It is often thought that the pursuit of profit maximization is the unifying characteristic of all private sector business organizations and, indeed, economic theory is very much based on the notion of the profit maximizing firm.

However, simple models of profit maximization are open to question, even if it is recognized for the moment that profit may be of only marginal relevance to organizations that exist largely for their members' or society's benefit. These are some of the more important limitations on profit maximizing theories:

1. The profit maximizing objective must be qualified by a time dimension. A firm pursuing a short-term profit maximizing objective may act very differently to one that seeks to maximize long-term profit. This may be reflected in a differing emphasis on research and development, new product development and market development strategies. Whether an organization is able to pursue long-term profit maximizing objectives will be influenced by the nature of the environment in which it operates. The financial environment of the United Kingdom and the emphasis on short-term results has caused UK organizations to pursue much more short-term profit goals than organizations in, for example, Japan, where the nature of organizational funding allows a longer time for projects to achieve profits. Similarly, an organization operating in a relatively regulated environment—such as patented medicines—will be in a stronger position to plan for long-term profit maximization than one that is operating in a relatively unpredictable and uncertain deregulated market.
2. A second major criticism of the dominance of profit maximization as a business objective is that maximization is not observed to occur in practice. In most organizations, there is a separation of ownership from management where the managers of the company have little or no stake in the ownership of the company. Thus, the managers may be able to pursue policies more in line with their own self-interests so long as they make sufficient profit to keep their shareholders happy. Instead of pursuing maximum profits, the managers of the company may pursue a policy of maximizing sales turnover, subject to achieving a *satisfactory* level of profits.
3. In practice, it can be very difficult to quantify the relationship between production costs, selling prices, sales volumes and profit. Managers may have inadequate knowledge about these linkages with which to pursue profit maximization effectively.

4.2.2   Market share maximization

Market share maximization may coincide with profit maximization, in cases where there is a close correlation between market share and return on investment. It has been suggested that this occurs in many sectors, such as UK grocery retailing. There are other instances, however, where there is a less straightforward relationship between market share and profitability. For example, in the UK retail travel agency sector, both the market leader and small specialist retailers have achieved reasonable returns on investment, but many medium-sized firms have faced below average returns.

There are circumstances and reasons why a firm may pursue a policy of maximizing market share independently of a profit maximizing objective. Domination of a particular market may give stability and security to the organization. This might be regarded as a more attractive option for the management than maximizing profits. Building market share may itself be seen as a short-term strategy to achieve longer term profits, given that there may be a relationship between the two.

Pursuing a market share growth objective may influence a number of aspects of a firm's marketing mix, for example it may cut prices and increase promotional expenditure, accepting short-term losses in order to drive its main rivals out of business, leaving it free to exploit its market.

4.2.3   Corporate growth

As an organization grows, so too does the power and responsibility of individual managers. In terms of salaries and career development, a growth strategy may appear very attractive to these people, not only for their own self-advancement but also as an aid to attracting and retaining a high calibre of staff, attracted by the prospects of career development. However, such enthusiasm for growth could lead the owners of the business to pursue diversification into possibly unknown and unprofitable areas. This happened during the economic boom of the late 1980s when many companies expanded too rapidly into often unknown areas. Shareholders were happy to back the management and take risks when times were good but could have benefited in the longer term by being more cautious and critical of its management's recommendations.

4.2.4   Satisficing

Given that the managers of a business are probably not going to benefit directly from increased profits, the argument has been advanced that managers aim for satisfactory rather than maximum possible profits. Provided that sufficient profit is made to keep shareholders happy, managers may pursue activities that satisfy their own individual needs, such as better company cars for themselves, or may pursue business activities that give them a relatively easy life or add to their ego. To achieve these diverse individual objectives, part of the organization's profit that could be paid out to shareholders is diverted and used to pay for managerial satisfaction. The extent to which satisficing represents an important business objective can be debated. It can be argued that in relatively competitive markets, competitive pressures do not allow companies to add the costs of these management diversions to their selling prices. If they did, they would eventually go out of business in favour of companies whose shareholders exercised greater control over the costs of their managers. Only in stable and relatively less competitive markets can these implied additional costs be borne by adding to prices.

There has been a growing tendency for the owners of a business to give senior managers of the business contracts of employment that are related to profit performance. While this may lessen the extent of the apparent conflict of objectives for management, a trade-off may still have to be made where, for example, a decision has to be made on whether to spend more money on better company cars for managers. Should they spend the money and get all of the benefit for themselves, or save costs in order to increase profits, of which they will receive only a share?

Satisficing behaviour can have a number of implications for marketing. Buying behaviour in any organization is likely to be complex, but companies that are satisficing are likely to attach relatively greater importance to the intangible decision factors such as ease of order, familiarity with a sales representative and the level of status attached to a particular purchase, rather than the more objective factors such as price and quality.

4.2.5   Survival

For many organizations, the objective of maximizing profit is a luxury for management and shareholders alike—the overriding problem is simply to stay in business. Many businesses have had to close not because of poor profitability—their long-term profit potential may have been very good—but because they have run out of short-term cash flow. Without a source of finance to pay for current expenses, a longer term profit maximizing objective cannot be achieved. Cash flow problems could come about for a number of reasons, such as unexpected increases in costs, a fall in revenue resulting from unexpected competitive pressure or a seasonal pattern of activity that is different to that which was predicted.

Survival as a business objective can influence marketing decisions in a number of ways. Pricing decisions may reflect the need to liquidate stock regardless of the mark-up or contribution to profit. This was evident during the Gulf War when many airlines were brought close to bankruptcy by the combination of falling volume of passenger business and increased fuel prices. In order to survive what many airlines thought would be a temporary blip, many offered very low fares just to keep cash flowing in order to cover their overheads. The need to survive can also affect organization's promotional activities. An advertising campaign to build up long-term brand loyalty may be sacrificed to a cheaper sales promotion campaign which has a shorter payback period.

4.2.6 Loss making

A company may be part of a group that needs a loss maker to set off against other companies in the group who are making profits that are heavily taxed by the Inland Revenue. Situations can arise where a subsidiary company makes a component that is used by another member of the group and although that subsidiary may make a loss, it may be more tax efficient for the company as a whole to continue making a loss rather than buying in the product at a cheaper price from an outside organization.

4.2.7 Personal objectives

Many businesses, especially smaller ones, appear to be pursuing objectives that have no economic rationality. They do not pursue maximum profits, and indeed may be quite happy making no profits at all. They may have no desire to grow and may be in no immediate danger of failure. Many small businesses are created to satisfy a variety of personal objectives. This was illustrated by the results of a survey undertaken by National Westminster Bank in 1995 into the reasons why individuals set up their own business. It was claimed by 31 per cent that their main reason was a desire for independence, while only 26 per cent saw an opportunity to make money as the primary motivation. About 15 per cent were tempted into setting up their own business because they had been made redundant. Many new business owners also sought to combine a business with a hobby activity, a desire to remain active and the opportunity for friendly encounters with customers.

Many small businesses are set up by individuals using a capital lump sum which they have received (such as an inheritance or a redundancy payment). Many people in such circumstances have used their lump sum to invest in what are perceived as relatively pleasant and enjoyable businesses such as antique shops, tea rooms and restaurants. Many fail in a competitive environment where personal objectives cannot be achieved without undue economic sacrifice (e.g. it has been estimated that over 80 per cent of all new restaurants fail within two years of opening). However, many others continue to provide goods and services for an acceptable sacrifice from the owners in a market-place where profit-motivated companies would be unable to meet their objectives. This may partly explain the domination of UK antique shops by small owner-managers and the absence of large chains of profit-motivated businesses.

4.2.8 Social objectives of commercial organizations

Occasionally, commercial organizations have overt social objectives of one form or another, usually alongside a resource objective, for example a requirement that the organization must at least break even. Charities such as Oxfam, while having clear objectives in maximizing their revenue, also state their objectives in terms of which groups they seek to benefit. Where they engage in trading activities (such as Oxfam shops), their social objectives may result in buying supplies from disadvantaged groups, even though this may not be the most commercially profitable.

Traditionally, many owners of commercial companies have adopted social objectives. For example, Quakers such as Cadbury and Rowntree sought to maximize the moral welfare of their work-force. In modern times, the Body Shop has an objective of not supporting experiments on animals, an objective that pervades many aspects of the company's marketing, including new product development and promotion. Even organizations which for the most part are pursuing profit objectives may pursue social objectives in some small areas of activity, as where an organization runs a sports or social club for its employees at a loss. The social responsibility of organizations, and the views of critics who are cynical about firms' social objectives, are considered in Chapter 9.

4.2.9 Maximizing benefits to consumers

An overriding objective of a marketing-oriented organization is to maximize consumer satisfaction. However, this has to be qualified by a second objective which requires the organization to meet its financial objectives. In the case of consumer co-operatives, maximizing the benefits to their customers has had a significance beyond the normal marketing concept of maximizing consumer satisfaction. The co-operative movement was originally conceived to eliminate the role of the outside shareholder, allowing profits to be passed back to customers through a dividend which is related to a customer's spending rather than their shareholding. Any action that maximized the returns to the business by definition maximized the benefits to consumers.

The importance of consumer co-operatives has declined since the 1950s for a number of reasons. Consumer co-operatives could appear very attractive to consumers at a time when firms were essentially production orientated and when the demand for goods exceeded their supply. With the reversal of this situation, other retailers with greater organizational flexibility and a more overt marketing orientation have attracted custom by offering additional services to customers, often associated with lower prices.

4.2.10 Maximizing public benefits

In many government and charity organizations, it is difficult to talk about the concept of profit or revenue maximization. Instead, the organization is given an objective of maximizing specified aspects of public benefit, subject to keeping within a resource constraint. Public sector hospitals are increasingly embracing the marketing concept, but it is recognized that it would be inappropriate for them to be given a strictly financial set of objectives. Instead, they might be given the objective of maximizing the number of operations of a particular kind within a resource constraint. Similarly, a charity campaigning for improved road safety may set an objective of maximizing awareness of its cause among important opinion formers.

There is frequently a gap between the publicly stated objectives of a public sector organization and the interpretation and implementation of these objectives by the staff concerned. As in a private sector organization, management in the public sector could promote secondary objectives that add to their own individual status and security, rather than maximizing the public benefit. A manager of a hospital may pursue an objective of maximizing the use of high technology because this may be perceived as enhancing his or her career, even though the public benefit could be maximized more efficiently with simpler technology.

In recent years, more pressure has been put on public services such as education and defence to operate according to business criteria. Marketing has begun to assume greater importance in a number of ways. As suppliers of services, public sector organizations are increasingly being set quantified objectives that reflect the needs of their clients. Improved research methods to find out more about client needs and more effective communication of their offering to clients have been part of this process towards greater marketing orientation. Many public services have themselves become major consumers of services as peripheral activities such as cleaning and catering have been subcontracted out. This has resulted in the growth of a market-orientated service sector. Very often, the management and staff previously providing an ancillary service within a public sector organization have bought out the operation from their employer and now have to sell the service back to the authority. Their objectives have changed from a vague notion of maximizing public benefit to one of maximizing their own profit.

4.2.11 Complexity of objectives

A number of possible objectives for organizations have been suggested above. In practice, an organization is likely to be pursuing multiple objectives at any one time. Furthermore, objectives are likely to change through time. A marketer needs to be able to identify the objectives that are influencing the behaviour of an organization and this can present a number of practical problems.

The first place to look for a statement of an organization's objectives might be its Memorandum and Articles of Association. This statement is required by the Companies Acts for all limited companies and includes an objects clause. In practice, companies frequently draw up their objects clause in a way that is so wide that the company can do almost anything.

A more up to date statement of objectives may be found in the annual report and accounts which all companies must produce annually and submit to Companies House where it is avaliable for public inspection. The report must include a Directors' report which may give an indication of the goals that the company is working towards. Many companies publish a mission statement, which gives a broad statement of the anticipated future direction that its business will take.

Beyond this, the true objectives may be difficult for an outsider to determine. Indeed, clearly stating objectives in too much detail may put a firm at a commercial disadvantage when competitors adapt their behaviour accordingly. Even insiders may have difficulty identifying whether an organization is pursuing very short-term profits or directing strategy towards longer-term profitability.

4.3 GROWTH OF ORGANIZATIONS

It was noted earlier that organizations, like most living organisms, have an inherent tendency to grow. In this section, the reasons for growth and the options for growth that are open to business organizations are explored.

4.3.1 Reasons for growth

An organization can grow in size for a number of reasons:

1. The markets in which the organization operates may be growing, making growth in output relatively easy to achieve. In addition, in a rapidly growing market, if an organization was to maintain a constant output, its market share would be falling. Growth may be considered not so much of a luxury as a necessity if it is to maintain its position in the market-place. This could be particularly important for industries where economies of scale are an important consideration.
2. A critical mass may exist for the size of firms in a market, below which they are at a competitive disadvantage. For example, a retail grocery chain which is aiming for a broad market segment will need to achieve a sufficiently large size in order to obtain bulk discounts from suppliers which can in turn be passed on in lower prices to customers. Size could also give economies of scale in many other activities such as advertising, distribution and administration. Many new businesses may include in their business plan an objective to achieve a specified critical mass within a given time period.
3. An overt policy of growth is often pursued by organizations in an attempt to stimulate staff morale. A growing organization is likely to be in a strong position to recruit and retain a high calibre of staff.

4. In addition to the formal goals of growth, management may in practice pursue objectives that result in growth. Higher rates of growth can bring greater status and promotion prospects to managers of an organization, even if a more appropriate long-term strategy may indicate a slower rate of growth.
5. Some organizations may grow by acquiring competitors in order to limit the amount of competition in a market where this is considered to be wasteful competition. An important reason behind the merger between British Airways and British Caledonian Airways was the desire to reduce excess capacity over common sections of route.

4.3.2   Types of organizational growth

Growth of organizations can be analysed in terms of:

1. The object of the growth, which can be defined in terms of the development of new markets and/or new products
2. Organizational issues about *how* the growth is achieved

The first of these issues can be analysed with the help of growth option matrices. For the second, two basic growth patterns for organizations can be identified—organic growth and growth by acquisition— although many organizations grow by a combination of the two processes.

4.3.3   Product/market expansion

An organization's growth can conceptually be analysed in terms of two key development dimensions: markets and products. This conceptualization forms the basis of the product/market expansion grid proposed by Ansoff (1957). Products and markets are each analysed in terms of their degree of novelty to an organization and growth strategies identified in terms of these two dimensions. In this way, four types of growth strategy can be identified. An illustration of the framework, with reference to the specific options open to a seaside holiday hotel, is shown in Figure 4.1.

The four growth options are associated with differing sets of problems and opportunities for organizations. These relate to the level of resources required to implement a particular strategy and the level

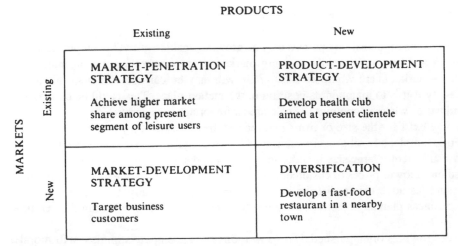

Figure 4.1   An application of Ansoff's growth matrix to a hotel operator

of risk associated with each. It follows, therefore, that what might be a feasible growth strategy for one organization may not be for another. The characteristics of the four strategies are described below:

1. *Market penetration strategies* This type of strategy focuses growth on the existing product range by encouraging higher levels of take-up among the existing target markets. In this way a specialist tour operator in a growing sector of the holiday market could—all other things being equal—grow naturally, simply by maintaining its current marketing strategy. If it wanted to accelerate this growth, it could do this firstly by seeking to sell more holidays to its existing customer base and secondly by attracting customers from its direct competitors. If the market was in fact in decline, the company could only grow by attracting customers from its competitors through more aggressive marketing policies and/or cost reduction programmes. A market penetration strategy offers the least level of risk to an organization—it is familiar with both its products and its customers.

2. *Market development strategies* This type of strategy builds upon the existing product range that an organization has established, but seeks to find new groups of customers for them. In this way a specialist regional ski tour operator that has saturated its current market might seek to expand its sales to new geographical regions or aim its marketing effort at attracting custom from groups beyond its current age/income groups. While the organization may be familiar with the operational aspects of the product that it is providing, it faces risks resulting from possibly poor knowledge of different buyer behaviour patterns in the markets which it seeks to enter. As an example of the potential problems associated with this strategy, many UK retailers have sought to offer their UK shop formats in overseas markets only to find that those features that attracted customers in the United Kingdom failed to do so overseas.

3. *Product development strategy* As an alternative to selling existing products into new markets, an organization may choose to develop new products for its existing customers. For example, a ski tour operator may have built up a good understanding of the holiday needs of a particular market segment, such as the 18 to 35 year old affluent aspiring segment, and then seeks to offer a wider range of services to them than simply skiing holidays. It might offer summer activity holidays in addition. While the company minimizes the risk associated with the uncertainty of new markets, it faces risk resulting from lack of knowledge about its new product area. Often a feature of this growth strategy is collaboration with a product specialist who helps the organization produce the service, leaving it free to market it effectively to its customers. A department store wishing to add a coffee shop to its service offering may not have the skills and resources within its organization to run such a facility effectively, but may subcontract an outside catering specialist, leaving it free to determine the overall policy that should be adopted.

4. *Diversification strategy* Here, an organization expands by developing new products for new markets. Diversification can take a number of forms. The company could stay within the same general product/market area, but diversify into a new point of the distribution chain. For example, an airline that sets up its own travel agency moves into a type of service provision that is new to the organization, as well as dealing directly with a segment of the market with which it had previously probably had few sales transactions. Alternatively, the airline might diversify into completely unrelated service areas aimed at completely different groups of customers—by purchasing a golf course or car dealership, for example. Because the company is moving into both unknown markets and unknown product areas, this form of growth carries the greatest level of risk from a marketing management perspective. Diversification may, however, help to manage the long-term risk of the organization by reducing dependency on a narrow product/market area.

In practice, most growth that occurs is a combination of product development and market development. In very competitive markets, organizations would probably have to slightly adapt their products if they are to become attractive to a new market segment. For the leisure hotel seeking to capture new business customers, it may not be enough to simply promote existing facilities; in order to meet business peoples' needs, it might have to offer refurbished facilities to make them more acceptable to business customers and offer new facilities (e.g. the facility for visitors to pay by account).

4.3.4   Organic growth

Organic growth is considered to be the more natural pattern of growth for an organization. The initial investment by the organization results in profits, an established customer base and a well-established technical, personal and financial structure. This provides a foundation for future growth. In this sense, success breeds success, for the rate of the organization's growth is influenced by the extent to which it has succeeded in building up internally the means for future expansion. All aspects of the organization can be said to evolve gradually. For example, the accounting and finance function may initially be under the day-to-day control of one person, but as the organization expands, so it becomes necessary to develop specialist areas within accounting, each with its own section head.

In terms of marketing, an organization may grow organically by tackling one segment at a time, using the resources, knowledge and market awareness it has gained in order to tackle further segments. A firm may grow organically into new segments in a number of ways. Many retail chains have grown organically by developing one region before moving on to another—Sainsburys grew organically from its southern base towards the northern regions, while Asda grew organically during the 1970s and early 1980s from its northern base towards the south. Other organizations have grown organically by aiming a basically similar product at new segments of the market—as Thomson Holidays has done in developing slightly differentiated holidays aimed at the youth and elderly markets. An example of an organization that has succeeded beyond this stage to offering new products for its existing customers is Marks and Spencers, who after attacking new geographical segments has offered new products in the form of financial services to its established customer base.

Where new market opportunities suddenly appear, an organization may not have the specialized resources that would allow it to grow organically. Within the financial services sector, a study by Ennew, Wong and Wright (1992) found that many of the assets of companies, such as specialized staff and distribution networks, were quite specific to their existing markets and could not easily be adapted to exploit new markets. Growth by acquisition was in many cases considered to be a better method of expansion.

4.3.5   Growth by acquisition

The rate of organic growth is constrained by a number of factors, for example the rate at which the market that an organization serves is growing. An organization seeking to grow organically in a slowly developing sector such as food manufacture will find organic growth more difficult than an organization serving a rapidly growing sector such as on-line computer information services. In some cases, organic growth is difficult because of a scarcity of resources (e.g. prime locations for retail sites), and growth by acquiring other companies is the easiest way of acquiring those resources. Also, companies with relatively high capital requirements will find organic growth relatively difficult.

Growth by acquisition may appear attractive to organizations where organic growth is difficult. In some cases it may be almost essential in order to achieve a critical mass which may be necessary for survival. The DIY retail sector in the United Kingdom is one where chains have needed to achieve a critical size in order to exploit economies in buying, distribution and promotion. Small chains have not been able to grow organically at a sufficient rate to achieve a critical mass, resulting in their take-over or merger to form larger chains. Sainsburys, owners of the Homebase chain of DIY outlets, sought to challenge the market leader B&Q. Organic growth would have involved considerable expenditure in new sites in a sector that was becoming saturated. Instead it sought to achieve economies of scale by acquiring its competitor Texas Homecare. Texas had itself grown by acquiring a number of smaller chains, such as Unit Sales.

A major problem for firms seeking to grow within the service sector by acquisition lies in the fact that often the main assets being acquired are the skills and knowledge of the acquired organization's employees. Unlike physical assets, key personnel may disappear following the acquisition, reducing the earning ability of the business. Worse still, key staff could defect to the acquiring company's competitors. There is evidence that much of the investment of financial institutions in acquiring estate agencies during the late 1980s was lost when key personnel left with their list of contacts to set up rival agencies.

Growth by acquisition may occur where an organization sees its existing market sector contracting and it seeks to diversify into other areas. The time and risk associated with starting a new venture in an alien market sector may be considered too great—acquiring an established business could be less risky, allowing access to an established client base and technical skills.

It was noted earlier that growth in itself may be seen as good for developing staff morale in allowing career progression. The organization may formally encourage growth by acquisition for this very reason, while staff may have informal objectives directed towards this end. Acquiring new subsidiaries could satisfy this objective for a company that is operating in otherwise static markets.

Growth by acquisition can take a number of forms. The simplest form is the agreed take-over whereby one firm agrees to purchase the majority of the share capital of another company. Payment can be in the form of cash or shares in the acquiring company, or some combination of the two. A take-over can be mutually beneficial where one company has a sound customer base but lacks the financial resources to achieve a critical mass while the other has the finance but needs a larger customer base. Many take-overs occur where the founder of a business is seeking to retire and to liquidate the value of the business.

While the majority of take-overs are mutually agreed, circumstances often arise where a take-over is contested. This particularly affects public companies whose shares can be bought and sold openly. Typically a cash-rich firm would identify another company that it recognizes as underperforming because of poor management. Its argument for a take-over is based on the appeal of its proven management style being applied to the underperforming assets of the target company, increasing the profitability of the latter's assets. Disputed take-overs can become very bitter affairs, with each side trying to prove its own performance while denigrating that of the other party. The battle is often made even more vitriolic because of contrasting cultural styles—for the target company, exposure of its management style and practices may be a new and unwelcome event, and represents a desire to remain independent.

During a contested take-over bid, the marketing strategy of both target and bidding companies can be significantly affected during the short term. To prove the ability of the existing management, the target company's marketing programmes may focus on boosting short-term market share, possibly at the expense of long-term brand building. Communication programmes can become aimed at the financial community as much as the final consumer, as in the contested take-over bid for Allied Lyons by the Australian Elders IXL, where adverts for the firm's diverse product range were amended to include the Allied Lyons name, aimed at associating the company with a much broader portfolio of brands than may have been appreciated by members of the financial community. New product launches may be brought ahead of the ideal launch date in order to impress the financial community.

For public companies, the Stock Exchange imposes strict rules about how a take-over bid may be conducted, covered by the City Code on Take-overs and Mergers and monitored by the Panel on Take-overs. Thus an acquiring company cannot simply quietly acquire shares in a company until it has achieved a majority shareholding. It must declare its holding once it has reached a 10 per cent holding and must make a formal take-over offer once it has acquired 30 per cent. The offer document itself is tightly prescribed in terms of the information that it must contain.

GROWTH STRATEGIES BRING PROBLEMS FOR
UK BUILDING SOCIETIES

The marketing environment of UK financial services organizations was very turbulent during the latter part of the 1980s, resulting in many organizations developing growth strategies that they were later to regret.

Prior to 1986, the marketing strategy of building societies was significantly influenced by the various Building Societies Acts. Legislation recognized that building societies had essentially been set up by members for the benefit of fellow members—they were a means of circulating funds from individual members who wished to invest their savings securely to those members who wished to borrow to finance house purchase. The system was regulated to ensure that building societies only lent their funds for low-risk investments and were not dependent on large investors who could withdraw their funds at short notice. In times of capital shortages, building societies assumed an almost social responsibility for rationing scarce mortgages between competing borrowers.

The Building Societies Act of 1986 came amid a general air of deregulation in financial markets. The Act allowed building societies for the first time to offer services that they had previously been prevented from offering, for example current bank accounts. Deregulation came at a time when the commercial banks were becoming successful at offering mortgages—the core of the building societies' business. Faced with such competition at their core, most building societies launched new product lines, often in association with other financial services companies. As well as cheque accounts, the larger societies launched their own credit cards, insurance policies, pension schemes and personal unsecured loans. The Abbey National—which had taken advantage of the legislation to convert itself from building society to public limited company status—was able to pursue an even greater product diversification policy. It invested heavily in a new chain of 'Cornerstone' estate agents and set up a

European subsidiary to offer U.K. style mortgages abroad. Smaller societies tended to deepen their existing product lines rather than add new ones. Societies such as the Heart of England, Leamington Spa and Town and Country offered a range of mortgages by which borrowers were able to borrow a very high percentage—if not all—of the value of a property against which the mortgage was secured.

By the time that the recession of the early 1990s had set in, building societies' diversification policies were being questioned. Some of the bolder diversifications turned into millstones round the neck of their owners. By 1992, Abbey National's estate agencies and European operations were making heavy losses and were eventually sold off at a loss to the company. Assumptions that building societies had made about customer loyalty and the possibilities for cross-selling of products seemed to have misjudged the ability of consumers to shop around for the best deal.

Nor was deepening a product line necessarily a safe way of expanding. Many of the smaller societies which had offered increasingly complex and risky mortgages ran into financial difficulties. During 1991, the Leamington Spa Society had to be rescued by the Bradford and Bingley Building Society when a large number of its borrowers became unable to repay their mortgages which in many cases exceeded the value of the property.

By the mid 1990s, a new type of growth appeared to be gaining ground as societies merged and some, such as the Halifax and Leeds Building Societies, chose to convert to public limited company status. Some societies, however, publicly stated their determination to remain mutual societies owned by their members. By remaining mutual, growth options were undoubtedly curtailed, but in view of the failure of much of the earlier diversification, many members felt that this probably wasn't a bad thing.

QUESTIONS

1. How could building societies have avoided getting into the difficulties described in the case study?
2. What advantages does PLC status offer to a building society?
3. Do customers of building societies benefit from their mutual status or are they put at a disadvantage compared to customers of PLC banks?

4.3.6   Mergers

A merger is a variation on a take-over where two existing companies agree to set up one new company which issues shares to the shareholders of each of the existing companies in agreed proportions and in exchange for existing shareholdings. Many agreed take-overs show characteristics of a merger and it is difficult to strictly distinguish between the two. Mergers can be illustrated by reference to the UK DIY sector. Both the Boots company and WH Smith had been expanding their separate chains of DIY stores (Payless and Do It All respectively) organically. This method of growth had failed to achieve the critical mass necessary to compete effectively with the market leader, B&Q. The two owners therefore agreed to merge the two companies with a new board of directors and shares allocated equally between the two parent organizations.

4.3.7   Joint ventures

Diversification into new business areas can be risky, even for a cash-rich business. It may lack the management skills necessary in the market that it seeks to enter, while the barriers to entry may present an unacceptably high level of risk to the company. One way forward is to set up a joint venture where companies with complementary skills and financial resources join together. A new limited company is usually formed with shares allocated between the member companies and agreement made on where the financial and human resources are to come from. There are many examples of joint ventures to be found in new high-technology, high-capital sectors such as telecommunications and broadcasting. British Sky Broadcasting was formed out of a merger of Sky Television and British Satellite Broadcasting, of which the latter was a joint venture made up of a consortium of electronics and publishing companies. Sometimes regulatory requirements may favour a joint venture rather than direct market entry. Although British Telecom could probably have succeeded by itself in launching a mobile telephone service in the United Kingdom, fear by regulatory agencies of market domination limited the company to membership of a joint venture with Securicor to launch Cellnet.

A joint venture is commonly used where a company seeks to enter an overseas market by matching its technical and financial resources with the local market knowledge of a company based in the target market. For example, when the Hong Kong based Hutchinson Telecom sought to expand its mobile telecommunications business in the United Kingdom, it formed a joint venture with British Aerospace to develop the Orange mobile phone network.

Where joint ventures are a success, the partners often seek to liquidate their investment by 'floating' the joint venture as a public limited company in its own right. This happened, for example in the flotations of British Sky Broadcasting and Orange.

4.3.8   Horizontal and vertical integration

Amalgamations between firms can take the form of horizontal integration, vertical integration or diversification. Horizontal integration occurs where firms involved in the same stage of manufacture of a product amalgamate to achieve greater economies of scale and—subject to Monopolies and Mergers Commission approval—to reduce the level of wasteful competition in a market. The merger between Sky Television and British Satellite Broadcasting fell into this category. Vertical integration occurs where a company acquires either its suppliers (backward integration) or its distributors (forward integration). Tour operators integrating backwards have ensured provision of aircraft capacity by acquiring or setting up their own airline, while others have integrated forwards by acquiring travel agents. Diversification occurs where firms acquire another firm operating in unrelated business areas, the main purpose of the acquisition often being to spread risk through a balanced portfolio of activities. Figure 4.2 depicts possible growth patterns for a brewery.

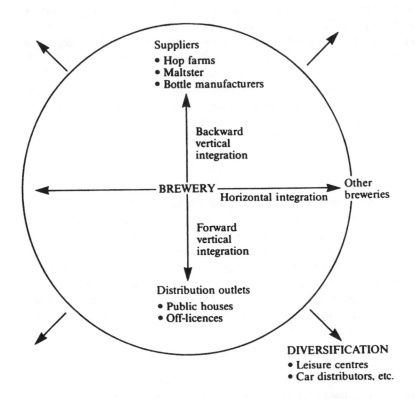

Figure 4.2   Possible growth patterns for a brewery

4.4   SOURCES OF FINANCE FOR GROWTH

As far as the private sector is concerned, there are two basic methods of financing growth. On the one hand, companies can raise risk capital (often referred to as *equity* capital) from shareholders for which a relatively high rate of return will be required. To supplement this, companies use a second and relatively less expensive form of *loan* finance. This must be repaid regardless of the fortunes of the company. The relationship between the two is referred to as gearing—a company which has a high amount of loan finance relative to equity capital is said to be highly geared. An optimum balance exists between the two types of finance, although this varies between different industry sectors.

4.4.1   Methods of raising equity capital

One method by which a sole trader or partnership can raise fresh capital is by forming a private limited company and selling shares in the company. For a private limited company, the sale of shares cannot be advertised to the public, so they have to be placed privately. For smaller companies, blocks of shares are often sold to relations or business associates. New opportunities to gain access to equity share capital have been provided through a relatively new type of intermediary—the venture capital company. These intermediaries develop an understanding of the opportunities for investment in smaller private companies and provide the link—and often also the management support—through which investment from cash-rich individuals and organizations such as pension funds is provided.

To gain access to significant amounts of new equity capital from a much wider financial community, a private company may 'go public' by forming a public limited company. Becoming a public company requires a special resolution to be passed by the shareholders and the Articles of Association to be amended to take out those restrictions that apply to a private company.

To acquire a full listing on the Stock Exchange, a considerable amount of time and money must be spent to meet the requirements of the Stock Exchange Council. These basically aim to ensure that anybody considering buying shares in the company is adequately informed about the record, current position and future prospects of the company. A detailed prospectus, including five years trading figures, with audited accounts must be produced. The actual sale of shares can take place in a number of ways, the most important of which are:

- An Offer for Sale to the general public, where a specified number of shares is offered at a fixed price, usually underwritten to guarantee the share income to the company. This tends to be an expensive method of raising equity capital
- Sale by Tender which involves selling the shares to the highest bidders
- Placement with financial institutions without the formality of a public offer for sale

The cost of raising fresh equity through a share issue can be considerable, reflecting the work of the accountants, bankers, solicitors and underwriters involved. For a typical share sale valued at £10 million, between 5 and 10 per cent would be lost in issuing expenses.

Obtaining access to equity capital through the stock market can be very expensive for smaller companies who can be caught in a dilemma. Small, rapidly growing businesses in fast-growing sectors may need fresh capital to sustain their growth. However, until they have achieved successful operation for a number of years, they cannot seek funding to bring about that growth. The stock markets in many countries have recognized this dilemma by creating secondary markets for capital which fall short of the high standards normally imposed on companies dealing on the main market. At the same time, such secondary stock markets provide opportunities for investors who are more willing to take a speculative risk in a company that could produce a spectacular return, or could just as easily prove to be a complete failure.

In the United Kingdom, an alternative to obtaining a full listing on the Stock Exchange is to seek one on the Alternative Investment Market (AIM), which replaced the earlier Unlisted Securities Market. This is much less costly to companies seeking to raise fresh finance. The Alternative Investment Market is a higher risk to investors as the information companies are required to submit is lower. However, each company must warn potential investors of their risks and must have a nominated adviser approved by the Stock Exchange. The role of the adviser is central to AIM, as the Stock Market does not look at companies' prospectuses. Advisers are required to confirm to the Exchange that the directors of a company have been guided on their responsibilities and obligations in respect of the AIM rules and that the rules have been obeyed. Advisers can be fined for poor performance. The stock markets of many countries have developed similar schemes to promote small, relatively high risk business ventures (e.g. France's Nouveau Marche).

An alternative method of raising fresh equity capital for an established business is to call on existing shareholders to subscribe for additional shares. This is known as a *rights issue* and shareholders are given the right to purchase additional shares at a specified price in proportion to their existing shareholding. Where a company is in financial difficulty with excessive debt, it may renegotiate with its creditors to turn some of its loans into equity capital. Shares are then given to creditors in return for cancelling part of the loans outstanding to them. This has happened with the financially beleaguered Eurotunnel company, whose shareholders have seen the value of their shares fall as new shares have been created to pay off debts rather than to invest in new revenue-generating assets.

4.4.2   Retained earnings

Free enterprise idealists would argue that a company's profits should be entirely distributed to its shareholders so that they can decide how they should be reinvested. In practice, companies tend to retain a proportion of profits for reinvestment within the business, encouraged by tax advantages. The amount distributed to shareholders in the form of a dividend tends to be kept at a stable level, meeting a norm for that particular industry and the expectations of shareholders. While retained earnings may seem an easy source of finance for a company, there is a danger that if it does not achieve an adequate internal return on these retained earnings, it may become the subject of a take-over bid from another company that considers that it could manage the capital of the business more effectively.

4.4.3   Loan capital

For the small business, loans for expansion may be obtained from family and friends. However, when loan requirements exceed the capabilities of these sources, commercial loans are sought and some form of security against the loan will usually be required. In many cases, the directors of a limited company will have to pledge their personal possessions as security for the company's loans, despite the separate legal identity of the company.

Debentures are loans to a company carrying interest at a fixed rate and are generally repayable on a specified date. Debenture holders receive priority over shareholders for annual income payments and when the assets of the business are liquidated. Some—called mortgage debentures—are backed by a particular fixed asset belonging to the company as security, while others are secured by a floating charge on the company's assets in general. In the event of default on payment, the lender has the right to take over the security offered and sell it in order to repay the outstanding loan. Others, known as loan stock, are unsecured, and their holders are in the same position as trade creditors in ranking for repayment in the event of liquidation, although still ahead of shareholders.

4.4.4   Management buy-outs

Management buy-outs (and the related idea of a 'buy-in') have been becoming increasingly popular and were very common during the economic boom of the late 1980s. A buy-out is an autonomous company which is created by the management and/or employees of a large group buying part of the business of their former employers. Funding a buy-out often leaves the company highly geared, with the management putting in relatively little of their own equity capital relative to the loan capital provided by a merchant bank. Such buy-outs often involve very complex financing, with the merchant bank seeking a route by which its minority shareholding could be liquidated by flotation very quickly afterwards, or assets of the newly formed business sold off to repay the loans. This method of financing growth was very attractive at a time of an expanding economy and relatively low interest rates, but high gearing has spelt difficulty for many new buy-outs when the state of the economy turned out to be below expectation and interest rates rose to above the level that had been budgeted for. Companies could not defer payment of interest on loans in the way that they could defer paying a dividend to the risk-taking shareholders. In Britain, many buy-outs were formed among retailers during the boom periods of the 1980s when consumer spending was at a historically high standard. Faced with a downturn in consumer spending a few years later, these companies did not have the flexibility to postpone payment of interest. Instead, they had to indulge in stock reductions and price discounting to keep cash flowing in. Sometimes they succeeded, but on other occasions receivership followed, as with Lewis's department stores and the jewellers Easthope & Co. In other cases, the finances of the business had to be restructured, usually to the detriment of the shareholders, as occurred in the case of the MFI furniture group during 1990.

4.5 MARKETING AND ORGANIZATIONAL SCALE

There is continuing debate about whether there is an 'ideal' size for business organizations. In fact, there are advantages and disadvantages of large firms and they can be found coexisting with much smaller firms in most sectors. This section reviews recent debate about the benefits of large organizations against small business units.

4.5.1 Economies of scale

In many sectors, large organizations have advantages over smaller ones. These are some of their principal advantages:

1. In some industries there are significant economies of scale in production processes. This is particularly true of industries where fixed costs of production are a high proportion of total costs. Therefore sectors such as car manufacture and banking allow large organizations to spread the high cost of capital equipment over a greater number of units of output, thereby pursuing what Porter (1980) describes as a cost leadership strategy. In sectors that use high technology, or that require highly trained labour skills, a learning curve effect may be apparent (also called a cost experience curve). By operating at a larger scale than its competitors, a firm can benefit more from the learning curve and thereby achieve lower unit costs. While this may be true of some industries, others face only a very low critical output at which significant economies of scale occur—niche retailing and hairdressing, for example. For organizations in these sectors, cost leadership would be a difficult strategy as many rival firms would also be able to achieve maximum cost efficiency.
2. As well as being more efficient at turning inputs into outputs, larger firms may be able to acquire their inputs on more advantageous terms in the first place. One reason for the success of large-scale retailers is the much greater bargaining power they have over suppliers, compared to smaller retailers. Often, smaller organizations have joined together in voluntary buying chains in order to increase their bargaining power with suppliers. Many farmers' co-operatives realize that a group of farmers can collectively achieve lower prices from suppliers than one farmer negotiating alone. As well as being able to bring greater bargaining power to negotiations with suppliers, buying on a large scale can give savings in the logistical costs of transferring goods from supplier to buyer.
3. Large-scale production can allow not only for lower cost production but also for better products to be offered. This can take the form of additional design features which could not be included if production was on a small scale (e.g. small manufacturers of food products may not be able to afford as much on designing eye-catching packaging as their larger competitors) or additional services that a firm is able to offer (large building societies may, for example, be able to offer a much more comprehensive range of investment services than their smaller competitors).
4. A company's promotion effort can be much more efficient where it is aimed at a large-volume national (or even international) market, rather than a purely local one. National television and press

advertising may be an efficient medium for a large-scale national company, which gives it a promotional advantage over smaller scale local producers who must rely on various local and regional
media.
5. Investors generally prefer companies that have a proven track record of stability. By being able to
diversify into a number of different products and market segments, companies are able to offer this
stability, resulting in 'blue chip' companies being able to obtain equity and loan capital at a lower
cost than smaller companies.
6. With relationship marketing becoming an important part of many organizations' strategy, the ability
to cross-sell related goods and services becomes crucial. By operating at a larger scale with a broad
portfolio of products, cross-selling can be facilitated.

4.5.2   Limits to growth

Most organizations pursue growth to a greater or lesser degree. However, there are limits to how far
and how fast a company can grow. Growth by acquisition—being relatively risky—can reveal limits
beyond which a company cannot sustain growth. Growth by acquisition is commonly associated with
high borrowings resulting in a high level of gearing. The use of relatively cheap debt capital may be
attractive while the company is profitable, but can leave the company dangerously exposed when
conditions deteriorate. Faced with a fixed charge for interest, the organization may be forced to liquidate some of its assets by disposing of subsidiaries, to raise cash to meet its interest payments. Many
companies that grew rapidly during the 1980s by acquisition using borrowed capital have been forced
to contract with the economic slowdown of the early 1990s. Examples include the Storehouse Group
which grew rapidly through its acquisition of British Home Stores and Mothercare and the conglomerate Polly Peck which grew very rapidly before going into receivership. Organizations that grew
organically at a slower rate without reliance on such a high level of borrowed capital have tended to
fare relatively better.

The ability of the management structure of a company to respond to growth sets a further limit to
growth. Many companies have benefited by having a dynamic personality leading during a period of
rapid growth, only to find that a large organization needs a much broader management base once it
passes a critical size. Organizations such as Next and Amstrad have suffered where the management
structure has not grown to meet the needs of a very different type of organization. If a company does
not restructure itself as it grows, diseconomies of scale may set in.

Legislative constraints may limit the ability of an organization to grow in its core markets. Most
countries have laws to prevent one firm dominating a market or having undue influence over it.
Legislation governing monopolies in the United Kingdom is considered in the next chapter.

4.5.3   De-mergers

Conglomerates sometimes reach a size and diversity that produce more problems than opportunities
for the group as a whole. A number of conglomerates have therefore split themselves up in a reversal
to the process of merging, sometimes referred to as de-merging. The initial cause of a de-merger is
often the recognition that shareholders' total share value would increase if they had shares in two or
more separate businesses rather than the one conglomerate holding company. Stock markets often have
difficulty placing a value on the shares of highly diversified companies, and many de-mergers have
seen the combined value of the de-merged companies' shares very quickly exceed the previous price
of the shares of the former holding company. This was true in the de-mergers of Racal and Vodaphone,
ICI and Zenecca, and BAT Industries and Argos.

The move to a de-merger may be strengthened by conflicts of interest within a conglomerate. A third
party buyer from a conglomerate may fear that purchases from one member company would prejudice

the confidentially in other areas of its business. This was one reason raised in the proposed de-merger of AT&T into three separate operating units responsible for telecommunications operations, equipment and information services. A rival telecommunications operator may have been suspicious about buying its equipment from a conglomerate whose telecommunication division was its arch rival.

Sometimes, de-mergers may arise from statutory intervention. In an earlier action by the American government, one of the largest de-mergers in corporate history occurred when AT&T was forced to sell off its local telephone companies (or 'Baby Bells') in order to create a more competitive market in telecommunications. In the United Kingdom, de-merging of part of a company's activities is often a condition for a take-over following a referral of a proposed take-over to the Monopolies and Mergers Commission.

4.5.4 The resurgence of small business

The term 'small business' is difficult to define. In an industry such as car manufacture, a firm with 100 employees would be considered very small, whereas among solicitors, a practice of that size would be considered large. The term small business is therefore a relative one, based typically on some measure of numbers of employees or capital employed. Within the European Union, the Eurostat definition of small companies is often used:

Micro-organizations:	0–9 employees
Small organizations:	10–99 employees
Medium-sized organizations:	100–499 employees
Large organizations:	500+ employees

Despite the tendency of firms to grow, there has been renewed interest in the role of small businesses within the economy. It is suggested that many of Britain's competitors can attribute the success of their economies to having a strong small business sector. The dynamic economies of the Far East have particularly strong small business sectors. During recent years, there has been a significant increase in the number of small businesses, especially in the expanding services sector.

In the United Kingdom, the Small Firms Report (DTI, 1995) highlighted a number of features of the small business sector:

1. There has been a significant growth in the number of small firms, up from around 2.4 million in 1980 to 3.6 million in 1994.
2. Despite the overall fall in employment in manufacturing in the United Kingdom between 1980 and 1992, jobs in companies with less than 100 employees have risen by 100 000. During this period, the percentage of manufacturing employment which these firms represent has risen from 19 to 29 per cent of the total, while the share of large firms fell from 68 to 52 per cent.
3. Although the number of small firms is increasing, large numbers of firms also go out of business. In 1994, although there was a net increase of 24 000 small firms, this represented 446 000 new start-ups, less 422 000 closures.
4. Small firms are concentrated in particular sectors. Of small firm employment 20 per cent is in the manufacturing sector. They are also dominant in construction (where 60 per cent of all firms are classified as 'microenterprises'), wholesale, retail and financial services.

Advocates of small business argue that they are important to the economy for a number of reasons:

1. They generally offer much greater adaptability than larger firms. With less bureaucracy and fewer channels of communications, decisions can be taken rapidly. A larger organization may be burdened

with constraints which tend to slow the decision-making process, such as the need to negotiate new working practices with trade union representatives or the need to obtain Board of Directors' approval for major decisions. As organizations grow, there is an inherent tendency for them to become more risk averse by building in systems of control which make them slower to adapt to changes in their marketing environment.

2. It is also argued that small businesses tend to be good innovators. This comes about through greater adaptability, especially where large amounts of capital are not required. This is often true of the service sector where typical low-cost innovations have included video film rental services and home delivery fast food services. Small firms can also be good innovators where they operate in markets dominated by a small number of larger companies and the only way in which a small business can gain entry to the market is to develop an innovatory product aimed at a small niche. The soap powder market in Britain is dominated by a small number of large producers, yet it was a relatively small company that identified a niche for environmentally friendly powders and introduced innovatory products to the market.

3. Most large firms started off as very small businesses, so it is important to the health of the economy that there is a continuing supply of growing companies to replace those larger firms that die.

The change in the structure and organization of industry and commerce, the growing emphasis on specialized services and the application of new technology have tended to encourage small business. Flexible manufacturing systems are increasingly able to allow a business to function at a much lower level of output than previously. An example is in printing, where new production processes have allowed entrepreneurs to undertake small print runs on relatively inexpensive machinery. The success of the small printer has been further encouraged by the proliferation of small business users of printed material requiring small print runs and a rapid turn-round of work. The tendency for large companies to subcontract functions such as cleaning and catering in order to concentrate on their core business has also given new opportunities to the small business sector.

It is not only small entrepreneurs who have been creating new small businesses, for larger organizations have also recognized their value and have tried to replicate them at a distance from their own structure. Many large manufacturing organizations operating in mature markets have created autonomous new small business units to serve rapidly developing or specialist niche markets, free of the bureaucratic culture of the parent organization. Local authorities have been required by the Local Government Act 1988 to set up their own Direct Labour Organizations which are effectively small units operating under the umbrella of the authority, albeit subject to rules and regulations specified in the Act. In the education sector, many universities have established small research companies at arms length from the universities' organizational structures.

While small business has certainly seen a resurgence in recent years, it should also be recognized that they have a very high failure rate. Conclusive evidence of the failure rate of small businesses is difficult to obtain, especially in view of the problem of identifying new businesses that do not need to register in the first place. However, one indication of failure rates comes from an analysis of VAT (value added tax) registrations, which show that during the early 1990s, only about one-third of businesses set up ten years previously were still registered. More detailed evidence was provided by the results of a survey undertaken by Warwick University in 1995 (Cressy and Storey, 1995). It found that less then 20 per cent of new small businesses survive more than six years, a poorer record than indicated by VAT returns, which exclude very small firms. The research suggested that it was very small firms that had the shortest lives, and described the characteristics of the small firm entrepreneur most likely to succeed. Businesses started by 50 to 55 year olds were found to be twice as likely to survive as those begun by people in their twenties, for example. Also significant were the number of proprietors, and whether they had a specific qualification and work experience in the same sector.

4.5.5 Government and small business

Governments in many countries have been keen to support small businesses. They have pointed to the successful small-business-led economies of the Far East and sought to emulate their growth through the creation of a strong domestic small business sector. The presence of large numbers of small businesses in a market is also useful for increasing the competitiveness of markets, thereby achieving government objectives of a more flexible economy and lower inflation.

Such motivations partly explain some of the concessions that governments have made to the small business sector. These include a lower rate of corporation tax for firms with a turnover of less than £300 000 p.a. (1994–5), allowing them to re-invest more of their profits. Small firms with a turnover of less than £46 000 p.a. (1994–5) are exempt from the need to charge VAT and have been freed from a wide range of duties that apply to larger companies, especially those relating to employment rights. To encourage the development of new businesses, many supportive innovations have been launched by central government, including various training schemes sponsored by Training and Enterprise Councils. Locally, Enterprise Agencies have given support to new businesses from existing firms.

Small business owners are often sceptical about governments' support for them, pointing out that government legislation often imposes disproportionate burdens on them. Cynics might argue that governments have seen the encouragement of small business as a simple means of getting unemployed people off the list of the unemployed. A survey of small businesses by the British Chambers of Commerce (1995) revealed the extent of small business owners' dissatisfaction with government regulations. More than 74 per cent of respondents complained about the burdens of VAT, which effectively makes businesses unpaid tax collectors for government. While larger firms may be able to afford a specialized accounting department, many small business owners are often left to add the submission of VAT returns as an additional job for them to have to undertake personally. Government has hoped to stimulate the small business sector through the compulsory competitive tendering (CCT) of local government services, but the 2000 plus regulations governing CCT have put many small businesses off bidding for contracts. In the BCC survey, 71 per cent of managing directors of small businesses claimed that the requirement to complete government forms was costing them between 1 and 2 per cent of their turnover. Governments frequently declare that they are going to cut the red tape and bureaucracy which imposes burdens on small businesses. However, the historic reality has often been in the opposite direction.

4.5.6 Organizational life-cycles

It is common to talk about products going through a life cycle from launch, through growth and maturity to eventual decline. Many have suggested that organizations also go through a similar type of life cycle. One analysis of services organizations by Sasser, Olsen and Wyckoff (1978) identified a number of stages in the life cycles of organizations:

- *Stage 1: entrepreneurial* In this stage, an individual identifies a market need and offers a product to a small number of people, usually operating from one location. While most entrepreneurs stay at this stage, some begin to think about growth, often entailing a move to larger and/or additional sites.
- *Stage 2: multisite rationalization* In this stage, the successful entrepreneur starts to add to the limited number of facilities. It is during this stage that the skills required for being a multisite operator begin to be developed. By the end of this stage, the organization gains a certain degree of stability at a level of critical mass. At this stage, franchising starts to be considered.
- *Stage 3: growth* Here the company's concept has become accepted as a profitable business idea. The company is now actively expanding through the purchase of competitors, franchising/licensing the concept, developing new company-operated facilities or a combination of the three. Growth is

not only influenced by the founder's desire to succeed but also from the pressures placed upon the company by the financial community.

● *Stage 4: maturity* The number of new outlets declines and revenues of individual facilities stabilize and in some cases decline. This tends to be caused by a combination of four factors: changing demographics within the firm's market, changing needs and tastes of consumers, increased competition and 'cannibalization' of older services by firms' newer products.

● *Stage 5: decline/regeneration* Firms can become complacent, and unless new products are developed or new markets found, decline and deterioration soon follows.

By identifying a company's position in the life cycle, the major objectives, decisions, problems and organizational transitions needed for the future can be anticipated. Thus firms can plan for necessary changes rather than react to a set of conditions that could have been predicted earlier.

TESCO STORES ADAPTS AS IT GROWS

Tesco Stores has grown to become a very profitable business and one of the UK's largest retailers. Today's Tesco is a long way from the humble barrow trading with which the business began, and an analysis of the company's growth illustrates the changes in form that Tesco has undergone in order to achieve its current market position.

The basis for the existing business of Tesco was founded shortly after the First World War when Jack Cohen left the flying corps with just £30 of capital available to him. His first taste of civilian entrepreneurship came with his decision to invest most of his £30 in the bulk purchase of tins of surplus war rations, which he proceeded to sell from a barrow in the street markets of London. As a sole trader, Jack Cohen needed the minimum of formality to get his business started. Furthermore, large capital investment was not required at a time when the typical retail unit was very small and selling through street markets was commonplace. The products that he sold were basic commodities which did not need large investment to create a distinctive and differentiated brand.

The name Tesco was first used by Cohen to differentiate the tea which he sold from that of his competitors. The name was derived by taking the first two letters of his own surname and prefixing it with the initials of the owner of the tea importing business from which he bought his tea—T. E. Stockwell. Jack Cohen was buying a commodity in bulk from the importer, re-packaging the tea and selling it under a brand name.

Further growth came by developing sales to other market traders in addition to the sales he made to final consumers. He acted as a middleman, or wholesaler, operating from a small warehouse. Success came from being able to spot a good bargain and to fill his warehouse with cheap goods that he would resell to London street traders. Channels of distribution at this time tended to be based on a push strategy in which entrepreneurs needed to actively sell products to the next stage in the chain of distribution.

It became clear to Cohen that he was capable of selling considerably more stock and making more profit if he had more outlets. In 1930 he therefore opened his first shop in an arcade in Tooting, south London. To do this and run his wholesale business would have been stretching the financial and managerial abilities of his sole trader status. He therefore decided to take on a partner—Sam Freeman—to buy and run the Tooting shop. The following year he formed another separate partnership with a nephew—Jack Vanger—to open a second shop in Chatham, followed by a third partnership to run a shop in London.

In 1932, Jack Cohen formed two private limited companies to run his two core businesses. Tesco Stores Ltd ran the retail business and by 1938 had grown to a chain of 100 shops. Growth had been fuelled by attracting private equity capital and using retained profits. The second company—J. E. Cohen Ltd—was created to run the growing wholesale business.

Backward vertical integration occurred when Jack Cohen became involved in businesses that supplied the wholesale and retail businesses. In 1942 Railway Nurseries (Cheshunt) Ltd was set up by buying farmland to supply Tesco with fresh vegetables. A couple of years later, Goldhanger Fruit Farms Ltd in Essex was created to supply Tesco with fresh and canned fruits, as well as supplying other retailers.

Numerous private companies now existed to run the Tesco businesses and in 1947 these were brought together in one holding company—Tesco Stores (Holdings) Ltd. The holding company held the share capital of the subsidiary companies that had been built up over the previous years. To provide additional equity capital for future growth, the holding company became a public company in December 1947 by offering 250 000 shares of 5p nominal value at 75p each to the general public. The money provided by the share issue was used to develop larger stores, in particular the new style of self-service store which was modelled on the American example and which proved increasingly successful for Tesco. The company had developed its own brands in a number of product areas such as tea and dairy products, but still relied on selling other manufacturers' products at lower prices than competing retailers. In the post-war period, the role of the retailer was changing as manufacturers sought to develop strong brands and to promote the benefits of their brands direct to the public. The power of the retailer to influence the decision of the customer was being reduced with the development of mass media aimed at the final consumer, particularly following the introduction of commercial television in the mid-1950s. Distribution strategies were changing from push to pull. Tesco aimed to make branded goods available to consumers at the lowest possible price—the company's motto became 'pile it high and sell it cheap'. The main constraint on offering lower prices was the existence of Resale Price Maintenance, which allowed manufacturers to control the price at which its products were sold to the public by retailers. The abolition of Resale Price Maintenance in 1964 was to be extremely beneficial to Tesco's marketing strategy, in which price was seen as a key element of the marketing mix. Further shares were sold during the 1950s and 1960s, allowing the company to expand rapidly and to open supermarkets in most towns throughout Britain. A major rights issue in January 1991 raised £572 million from existing shareholders to fund further expansion and to reduce the level of gearing. As the company's core business of selling groceries and household goods approached saturation, the company diversified into related areas such as the sale of petrol and the creation of in-store coffee shops.

The bulk of Tesco's growth has been organic in nature. As management abilities and financial reserves were built up, they were used to develop more stores and to enter different stages of the distribution process. On occasions, however, growth has come about by acquisition, for example the acquisition of the Hillards group in 1987 and the Scottish based William Low in 1994. The addition of William Low's outlets allowed Tesco to expand rapidly in Scotland where it was poorly represented at the time.

Tesco PLC has challenged Sainsburys for the distinction of being the largest grocery retailer in the United Kingdom, owning over 500 stores, employing a total of over 130 000 staff and selling 20 000 lines, of which about 3000 are own brand products. Market traders such as Jack Cohen's original business still exist alongside Tesco, and in reaching its present position it is possible to observe a number of changes that Tesco has had to go through. In order to grow, Tesco had to offer some unique advantage over its competitors. In the early days this was based on low price and this price orientation was emphasized as late as 1977 when Tesco initiated a price-cutting war among the major supermarkets. More recently, Tesco has sought to differentiate itself by offering a better quality of service. Most new developments of the 1980s were focused on large out-of-town superstores offering a wide choice of products with easy car parking facilities. A lot of money has been invested in developing the company's own brand products, of which many in the late 1980s were differentiated by being promoted as healthy life-style products. As it has grown, Tesco has been able to achieve greater economies of scale in distribution and promotion. It has also used size to exert greater power in the chain of distribution and to achieve competitive pricing. Instead of aggressively pushing goods though the chain, Tesco has sought to pull customers in to its own stores specifically by stressing the unique advantages of shopping at Tesco.

QUESTIONS

1. Identify the diversity of legal forms that Tesco has adopted at different stages of its development.
2. Summarize the strategies that have been used to bring about growth.
3. In what ways has the company's marketing mix adapted to changes in its marketing environment?

REVIEW QUESTIONS

1. (a) Prepare a short report outlining the main reasons why businesses of different sizes exist.
   (b) Are there any relationships between the size of the business and the market in which it operates?
   (CIM Marketing Environment examination, June 1995, Q.2)
2. What problems for the marketing management of a furniture manufacturer might arise from rapid growth?
3. In what ways have the objectives of newly privatized industries changed compared to those of the state-owned organizations that they replaced?
4. What are the problems and opportunities for marketing management arising from a policy of growth through diversification?
5. Explain the resurgence of interest in the small business sector.
6. Choose one industry sector with which you are familiar and examine how small and large firms have found roles in which they can coexist with each other.

REFERENCES

Ansoff, H. I. (1957) 'Strategies for Diversification', *Harvard Business Review*, vol. 25, no. 5, September–October, pp. 113–24.

British Chambers of Commerce (1995) *Small Firms Survey: Regulation*, BCC, London.

Cressy, R. and Storey, D. (1995) *Small and Medium Sized Enterprises*, Warwick University Business School.

DTI (1995) *Small Firms in Britain 1995*, Department of Trade and Industry, London.

Ennew, C., Wong, P. and Wright, M. (1992) 'Organisational Structures and the Boundaries of the Firm: Acquisitions and Divestments in Financial Services', *The Services Industries Journal*, vol. 12, no. 4, pp. 478–97.

Porter, M. (1980) *Competitive Strategy:Techniques for Analyzing Industries and Competitors*, Free Press, New York.

Sasser, W. E., Olsen, R. P. and Wyckoff, D. D. (1978) *Management of Service Operations:Texts, Cases, Readings*, Allyn and Bacon, Boston, Mass.

FURTHER READING

Davidson, I. and Mallin, C. (1993) *The Business Accounting and Finance Blueprint*, Blackwell, Oxford.

Gaughan, P. (ed.) (1994) *Readings in Mergers and Acquisitions*, Blackwell, Oxford.

Keasey, K. and Watson, R. (1993) *Small Firm Management*, Blackwell, Oxford.

Kohn, M. (1994) *Financial Institutions and Markets*, McGraw-Hill, Maidenhead.

Office of Fair Trading (1990) *An Outline of UK Competition Policy*, OFT, London.

Scott, M. (ed.) (1986) *Small Firms, Growth and Development*, Gower, Aldershot.

Storey, D. J. (1988) *Entrepreneurship and the New Firm*, Routledge, London.

Ward, K. (1994) *Strategic Issues in Finance*, Heinemann, Oxford.

CHAPTER FIVE

THE COMPETITION ENVIRONMENT

OBJECTIVES

After reading this chapter, you should understand:

- The importance of market structure to marketing decisions
- The characteristics of perfectly competitive markets and reasons why competitive markets are considered to be superior for meeting consumers' needs
- Causes of market imperfection and their implications for marketing management
- Legislative measures designed to preserve the competitive nature of markets

5.1 INTRODUCTION TO THE COMPETITIVE ENVIRONMENT

Competition is a crucial fact of life to most organizations operating in a commercial environment. Competition usually arises when companies seek to attract customers from rival companies by offering better products and/or lower prices. Competition can also arise in the acquisition of resources, and where these are scarce relative to the demand for them, rival buyers will bid up their price. However, competition in customer and resource markets can be complex and a full understanding of each market is needed if the effects of competition on an organization are to be fully appreciated. This chapter begins by reviewing the fundamentals of competitive markets which are characterized by 'perfect competition' (sometimes referred to as 'atomistic competition'). In fact, perfect competition is the exception rather than the norm and most markets have imperfections which allow some organizations in the market to have undue influence over it. It is because of these imperfections that governments have intervened, believing that, in general, competitive markets are better for consumers.

Markets are a central concern for students and practitioners of both economics and marketing. While marketers focus on the demand side of a market, economists define markets in terms of the interaction between two groups:

- Those seeking to buy products
- Those seeking to sell them

Economists distinguish between those economic influences that operate at the level of the individual firm and those that relate to the economy as a whole. The study of an organization and its customers/suppliers in isolation from the rest of the economy is generally referred to as microeconomic analysis. In this type of analysis, the national economy is assumed to be stable. However, this assumption is rarely true, so economists seek to understand the workings of the economy and, from this, the effects of changes in the national (and international) economy on individual organizations. This is generally referred to as macroenvironmental analysis.

This chapter is concerned primarily with microeconomic influences as they affect the decisions made by individual firms, for example with regard to their pricing and production levels. The following chapter will return to macroeconomic analysis.

5.1.1   Market structure

The market conditions facing suppliers of goods and services vary considerably. Customers of electricity and water companies may feel they are being exploited with high prices and poor service levels by companies who know that their customers have little choice of supplier. On the other hand, customers are constantly wooed by numerous banks and building societies who are all trying to sell basically similar products in a market that provides consumers with a lot of choice. Differences in the characteristics of buyers and sellers define the structure of a market.

The term market structure is used to describe:

● The number of buyers and sellers operating in a market
● The extent to which the market is concentrated in the hands of a small number of buyers and/or sellers
● The degree of collusion or competition between buyers and/or sellers

An understanding of market structure is important to marketers, not only to understand the consequences of their own actions but also the behaviour of other firms operating in it.

Market structures range from the theoretical extremes of perfect competition and pure monopoly. In practice, examples of the extremes are rare and analysis therefore focuses on levels of market imperfection between the two extremes (Figure 5.1).

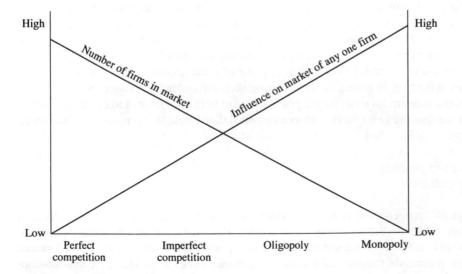

Figure 5.1   A continuum of market structures

5.2   PERFECT COMPETITION

This is the simplest type of market structure to understand and corresponds very much with most peoples' idea of what a very competitive market should be like. Government policy makers often pursue a vision of perfect competition as the ideal market structure. Although perfectly competitive markets in their theoretical extreme are rarely found in practice, a sound understanding of the way they work is essential for understanding competitive market pressures in general.

Perfectly competitive markets are attributed with the following principal characteristics:

1. There are a large number of small producers supplying to the market, each with similar cost structures and each producing an identical product.
2. There are also a large number of buyers in the market, each responsible for purchasing only a small percentage of total output.
3. Both buyers and sellers are free to enter or leave the market, that is there are no barriers to entry or exit.
4. In a perfectly competitive market, there is a ready supply of information for buyers and sellers about market conditions.

Some markets come close to having these characteristics, for example:

- Wholesale fruit and vegetable markets
- The 'spot' market for oil products
- Stock markets where shares are bought and sold

In reality, very few markets fully meet the economists' criteria for perfect competition and even those markets described above have imperfections (e.g. wholesale fruit and vegetable markets are increasingly influenced by the practice of large retailers contracting directly with growers).

Perfect competition implies that firms are *price takers* in that competitive market forces alone determine the price at which they can sell their products. If a firm cannot produce its goods or services as efficiently as its competitors, it will lose profits and eventually go out of business. Customers are protected from exploitative high prices, because as long as selling a product remains profitable, companies will be tempted into the market to satisfy customers' requirements. Eventually, competition between firms will result in excessive profits being eliminated so that an equilibrium is achieved where loss-making firms have left the market and the market is not sufficiently attractive to bring new firms into it.

Probably the most important reason for studying perfect competition is that it focuses attention on the basic building blocks of competition: demand, supply and price determination.

5.2.1   Demand

Demand refers to the quantity of a product that consumers are *willing* and *able* to buy at a specific price over a given period of time. In economic analysis, demand is measured not simply in terms of what people would *like* to buy—after all, most people would probably want to buy expensive holidays and cars. Instead, demand refers to how many people are actually able and willing to buy a product at a given price and given a set of assumptions about the product and the environment in which it is being offered. Demand is also expressed in terms of a specified time period, for example so many units per day.

In general, as the price of a product falls, so the demand (as defined above) can be expected to rise. Likewise, as the price rises, demand could be expected to fall. This relationship can be plotted on a

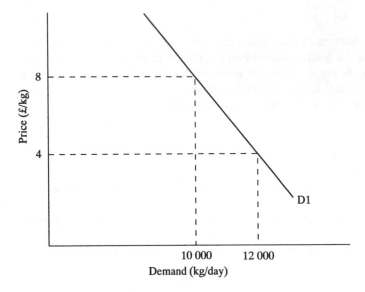

Figure 5.2   A demand curve for medium-fat cheddar cheese

simple graph. In Figure 5.2, a *demand curve* for medium-fat cheddar cheese is shown by the line D1. This relates, for any given price shown on the vertical axis, the volume of demand, which is shown on the horizontal axis. Therefore, at a price of £8.00 per kg, demand is 10 000 units per period within a given area, while at a price of £4.00, the demand has risen to 12 000 units.

It is important to note that the demand curve drawn here refers to total market demand from all consumers and is not simply measuring demand for one producer's output. The importance of this distinction will become clear later, as the implication of this is that firms have to make their price decisions based on overall market conditions.

The demand curve D1 is based on a number of assumptions. These include, for example, assumptions that the price of substitutes for cheese will not change or that consumers will not suddenly take a dislike to cheddar cheese. Demand curve D1 measures the relationship between price and market demand for *one given set of assumptions*. When these assumptions change, a new demand curve is needed to explain a new relationship between price and quantity demanded.

In Figure 5.3, two sets of fresh assumptions have been made and new demand curves D2 and D3 drawn, based on these new sets of assumptions. For new demand curve D2, more cheese is demanded for any given price level (or, alternatively, this can be restated in terms of any given number of consumers demanding cheese being prepared to pay a higher price). There are a number of possible causes of the shift of the demand curve from D1 to D2:

1. Consumers could have become wealthier, leading them to demand more of all goods, including cheese.
2. The price of substitutes for cheddar cheese (e.g. meat or other types of cheese) could have increased, thereby increasing demand for cheese.
3. Demand for complementary goods (such as savory biscuits) may increase, thereby leading to an increase in demand for cheese.
4. Consumer preferences may change. This may occur, for example, if cheddar cheese is found to have health-promoting benefits.
5. An advertising campaign for cheddar cheese may increase demand for cheese at any given price.

Similarly, a number of possible reasons can be put forward to explain the shift from demand curve D1 to D3, where for any given price level, less is demanded:

1. Consumers could have become poorer, leading them to demand fewer of all goods, including cheese.
2. The price of substitutes for cheddar cheese (e.g. meat or other types of cheese) could have decreased, thereby making the substitutes appear more attractive and reducing demand for cheese.
3. Demand for complementary products may fall.
4. Cheddar cheese may become associated with serious health hazards, leading to less demand at any given price.
5. An advertising campaign for substitute products may shift demand away from cheddar cheese.

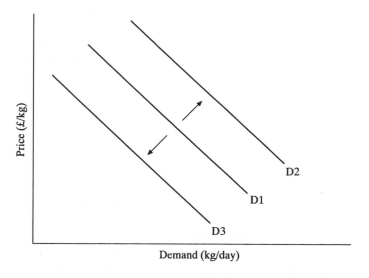

Figure 5.3   Alternative demand curves for cheese, based on differing assumptions

The demand curves shown in Figures 5.2 and 5.3 have both been straight, but this is a simplification of reality. In fact, demand curves would usually be curved, indicating that the relationship between price and volume is not constant for all price points. There may additionally be significant discontinuities at certain price points, as where buyers in a market have psychological price barriers, above or below which their behaviour changes. In many markets, the difference between £10.00 and £9.99 may be crucial in overcoming buyers' attitudes that predispose them to regard anything over £10 as being unaffordable and anything below it as a bargain.

Actually collecting information with which to plot a demand curve poses theoretical and practical problems. The main problem relates to the *cross-sectional* nature of a demand curve, that is it purports to measure the volume of demand across the ranges of price possibilities. However, this kind of information can often only be built up by a *longitudinal* study of the relationship between prices and volume over time. There is always the possibility that, over time, the assumptions on which demand is based have changed, in which case it is difficult to distinguish between a movement *along* a demand curve and a *shift* to a new demand curve. It is, however, sometimes possible for firms to conduct controlled cross-sectional experiments where a different price is charged in different areas and the effects on volume recorded. To be sure that this is accurately measuring the demand curve, there must be no extraneous factors in areas (such as differences in household incomes) that could partly explain differences in price/volume relationships.

The demand curves shown in Figures 5.2 and 5.3 slope downwards, indicating the intuitive fact that as price rises, demand falls and vice versa. While this is intuitively plausible, it is not always the case. Sometimes, the demand curve slopes upwards, indicating that as the price of a product goes up, buyers are able and willing to buy more of the product. Classic examples of this phenomenon occur where a product becomes increasingly desirable as more people consume it. A telephone network which has only one subscriber will be of little use to the first customer who will be unable to use a telephone to call anyone else. However, as more customers are connected, the value of the telephone network becomes greater to each individual who is correspondingly willing to pay a higher price. This phenomenon helps to explain why large international airports can charge more for aircraft to land than smaller regional airports. As the number of possible aircraft connections increases, airlines' willingness to pay high prices for landing slots increases.

Upward sloping demand curves can also be observed for some products sold for their 'snob' value. Examples include some designer label clothes where high price alone can add to a product's social status. Upward sloping demand curves can be observed over short time periods where a 'bandwagon' effect can be created by rapidly rising or falling prices. For example, in stock markets, the very fact that share prices are rising may lead many people to invest in shares.

5.2.2   Supply

Supply is defined as the amount of a product that producers are willing and able to make available to the market at a given price over a particular period of time. Like demand, it is important to note that at different prices there will be different levels of supply, reflecting the willingness and/or ability of producers to supply a product as prices change.

A simple supply curve for medium-fat cheddar cheese is shown in Figure 5.4. The supply curve slopes upwards from left to right, indicating the intuitively plausible fact that as market prices rise, more suppliers will be attracted to supply to the market. Conversely, as prices fall, marginal producers

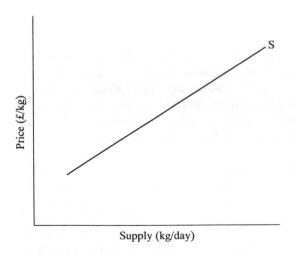

Figure 5.4   A supply curve for cheese

(such as those who operate relatively inefficiently) will drop out of the market, reducing the daily supply available.

It is again important to distinguish movements *along* a supply curve from *shifts* to a new supply curve. The supply curve S1 is based on a number of assumptions about the relationship between price and volume supplied. If these assumptions are broken, a new supply curve based on the new set of assumptions needs to be drawn. In Figure 5.5, two new supply curves, S2 and S3 are shown. S2 indicates a situation where, for any given price level, total supply to the market is reduced. This could come about for a number of reasons, including:

1. Changes in production technology, which result in cheddar cheese being produced more efficiently and therefore suppliers being prepared to supply more cheese at any given price (or, looked at another way, for any given volume supplied, suppliers are prepared to accept a lower price).
2. Extraneous factors (such as favourable weather conditions) could result in a glut of produce which must be sold and the market is therefore flooded with additional supply.
3. Governments may give a subsidy for each kilogram of cheese produced by suppliers, thereby increasing their willingness to supply to the market.

The new supply curve S3 indicates a situation where, for any given price level, total supply to the market is increased. This could come about for a number of reasons, including:

1. Production methods could become more expensive, for example because of more stringent health and safety regulations. Therefore, for any given price level, fewer firms will be willing to supply to the market as they will no longer be able to cover their costs.
2. Extraneous factors (such as abnormally bad weather) could result in producers having difficulty in getting their produce to market.
3. Governments may impose additional taxes on suppliers (e.g. extending the scope of business rates to cover agricultural property).

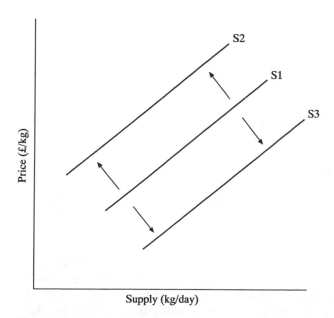

Figure 5.5 Alternative supply curves for cheese, based on differing assumptions

5.2.3 Price determination

An examination of the demand and supply graphs indicates that they share common axes. In both cases the vertical axis refers to the price at which the product might change hands, while the horizontal axis refers to the quantity changing hands.

It is possible to redraw the original demand and supply lines (D1 and S1) on a single graph (Figure 5.6). The supply curve indicates that the lower the price, the less cheese will be supplied to the market. Yet at these lower prices, customers are willing and able to buy a lot of cheese—more than the suppliers collectively are willing or able to supply. By following the supply curve upwards, it can be observed that suppliers are happy to supply more cheese, but at these high prices, there are few willing buyers. Therefore, at these high prices supply and demand are again out of balance.

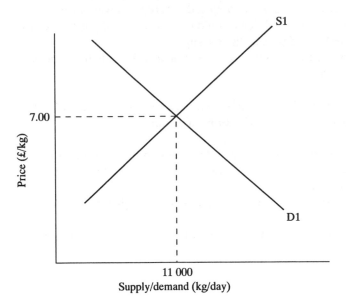

Figure 5.6   Supply and demand for cheese, showing the equilibrium market price

Between the two extremes there will be a price where the interest of the two groups will coincide. This balancing of supply and demand is the foundation of the theory of market price, which holds that in any free market there is an 'equilibrium price' that matches the quantity that consumers are willing and able to buy (i.e. demand) with the quantity that producers are willing and able to produce (i.e. supply).

In perfectly competitive markets, the process of achieving equilibrium happens automatically without any external regulatory intervention. Perfectly competitive markets do not need any complicated and centralized system for bringing demand and supply into balance, something which is difficult to achieve in a centrally planned economy, such as those which used to predominate in Eastern Europe.

In Figure 5.6, supply and demand are brought precisely into balance at a price of £7.00. This is the equilibrium price and, at this price, 11 000 kg of cheese per day will be bought and sold in the market. If a company wants to sell its cheese in the market, it can only do so at this price. In theory, if it charged a penny more, it would get no business because everybody else in the market is cheaper. If it sells at a penny less, it will be swamped with demand, probably selling at a price that is below its production costs.

It is important to remember that in a perfectly competitive market, individual firms are *price takers*. The market alone determines the 'going rate' for their product.

Changes in the equilibrium market price come about for two principal reasons:

● Assumptions about suppliers' ability or willingness to supply change, resulting in a shift to a new supply curve
● Assumptions about buyers' ability or willingness to buy change, resulting in a shift to a new demand curve

The effects of shifts in supply are illustrated in Figure 5.7. From an equilibrium price of £7.00 and volume of 11 000 kg, the supply curve has shifted to S2 (perhaps in response to the imposition of a new tax on production). Assuming that demand conditions remain unchanged, the new point of intersection between the demand and supply lines occurs at a price of £7.50 and a volume of 10 500 kg. This is the new equilibrium price. A similar analysis can be carried out on the effects of a shift in the demand curve, but where the supply curve remains constant. New equilibrium prices and trade volumes can be found at the intersection of the supply and demand curves. In practice, both the supply and demand curves may be changing at the same time.

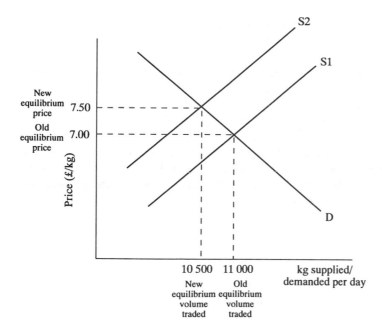

Figure 5.7   A shift in the supply curve for cheese, showing the new equilibrium market price

The speed with which a new equilibrium price is established is dependent upon how efficiently a market is working. In pure commodity markets where products are instantly perishable, rapid adjustments in price are possible. Where speculators are allowed to store goods, or large buyers and sellers are able to unduly influence a market, adjustment may be slower. The extent of changes in price and volume traded is also dependent on the elasticities of demand and supply, which are considered in the following sections.

5.2.4   Elasticity of demand

Elasticity of demand refers to the extent to which demand changes in relation to a change in price or some other variable such as income. What is important here is to compare the proportionate (or percentage) change in demand with the proportionate (or percentage) change in the other variable, over any given period of time.

The most commonly used measure of elasticity of demand is *price* elasticity of demand. Information on this is useful to business organizations to allow them to predict what will happen to volume sales in response to a change in price. This section is concerned with the responsiveness of a whole market to changes in price. It will be recalled that in a perfectly competitive market, firms must take their selling price from the market, so the only elasticity that is of interest to them is the elasticity of the market as a whole.

Price elasticity of demand refers to the ratio of the percentage change in demand to the percentage change in price. In other words, it seeks to measure how the sales of a product respond to a change in its price. This can be expressed as a simple formula:

$$\text{Price elasticity of demand} = \frac{\text{change in demand (\%)}}{\text{change in price (\%)}}$$

Where demand is relatively unresponsive to price changes, demand is said to be *inelastic* with respect to price. Where demand is highly responsive to even a small price charge, demand is described as being *elastic* with respect to price.

Two demand curves are shown in Figure 5.8. D1 is more elastic than D2, as indicated by the greater effect on volume of a change in price, compared with the effects of a similar price change with D2.

A number of factors influence the price elasticity of demand for a particular product. The most important is the availability of substitutes. Where these are readily available, buyers are likely to switch between alternative products in response to price changes. The absolute value of a product and its importance to a buyer can also influence its elasticity. For example, if infrequently purchased boxes of matches increased in price by 10 per cent from 10p to 11p, buyers would probably not cut back on their purchases. However, if the price of television sets increased by the same percentage amount from £300 to £330, many buyers may pull out of the market.

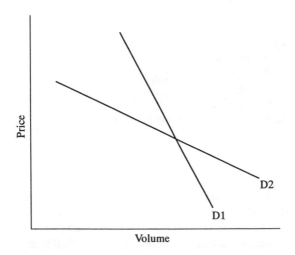

Figure 5.8   A comparison of a relatively inelastic demand function (D1) with a relatively elastic one (D2)

For any measure of elasticity, it is important to consider the time period over which it is being measured. In general, products are much more inelastic to changes in price over the short-term, when possibilities for substitution may be few. However, over the longer term, new possibilities for substitution may appear. This explains why petrol is very inelastic over the short-term but much more so over the long-term. Faced with a sudden increase in petrol prices (as happened in 1976), motorists have little choice other than paying the increased price. However, over the longer term, they can reduce their purchases of fuel by buying more fuel-efficient cars, rearranging their pattern of life so that they do not need to travel as much or sharing cars.

Further measures of elasticity of demand can be made by considering the responsiveness of demand to changes in the assumptions on which the demand curve is based. The most important of these is income elasticity of demand, which measures the responsiveness of demand to changes in buyers' combined incomes and can be expressed in the following way:

$$\text{Income elasticity of demand} = \frac{\text{change in demand } (\%)}{\text{change in income } (\%)}$$

In general, as a population's income rises, the demand for particular products rises, giving rise to a positive income elasticity of demand. Where there is a particularly strong increase in demand in response to an increase in incomes (or vice versa), a product can be said to have a high income elasticity of demand. This is true of luxuries such as long-haul air holidays and fitted kitchens, whose sales have increased during times of general economic prosperity, but declined during recessionary periods. On the other hand, there are some goods and services whose demand goes down as incomes increase. These are referred to as inferior goods and examples in most Western countries include local bus services and household coal.

It is useful for marketing managers to understand income elasticity of demand in order to plan a response to anticipated changes in aggregate income. If, for example, a general rise in consumer income looks likely to reduce the sales of a product that has a negative income elasticity, a business may seek to shift its resources to making products with a positive income elasticity. In trying to plan for the future, businesses rely on their own historical information about sales/income relationships, and also government and private forecasts about current and future levels and distribution of income.

A third measure of demand elasticity to note is a product's cross-price elasticity of demand. This refers to the percentage change in demand for product A when the price of product B changes. Where products are very close substitutes, this may be a very important measure to understand consumer demand. For example, the price of butter can have a significant effect on demand for margarine.

It is possible to identify numerous other *ad hoc* measures of elasticity of demand. Firms may be interested in the responsiveness of demand to changes in some measure of the quality of their product. For example, a railway operator may be interested in the effects on demand of improvements in service reliability or a bus operator may be interested in establishing the percentage increase in passenger demand resulting from a given percentage increase in frequency of a bus route.

5.2.5 Elasticity of supply

The concept of elasticity can also be applied to supply, so as to measure the responsiveness of supply to changes in price. Elasticity of supply is measured by the formula:

$$\text{Elasticity of supply} = \frac{\text{change in supply } (\%)}{\text{change in price } (\%)}$$

If suppliers are relatively unresponsive to an increase in the price of a product, the product is described as being inelastic with respect to price. If producers increase production substantially as prices rise, the product is said to be elastic.

As with price elasticity of demand, time is crucial in determining the elasticity of supply. Over the short term, it may be very difficult for firms to increase supply, making it very inelastic with respect to price. In the case of markets for agricultural products, elasticity is determined by the growing cycle and new supply may only be forthcoming in time for the next season. For many manufacturing processes, supplies can eventually be increased by investing in new productive capacity and taking on additional workers. Over the longer term, supply is more elastic.

5.2.6   Limitations of the theory of perfect competition

Although government policy makers often view perfectly competitive markets as an ideal to aim towards, the automatic balancing of supply and demand at an equilibrium price, as described above, is seldom achieved in practice. These are some of the more important reasons why perfect competition is rarely achieved in practice:

1. Where economies of scale are possible in an industry sector, it is always possible for firms to grow larger and more efficient, and thereby able to exercise undue influence in a market. In general, perfect competition only applies where production techniques are simple and opportunities for economies of scale are few.
2. Markets are often dominated by large buyers who are able to exercise influence over the market. The market for many specialized defence products may be competitive in terms of a large number of suppliers, but demand for their products is dominated by one government buying agency.
3. It can be naive to assume that high prices and profits in a sector will attract new entrants, while losses will cause the least efficient to leave. In practice, there may be a whole range of barriers to entry which could cover the need to obtain licences for production, the availability of trained staff and access to distribution outlets. Also, there are sometimes barriers to exit where firms are locked into long-term supply contracts or where it would be excessively expensive to lay off resources such as labour.
4. A presumption of perfectly competitive markets is that buyers and sellers have complete information about market conditions. In fact, this is often far from the truth. On the simple point of making price comparisons, much research has been undertaken to show that buyers often have little knowledge of the going rate price for a particular category of product. The use of bar scanning equipment by retailers has resulted in many products no longer carrying a price label, weakening customers' retained knowledge of prices. Sometimes, as in the case of telephone call tariffs or credit card interest charges, prices are very difficult to comprehend.

5.3   MONOPOLISTIC MARKETS

At the opposite end of the scale to perfect competition lies pure monopoly. In its purest extreme, monopoly in a market occurs where there is only one supplier to the market, perhaps because of regulatory, technical or economic barriers to entry which potential competing suppliers would face. Literally speaking, a monopoly means that one person or organization has complete control over the resources of a market. However, this rarely occurs in practice. Even in the former centrally planned economies of Eastern Europe, there have often been active 'shadow' markets which have existed alongside official monopoly suppliers.

Sometimes, monopoly control over supply comes about through a group of suppliers acting in collusion together in a 'cartel'. As with the pure monopoly, companies would join a cartel in order to try and protect themselves from the harsh consequences (for suppliers) of competition. The best example of a cartel is OPEC (oil producing exporting countries) which during the 1970s and 1980s had significant monopoly power over world oil price and output decisions.

Government definition of a monopoly is much less rigorous than pure economic definitions. In the United Kingdom, two types of monopoly can occur:

1. A *scale* monopoly occurs where one firm controls 25 per cent of the value of a market.
2. A *complex* monopoly occurs where a number of firms in a market together account for over 25 cent of the value of the market and their actions have the effect of limiting competition.

It can, however, be difficult to define just what is meant by 'the market'. While in Britain there may be just a few companies who between them have a near monopoly in the supply of bananas, when looked at in the context of the fruit market more generally, monopoly power diminishes. Also, is it most appropriate to confine attention to the UK market or to include overseas markets in a definition of monopoly? A firm may have a dominant market position at home, but may face severe competition in its overseas markets. In fact, the European Community now takes a Europe-wide perspective for assessing monopoly power for many products which can only sensibly be marketed Europe-wide. Thus, although British Aerospace has a dominant position in a number of its UK markets, when seen in a European context, it does in fact face severe competitive pressure.

5.3.1   Effects on prices and output of monopoly

A monopolist can determine the market price for its product and can be described as a 'price maker' rather than a 'price taker'. Where there are few substitutes for a product and where demand is inelastic, a monopolist may be able to get away with continually increasing prices in order to increase its profits.

In a pure monopoly market, consumers would face prices that are higher than would have occurred in a perfectly competitive market. Furthermore, because prices are higher, a downward sloping demand curve would indicate that output would be lower than in a competitive market. It is therefore commonly held that monopolies are against the public interest by leading to higher prices and lower output. Although there are occasionally circumstances where monopoly yields greater public benefit than free competition (discussed later in this chapter), the general policy of governments towards monopoly has been to restrict their power.

5.3.2   Marketing implications of monopoly

In a pure monopoly, a firm's output decisions would be influenced by the elasticity of demand for its products. So long as demand remained elastic, it could continue raising prices and thereby its total revenue. While a firm may have monopoly power over some of its users, it may face competition if it wishes to attract new segments of users. It may therefore resort to differential pricing when targeting the two groups. As an example, British Rail Network South East has considerable monopoly power over commuters who need to use its trains to arrive at work by 9.00 a.m. on weekdays. For such commuters, the alternatives of travelling to work by bus or car are very unattractive. However, leisure travellers wishing to go shopping in London at off-peak fares may be much more price sensitive. Their journey is optional to begin with and their flexibility with respect to their time of travel is greater. For them, the car or bus provides a realistic alternative. As a result, Network South East offers a range of price incentives aimed at off-peak leisure markets, while charging full fare for its peak period commuters.

Marketing managers who think strategically will be reluctant to fully exploit monopoly power. By charging high prices in the short-term, a monopolist could give signals to companies in related product fields to develop substitutes that would eventually provide effective competition. Blatant abuse of monopoly power could also result in a referral to the regulatory authorities (see below).

5.4   IMPERFECT COMPETITION

Perfectly competitive markets may be ideal for consumers because they have a tendency to minimize prices and maximize outputs. However, lower prices are not attractive to suppliers, because, for any given level of output, lower prices mean lower revenue and therefore profit. It is not surprising therefore that firms seek to limit the workings of perfectly competitive markets. It could be argued that most firms would like to be in the position of a monopolist and able to control the price level and output of their market. This is an unrealistic aim for most firms, but, in practice, firms can create imperfections in markets that give them limited monopoly power over their customers.

One of the assumptions of perfect competitions is that products offered in a particular market are identical. An entrepreneur can seek to avoid head-on competition with its competitors by trying to sell something that is just a little bit different compared to its competitors. Thus, in a market for fresh vegetables, a vegetable trader may try and get away from the fiercely competitive market for fresh potatoes, for which the price is determined by the market, by slightly differentiating its product. These are some possible differentiation strategies it could pursue:

- The trader might concentrate on selling specially selected potatoes, for example ones that are particularly suited to baking.
- A delivery service might be provided for customers.
- The potatoes could be packed in materials that prevent them being bruised.
- The trader might offer a no-quibble money-back guarantee for people who buy potatoes that turn out to be bad.
- The potatoes could be baked and offered with a range of fillings.
- If the trader was very ambitious, the potatoes might be processed into tinned or dried potatoes.
- As a result of any of the above actions, the trader could develop a distinct brand identity for the potatoes, so that buyers do not ask just for potatoes but for 'Brand X' potatoes by name.

In the example above, the trader has taken steps to turn a basic commodity product into something that is quite distinctive, so it has immediately cut down the number of direct competitors that it faces. In fact, if its product really was unique, it would have no direct competition; in other words, it would be a monopoly supplier of a unique product. However, it must not be forgotten that although the way the trader presented the potatoes may be unique, they are still broadly similar to the potatoes that everybody else is selling. The trader therefore still faces indirect competition, including competition from other foods such as rice and pasta which provide a substitute for potatoes.

If a trader has successfully differentiated its product, it is no longer strictly a price taker from the market. It may be able to charge 2p a pound more than the going rate for its selected and packaged potatoes, if customers think that the higher price is good value for a better product. It will be able to experiment to see just how much more buyers are prepared to pay for its differentiated product.

5.4.1   The role of brands

The process of branding is at the heart of organizations' efforts to remove themselves from fierce competition between generic products. Summarizing previous research, Doyle (1989) described brand building as the only way for a firm to build a stable, long-term demand at profitable margins. Through adding values that will attract customers, firms are able to provide a base for expansion and product development and to protect themselves against the strength of intermediaries and competitors. There has been much evidence linking high levels of advertising expenditure to support strong brands with high returns on capital and high market share (Buzzell and Gale, 1987).

Branding simplifies the decision-making process by providing buyers with a sense of security and consistency which distinguishes a brand from a generic commodity. There have been many conceptualizations of the unique positioning attributes of a brand. These usually distinguish between tangible dimensions that can be objectively measured (such as taste, shape, reliability) and the subjective values that can only be defined in the minds of consumers (such as the perceived personality of a brand). With increasing affluence, the non-functional expectations of brands have assumed increasing importance. A number of dimensions of a brand's emotional appeal have been identified, including trust, liking and sophistication and it has been shown that products with a high level of subjective emotional appeal are associated with a high level of customer involvement (Laurent and Kapferer, 1985). This has been demonstrated, for example, in the preference shown for branded beer compared to a functionally identical generic beer. As consumers buy products, they learn to appreciate their added value and begin to form a relationship with them. For example, as Pitcher (1985) observed, there are many companies selling petrol and credit cards, but individual companies such as Shell and American Express have created brands with which customers develop a relationship and guide their choice in a market dominated by otherwise generic products.

The traditional role of branding has been to differentiate products, but brands have been increasingly applied to organizational images too. This has occurred particularly with services where the intangibility of the product causes the credentials of the provider to be an important choice criterion.

In recent years there has been a growth in the number of 'own label' or 'private label' products sold by retailers. The suggestion that the growth of generic products is challenging traditional product branding strategy can be partly explained by a shift in buyers' brand allegiance, away from those of manufacturers and towards those of intermediaries. Through continued investment, retailers have developed products that have comparable functional qualities to manufacturers' branded products (McGoldrick, 1990). In many cases, retailers' own label products have developed a sufficiently strong brand reputation that they can command a price premium over other manufacturers' branded products.

However, both the functional and emotional dimensions of brands have come under more general environmental pressure. Research has suggested that consumers are becoming increasingly critical of the messages of brand building advertising, especially those aimed at creating abstract brand personalities. It is also claimed that consumers are becoming increasingly confident, ready to experiment and to trust their own judgement and less tolerant of products that do not contribute to their own values. The functional qualities of brands have come under pressure from increasing levels of consumer legislation. Characteristics such as purity, reliability and durability may have traditionally added value to a brand, but these are increasingly enshrined in legislation and therefore less capable of being used to differentiate one product from another. An example of the effects of legislation on brand loyalty can be observed in the taxi market by contrasting buyer behaviour in areas with strict licensing (e.g. London) with areas where a relatively free and unregulated market exists. In the former case, differentiation of the core service is difficult, and one black London taxi is very much like another. Where markets are unregulated, buyers seeking a taxi are more likely to seek the reassurance of a branded operator.

5.4.2 Imperfect competition and elasticity of demand

The analysis of price decisions for firms in a competitive market indicated that, for any one firm, price is given by the market. An individual firm cannot increase profits by stimulating demand through lower prices, nor would it gain any benefit by seeking to raise its prices. This changes in an imperfectly competitive market where a firm acquires a degree of monopoly power over its customers. Each firm now has a demand curve for its own unique product.

Firms face a downward sloping demand curve for their products, indicating that, as prices fall, demand increases and vice versa. In fact, a number of demand curves describing a firm's market can be described, ranging from the general to the specific brand. For example, in the market for breakfast cereals, the demand curve for cereals in general may be fairly inelastic, on the basis that people will always want to buy breakfast cereals of some description (Figure 5.9). Demand for one particular type of cereal, such as corn flakes, will be slightly more elastic as people may be attracted to corn flakes from other cereals such as porridge oats on the basis of their relative price. Price becomes more elastic still when a particular brand of cereals is considered. To many people, Kellogg's corn flakes can be easily substituted with other brands of corn flakes, so if a price differential between brands developed, switching may occur.

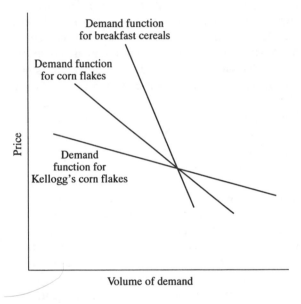

Figure 5.9   A comparison of elasticities of demand for breakfast cereals at different levels of product specificity

By lowering its price, a firm may be able to increase its sales, but what is important to firms is that they increase their total revenue (and, thereby, profits). Whether this happens depends upon the elasticity of demand for the product in question.

Total revenue is a function of total sales multiplied by the selling price per unit. Table 5.1 summarizes the effects on total revenue of changes in price, given alternative assumptions about elasticity:

Table 5.1 Effects of elasticity of demand and price changes on total revenue

Price elasticity of demand	Price change	Revenue effect
High (elastic demand)	+	−
	−	+
Low (inelastic demand)	+	+
	−	−

BRITISH RAIL ARRIVES AT MARKET-BASED PRICES

The environment in which transport services are provided ranges from perfectly competitive to monopolistic. As in other sectors of the economy, examples of perfect competition are relatively rare within the transport sector, but can be seen in such instances as the spot market for shipping or the haggling that accompanies hiring a taxi in many unregulated markets. In general, as the technology and capital intensiveness of a method of transport increases, so too does the possibility of transport monopolies developing. In addition, governments have often been happy to support, or even to actively encourage, transport monopolies on the grounds of resulting public benefits.

British Rail has been gradually making the transition from a monopoly supplier of transport to one operating in highly competitive markets. During this transition, the basis for price determination has changed significantly.

The political environment has had an important effect on British Rail's pricing policies. Before the 1960s, railways were seen as essentially a public service, reflecting an age before the advent of mass bus, car and truck transport when rail users had little choice of transport. Prices were set on a seemingly equitable basis related to production costs, with fares being charged strictly on a cost per mile basis. A distinction was made between first and second class, and a system of cheap day returns existed largely through tradition. From the 1960s, British Rail moved away from social objectives with the introduction of business objectives. With this has come a recognition that pricing must be used to maximize revenue rather than to provide social equality.

Market segmentation has replaced social planning as a basis for determining railway fares. A number of market segments for rail passenger travel have been identified and a distinctive marketing mix developed for each. The business traveller typically has a need for the flexibility of travelling at any time of the day and because an employer is often picking up the bill; demand from this segment tends to be relatively inelastic with respect to the price charged. Some segments of the business market demand higher standards of quality and are prepared to pay a higher price for first class

travel or for an executive package that includes additional services such as meals and car parking. Leisure segments are on the whole more price sensitive and may be prepared to accept a lower standard of service offered in return for a lower price (e.g. the student segment is offered lower fares in return for accepting restrictions on the number of trains on which tickets can be used).

Competitors have an increasingly important effect on the pricing of rail services and the nature of the competition varies from one market segment to another. For example, students are more likely than the business person to accept the coach as an alternative and therefore student rail fares are often pitched just above the equivalent student coach fare, the higher rail fare being justified on the basis of a superior service offering. For the business traveller, a key comparison is with the cost of running a car, parking and, more importantly, the cost of an employed person's time. Against these costs, the full first class fare may appear to be relatively good value. For the family market, the most serious competition is presented by the family car, so a family discount railcard allows the family as a unit to travel for the price of little more than two adults. For commuters to central London, British Rail has maintained a certain amount of monopoly power among segments of users who have little realistic short-term alternative to the train for getting to work. Over recent years, season ticket prices for commuters have tended to rise faster than average, reflecting the price inelasticity of such 'captive' customers, as well as the high cost of catering for peak hour demands. In some cases, the unprofitability of serving particular segments has led train operators to charge very high prices in a bid to 'choke-off' unprofitable demand. As an example of this, the train operator South-West Trains received a lot of bad publicity during 1995 when it doubled the price of season tickets on a route in Devon, apparently to reduce demand from school children travelling to school. It was claimed that investing in additional capacity to cater for these users would have been unprofitable.

With the advent of rail privatization, competitor-orientated pricing acquired additional significance as newly formed train operating companies found themselves competing against each other on price and service levels. Direct competition has occurred on some routes such as London to Gatwick Airport where a number of train operators provide a parallel service. More indirect competition has occurred where routes overlap, for example Chiltern Trains has competed with InterCity for passengers between Birmingham and London. However, the prospects for serious price competition occurring between rival train operators seem remote. The barriers to entry remain high, with major financial and regulatory hurdles facing new entrants attracted to the industry. In a network of interconnecting services, train operators are often dependent on one another for through ticketing. For consumers, the prospect of competition may bring about even more confusion over the range of fares available and it would seem unlikely that the perfectly competitive market requirement for complete knowledge about all competing alternatives could be attained.

QUESTIONS

1. Should governments intervene to regulate rail fares?
2. What are the benefits to rail operators of offering reduced fares to students?
3. Are train fares too expensive?

5.4.3 Oligopoly

One step on from imperfect competition is a market structure often referred to as *oligopoly*. It lies somewhere between the two extremes of perfect competition and pure monopoly. An oligopoly market is one that is dominated by a small number of sellers who provide a large share of the total market output. The crucial point about oligopoly markets is that all suppliers in the market are interdependent. One company cannot take price or output decisions without considering the specific possible responses of other companies.

Oligopoly is a particularly important market structure in industries where economies of scale are significant. They are typical of oil refining and distribution, pharmaceuticals, car manufacturing and detergents. Customers of oligopoly organizations may not immediately appreciate that the products they are buying come from an oligopolist as such firms often operate with a variety of brand names (the detergent manufacturers Unilever and Proctor and Gamble between them have over 50 apparently competing detergent products on sale in the United Kingdom).

Oligopolists generally understand their relationship to one another and there is often a reluctance to 'rock the boat' by upsetting the established order. One firm is often acknowledged as the price leader and firms wait for their actions before adjusting their prices. In the UK car market, it has often been suggested that other manufacturers wait for Ford to adjust its prices before making their own price decisions. It has been suggested that firms may not match upward price movements, in the hope of gaining extra sales, but they would match downward price changes for fear of losing market share. Price wars between oligopplists can be very expensive to participants, so there is a tendency to find alternative ways to compete for customers, such as free gifts, coupons, added value offers and sponsorship activities.

Oligopolists have often been accused of collusion and creating barriers to entry for newcomers (such as signing exclusive distribution rights with key retailers). It has therefore been suggested that an oligopoly market structure is against the public interest. Against this argument, the public interest may benefit from economies of scale which allows products to be made at a lower unit cost than would be achievable by smaller scale companies. Furthermore, while oligopolists may have a cosy market in their home country, they may face severe competition as an outsider in overseas markets. The benefits of scale in their domestic market can give them the resources and low unit costs with which to tackle an overseas market, thereby helping a country's balance of trade and creating additional employment.

5.5   COMPETITION POLICY

The vision of competitive markets that bring maximum benefit to consumers is often not achieved. The imperfections described above can be summarized as resulting from:

- The presence of large firms that are able to exert undue influence over participants in a market, for example through scale economies
- Collusion between sellers (and sometimes buyers) which has the effect of restricting price competition and the availability of products
- Barriers to market entry and restraints on trade which may prevent a company moving into a market (e.g. a manufacturer may prevent a retailer from selling competing manufacturers' products)
- Rigidity in resource input markets which prevent supply moving to markets of strong demand (e.g. labour inflexibility may prevent a company from exploiting markets that have high levels of profitability)

Because of the presumed superiority of competitive markets, the law of most developed countries has been used to try and remove market imperfections where these are deemed to be against the public interest. This section initially considers the common law of England as a method by which anticompetitive practices have been curbed. More significantly, a growing body of legislation based on statute law is now available to governments and organizations seeking to curb anticompetitive practices.

5.5.1   Common law approaches to improving market competitiveness

Common law evolves over time on the basis of case judgements which set a precedent for subsequent cases to follow (see Chapter 10). There is case law that holds that agreements between parties that have the effect of restraining free trade are unlawful.

Sometimes, it may appear to be sensible for a business person to make a contract with another company by which he or she agrees to limit the parties with whom they can trade in the future. In return for an exclusivity clause, the business person may receive preferential treatment from the other party. Such agreements have often been referred to as 'solus agreements' and have been frequently used, for example in contracts between oil companies and petrol station owners. Such an agreement normally contains a tying covenant by which the station owner agrees, in return for a rebate on the price, to sell only the supplier's brand of petrol, a compulsory trading covenant that obliges the garage owner to keep the garage open at reasonable hours and a continuity covenant that requires him or her, if the business is sold, to obtain the acceptance of the agreement by the purchaser. In one important case, a garage owner had two garages and a solus agreement in respect of each, one for 4½ years and the other for 21 years. The garage owner felt that the actions of the oil company were threatening its profits and sought to obtain its petrol from a cheaper source, in defiance of his agreement. The case came before the House of Lords who held that the essence of the solus agreements was to unreasonably restrict the garage proprietor's freedom of trading.

It is important to note the word 'reasonable'. In deciding whether the agreement between the oil company and petrol station owner was reasonable and therefore valid, the Law Lords stressed the importance of taking into account the public interest and held the 4½ year agreement reasonable but the 21 year agreement too long and therefore unreasonable and invalid. The petrol station owner was therefore free to buy his fuel from another source, regardless of the agreement.

The 'public interest' is important in deciding whether a restrictive agreement is reasonable or not. The courts may feel that by tying a company to a supplier for 21 years, effective competition in a market is reduced, thereby resulting in higher prices for everybody.

While the case of the petrol station dated from the 1960s, more recent examples have been reported of firms seeking to rely on the common law to break free from a restrictive agreement. In the United

Kingdom, tenants of pubs often sign agreements with breweries that prevent them buying much of their beer from third parties, in return for which the brewery may provide a tenancy agreement and other support for the tenant. A number of tenants have approached the courts to have clauses restricting their rights to make third party purchases of beer set aside, on the grounds that they have the effect of unreasonably restricting trade. To independent brewers seeking new outlets for their beer, it is important that such restraints on trade are removed to allow them access to the market.

A claim of restraint of trade can also be made against a company buying a business that restricts the future business activity of the person from whom they have bought the business. An individual who has set up a successful business may often be tempted by a take-over bid from another company. The acquiring company may be keen to grow so that it can achieve economies of scale, or it may simply want access to the target company's customers. Whatever the reason for the take-over, the acquiring company will often seek a clause restricting the seller of the business from going straight back into the market-place and setting up another business which is in competition with the one that it has just sold. During the 1980s, banks and building societies in the United Kingdom were keen to expand into the estate agency business for a number of reasons. Rather than growing organically, most chose to buy existing agencies that had an established local loyalty. The owners of such businesses were usually required to agree to a clause that limited their rights to set up another estate agency business in competition with that of the acquiring company.

Again, any clause has to be 'reasonable'. A clause prohibiting the seller of a business from setting up an estate agency chain within a 25 mile radius of its base for a period of 3 years from the date of sale would almost certainly be considered to be reasonable. A clause prohibiting the seller from entering into any form of business anywhere in the country within 10 years would almost certainly be deemed to be unreasonable.

If a clause in an agreement is deemed by a court to be unreasonable, it may remove it from the contract. It can however, be difficult to know what a court will consider to be 'reasonable' in the circumstances of a particular case.

5.5.2   Statutory intervention to create competitive markets

As the economy has become more complex, common law has proved inadequate on its own to preserve the competitiveness of markets. Common law has therefore been supplemented by statutory legislation, that is laws passed by government as an act of policy. In the United Kingdom, the most significant pieces of legislation that have affected the competitiveness of markets are:

- The Competition Act 1980
- The Resale Prices Act 1964
- Articles 85 and 86 of the Treaty of Rome

One outcome of statutory intervention has been the creation of a regulatory infrastructure, which in the United Kingdom includes the Office of Fair Trading, the Monopolies and Mergers Commission and regulatory bodies to control specific industries.

5.5.3   The Competition Act 1980

This piece of legislation supplements the common law and builds upon the Restrictive Trade Practices Act of 1976. Section 2 of the Competition Act 1980 defines an anticompetitive practice as a course of conduct which restricts, distorts or prevents competition in the production or acquisition of goods or services in the United Kingdom. One-off acts of anticompetitive behaviour and actions by smaller firms with a turnover of less than £5 million escape the provisions of the Act.

The Restrictive Trade Practices Act makes it a criminal offence for companies or individuals to come to an agreement that has the effect of restricting trade. The restriction could refer to agreements on prices, the allocation of sales territories, product design or anything else that has the effect of restricting consumers' choice. The Restrictive Practices Court is responsible for determining whether parties to an agreement are guilty of a restrictive trade practice.

Many covert price-fixing agreements have been alleged by the Director General of Fair Trading and referred to the Restrictive Practices Court where such activities have been declared illegal. As an example, during 1984, the court sought injunctions to stop the ferry operators Sealink and Townsend Thoresen fixing fares on routes between Northern Ireland and Scotland, while two years later an agreement between the four largest betting shop operators to not compete on price was declared illegal.

At a local level, many service providers have understandings—if not outright agreements—that have the effect of limiting price competition. In this way, local estate agents and building contractors have frequently been accused of covert collusion. For example, building contractors may agree a rota by which they take it in turns to bid for local authority contracting work, thereby reducing price competition among themselves. Similarly, there may be an informal agreement between estate agents in a local area that they will charge a standard rate for specified services. Inevitably, obtaining evidence of such informal collusive agreements can be very difficult for the court.

Restrictive trade practices must be registered with the Restrictive Trade Practices Court and may be allowed where it can be shown that, on balance, they are in the public interest. Parties to a restrictive practice must show that one or more of a number of 'gateways' apply to the practice. Gateways may allow for a restrictive practice where, for example, it can be shown that the practice is required to prevent injury to the public (a case argued by pharmaceutical companies for restricting sales of drugs through pharmacies); removal of the restrictive practice would deny benefits to the public; and export business would be harmed by removing the restrictive agreement. Thus an investigation in 1992 into car retailing acknowledged that restrictive manufacturer–dealer franchises had the effect of keeping prices higher than in many other countries, but essentially recommended retaining the present system on account of compensating benefits to the public. These benefits included better after-sales service and greater availability of replacement components.

5.5.4 The Resale Prices Act 1976

This legislation consolidated earlier legislation relating to resale price maintenance, principally the Resale Price Maintenance Act 1964. Manufacturers of goods often like to be able to control the price of their products as they pass through a value chain, but this can have the effect of restricting competition between distributors. A manufacturer of hi-fi equipment that has positioned its equipment as exclusive, high-value products may seek to prevent retailers 'piling it high and selling it cheap'. Given a high elasticity of demand, the retailer may increase its sales and profitability. However, for the manufacturer, the discount strategy may devalue the image of its hi-fis and merely switch sales away from retailers who give good promotional support and service to a retailer who concentrates all efforts on cutting costs.

Although the hi-fi manufacturer would like to be able to force discount retailers to charge the full recommended price, it will find an obstacle in the Resale Prices Act. This prevents a manufacturer insisting on a price at which a retailer or wholesaler must sell its products to customers. The purpose of the legislation is to stimulate price competition between retailers. It is illegal for manufacturers to do anything that has the effect of limiting retailers' ability to charge whatever prices they think fit. For example it would be illegal for the manufacturer to withhold supplies unless there was another non-price-related reason for doing so.

Resale price maintenance is only allowed where it can be shown to be in the public interest. The best example where this has been true is the book industry where, until September 1995, publishers were able to insist that bookshops sell books at the publishers' recommended retail price (through the 'Net Book Agreement'). Even the market-led Conservative government of the late 1980s saw advantages in retaining the Net Book Agreement, which focused on encouraging specialist book shops to stock a wide range of titles. The argument was put forward that if they could not make profits by selling 'best sellers' at full price, they would not be able to cross-subsidize the specialist titles which would be in the public interest to make available.

5.5.5   Articles 85 and 86 of the Treaty of Rome

Domestic legislation is used to control anticompetitive practices where their effects are confined within national boundaries. Where restrictive practices exceed these limits, Articles 85 and 86 of the Treaty of Rome can be applied. Article 85 prohibits agreements between organizations and arrangements between organizations that affect trade between member states of the European Union and in general prohibits anticompetitive practices, such as price fixing, market sharing and limitations on production. However, Article 85(3) provides for exemptions where restrictions on competition may be deemed to be in the public interest.

Article 86 prohibits the abuse of a dominant market position within the European Community insofar as it may affect trade between member states; the fact that a business has a monopoly position is not in itself prohibited.

The European Commission—which oversees implementation of Articles 85 and 86—can prohibit mergers where the combined turnover exceeds ECU 200 million or where the company will have over 25 per cent of a national market and the merger will have an adverse effect on competition. In the United Kingdom, the European Commission has intervened to force British Airways to sell some of its routes which it acquired from British Caledonian, even though the take-over had previously been approved by the domestic regulatory authorities.

Both Articles are increasingly influencing trade within Britain. For example, the opponents of restrictions on Sunday shop opening in England used a circuitous argument to claim that these articles had the effect of restricting trade to the detriment of overseas suppliers.

5.5.6   Control on price representations

One of the assumptions of a perfectly competitive market is that participants in it have complete information about competing goods and services. In reality, buyers may find it very difficult to judge between competing suppliers because prices are disclosed in a deceptive or non-comparable manner. Legislation, such as the Consumer Protection Act 1987, makes it illegal for a company to give misleading statements about the price of goods or services. This not only helps to protect consumers from exploitation, but also helps to preserve the competitiveness of a market. Consumer protection legislation is considered in more detail in Chapter 10.

5.6   REGULATORY AGENCIES

A number of agencies have responsibility for preserving the competitiveness of markets. In the United Kingdom, the most important are:

- The Director General for Fair Trading
- The Monopolies and Mergers Commission
- Public utility regulators

In addition, a number of other organizations are active in either using legislation to protect the competitiveness of markets or by drawing attention to abuses in monopoly power. At a local level, Trading Standards Departments have powers to prosecute companies using misleading prices, among other things. Consumer champions who can draw attention to anticompetitive practices include Citizens Advice Bureaux, Ombudsmen and the media (discussed in more detail in Chapter 10).

5.6.1   The Office of Fair Trading

The Office of Fair Trading (OFT) is headed by the Director General of Fair Trading and has a general duty to keep under review commercial activities in the United Kingdom. On the advice of the OFT, the Secretary of State for Trade may make an order to prohibit harmful consumer trade practices, infringement of which is a criminal offence. Trading Standards Departments of Local Authorities can report persistent offenders to the OFT which may prosecute in serious cases. It may also refer a case to the Monopolies and Mergers Commission.

5.6.2   The Monopolies and Mergers Commission

The Monopolies and Mergers Commission (MMC) has no power to initiate its own investigations. Instead, it responds to referrals which can be made by the following bodies:

- The Secretary of State for Trade
- The Director General of Fair Trading
- Public utility regulators
- The Independent Television Commission

An investigation by the MMC is normally completed within 3 months. The Commission only has power to make recommendations to the referring body. It is up to the latter whether the recommendations should be implemented. In the case of existing monopolistic situations, the Commission can recommend divestment of assets or other action to reduce the undesirable elements of monopoly power. A recent example of a company forced to divest assets involved the Rank Organization. Rank acquired Mecca Leisure during 1990, giving it significant monopoly power in the operation of bingo halls and clubs within the London area. In order to reduce this monopoly position, Rank was forced to sell off some of its London Bingo halls.

To illustrate the work of the Monopolies and Mergers Commission in curbing anticompetitive practices, a few examples of the findings of recent reports are presented here.

- In a 1994 report, the MMC found evidence of a 'complex' monopoly in private health care services which served to strengthen the British Medical Association's role in helping to fix consultants' fee levels. The Association had published a list detailing prices that should be charged by its members for a range of operations, ranging from £310 for the removal of a wisdom tooth to £5825 for a liver transplant. The MMC's report concluded that the BMA's price guidelines resulted in consultants charging more than would be the case had they arrived at their own prices. The Commission recommended that the use of a standard price list should end. The government gave its full backing to the report and the price guidelines were withdrawn.
- In 1990, the Commission found that British Gas had been using its monopoly power among industrial users to charge high prices. Where industrial customers had no realistic alternative to the use of gas, the Commission found that British Gas had been charging relatively high prices for each unit of gas consumed, in contrast to a lower unit price charged to companies who could effectively use electricity as an alternative. The Commission recommended that British Gas should be required to publish and use a standard tariff for all industrial users of gas. The gas industry's

regulator accepted the report and British Gas charged its industrial users according to a published tariff.

- The MMC does not just involve itself with national organizations—it also investigates local abuse of monopoly power. Since the deregulation of the UK bus industry, the MMC has investigated several alleged anticompetitive practices by bus companies. For example, during 1994 in an investigation of bus services in Darlington, the MMC found a scale monopoly that acted in favour of the Stagecoach and Go-Ahead Northern bus companies. It found that Stagecoach recruited most of the drivers of the ailing Darlington Transport Company, registered services on all its routes and then ran free services, causing the sale of the municipal bus company to fall through and the company to collapse. The Director General of Fair Trading sought undertakings from Stagecoach and Go-Ahead Northern that they would maintain fares and service frequencies for three years after a competitor withdrew from a route, if their lower fares or increased frequencies had been responsible for the competitor withdrawing. The MMC eventually recommended a 12 month fares and frequencies freeze, despite protests by both companies that their behaviour had been in the public interest, pointing to their investment in new vehicles and staff training.

Whether an apparent monopoly should in fact be referred to the Monopolies and Mergers Commission often involves an element of political judgement. For example, following the Mirror Group Newspaper's proposed take-over of the *Independent* newspaper, there were many calls for the take-over to be referred to the MMC as Mirror Group Newspapers already-owned a number of other national newspaper titles. The Secretary of State for Trade refused this request, arguing that the *Independent* newspaper was losing money and an MMC referral may put the continuing existence of the title at risk.

5.6.3   Regulation of public utilities

During the 1980s, the privatization of many UK public sector utilities resulted in the creation of new private sector monopoly companies, including those providing gas, water, telephones and electricity. The United Kingdom led the way in privatizing public utilities and many other countries have now followed its example.

To protect the users of these services from exploitation, the government response has been twofold:

1. Firstly, government has sought to increase competition, in the hope that the invisible forces of competition will bring about lower prices and greater consumer choice. In this way, the electricity generating industry was divided into a number of competing private suppliers (National Power, Powergen, Nuclear Electric, Scottish Power and Scottish Hydro), while conditions were made easier for new generators to enter the market. The problem here is that there may be very real barriers to entry in markets where the capital cost of getting started can be very high, as in the case of water supply. In some cases, measures to increase competition have had only a limited effect, as in the very limited competition faced by the newly privatized British Telecom from Mercury Communications—the latter has only had a significant effect on moderating British Telecom prices in the highly competitive market for long distance calls by large business users. For many of the newly privatized monopolies, effective competition proved to be an unrealistic possibility.
2. Where competition alone has not been sufficient to protect the consumer's interest, government has created a series of regulatory bodies which can determine the level and structure of charges made by these utilities. The regulatory bodies can determine the pattern of competition within a sector by influencing relationships between competitors and easing barriers to entry. These are some of the more significant regulatory bodies in the United Kingdom:

Oftel—regulates the telecommunications market
Ofgas—regulates the gas market
Offer—regulates the electricity market
Ofwat—regulates the water supply industry

In general, private sector companies operating in monopoly utility markets require a licence from their regulator to do so. The regulator takes a view as to what constitutes the public interest when reviewing operators' licences to trade. Prices charged, standards of service and speed of service are all factors that the regulator can insist the companies implement if they are to carry on trading. Unresolved issues can be referred from a regulator to the Monopolies and Mergers Commission. This occurred, for example, in 1995 when Oftel and British Telecom were unable to reach an agreement about the portability of customers' telephone numbers, which would have had the effect of increasing the competitiveness of the telephone market.

In utility markets where competition is absent, regulators have to balance what is desirable from the public's point of view with the companies' need to make profits, which will in turn provide new capital for investment in improvements. Over the long term favouring consumers may result in lower investment in a sector leading to supply shortages. Regulators are trying to combine market forces with a degree of centralized planning and there are growing concerns about the difficulties of achieving this.

REGULATING PRICES AT BT

British Telecom prices—an example of monopoly regulation

British Telecom (BT) continues to enjoy strong monopoly power. Eight years after privatization, it still accounted for over 80 per cent of the turnover of the telecommunications sector in the United Kingdom, and was particularly dominant in the non-business sector. BT has often been accused of having a licence to print money through its domination of the market. In arriving at pricing decisions, BT has to balance a number of factors. In the short term, it has a relatively protected market with very little price pressure from competitors. However, this protected market will not last for ever, especially as increasing competition from newly licensed cable and portable telephone networks is likely to put greater pressure on its prices during the next decade. BT has therefore sought to set its prices to make the most of its monopoly while it enjoys it. Against this, most of its prices are regulated by the government watchdog Oftel, which has the power to regulate telephone charges and must respond to public and political pressure. A widespread feeling that BT prices are higher than in many Western countries, plus reports of very large salaries earned

by the senior executives of BT, has caused BT to act cautiously for fear of provoking the regulator to impose unduly harsh price controls on the company. Some price incentives, such as its provision of the free 'Childline' telephone service, are designed to present a better image of a caring BT in an attempt to fend off more extreme demands for price controls. Other initiatives, such as lower charges on trunk routes or off-peak reductions at weekends, are designed to boost revenue against competitive pressure or where demand is price sensitive.

Nevertheless, BT recognizes the power that its regulating body has over its prices, but has generally sought to agree these with Oftel rather than to have them imposed. In June 1992, Oftel accepted a proposal from BT that affected its prices in a number of ways:

1. Increases in a basket of all BT services were to be limited to the increase in the Retail Price Index (RPI) less 7.5 per cent.
2. Rental charge increases for ordinary exchange lines were to be limited to RPI less 2 per cent.
3. For all other individual services within the basket of services, no single item was to be raised by greater than the level of RPI. This

agreement was included in response to previous complaints that average price increases had hidden the fact that this still allowed some individual prices to increase quite significantly, often hitting captive groups of customers.

4. To protect infrequent users of telephone services, a low-user scheme was revised to benefit those private customers who use less than 240 units per quarter.

BT has generally tried to voluntarily agree licence conditions with Oftel, rather than to have them imposed. This has generally worked well, as BT recognizes that a referral to the Monoplies and Mergers Commission would take up a lot of its managers' time which could have been more usefully applied elsewhere. In its discussions with Oftel about the portability of customers' telephone numbers, BT was unable to agree a formula for sharing the cost of switching re-routed calls, so an MMC investigation followed.

The effects of government regulation may be to extend or shorten the period during which a company has a protected market for its new market. The announcement by the British government in 1991 that it was to licence a number of new cellular telephone networks had the effect of bringing forward the time when the existing operators have to face direct competition on price.

QUESTIONS

1. Is it necessary for government to regulate telephone charges?
2. What alternatives are available to protect users against exploitative prices?
3. What new pricing opportunities are made available by deregulation of telecommunications markets?

5.6.4   Control of government monopolies

Although the UK government has gone a long way in privatizing and deregulating markets that were previously the preserve of state organizations, there are still many services that cannot be sensibly privatized or deregulated. It is difficult, for example to privatize roads or to expose them to serious competition. It would be almost impossible to deregulate social services or the police force. It used to be thought that because the government actually provided the service, the public interest was thereby automatically protected. Government and the public were considered one and the same thing. However, with an increasingly consumerist society, it has become clear that what government thinks is good for the public is not necessarily what the public actually wants. Therefore, where it is impractical to privatize publicly provided services, government has taken a number of measures to try and protect consumers from exploitation. These are some of the methods that have been used:

1. *Arms length organizations* It was noted in Chapter 4 that agencies (such as QUANGOs) that are at 'arms length' from government have grown in numbers in recent years. With these types of organizations, managers are given clearly defined targets which are intended to reflect the interests of the users of the service, rather than just the narrower interests of government.
2. *Market testing* Sometimes, local and central government tests the market to see whether part of the work of a department can be subcontracted to an outside organization. Even some specialized services, such as accounting, architectural and legal services, have been put out to market tender. It is sometimes argued that a clear producer–buyer division makes it much easier for the body providing money for a service to exercise control over standards of performance and to create a market at the point of production, even if not at the point of consumption. For example, a local authority producing its own refuse collection services has to balance the needs of consumers with its need for good industrial relations, etc. By contracting out the service, the authority can concentrate single-mindedly on ensuring that the contractor is performing to the agreed standard.

3. *Citizens Charters* These have become popular as a method of providing consumers of public services with standards of service which government organizations are expected to meet. They have been introduced to protect rail passengers, health service patients and parents of school children against poor service provided by a public sector monopoly organization. Cynics have dismissed them as government hype which conceals underlying expenditure cuts and unnecessarily raises consumers' expectations. However, by setting out standards of performance, a charter gives a clear message to the management and employees of a state organization about the standards that users expect of them.

REVIEW QUESTIONS

1. In the context of market structure analysis, what are the options available to firms in a highly competitive market to improve profitability. (12 marks)
   Select one of the options and discuss it, making clear how lasting the profit improvement is likely to be in the long run.   (8 marks)
   (CIM Marketing Environment Examination, December 1994, Q.9)
2. Identify the impact and discuss the likely marketing response to two of the following environmental changes affecting a major oil refining and distributing company:
   - The introduction of a carbon tax
   - A breakthrough in cost-effective solar power stations
   - A well-financed new entrant entering its main market
   - Teleconferencing and telecommunications growing rapidly
   - Cut-price supermarket petrol sales expanding significantly
   (CIM Marketing Environment Examination, December 1994, Q.10)
3. You have been asked by your marketing director to provide a brief report analysing the profitability of your industry.
   (a) Selecting an industry of your choice, identify the key elements of its structure and summarize the forces that determine its long run profitability.   (12 marks)
   (b) Append your recommendations on the strategies a company could adopt in order to maintain or improve profitability.   (8 marks)
   (Based on CIM Marketing Environment Examination, June 1995, Q.4)
4. (a) Show, using diagrams, what would happen to the market price of compact discs if a new technological development suddenly allowed CDs to be produced at a much lower cost than previously.
   (b) What factors might cause the demand curve for CDs to shift upwards?
5. In a medium-sized English town, one bus company recently agreed to buy the operations of another operator, giving the acquiring company over 80 per cent of the local market for scheduled bus services. In view of a possible referral of the take-over by the Office of Fair Trading to the Monopolies and Mergers Commission, assess the advantages and disadvantages to the public of the existence of a local monopoly.
6. Summarize the problems facing the government in its attempts to control the price of public water supply.

REFERENCES

Buzzell, R. D. and Gale, B. M. (1987) *The PIMS Principle*, Free Press, New York.
Doyle, P. (1989) 'Building Successful Brands: The Strategic Options', *Journal of Marketing Management*, vol. 5, no. 1, pp. 77–95.
Laurent, Giles and Kapferer, Jean-Noel (1985) 'Measuring Consumer Involvement Profiles', *Journal of Marketing Research*, vol. 22 (February), pp. 41–53.
McGoldrick, P. J. (1990) *Retail Marketing*, McGraw-Hill, Maidenhead.
Pitcher, A. (1985) 'The Role of Branding in International Advertising', *International Journal of Advertising*, vol. 4, no. 3, pp. 241–6.

FURTHER READING

Davies, S., Lyons, B., Geroski, P. and Dixon, H. (1991) *Economics of Industrial Organizations*, Longman, Harlow.

Dick, Alan S. and Basu, K. (1994) 'Customer Loyalty: Toward an Integrated Conceptual Framework', *Journal of the Academy of Marketing Science*, vol. 22, no. 2, pp. 99–113.

Ernst J. (1994) *Whose Utility? The Social Impact of Public Utility Privatization and Regulation in Britain*, Open University Press, Buckingham.

King, S. (1991) 'Brand Building in the 1990s', *Journal of Marketing Management*, vol. 7, no. 1, pp. 3–13.

Korah, V. (1994) *An Introductory Guide to EC Competition Law and Practice*, 5th edn, Sweet and Maxwell, London.

Lipsey, R. G. and Chrystal K. A. (1995) *An Introduction to Positive Economics*, 8th edn, Oxford University Press, Oxford.

Stanlake, G. F. and Grant, S. J. (1995) *Introductory Economics*, 6th edn, Longman, Harlow.

THE NATIONAL ECONOMIC ENVIRONMENT

OBJECTIVES

After reading this chapter, you should understand:

- The concept of economic structure
- The interrelatedness of producers, consumers and government in the circular flow of income
- Commonly used measures of economic activity
- The role of government in influencing the macroeconomic environment
- The marketing implications of government economic policy

6.1 MACROECONOMICS AND MARKETING

In the previous chapter, microeconomic analysis of a firm's competitive environment made a number of assumptions about the broader economic environment in which the firm operates. Thus, in the analysis of supply and demand in any given market, changes in household incomes or government taxation were treated as an uncontrollable external factor to which a market responded. For most businesses, a sound understanding of this broader economic environment is just as important as understanding short-term and narrow relationships between the price of a firm's products and demand for them.

An analysis of companies' financial results will often indicate that business people attribute their current success or failure to the state of the economy. For example, a retail store that has just reported record profit levels may put this down to a very high level of spending by consumers, while a factory that has just laid off workers may blame a continuing economic recession for its low level of activity.

Few business people can afford to ignore the state of the economy because it affects the willingness and ability of customers to buy their products. It can also affect the price and availability of its inputs. The shop that reported record profits may have read economic indicators correctly and prepared for an upturn in consumer spending by buying in more stocks or taking on more sales assistants.

Many people are quite bewildered by the workings of the economy, but it is very important that a marketing manager has a sound grasp of how the national economy works. This chapter is concerned with what has often been described as 'macroenvironmental' analysis. Although the workings of the economy at a national level are the focus of this chapter, it must be remembered that even national economies form part of a larger international economic environment. Issues of international economic analysis will be returned to in Chapter 12.

This chapter begins by analysing the structure of the national economy and the interdependence of the elements within this structure. The national economy is a complex system whose functioning is influenced by a range of planned and unplanned forces. While unplanned forces (such as turbulence in the world economic system) can have significant impacts on the national economic system, marketing managers are particularly keen to understand the planned interventions of governments, who seek to influence the economy for a variety of social and political reasons.

6.2 THE STRUCTURE OF THE ECONOMY

Most analyses of national economies divide the productive sectors into three categories:

1. The primary sector which is concerned with the extraction and production of basic raw materials from agriculture, mining and oil exploration, etc.
2. The secondary sector which transforms the output of the primary sector into products that consumers can use (e.g. manufacturing, construction, raw material processing, etc.)
3. The tertiary sector which comprises services

Comparisons can be drawn between the three sectors described above and value chains described in Chapter 2. In general, these three sectors add progressively higher levels of value to a product.

A further division in the economy occurs between the productive sector and the consumption sector. Intervening as both a producer and a consumer, government provides a third element of an economy. The relationship between producers and consumers is the basis for models of the circular flow of income, discussed later in this chapter.

6.2.1 Measures of economic structure

The relative importance of the three productive sectors described above has been changing. Evidence of this change is usually recorded by reference to three key statistics:

1. The share of gross domestic product (GDP) which each sector accounts for
2. The proportion of the labour force employed in the sector
3. The contribution of the sector to a nation's balance of payments

A key trend in Britain, like most developed economies, has been the gradual decline in importance of the primary and manufacturing sectors, and the growth in the tertiary, or services, sector. The extent of the change in the UK economy, when measured by shifts in GDP and employment, is indicated in Table 6.1.

Table 6.1 Composition of the UK productive sector

		1969	1979	1989	1993
Primary	Share of GDP (%)	4.3	6.7	4.2	4.1
	Workforce (%)	3.6	3.0	2.1	1.8
Secondary	Share of GDP (%)	42.0	36.7	34.5	29.5
	Workforce (%)	46.8	38.5	28.9	25.4
Tertiary	Share of GDP (%)	53.0	56.5	61.3	66.4
	Workforce (%)	49.3	58.5	69.0	72.8

Source: compiled from 'Economic Trends', *Employment Gazette.*

While the statistics in Table 6.1 appear to show a number of clear trends, the figures need to be treated with a little caution for a number of reasons:

1. Fluctuations in the value of GDP for the primary sector often have little to do with changes in activity levels, but instead reflect changes in world commodity levels. Oil represents a major part of the UK's primary sector output, but the value of oil produced has fluctuated from the very high levels of the early 1980s to the very low levels of the 1990s, largely reflecting changes in oil prices.
2. The level of accuracy with which statistics have been recorded has been questioned, especially for the services sector. The system of Standard Industrial Classifications (SICs) for a long while did not disaggregate the service sector in the same level of detail as the other two sectors.
3. Part of the apparent growth in the services sector may reflect the method by which statistics are collected, rather than indicating an increase in overall service level activity. Output and employment is recorded according to the dominant business of an organization. Within many primary and secondary sector organizations, many people are employed producing service-type activities, such as cleaning, catering, transport and distribution. Where a cook is employed by a manufacturing company, output and employment is attributed to the manufacturing sector. However, a common occurrence during the 1980s has been for manufacturing industry to contract out many of these service activities to external contractors. Where such contracts are performed by contract catering, office cleaning or transport companies, the output becomes attributable to the service sector, making the service sector look larger, even though no additional services have been produced—they have merely been switched from internally produced to externally produced.

Nevertheless, the figures clearly indicate a number of significant trends in the economy:

1. The primary sector in the United Kingdom, like most developed economies, has been contracting in relative importance. There are supply and demand side explanations of this trend. On the supply side, many basic agricultural and extractive processes have been mechanized, resulting in them using less employees and thereby consuming a lower proportion of GDP. Many primary industries have declined as suppliers have been unable to compete with low-cost producers in countries that are able to exploit poor employment working conditions. On the demand side, rising levels of affluence have led consumers to demand increasingly refined products. In this way, consumers have moved from buying raw potatoes (essentially a product of the primary sector) to buying processed potatoes (e.g. prepared ready meals) which involve greater inputs from the secondary sector. With further affluence, potatoes have been sold with added involvement of the service sector (e.g. eating cooked potatoes in a restaurant).
2. Output of the secondary sector in the United Kingdom fell from 42 per cent of GDP in 1969 to 29 per cent in 1993, reflecting the poor performance of manufacturing industry. This can again be partly explained by efficiency gains by the sector, requiring fewer resources to be used, but more worryingly by competition from overseas. The emergence of newly industrialized nations with a good manufacturing infrastructure and low employment costs, rigidities in the UK labour market, declining research and development budgets relative to overseas competitors and the effects of exchange rate policy have all contributed to this decline.
3. In respect of its share of GDP, the services sector saw almost continuous growth during the period 1969–94. With the exception of transport and distribution where output fell between 1979 and 1981, and public administration, where the same occurred between 1981 and 1986, most subsectors experienced increases in output over the period, with banking, finance, insurance, business services, leasing and communications being particularly prominent. In 1993, the tertiary sector accounted for 66 per cent of GDP, up from 53 per cent in 1969.

6.2.2   Towards a service economy?

The United Kingdom, like many developed economies, has traditionally run a balance of trade deficit in manufactured goods (i.e. imports exceed exports) but has made up for this with a surplus in 'invisible' service 'exports'. In 1993, while the UK's visible balance was in deficit by £13 209 million, there was an invisible surplus of £2898 million.

During the recession of the early 1980s, the service sector was seen by many as the salvation of the economy. Many politicians were keen to promote the service sector as a source of new employment to make up for the diminishing level of employment within the primary and secondary sectors. A common argument during this period was that the United Kingdom no longer held a competitive cost advantage in the production of goods and therefore these sectors of the economy should be allowed to decline and greater attention paid to those services that showed greater competitive advantage. The logic of this argument can be pushed too far, in particular:

- A large part of the growth in the service sector during the 1980s reflected the buoyancy of the primary and secondary sectors during that period. As manufacturing industry increases its level of activity, the demand for many business-to-business services such as accountancy, legal services and business travel increases. The sudden decline of many financial services sectors after 1989 reflected the downturn in manufacturing activity, resulting in lower demand for business loans and export credits, etc.
- The assumption that the United Kingdom has a competitive cost advantage in the production of services needs to be examined closely. In the same way that many sectors of UK manufacturing industry lost their competitive advantage to developing nations during the 1960s and 1970s, there is evidence that the once unquestioned supremacy in certain service sectors is being challenged. Financial services markets which achieved prominence in London when the United Kingdom was the world's most important trading nation are increasingly following world trade to its new centres such as Tokyo and Frankfurt. High levels of training in some of Britain's competitor nations have allowed those countries to firstly develop their own indigenous services and then to develop them for export. Banking services which were once a net import of Japan are now exported throughout the world.
- Over-reliance on the service sector could pose strategic problems for the United Kingdom. A diverse economic base allows a national economy to be more resilient to changes in world trading conditions.

PHILIPPINES GETS A SHARE OF EMERGING WORLD TRADE IN DATA

Improvements in technology, changes in users' needs and the emerging information age illustrate how whole new categories of service industries can appear very quickly with subsequent major effects on national economies.

Data processing was just such a service industry which emerged almost from nowhere during the 1980s as organizations of all kinds found increasing need to enter data into computerized databases—records of customer sales, services performed, details of rolling stock movements, to name but a few. Many organizations were just beginning to appreciate the huge amount of data they were letting slip by, instead of analysing it to build up customer databases or analyse performance levels, etc. In the early days, most firms regarded this as a back-room function that they could perform most cost effectively by using their own staff on their own premises. With time, an increasing volume of data to be processed and the growing sophistication of data analysis systems, many service companies emerged to take the burden of data processing from client companies.

At first, most data processing companies operated close to their clients—closeness was demanded by the limitations of data communication channels. However, by the late 1980s, the rapid pace of development in the telecommunications industry—especially the development of satellites and fibre optic links—allowed large volumes of data to be transmitted over long distances much more cheaply and reliably than ever before. This opened the door to an international trade in data processing and operators around the world soon stepped in to exploit their comparative cost advantages. In particular, the development of telecommunications allowed companies to operate in overseas countries where labour costs were low, working regulations relaxed and trades unions virtually non-existent.

Data processing has established itself as a significant new sector of economies in the Caribbean, the Philippines and the Irish Republic. Each of these countries is characterized by relatively low wage rates with skills that are at least as good as those of workers in more developed countries.

The development of the Kansas, USA-based Saztec Company illustrates the way in which new service sectors emerge and can create new service sectors in developing economies. Saztec has won contracts to process the data of many major organizations throughout the world, including a number of Federal government agencies in the United States and the Home Office in the United Kingdom. Yet these services are generally produced far away from either the company's or the client's base. The company employs over 800 people in the Philippines, who earn an average of $50 per month—one-fifth of the salary paid to its staff at Kansas. Staff turnover, at less than 1 per cent is much lower than the 35 per cent annual rate at Kansas. Furthermore, the company is able to obtain a higher quality of output by the military style organization and control of its staff—something that would not be accepted in the United States.

The Philippines has become an important exporter of data processing services by exploiting its comparative cost advantage in labour inputs, something that is useful in capturing high-volume, basic data input where accuracy and cost are paramount. Another country that has developed this service sector in a big way is Jamaica, which in addition to exploiting its low labour costs offers the advantages of a sophisticated infrastructure—such as satellite links—and generous tax incentives. Ireland, by contrast, has exploited the fact that it has a relatively highly educated and English-speaking work-force who earn about half what their counterparts would earn in the United States or the United Kingdom. A number of firms, such as Wright Investor Services, have been set up in Ireland to do more sophisticated financial analysis on behalf of the big London-based banks and insurance companies.

QUESTIONS

1. Why has data processing emerged as a major new service sector within the Philippines economy?
2. What other service sectors have emerged during the past two decades? What factors explain their emergence?
3. What are the advantages to the Philippines economy of developing its data processing industry? Are there any disadvantages?

6.2.3   International comparisons

The Organization for Economic Co-operation and Development (OECD) reported in the 1980s that the services sector had accounted for most of the world-wide growth in employment since the oil crisis of 1973. However, there are still significant structural differences between economies in terms of the relative importance of primary, secondary and services sectors. There appears to be a high level of correlation between the level of economic development in an economy (as expressed by its GDP per capita) and the strength of its services sector. It is debatable whether a strong services sector leads to economic growth or is a result of that economic growth. The debate can be partly resolved by dividing services into those that are used up in final consumption and those that provide inputs to further business processes (see below).

The International Labour Office's *Year Book of Labour Statistics* (ILO, 1991) illustrates the magnitude of these differences in 1990 (or the most recent year for which figures were available at that date). The more highly developed economies were associated with high percentages of workers employed in the services sector, for example the United States (75.6 per cent), Canada (75.2 per cent), Australia (74.2 per cent), the United Kingdom (70.6 per cent) and Switzerland (69.0 per cent). Western countries that are considered to be less developed have proportionately fewer employed in their services sector, for example Spain (59.7 per cent), Portugal (53.2 per cent), Ireland (53.0 per cent) and Greece (49.9 per cent). The lowest levels of services employment are found in the less-developed countries, for example Mexico (29.9 per cent), Bangladesh (28.3 per cent) and Ethiopia (9.7 per cent).

6.2.4 Consumer, producer and government sectors

Consumer goods and services are provided for individuals who use up those goods and services for their own enjoyment or benefit. No further economic benefit results from the consumption of the product. In this way, the services of a hairdresser can be defined as consumer services. On the other hand, producer goods and services are those that are provided to other businesses in order that those businesses can produce something else of economic benefit. In this way, a road haulage company sells services to its industrial customers in order that they can add value to the goods that they produce, by allowing their goods to be made available at the point of demand.

The essential difference between production and final consumption sectors is that the former creates wealth while the latter consumes it. Traditionally, economic analysis has labelled these as 'firms' and 'households' respectively. The discussion later in this chapter will indicate problems that may arise where an apparently prosperous household sector is not backed by an equally active production sector.

There has been continuing argument about the role of government in the national economy which has led to shifts in the proportion of GDP accounted for by the public sector. During the 1980s, the UK government regarded the public sector almost as a burden on the country and set about dismantling a lot of the state's involvement in the economy. Privatization and the encouragement of private pensions were just two manifestations of this. By the mid 1990s, the proportion of UK government expenditure as a proportion of total GDP appeared to have stabilized at about 41 per cent, with increasing social security spending offsetting much of the reduction in expenditure accounted for by state-owned industries.

Governments do not always take such a 'hands-off' approach. The economies of Eastern Europe have in the past been dominated by central planning in which the government determined the lion's share of income and expenditure in the economy. Even in Britain shortly after the war, the government assumed a very major role in the economy, with the nationalization of many essential industries.

Marketers need to keep their eyes on political developments which shift the balance of resources between public and private sectors. A company that is involved in the marketing of health service products, for example, will be very interested in the government's view about the respective roles to be played by the private sector and the National Health Service.

6.3 THE CIRCULAR FLOW OF INCOME

Households, firms and government are highly interdependent and the level of wealth created in an economy is influenced by the interaction between these elements. To understand the workings of a national economy, it is useful to begin by developing a simple model of a closed economy comprising just two sectors—firms and households—which circulate money between each other.

The simplest model of a circular flow of income involves a number of assumptions:

- Households earn all their income from supplying their labour to firms.
- Firms earn all their income from supplying goods and services to households.
- There is no external trade.
- All income earned is spent (i.e. households and firms do not retain savings).

In this simple model, the income of households is exactly equal to the expenditure of firms and vice versa. It follows that any change in income from employment is directly related to changes in expenditure by consumers. Similarly, any change in sales of goods and services by firms is dependent upon employment. In this simplified economy, income, output, spending and employment are all inter-related (Figure 6.1). Of course, this simplified model of the economy is almost impossible to achieve in practice, because most economies are affected by factors that upset this stable equilibrium pattern of income and expenditure.

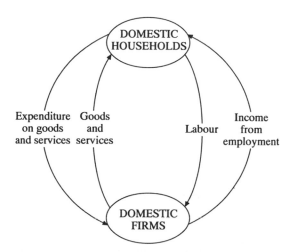

Figure 6.1   The circular flow of income based on a simplified model of a national economy

Instability in this static model can come about for two principal reasons: additional money can be *injected* into the circular flow, while money currently circulating can be *withdrawn*. Injections have the effect of increasing the volume and speed of circulation of money within this flow, while withdrawals have the opposite effects.

Withdrawals can take a number of forms:

- Savings by households which occur when income is received by them but not returned to firms.
- Government taxation, which removes income received by households and prevents them from returning it to firms in the form of expenditure on goods and services. Taxation of businesses diverts part of their expenditure from being returned to households.
- Spending on imported goods and services by households means that this money is not received by firms, who cannot subsequently return it to households in the form of wages.

The opposite of withdrawals are injections and these go some way to counter-balancing the effects described above in the following ways:

- Firms may earn income by selling goods to overseas buyers. This represents an additional source of income which is passed on to households.
- Purchases by firms of capital equipment which represents investment as opposed to current expenditure.
- Instead of reducing the flow of income in an economy through taxation, governments can add to it by spending on goods and services.

A revised model of the circular flow of income, incorporating these modifications, is shown in Figure 6.2.

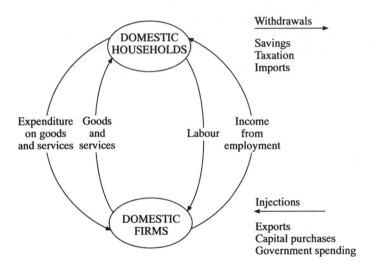

Figure 6.2   A modified circular flow of income incorporating injections and withdrawals

This modified model of the economy still involves a number of fairly unrealistic assumptions (e.g. that consumers do not borrow money). In addition, it is unrealistic to assume that households only earn income from employment activity. They also receive it from returns on investments, property rentals and self-employment. However, it serves to stress the interdependence of the different sectors of the economy and the fact that, through this interdependence, changes in behaviour by one group can result in significant changes in economic performance as a whole. Of particular interest to government policy makers and marketers alike is the effect on total economic activity of changing just one element in the circular flow. This is commonly referred to as the multiplier effect (described below).

6.3.1   The Phillips machine model of the economy

In an attempt to demonstrate the workings of the economy, the Phillips machine model draws on the principles of fluid dynamics. The basic principle of the model is that water circulates around the machine's tubes in an analogous way to money circulating around the economy (Figure 6.3).

One starting point for the machine is to consider the holding tank which contains the total amount of money available for transactions. The fuller the tank, the greater the amount of money that flows into the neighbouring chamber as incomes. These are then pumped to the top of the machine from where they cascade down through the machine's central chambers. Some of this is taken out of the flow as government taxation, while additional money re-enters the flow as government expenditure. Further amounts are drawn off as some households choose to save some of their incomes. These savings flow into a tank holding households' surplus balances, some of which are used to finance spending on investment, which re-enters the main flow later. The higher the level of surplus balances available for investment, the lower the interest rate and the greater the amount of new investment. Interest rates can be held constant by drawing some of the surplus funds into a spare tank at the back of the machine. The main flow now comprises consumers' spending, some of which goes on imports, thereby building up foreigners' holdings of sterling in another tank, thereby lowering the value of sterling. The fuller the tank, and therefore the lower the exchange rate, the greater the flow out of the pipe at the bottom which comprises exports. The exchange rate can be held constant by diverting foreign-held sterling into another tank at the back.

The main flow now represents total national expenditure, which equals total national income. It falls back into the bottom tank from which it started, thereby topping up balances available for transactions. The flow throughout the system can be modified by inserting partial blockages at strategic points. The resulting flows move pens which record the impact on key variables such as domestic expenditure and exports.

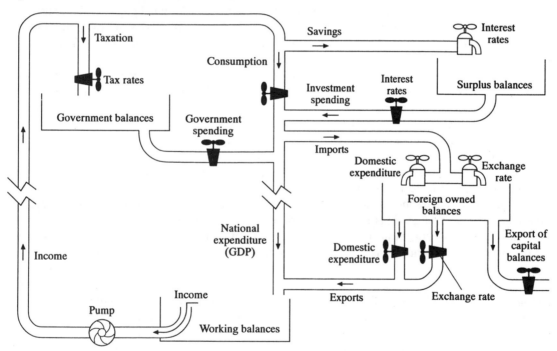

Figure 6.3 The Phillips machine model of the economy

6.3.2 The multiplier effect

The multiplier effect can be compared to the effects of throwing a stone into a pond of water. The impact of the stone with the water will cause an initial wave to be formed, but beyond this will be waves of ever-decreasing strength. The strength of these ripples will lessen with increasing distance from the site of original impact and with the passage of time. Similarly, injecting money into the circular flow of income will have an initial impact on households and businesses directly affected by the injection, but will also be indirectly felt by households and firms throughout the economy.

The multiplier effect can be illustrated by considering the effects of a major capital investment by private sector firms or by government. The firm making the initial investment spends money buying in supplies from outside (including labour) and these outside suppliers in turn purchase more inputs. The multiplier effect of this initial expenditure can result in the total increase in household incomes being much greater than the original expenditure. A good example of the multiplier effect at work in the United Kingdom is provided by the National Garden Festivals held during the 1980s at Liverpool, Stoke-on-Trent, Glasgow and Gateshead. While these government-inspired events initially created direct employment within the events themselves, demand rippled out to other business sectors, such as hotels and transport. The level of activity generated additional demand for local manufacturing industry, for example visitors require food that may be produced locally, the producers of which may in turn require additional building materials and services to increase production facilities.

The extent of the multiplier effects of initial expenditure is influenced by a number of factors. Crucial is the extent to which recipients of this initial investment recirculate it back into the national economy. If large parts of it are saved by households or used to buy imported goods (whether by firms or by households), the multiplier effects to an economy will be reduced. In general, income that is received by individuals who have a high propensity to spend each additional pound on basic necessities is likely to generate greater multiplier benefits than the same money received by higher income households who have a greater propensity to save it or to spend it on imported luxuries. The implications of this for government macroeconomic policy will be considered later.

The multiplier effect can be used to analyse the effects of withdrawals from the circular flow as well as injections. Therefore, if firms spend less on wages, household income will fall as a direct result, leading indirectly to lower spending by households with other domestic firms. These firms will in turn pay less to households in wages, leading to a further reduction in spending with firms, and so on.

Multiplier effects can be studied at a local as well as a national level. Government capital expenditure is often made with a view to stimulating areas of severe unemployment (e.g. the National Garden Festivals were aimed at stimulating areas where the closure of traditional industries had created significant local unemployment). However, whether the local economy is helped will depend upon how much subsequent expenditure is retained within the area. In one study of the regional multiplier effects of large firms setting up provincial administrative service centres, it was found that firms frequently bought in many of their supplies, often including their staff from outside the region, or even the country, thus lessening the local benefits of this form of services development (Marshall, 1985).

As well as examining the general macroeconomic effects of spending by firms on household income and vice versa, multiplier analysis can also be used to assess the impact of economic activity in one business sector upon other business sectors. Many economies suffer because vital economic infrastructure remains undeveloped, preventing productivity gains in other sectors. The availability of transport and distribution services have often had the effect of stimulating economic development at local and national levels, for example following the improvement of rail or road services. The absence of these basic services can have a crippling effect on the development of the primary and manufacturing sectors —one reason for Russian agriculture not having been fully exploited has been the ineffective distribution system available to food producers.

One approach to understanding the contribution of one business sector to other sectors of the economy is to analyse input–output tables of production and data on labour and capital inputs. In one study (Wood, 1987) these were used to estimate the effects that productivity improvements in all of the direct and indirect supply sectors had on the productivity levels of all other sectors. Thus, some apparently high productivity sectors (such as chemicals) were shown to be held back by the low productivity of some of their inputs. On the other hand, efficiency improvements in some services such as transport and distribution were shown to have had widespread beneficial effects on the productivity contribution of other sectors.

LOTTERY FEVER LINKED TO CHANGES IN NATIONAL ECONOMY

For many years, UK government policy had been cautious towards gambling, viewing it as a bad influence in society which needed to be controlled by legislation. By the early 1990s, popular mood had been changing, helped not least by the sight of major national lotteries in other countries of Europe and the United States. A 1992 White Paper on lotteries led to the licensing of the UK's first National Lottery by the government's newly created Office of National Lottery (Oflot). Within a year of its launch in 1994, observers were suggesting that the lottery was having a significant effect on the national economy as a whole.

For the licensed lottery operator Camelot (owned by a consortium of Cadbury Schweppes, De La Rue, GTech and ICL), forecasting demand for lottery tickets was very difficult. The only evidence that could be drawn on was large national lotteries overseas (where differing cultural attitudes may have limited extrapolation to the United Kingdom) and smaller local lotteries in the United Kingdom which had much smaller prizes than those anticipated by Camelot (and therefore didn't create any major publicity impact). Although the UK gaming market (covering activities from football pools to casinos) was then currently worth an estimated £15 billion a year, the question remained how much National Lottery income would be derived from customers switching from other forms of gambling and how much would be switched from completely different forms of consumer expenditure.

In the event, weekly sales of lottery tickets shortly after launch were about £60 million per week, slightly ahead of forecast. This increased significantly with the launch of 'Instant' scratch cards, which were expected to achieve annual sales of around £1 billion a year. Within six months of launch, research had shown that 25 million people (out of an eligible total of 44 million) played the National Lottery every week. The Saturday afternoon queues at Lottery retailers seemed to have become a ritual for many, hoping that their 1 in 14 million chance of winning the Jackpot in the Saturday evening draw would come good.

Before long, critics of the National Lottery were pointing to its harmful economic side-effects, in addition to religious groups who had traditionally seen gambling as immoral. The most vociferous critics were companies involved in other gambling activities, with attendance at bingo halls and participation in football pools significantly down. The National Lottery was directly blamed for the Littlewoods Pools company's decision to lay off about 10 per cent of its work-force shortly after its launch. Beyond this, many more companies from consumer goods and services sectors blamed the National Lottery for diverting consumer expenditure away from their products. Research had shown that previous non-gamblers had been drawn to the National lottery and the average weekly stake money of about £2.50 was causing diversion of expenditure from other consumer goods and services. It effectively represented a withdrawal from the circular flow of income and was blamed for prolonging the economic recession at a time when consumer confidence and expenditure remained low. Worse still, research showed quite clearly that the most important purchasers of lottery tickets were people from relatively low income groups. This group's purchases of lottery tickets was particularly harmful as people with low incomes have a higher propensity to spend their money rather than to save it. Whereas a high income person may buy lottery tickets using money that would otherwise have been saved, lower income groups are more likely to divert expenditure from other products. Total national income could be further reduced by a multiplier effect.

Although the initial effect of the Lottery was to take money out of the circular flow of income, over the longer term, the distribution of its income could help to stimulate the economy. Income from the National Lottery is distributed in a number of ways. For each £1 lottery ticket, 50p is returned to the public in the form of prizes. The large size of the top prizes (up to £17.8 million for the top prize one week in early 1995) has given individuals income beyond a level that they could realistically immediately return to the domestic circular flow of income. Faced with such large prize winnings, much has been saved, or in many cases, invested in overseas assets.

For the remainder of the £1 lottery stake, 12p is taken by the Treasury, representing a further withdrawal. The lottery operator and retailers each take 5p, leaving 28p to be given to good causes (sports, arts, charities, the national heritage and the Millennium Fund). The distribution of money to good causes may go some way to generating more positive multiplier effects. In addition to numerous grants to local organizations (e.g. grants to sports clubs to renew their facilities), a number of larger grants have been given by the five grant-giving bodies. One of the earliest large grants was one for £7 million from the Millennium Fund for the restoration of the waterfront at Portsmouth. The Millennium Commission (which administers grants by the Millennium Fund) insisted, like the other grant-giving bodies, that all payments should go towards new capital projects, rather than being used to fund current expenditure.

What was initially seen by many as little more than a game has had significant redistributive effects on the national economy. Millions of people have diverted expenditure from routine goods and services. A few new millionaires have been created and grants paid for out of prize money will create multiplier benefits in the areas where they are used.

QUESTIONS

1. Does the National Lottery benefit the national economy overall?
2. What would be the effect on the national economy of replacing a small number of very large weekly prizes with a large number of relatively small ones?
3. What would you expect to be the overall effect of the National Lottery on charity organizations?

6.3.3   The accelerator effect

Changes in the demand for consumer goods can lead, through an accelerator effect, to a more pronounced change in the demand for capital goods. This phenomenon is known as the accelerator effect. A small increase in consumer demand can lead to a sudden large increase in demand for plant and machinery with which to satisfy that demand. When consumer demand falls by a small amount, demand for plant and machinery falls by a correspondingly larger amount.

The accelerator effect is best illustrated by reference to an example (Figure 6.4) based on consumers' demand for air travel and airlines' demands for new aircraft. In this simplified example, an airline operates a fleet of 100 aircraft and during periods of stable passenger demand buys 10 new aircraft and retires 10 older aircraft, retaining a stable fleet size of 100 aircraft. Then, some extraneous factor may cause the airline's passenger demand to fall by 3 per cent p.a. The airline responds to this by reducing its capacity by 3 per cent to 97 aircraft (assuming that it can reschedule its aircraft so that it is able to accommodate all of its remaining passengers). The easiest way to achieve this is by reducing its annual order for aircraft from 10 to 7. If it continued to retire its 10 oldest aircraft, this would have the effect of reducing its fleet size to 97, in line with the new level of customer demand. What is of importance here is that while consumer demand has gone down by just 3 per cent, the demand facing the aircraft manufacturer has gone down by 30 per cent (from 10 aircraft a year to 7). If passenger demand settles down at its new level, the airline will have no need to cut its fleet any further, so will revert to buying 10 aircraft a year and selling 10 old ones. If passenger demand picks up once more, the airline may seek to increase its capacity by ordering not 10 aircraft, but, say, 13.

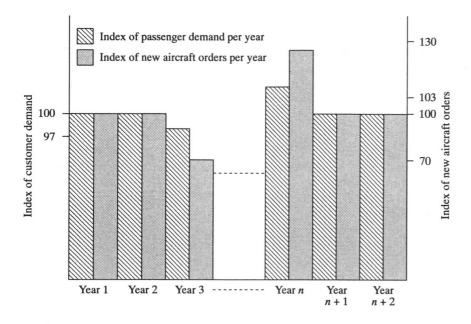

Figure 6.4   The accelerator effect on new aircraft orders of changes in passenger demand

6.3.4   Inflation

It should be apparent that multiplier effects could easily result in injections to the circular flow of income, causing more money to chase a fixed volume of goods and services available for consumption. This leads to the classic case of *demand pull* inflation, when excessive demand for goods and services relative to their supply results in an increase in their market price level. Demand pull inflation can result from an increase in the availability of credit, excessive spending by government and tax cuts that increase consumers' disposable incomes, so allowing them to buy more goods and services.

An alternative cause of inflation is referred to as *cost push* inflation. On the supply side, increases in production costs (such as higher wage costs, rising raw material costs, higher overheads, additional costs of health and safety legislation) may push up the price at which companies are prepared to supply their goods to the market, unless they are offset by increases in productivity.

An inflationary spiral can be created where higher wages in an economy result in greater spending power, leading to demand pull inflation. The resulting higher cost of consumer goods leads workers to seek wage increases to keep them ahead of inflation, but these increases in wage costs add a further twist to cost-plus inflation, and so on. Because markets are seldom perfectly competitive and therefore unable to correct for inflation, governments are keen to intervene to prevent inflationary processes building up in an economy (see below).

6.3.5   Complex models of the economy

The simple model of the economy presented above is based on many assumptions which need to be better understood if model making is to make a useful contribution to policy making. It is important for governments to have a reasonably accurate model of how the economy works so that predictions can be made about the effects of government policy. A model should be able to answer such questions as:

● What will happen to unemployment if government capital expenditure is increased by 10 per cent?
● What will happen to inflation if income tax is cut by 2p in the pound?
● What will be the net effect on government revenue if it grants tax concessions to firms investing in new capital equipment?

Marketers in the private sector also take a keen interest in models of the economy, typically seeking to answer questions such as:

● What effect will a cut in income tax have on demand for new car purchases by private consumers?
● How will company buyers of office equipment respond to reductions in taxation on company profits?
● Will the annual budget create a feeling of confidence by consumers which is sufficiently strong for them to make major household purchases?

Developing a model of the economy is very different from developing a model in the natural sciences. In the latter case, it is often possible to develop closed models where all factors that can affect a system of interrelated elements are identifiable and can be measured. Predicting behaviour for any component of the model is therefore possible, based on knowledge about all other components. In the case of economic models, the system of interrelated components is open rather than closed. This means that not only is it difficult to measure components, it can be difficult to identify what elements to include as being of significance to a national economy. For example, few models accurately predicted that a sudden rise in oil prices by OPEC producers would have a major effect on national economies throughout the world. Furthermore, it is very difficult to develop relationships between variables that remain constant through time. Whereas the relationship between molecules in a chemistry model may be universally true, given a set of environmental conditions, such universal truths are seldom found in economic modelling. This has a lot to do with the importance of *attitudes* of firms and consumers which change through time for reasons that may not become clear until after the event. For example, a 2 per cent cut in income tax may have achieved significant increases in consumer expenditure on one occasion, but resulted in higher levels of savings or debt repayment on another occasion. The first time round, factors as ephemeral as good weather and a national success in an international football championship could have created a 'feel good' factor which was absent the following time round.

6.4   THE BUSINESS CYCLE

From the discussion in the previous sections, it should become quite apparent that national economies are seldom in a stable state. The situation where injections exactly equal withdrawals can be described as a special case with the normal state of affairs being for one of these to exceed the other. An excess of injections will result in economic activity increasing, while the opposite will happen if withdrawals exceed injections. This leads to the concept of the business cycle which describes the fluctuating level of activity in an economy. Most developed economies go through cycles that have been described as:

● Recession–prosperity
● Expansion–contraction
● Stop–go and
● 'Boom and bust'

Figure 6.5 shows the pattern of the business cycle for the United Kingdom, as measured by fluctuations in the most commonly used indicator of economic activity—the gross domestic product (described below).

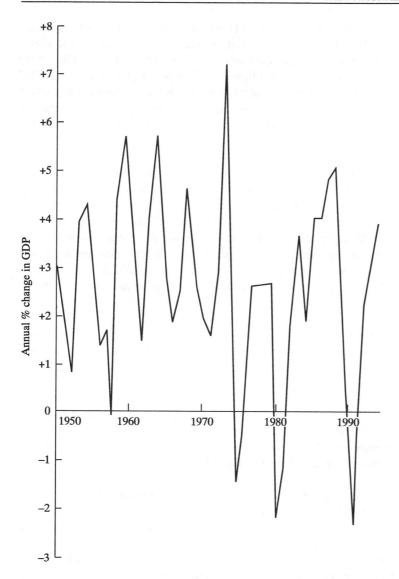

Figure 6.5   Annual rate of change of UK Gross Domestic Product
(*Source*: based on *Annual Abstracts of Statistics*)

6.4.1   Measuring economic activity

GDP is just one indicator of the business cycle. In fact, there are many indicators of economic activity which may move at slightly different times to each other. Some 'leading' indicators may be used as early warning signs of an approaching economic recession, with other indicators—if not corrected by government intervention—following a similar trend in due course. Some of the more commonly used indicators of the business cycle are described below.

Gross domestic product (GDP)   This index measures the total value of goods and services produced within the economy and can be used to compare economic performance over time and to compare performance between countries. In a typical year, the economies of Western Europe countries may expand by 2–3 per cent p.a., although this was higher in the boom years of the early 1980s and many countries temporarily suffered a fall in GDP with the onset of the recession at the end of the 1980s. Developing countries of the Far East have in the recent past often sustained growth rates of GDP in the order of 5–8 per cent p.a. One derivative of this index is a figure for GDP per capita. Therefore, if GDP is going up by 2 per cent a year and the population is constant, it means that, on average, everybody is 2 per cent better off. Whether this is true in reality, of course, depends not only on how the additional income is distributed but also on an individual's definition of being better off (GDP takes no account of 'quality of life').

Unemployment rates   Because of the profound social and economic implications of high levels of unemployment, governments normally monitor changes in unemployment levels closely. Unemployment tends to rise as the economy enters a general economic recession and falls as it enters a period of recovery. Unemployment occurs where firms are unable to sell their output and seek to scale back their work-force, either by laying off existing workers or not recruiting new ones. This results in less spending by the growing number of unemployed people, thereby exacerbating firms' sales difficulties. Actually measuring trends in unemployment over time can be difficult, as definitions used by governments frequently change. Cynics would say that this is done to hide the true level of unemployment, for example by excluding people who are on job training schemes.

Output levels   The output of firms is an important indicator of the business cycle, and is closely watched because of its effects on employment and the multiplier effects of firms spending less with their suppliers. In the United Kingdom, the government's *Business Monitor* publishes regular indicators of outputs for different sectors. Another widely quoted source of data on output is the Confederation of British Industry (CBI) which publishes monthly and quarterly surveys on industry's output, investment and stock levels. This provides a good indication of changes in different sectors of the economy and possible future business trends. In addition to these widely used and formalized methods of measuring output, a number of *ad hoc* approaches have been used, which it is claimed give early indicators of an economic recovery or downturn. Examples include:

● Sales of first class tickets by British Rail, where a fall in sales is often an early indication of firms cutting back expenditure ahead of major cuts in output.
● The number of commercial vehicles crossing the Severn Bridge between England and Wales has been correlated with output of the manufacturing sector in general.
● Sales of Ford Transit vans have been associated with a revival in fortunes by the small business sector and rising sales of heavy trucks with growing confidence by firms to invest in capital equipment.

Average earnings   Unemployment figures record the extreme case of workers who have no employment. However, under-employment can affect the national economy just as importantly as unemployment as workers are put on short-time working or lose opportunities for overtime working. Conversely, average earnings may rise significantly during the early years of a boom as firms increase overtime working and bid up wage rates in an attempt to take on staff with key skills.

Disposable income   Average diposable income refers to the income that individuals have available to spend after taxation. It follows that as taxes rise, disposable income falls. A further indicator of household wealth is *discretionary income*, which is a measure of disposable income less expenditure on the necessities of life, such as mortgage payments. Discretionary income can be significantly affected by sudden changes in the cost of mortgages and other items of expenditure, such as travel costs, which form a large component of household budgets.

Consumer spending   Trends in consumer spending may diverge from trends in discretionary income on account of changes in consumers' propensity to borrow or save. When consumer spending runs ahead of discretionary income, this can be explained by an increase in borrowing. Conversely, spending may fall faster than discretionary income, indicating that consumers are repaying debts and/or not borrowing additional money.

There are numerous indicators of consumer spending, including the government's Family Expenditure Survey. More up to date information is supplied by the Credit Card Research Group (CCRG), an organization representing the main UK credit card issuers. After making a number of assumptions about changing card-using habits, CCRG is able to monitor changes in the volume of consumer spending using credit cards. It is also able to monitor consumer borrowing using credit cards and net repayments of credit card debts.

Savings ratio   The savings ratio refers to the proportion of individuals' income that is saved rather than spent. Saving/borrowing levels are influenced by a number of factors, including the distribution of income in society (poorer people tend to save less, therefore any redistribution of income to this group would have the effect of reducing net savings) and consumers' level of confidence about the future (see below). During periods of high consumer confidence, savings ratios tend to fall as consumer borrowing rises. During the economic boom of the mid 1980s, savings ratios reached historically low levels, but increased during the subsequent recession. Businesses look to a fall in savings ratios as an early indicator of increasing consumer confidence.

Confidence levels   Private individuals and businesses may have a high level of income and savings, but there is no guarantee that they will spend that money or take on new debt in making purchases of expensive items. They may only be happy about making major spending decisions if they feel confident about the future. Higher confidence may result, for example, from consumers feeling that they are not going to be made unemployed, that their pay is going to keep up with inflation and that the value of their assets is not going to fall. A number of confidence indices are now published, for example by Chambers of Commerce and the CBI, covering both private consumers and businesses.

Inflation rate   Inflation refers to the rate at which prices of goods and services in an economy are rising. A commonly used general indicator of inflation in the United Kingdom is the Retail Prices Index (RPI) which is based on information collected about the prices of goods and services consumed by an average household. This is a commonly used 'headline' rate of inflation which is frequently used by employees as a basis for wage negotiations and is used by the UK government for adjusting the value of a number of social security benefits. The RPI may be too general to be of relevance to the spending patterns of certain individuals or organizations, so there are numerous alternative indices covering specific sectors. Many building societies, for example, produce indices of house price inflation, while specialized indices are available for new car purchases and construction costs, among others. The government publishes a monthly producer prices index which measures changes in the prices of goods bought by manufacturing firms. A rise in this indicator can signal later increases in the RPI when the components are incorporated into finished goods bought by households.

Inflation affects different groups of consumers with different effects. During a period of falling interest rates and fuel prices, a home-owning, car-using household may experience negative inflation, leaving it with greater discretionary income. At the same time, the cost of public transport and rented housing may be increasing, leaving groups dependent on public transport and council accommodation facing a high level of inflation, thereby leaving less discretionary income.

Interest rates   Interest rates represent the price that borrowers have to pay to a lender for the privilege of using their money for a specified period of time. Interest rates tend to follow a cyclical pattern which is partly a reflection of the level of activity in the economy. During periods of recession, the supply of funds typically exceeds demand for them (caused, for example; by consumers being reluctant to spend, thereby building up their savings, and by the unwillingness of consumers and firms to borrow to pay for major expenditure items). In these circumstances, interest rates typically fall. During a period of economic prosperity, the opposite holds true, and interest rates have a tendency to rise. In reality, the determination of interest rates is affected by more than the market supply and demand for money. Rates are also influenced by government intervention as governments use them as a tool of economic management. In general, low interest rates are seen as desirable because they reduce the cost of firms' borrowings and increase consumers' level of discretionary income through lower mortgage costs. However, during periods of unhealthily excessive demand in the economy, governments use high interest rates to try and dampen down demand from firms and consumers.

Overseas trade figures The monthly overseas trade figures indicate the difference between a country's imports and exports. A lot of attention is given to the 'current account' which measures overseas transactions in goods and services but not capital (discussed further in Chapter 12). In general, a current account surplus is considered good for an economy, suggesting that an economy's production sector is internationally competitive. A detailed analysis of overseas trade figures indicates trends that can often be related to the business cycle and can be used to predict future levels of activity in the economy. At the height of a boom cycle, imports of manufactured goods may rise much faster than corresponding exports, possibly suggesting unsustainable levels of household consumption. Rising imports of capital equipment may give an indication that firms are ready to invest in additional domestic productive capacity following the end of a period of recession.

Exchange rates The exchange rate is the price of one currency in terms of another (e.g. an exchange rate of £1 = DM 2.35 means that £1 costs 2.35 Deutschmarks). A number of factors influence the level of a country's exchange rate, but as an economic indicator the rate is often seen as an indication of the willingness of overseas traders and investors to hold that country's currency. Falling rates of exchange against other currencies may be interpreted as overseas investors losing their confidence in an economy or its government, leading them to sell their currency holdings and thereby depressing its price.

The theory of exchange rate determination and the implications for business are discussed in more detail in Chapter 12.

6.4.2   Tracking the business cycle

It is easy to plot business cycles with hindsight. However, businesses are much more interested in predicting the cyclical pattern in the immediate and medium term future. If the economy is at the bottom of an economic recession, that is the ideal time for firms to begin investing in new productive capacity. In this case, accurate timing of new investment can have two important benefits:

1. Firms will be able to cope with demand as soon as the economy picks up. At the end of previous economic recessions, demand has often initially outstripped the restricted supply, leading many domestic firms and consumers to buy from overseas. Firms have often only invested in new capacity once overseas competitors have built up market share, and possibly created some long-term customer loyalty too.
2. At the bottom of the business cycle, resource inputs tend to be relatively cheap. This particularly affects wage costs and the price of basic raw materials such as building materials. Good timing can allow a firm to create new capacity at a much lower cost than it would incur if it waited until it was well into the upturn, when rising demand would push up resource costs.

Analysing turning points in the business cycle has therefore become crucial to marketers. To miss an upturn at the bottom of the recession can result in a firm missing out on opportunities when the recovery comes to fruition. On the other hand, reacting to a false signal can leave a firm with expensive excess stocks and capacity on its hands. A similar problem of excess capacity can result when a firm fails to spot the downturn at the top of the business cycle.

It is extremely difficult to identify a turning point at the time when it is happening. Following the recession of the early 1990s, there have been a number of false predictions of an upturn, some politically inspired by governments keen to encourage a 'feel-good' factor ahead of an election. There was a widespread feeling in 1994·that the UK economy had reached a turning point and many companies began investing in new stock and capacity in expectation of this upturn. When the predicted revival in domestic consumer expenditure failed to transpire, companies in product fields as diverse as cars, fashion clothing and electrical goods were forced to sell off surplus stocks at low prices.

Getting out of a trough in the business cycle is very dependent upon the confidence of firms and individuals about the future. Cynics may argue that governments are acting in a politically opportunistic way by talking about the onset of recovery. However, if the government cannot exude any confidence for the future, there is less likelihood of firms and individuals being prepared to invest their resources for the future.

From a marketing perspective, firms try to react to turning points as closely as possible:

- Companies that are highly dependent on the business cycle frequently subscribe to the services of firms that have developed complex models of the economy and are able to make predictions about future economic performance. Some of these models (such as those developed by major firms of stockbrokers) are general in their application and based on models of the economy used by government policy makers in the Treasury. Specialized models seek to predict demand for more narrowly defined sectors, such as construction.
- Companies can be guided by key lead indicators which have historically been a precursor of a change in activity levels for the business sector. For a company manufacturing heavy trucks, the level of attendance at major trade exhibitions could indicate the number of buyers who are at the initial stages in the buying process for new trucks.
- Instead of placing all their hopes in accurate forecasts of the economy, companies can place greater emphasis on ensuring that they are able to respond to economic change very rapidly when it occurs. At the bottom of the cycle, this can be facilitated by developing flexible production methods, for example by retaining a list of trained part-time staff who can be called on at short notice, or having facilities to acquire excess capacity from collaborating firms overseas at very short notice. At the top of the cycle, the use of short-term contracts of employment can help a company to downsize rapidly at minimum cost.

6.5   MACROECONOMIC POLICY

The national economy has been presented as a complex system of interrelated component parts. To free market purists, the system should be self-correcting and need no intervention from governments. In reality, national economies are not closed entities and equilibrium in the circular flow can be put out of balance for a number of reasons, such as:

- Increasing levels of competition in the domestic market from overseas firms who have gained a cost advantage
- Changes in a country's ratio of workers to non-workers (e.g. the young and elderly)
- Investment in new technology which may replace firms' expenditure on domestic wages with payments for capital and interest to overseas companies

Most Western governments have accepted that the social consequences of free market solutions to economic management are unacceptable and they therefore intervene to manage the economy to a greater or lesser extent.

6.5.1 Policy objectives

This section begins by reviewing the objectives governments seek to achieve in their management of the national economy.

Maintaining employment   However unemployment is defined, its existence represents a waste of resources in an economy. Individuals who have the ability and willingness to work are unable to do so because there is no demand from employers for their skills. Workers' services are highly perishable in that, unlike stocks of goods, they cannot be accumulated for use when the economy picks up. Time spent by workers unemployed is an economic resource that is lost for ever. Most developed economies recognize that unemployed people must receive at least the basic means of sustenance, so governments provide unemployment benefit. Rising unemployment increases government expenditure.

As well as representing a wasted economic resource, unemployment has been associated with widespread social problems, including crime, alcoholism and drug abuse. High levels of unemployment can create a divided society, with unemployed people feeling cut off from the values of society while those in employment perceive many unemployed as being lazy or unwilling to work.

In general, governments of all political persuasions seek to keep unemployment levels low, in order to avoid the social and economic problems described above. However, many suspect that governments with right-wing sympathies are more likely to tolerate unemployment on the grounds that a certain amount of unemployment can bring discipline to a labour market which could otherwise give too much economic bargaining power to workers. An excess of labour supply over demand would result in wages paid to workers falling, at least in a free market. This may itself be seen as a desirable policy objective by lowering prices for consumers and increasing firms' competitiveness in international markets.

In their attempts to reduce unemployment, governments must recognize three different types of unemployment which each require different solutions:

1. *Structural unemployment* occurs where jobs are lost by firms whose goods or services are no longer in demand. This could come about through changing fashions and tastes (e.g. unemployment caused by the closure of many traditional UK seaside hotels); because of competition from overseas (for example, many jobs in the textile, ship building and coal mining industries have been lost to lower-cost overseas suppliers); or a combination of these factors. Where a local or national economy is very dependent upon one business sector and workers' skills are quite specific to that sector, the effects of structural employment can be quite severe, as can be seen in the former ship building areas of Tyneside or coal mining areas of South Wales. Governments have tackled structural employment with economic assistance to provide retraining for unemployed workers and Regional Assistance Grants to attract new employers to areas of high unemployment.

2. *Cyclical unemployment* is associated with the business cycle and is caused by a general fall in demand, which may itself be a consequence of lower spending levels by firms. Some business sectors, such as building and construction, are particularly prone to cyclical patterns of demand, and hence cyclical unemployment. The long-term cure for cyclical employment is a pick-up in demand in the economy, which governments can influence through their macroeconomic policy.

3. *Technological unemployment* occurs where jobs are replaced by machines and has had widespread implications in many industrial sectors such as car manufacture, banking and agriculture. Governments have to accept this cause of unemployment, as failure to modernize will inevitably result in an industry losing out to more efficient competition. For this reason, attempts to subsidize

jobs in declining low-technology industries are normally doomed as overseas competitors gain market share, and eventually lead to job losses which are greater than they would have been had technology issues been addressed earlier. Where a low-technology sector is supported by import controls, consumers will be forced to pay higher prices than would otherwise be necessary. Where the goods or services in question are necessities of life, consumers' discretionary income will effectively fall, leading to lower demand for goods and services elsewhere in the economy. Although technological unemployment may be very painful to the individuals directly involved, the increasing use of technology usually has the effect of making necessities cheaper, thereby allowing consumers to demand new goods and services. One manifestation of this has been the growth in services jobs, as consumers switch part of their expenditure away from food and clothing (which have fallen in price in real terms) towards eating out and other leisure pursuits.

Stable prices   Rapidly rising or falling prices can be economically, socially and politically damaging to governments. Rapidly rising prices (inflation) can cause the following problems:

- For businesses, it becomes difficult to plan ahead when selling prices and the cost of inputs in the future are not known. In many businesses, companies are expected to provide fixed prices for goods and services which will be made and delivered in the future at unknown cost levels.
- Governments find budgeting difficult during periods of high inflation. Although many government revenues rise with inflation (e.g. value added tax), this may still leave an overall shortfall caused by higher costs of employing government workers and higher contract costs for new capital projects.
- Inflation can be socially divisive as those on fixed incomes (e.g. state pensioners) fall behind those individuals who are able to negotiate wage increases to compensate for inflation. Inflation also discriminates between individuals who own different types of assets. While some physical assets such as housing may keep up with inflation, financial assets may be eroded by inflation rates that exceed the rate of interest paid. In effect, borrowers may be subsidized by lenders.
- High levels of inflation can put exporters at a competitive disadvantage. If the inflation level of the United Kingdom is higher than competing nations, UK firms' goods will become more expensive to export, while the goods from a low inflation country will be much more attractive to buyers in the United Kingdom, all other things being equal. This will have an adverse effect on UK producers and on the country's overseas balance of trade (assuming that there is no compensating change in exchange rates).

High levels of inflation can create uncertainty in the business environment, making firms reluctant to enter into long-term commitments. Failure to invest or reinvest can be ultimately damaging for the individual firm as well as the economy as a whole.

This is not to say that completely stable prices (i.e. a zero rate of inflation) is necessarily good for a national economy. A moderate level of price inflation encourages individuals and firms to invest in stocks, knowing that their assets will increase in value. A moderate level of inflation also facilitates the task of realigning prices by firms. A price reduction can be achieved simply by holding prices constant during a period of price inflation. Where price inflation causes uncertainty for firms purchasing raw materials, this uncertainty can often be overcome by purchasing on the 'futures' market. Such markets exist for a diverse range of commodities such as oil, grain and metals and allow a company to pay a fixed price for goods delivered at a specified time in the future, irrespective of whether the market price for that commodity has risen or fallen in the meantime.

The opposite of inflation is deflation, and this too can result in social, economic and political problems:

- Individuals and firms who own assets whose value is depreciating perceive that they have become poorer and adjust their spending patterns accordingly. In Britain during the early 1990s, many individuals saw their most important asset—their house—falling in value as part of a general fall in property prices. In extreme cases, individuals felt 'locked' into their house as they had borrowed more to buy it than the house was currently worth. They therefore had difficulty trading up to a larger house, thereby possibly also creating demand for home-related items such as fitted kitchens. More generally, falling property prices undermined consumers' confidence, in sharp contrast to the 1980s when rising house prices created a 'feel good' factor, fuelling spending across a range of business sectors.
- Individuals and firms will be reluctant to invest in major items of capital expenditure if they feel that, by waiting a little longer, they could have obtained those assets at a lower price.
- Deflation can become just as socially divisive as inflation. Falling house prices can lead many people who followed government and social pressures to buy their house rather than renting to feel that they have lost out for their efforts.

Economic growth   Growth is a goal shared by businesses and governments alike. It was suggested in Chapter 3 that businesses like to grow, for various reasons. Similarly, governments generally pursue growth in gross domestic product for many reasons:

- A growing economy allows for steadily rising standards of living, when measured by conventional economic indicators. In most Western economies, this is indicated by increased spending on goods and services that are considered luxuries. Without underlying growth in GDP, increases in consumer spending will be short lived.
- For governments, growth results in higher levels of income through taxes on incomes, sales and profits. This income allows government to pursue socially and politically desirable infrastructure spending, such as the construction of new hospitals or road improvements.
- A growing economy creates a 'feel good' factor in which individuals feel confident about being able to obtain employment and subsequently feel confident about making major purchases.

Economic growth in itself may not necessarily leave a society feeling better off as economic well-being does not necessarily correspond to quality of life. There is growing debate about whether some of the consequences of economic growth, such as increased levels of pollution and traffic congestion, really leave individuals feeling better off. There is also the issue of how the results of economic growth are shared out between members of a society.

Distribution of wealth   Governments overtly and covertly have objectives relating to the distribution of economic wealth between different groups in society. In the United Kingdom, the trend since the Second World War has been for a gradual convergence in the prosperity of all groups, as the very rich have been hit by high levels of income, capital gains and inheritance tax, while the poorer groups in society have benefited from increasing levels of social security payments. During periods of Labour administrations, the tendency has been for taxes on the rich to increase, tilting the distribution of wealth in favour of poorer groups. However, the Thatcher years of the 1980s saw this process put into reverse as high income groups benefited from the abolition of higher rates of income tax and the liberalization of inheritance taxes. At the same time, many social security benefits have been withdrawn or reduced in scope or amount, leaving many lower or middle income groups worse off.

The effects of government policy objectives on the distribution of income can have profound implications for marketers. During most of the post-war years, the tendency was for mid-market segments to grow significantly. In the car sector, this was associated with the success of mid-range cars such as the Ford Escort and Sierra. During periods of Labour administration, the sale of luxury cars tended to suffer. However, the boom of the late 1980s and the rapid rise in income of the top groups in society resulted in a significant growth in the luxury car sector. Manufacturers such as BMW, Mercedes Benz and Jaguar benefited from this trend. At the same time, the worsening of the fortunes of many lower income groups partly explained the growth in very low priced basic cars such as those manufactured by Lada, Skoda and FSO.

Stable exchange rate A stable value of sterling in terms of other major currencies is useful to businesses who are thereby able to accurately predict the future cost of raw materials bought overseas and the sterling value they will receive for goods and services sold overseas. Stable exchange rates can also help consumers, for example in budgeting for overseas holidays. It is, however, debatable just what the 'right' exchange rate is that governments should seek to maintain (this is discussed further in Chapter 12).

An important contributor to maintaining a stable exchange rate is the maintenance of the balance of payments. Governments avoid large trade deficits, which can have the effect of lowering the exchange rate. From a business perspective, balance of trade surpluses tend to benefit the economy through the creation of jobs, additional economic growth and a general feeling of business confidence. Surpluses created from overseas trade can be used to finance overseas lending and investment, which in turn generate higher levels of earnings from overseas in future years.

Government borrowing Government borrowing represents the difference between what it receives in any given year from taxation and trading sources and what it needs in order to finance its expenditure programmes. The difference is often referred to as the public sector borrowing requirement (PSBR). The level of PSBR is partly influenced by political considerations, with right wing free market advocates favouring a reduced role for the government, reflected in a low level of PSBR. Advocates of intervention are happier to see the PSBR rise. Government borrowing tends to rise during periods of economic recession and fall during periods of boom. This can be explained by income (especially from income and profits taxes) rising relative to expenditure during a boom and expenditure (especially on social security benefits) rising relative to income during a recession.

6.5.2 Government management of the economy

From government policy objectives come strategies by which these policy objectives can be achieved. This is an area where it can be possible to line up a dozen economists and get a dozen different answers to the same problem. Sometimes, political ideology can lead to the strategy being considered to be just as important as the policy objectives with supporters of alternative strategies showing very strong allegiance to them.

In trying to reconcile multiple objectives, governments invariably face a dilemma in reconciling all of them simultaneously. Of the three principal economic objectives (maintaining employment, controlling inflation and economic growth), satisfying objectives for any two invariably causes problems with the third (see Figure 6.6). It is therefore common for governments to shift their emphasis between policy objectives for political and pragmatic reasons. However, many surveys of business leaders have suggested that what they consider important above all else is *stability* in governnment policy. If the government continually changes the economic goal posts, or its economic strategy, businesses' own planning processes can be put into confusion.

Sometimes, policy can be implemented in pursuit of one objective, only for adverse side effects to appear leading to policy being directed to solving this second problem. During the early 1990s, the UK government put the reduction in inflation as its top economic policy priority and achieved this through high interest rates, among other things. However, high interest rates created a recession, signified by falling demand, rising unemployment and reduced levels of investment. Resolving these problems became a priority for government policy.

Policy goals

	Economy: steady increase in GDP	Employment: maintain full employment	Inflation: maintain stable currency
Economy	—	Full employment contributes to GDP growth	Desire to retain low level of inflation may curb economic growth
Employment	Rapid GDP growth can lead to 'over-full' employment and skill shortages	—	Desire to retain low level of inflation may limit employment opportunities
Inflation	Economic growth may lead to excessive demand relative to supply, resulting in inflation	Full employment can lead to an inflationary spiral of wage increases	—

Possible effects of policy goals

Figure 6.6   Problems in reconciling conflicting economic policy objectives

Two commonly used approaches to economic management can be classified under the headings of:

1. Fiscal policy, which concentrates on stimulating the economy through changes in government income and expenditure
2. Monetary policy, which effectively influences the circular flow of income by changes in the supply of money and interest rates.

Fiscal policy   Government is a major element of the circular flow of income, both as tax collector and as a source of expenditure for goods and services and payments to households. Increases in government spending have the effect of injecting additional income into the circular flow and, through the multiplier effect, thereby increasing the demand for goods and services. Reductions in government spending have the opposite effect. Changes in taxation can similarly affect the circular flow of income (e.g. a cut in income tax effectively injects more money into the economy).

The use of fiscal measures to regulate the economy achieved prominence with the economist John Maynard Keynes, whose followers are generally referred to as Keynsians. Keynes developed his ideas as a means of overcoming the high levels of unemployment and falling commodity prices which were associated with the Great Depression of the 1930s. Conventional economics had failed to return resource markets to equilibrium, largely because of rigidities that had built up in markets. Instead, Keynes advocated the use of fiscal policy to increase the level of aggregate demand within the economy. Through a multiplier effect, spending by workers employed on government 'pump-priming' projects would filter through to private sector suppliers, who would in turn employ further workers, thereby eventually eradicating unemployment. If the economy showed signs of becoming too active, with scarcity in resource markets and rising price levels, suppression of demand through fiscal actions would have the effect of reducing inflationary pressures (Figure 6.7).

In the 1930s, fiscal measures were considered quite revolutionary and resulted in such projects as the electrification of railways and the construction of the National Grid being undertaken not just for the end result but also for the multiplier benefits of carrying out the construction tasks. More recently, road building and government funded construction in general have been used as a regulator of the economy, on account of their high employment content and low levels of initial 'leakage' to imported supplies. This has, however, served to increase the cyclical pattern of demand facing the construction sector.

Critics of fiscal policy have argued that fiscal intervention is a very clumsy way of trying to return the economy to equilibrium and a method that achieves temporary rather than permanent solutions to underlying economic problems. Keynsian policies call for bureaucratic civil servants to make quasi-commercial decisions which they are generally ill equipped to do. There is much evidence of failed fiscal policy at a local level where government grants and tax incentives have been given to attract industry to depressed areas, only for those industries to close down after a few years (e.g. car factories built in Northern Ireland, Merseyside and Glasgow with government grants and tax concessions have proved to be commercial failures). Critics of fiscal policy look to monetarist policies as an alternative.

Monetary policy   By contrast, the monetarist approach uses changes in the volume of money supply to influence aggregate demand in the economy. Monetarism achieved prominence with the work of Milton Freedman and found favour with the Thatcher government of the 1980s. The basic proposition of monetarism is that government need only regulate the supply of money in order to influence the circular flow of income. From this, adjustments in the economy happen automatically by market forces without the need for intervention by government in the running of business organizations (Figure 6.7). If government wishes to suppress demand in the economy, it would do this by restricting the volume of money in circulation in the economy (e.g. by raising interest rates or restricting the availability of credit). It would do the opposite if it wished to stimulate the economy.

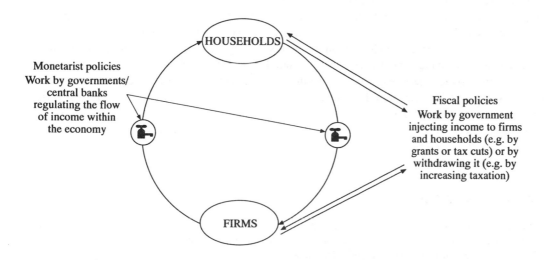

Figure 6.7   The monetarist and fiscal approaches to management of the economy

Monetarism appeals to free market purists because of the limited government hands-on intervention that is required. However, governments have found it politically unacceptable to pursue monetarist policies to their logical conclusion. Suppressing demand by controlling the availability of money alone could result in unacceptably high levels of interest rates.

6.5.3   Limitations of government intervention in the national economy

At a practical level, critics of both monetarist and fiscal approaches to economic management have pointed to their failure to significantly influence the long-term performance of an economy. More recently, the fundamental concept of government intervention has been challenged in an emerging body of theoretical and empirical research which is commonly referred to as rational expectations theory. Proponents of the theory claim that it is too simplistic to regard government economic intervention in terms of simple stimulus–response models. It is naive, for example, to assume that private companies will take an increase in government capital spending as a cue to increase their own productive capacity. Instead, firms rationally assess the likely consequences of government intervention. Therefore an increase in government capital expenditure may lead to an expectation of eventually higher interest rates and inflation. Faced with this rational expectation, firms may decide to cut back their own expenditure, fearing the consequences for their own business of high inflation and interest rates. This is the opposite of the government's intended response. The theory of rational expectations holds that business people have become astute at interpreting economic signals and, because of this, government's ability to manage the national economy is significantly reduced.

6.5.4   The central bank

A nation's central bank plays an important role in the management of the national economy. In the United Kingdom, the Bank of England acts as a lender of last resort and has responsibility for regulating the volume of currency in circulation within the economy. Through its market operations, it intervenes to influence the exchange rate for sterling. The Bank of England also has a supervisory role in respect of privately-owned banks within the United Kingdom.

Countries differ in the extent to which powers of the central bank are separated from government. In the United States and Germany, for example, granting the central bank a quasi-autonomous status and allowing it freedom to make decisions on monetary policy has been regarded as a means of guaranteeing prudent management of the money supply against political intervention for possibly short-term opportunistic objectives. Against this, the argument is put forward that central banks should be politically accountable and should be influenced by the social and political implications of their actions and not just the more narrowly defined monetary ones. In the United Kingdom, the Bank of England has traditionally been influenced by the Treasury arm of government. Business leaders remain divided on the relative merits of a politically influenced central bank and one that is above narrow political interests.

REVIEW QUESTIONS

1. 'Economic policy is the product of the conflicting desires of governments for price stability and full employment stability.' Discuss this statement in the context of your government's economic policies.
   (CIM Marketing Environment Examination, December 1994, Q.7, part i)
2. What would be the marketing implications of your current government's current economic policies?
   (CIM Marketing Environment Examination, December 1994, Q.7, part ii)
3. During 1993, the UK government announced that it would fund the creation of a new University in Northern Ireland. What multiplier benefits are likely to be associated with this project?
4. Identify some of the consequences for a UK vehicle manufacturer of a UK inflation rate of 5 per cent p.a., compared to a European Union average of 2 per cent.
5. Contrast the effects of 'tight' fiscal and tight monetary policies on the construction sector.
6. In the context of 'rational expectations' theory, what evidence could you suggest to indicate that business people 'see through' the short-term implications of government economic policies?

REFERENCES

International Labour Office (1991) *Year book of labour statistics*, Geneva.

Marshall, J. N. (1985) 'Business Services, the Regions and Regional Policy', *Regional Studies*, vol. 19, pp. 353–63.

Wood, P. A. (1987) 'Producer Services and Economic Change, Some Canadian Evidence', in *Technological Change and Economic Policy*, eds K. Chapman and G. Humphreys, Blackwell, London.

FURTHER READING

Artis, M. J. (ed.) (1994) *Prest and Coppock's The U.K. Economy: A Manual of Applied Economics*, 13th edn, Oxford University Press, Oxford.

Dunnett, A. (1992) *Understanding the Economy*, 3rd edn, Longman, Harlow.

Griffiths, A. and Wall, S. (eds) (1995) *Applied Economics: An Introductory Course*, 6th edn, Longman, Harlow.

Hildebrand, G. (1992) *Business Cycle Indicators: A Complete Guide to Interpreting the Key Economic Indicators*, Probus Publishing, Chicago, Ill.

Miller, P. J. (ed.) (1994) *The Rational Expectations Revolution: Readings from the Front Line*, MIT Press, Cambridge, Mass.

Mullineux, A., Dickinson, D. and Peng, W. (1993) *Business Cycles: Theory and Evidence*, Blackwell, Oxford.

Van der Ploeg, F. (ed.) (1994) *Handbook of International Macroeconomics*, Blackwell, Oxford.

THE POLITICAL ENVIRONMENT

OBJECTIVES

After reading this chapter, you should understand:

- The basis of government in the United Kingdom
- The respective roles of local, national and European government
- The two-way interaction between organizations and their political environment
- The reasons why it is important for marketers to appreciate the political environments in which they operate

7.1 DEFINING THE POLITICAL ENVIRONMENT

All aspects of an organization's marketing environment are interrelated to some extent, and this is especially true of the political environment. Inter-linkages occur in many ways, for example:

1. Political decisions inevitably affect the economic environment, for example in the proportion of GDP accounted for by the state and the distribution of income between different groups in society (Chapter 6).
2. Political decisions also influence the social and cultural environment of a country (Chapter 8). For example, governments create legislation which can have the effect of encouraging families to care for their elderly relatives or allowing shops to open on Sundays. In short, the actions of politicians are both a reflection of the social and cultural environment of a country and also help to shape it.
3. Politicians can influence the pace at which new technologies appear, for example through tax concessions on research and development activity (Chapter 11).

The political environment is one of the less predictable elements in an organization's marketing environment. Although politicians issue manifestos and other policy statements, these have to be seen against the pragmatic need of governments to modify their policies during their period in office. Change in the political environment can result from a variety of internal and external pressures. The fact that democratic governments have to seek re-election every few years has contributed towards a cyclical political environment. Turbulence in the political environment can be seen by considering some of the major swings that have occurred in the political environment in the United Kingdom since the Second World War:

- During the late 1940s, the political environment stressed heavy government intervention in all aspects of the economy, including ownership of a substantial share of productive capacity.

- During the 1950s, there was a much more restrained hands off approach in which many of the previously nationalized industries were deregulated and sold off.
- During the 1960s and 1970s the political environment oscillated in moderation between more and less government involvement in the ways businesses are run.
- The 1980s saw a significant change in the political environment, with the wholesale withdrawal of government from ownership and regulation of large areas of business activity.
- More recently, marketers monitoring the political environment have detected a shift away from the radicalism of the 1980s to the idea of a social market economy in the 1990s.

7.1.1   Importance of monitoring the political environment

The marketer needs to monitor the changing political environment because it impinges on the marketing function of businesses in a number of ways:

1. At the most general level, the stability of the political system affects the attractiveness of a particular national market. While radical change rarely results from political upheaval in most Western countries, the instability of many Eastern European governments leads to uncertainty about the economic and legislative framework in which goods and services will be provided.
2. At a national level, government passes legislation that directly affects the relationship between the firm and its customers and between itself and other firms. Sometimes legislation has a direct effect on marketers, for example a law giving consumers rights against the seller of faulty goods. At other times, the effect is less direct, as where legislation requiring local authorities to put out to tender some of their duties has the effect of creating more competitive relationships between firms in a market.
3. The government is additionally responsible for protecting the public interest at large, imposing further constraints on the activities of firms, for example where the government lays down design standards for cars to protect the public against pollution or road safety risks.
4. The economic environment is directly affected by the actions of government. It is responsible for formulating policies that can influence the rate of growth in the economy and hence the total amount of spending power. It is also a political decision as to how this spending power should be distributed between different groups of consumers and between the public and private sectors.
5. Government at both a central and local level is itself a major consumer of goods and services, currently accounting for about 41 per cent of the UK's gross domestic product.
6. Government policies can influence the dominant social and cultural values of a country, although there can be argument about which is the cause and which is the effect. UK government policies of the 1980s emphasized wealth creation as an end in itself and also had the effect of generating a feeling of confidence among consumers. This can be directly linked to an increase in consumer spending at a higher rate than earnings growth and a renewed enthusiasm for purchasing items of ostentatious consumption.

It should be remembered that marketers have to not only monitor the political environment, they are also often involved in contributing to it. This can happen where organizations feel threatened by change and lobby government to intervene to pass legislation that will protect their interests.

To understand the nature of the political environment more fully and its impact on marketing, it is necessary to examine the different aspects of government. Government influence in the United Kingdom can be divided into the following categories:

- Central government
- Local government

- European Union (EU) government
- Supranational government

7.2 CENTRAL GOVERNMENT

The government system of most countries can be divided into four separate functions. In the United Kingdom, these are the legislature, the executive, the civil service and the judiciary. These collectively provide sovereign government within the United Kingdom, although as will be seen later, this sovereignty is increasingly being subjected to the authority of the European Community.

7.2.1 Parliament

Parliament provides the supreme legislative authority in the United Kingdom and comprises the Queen, the House of Commons and the House of Lords. The House of Commons is the most important part of the legislature as previous legislation has curtailed the authority in Parliament of the monarch and the House of Lords. It is useful to be aware of the procedures for enacting new legislation so that the influences on the legislative process can be fully understood (Figure 7.1)

New legislation starts life as a Bill and passes through parliamentary processes to the point where it becomes an Act of Parliament. Most Bills that subsequently become law are government sponsored and often start life following discussion between government departments and interested parties. On

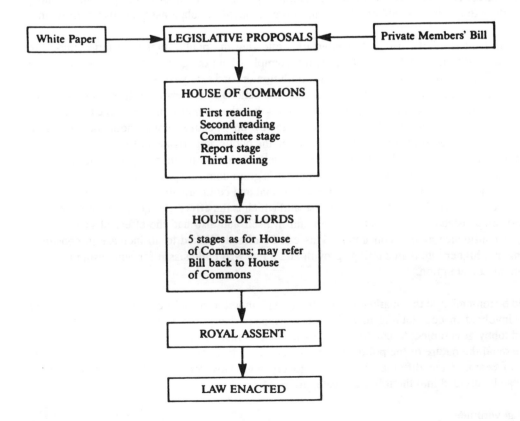

Figure 7.1 The progress of legislation through parliament

some occasions, these discussions may lead to the setting up of a Committee of Enquiry or (less frequently) a Royal Commission which reports to the government. The findings of such a committee can be accepted, rejected or amended by the government which puts forward ideas for discussion in a green paper. Following initial discussion, the government would submit definite proposals for legislation in the form of a White Paper. A Parliamentary Bill would then be drafted, incorporating some of the comments that the government has received in response to the publication of the White Paper. The Bill is then formally introduced to Parliament by a first reading in the House of Commons at which a date is set for the main debate at a second reading. A vote is taken at each reading, and if it is a government bill, it will invariably pass at each stage. If it passes the second reading, the Bill will be sent to a Standing Committee for a discussion of the details. The Committee will in due course report back to the full House of Commons and there will be a final debate where amendments are considered, some of which originate from the Committee and some from members of the House of Commons in general. The Bill then passes to the House of Lords and goes through a similar five stages. The Lords may delay or amend a Bill, although the Commons may subsequently use the Parliament Act to force the Bill through. Finally, the Bill goes to the monarch to receive the Royal Assent, upon which it becomes an Act of Parliament.

This basic model can be changed in a number of ways. Firstly, in response to a newly perceived problem, the government could introduce a Bill with very few clauses and with the agreement of party managers could cut short the consultation stages, speed up the passage of the Bill through its various stages and provide Royal Assent within a matter of days, instead of the months that it could typically take. This has occurred, for example, in the case of a one clause Bill to prohibit trade in human organs, a measure that had received all-party support. A second variation on the basic model is provided by Private Members Bills. Most Bills start life with government backing. However, backbench Members of Parliament can introduce their own Bills, although the opportunities for doing this are limited and if they do not subsequently receive government backing, their chances of passing all stages of the Parliamentary process are significantly reduced.

In the chapter on the legal environment (Chapter 10), it is noted that the law affecting marketers comes from two principal sources—statute law and case law. Case law evolves gradually and is determined by judges who aim to be impartial and free from any sectional interest. The ability of the marketer to influence change in this aspect of the law is therefore very limited. However, this cannot be said of statute law passed by Parliament. The lobbying of Members of Parliament has become an increasingly important activity, brought about by individuals and pressure groups to try and protect their interests where new legislation is proposed which may affect them. During the early 1990s, proposals to give private leaseholders the right to purchase their freehold encountered fierce lobbying by commercial property owners, with the result, some would say, that the final legislation passed was very much a watered-down version of the government's original proposals. If marketers are to succeed in influencing their political environment, they need to identify the critical points in the passage of a Bill at which pressure can be applied and the critical members who should form the focus of lobbying.

7.2.2 The executive

Parliament comprises a collection of elected representatives whose decisions, in theory, are carried out by the executive arm of government. In practice, the executive plays a very important role in formulating policies which parliament then debates and invariably accepts. In the United Kingdom, the principal elements of the executive comprise the Cabinet and Ministers of State.

The Cabinet The main executive element of central government is made up of the Prime Minister and Cabinet, who determine policy and who are responsible for the consequences of their policies. The cabinet is headed by the Prime Minister who has many powers, including the appointment and dismissal of ministers and determining the membership of cabinet committees, chairing the Cabinet and setting its agenda, summarizing the discussions of the Cabinet and sending directives to ministers. The Prime Minister is also responsible for a variety of government and non-government appointments and can determine the timing of a general election. Many would argue that Britain is moving towards a system of presidential government by the Prime Minister, given the considerable powers at his or her disposal. There are, however, a number of constraints on the power of the Prime Minister, such as the need to keep the loyalty of the Cabinet and the agreement of Parliament, which may be difficult when the governing party has only a small majority in the House of Commons.

In practice, the Prime Minister is particularly dependent upon the support of a small inner cabinet of senior colleagues for advice and assistance in carrying policy through the party. In addition to this small inner cabinet surrounding the Prime Minister, recent years have seen the development of a small group of outside advisors on whose loyalty the Prime Minister can totally rely. Some are likely to be party members sitting in Parliament, while others may be party loyalists who belong to the business or academic community. There have been occasions when it has appeared that the Prime Minister's advisors were having a greater influence on policy than their cabinet colleagues.

The ideological background of the Prime Minister and the composition of the government may give some indication of the direction of government policy. On government attitudes towards aspects of the political environment, such as competition policy and personal taxation, marketers could study the composition of the government to try and predict future policy.

Ministers of State The government of the country is divided between a number of different departments of state (see Figure 7.2). Each department is headed by a Minister or Secretary of State who is a political appointee, usually filled by a member of the House of Commons. They are assisted in their tasks by junior ministers. The portfolio of responsibilities of a department frequently changes when a new government comes into being. Ministers are often given delegated authority by Parliament, as where an Act may allow charges to be made for certain health services, but the Minister has the delegated power to decide the actual level of the charges.

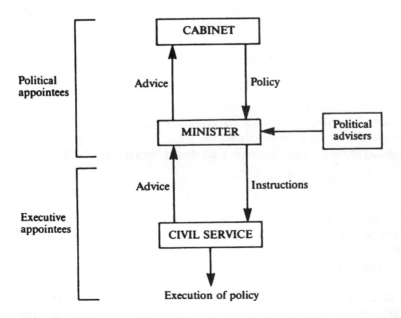

Figure 7.2 The UK government system of departmental administration: a simplified diagram

7.2.3   Political parties

The purpose of political parties is to advance the cause of their members. In general, the views of the members of political parties cross a range of policy issues, so political parties can be distinguished from single-interest groups such as the Campaign for Nuclear Disarmament. Because they represent a diverse range of issues, it is not surprising that leaders of political parties find it difficult to gain the unanimous support of all members on all issues. In the United Kingdom, members of the main political parties are divided on issues such as the level of involvement with the European Community, defence expenditure and educational policy. Nevertheless, a political party stands for a broad statement of values which its members can identify with. In the United Kingdom, the Conservative party has traditionally been identified with such core values as the self-reliance of individuals, less rather than more government and the role of law and order. The Labour party, by contrast, has traditionally stood for state intervention where market failure has occurred, protection of the weak in society from the strong and efforts to reduce inequalities in wealth. The Liberal Democrat party has traditionally appealed to people who believe in open democratic government in a market economy with government intervention where market mechanisms have produced inequalities or inefficiencies.

The Conservative party has traditionally been seen as the party of business and the Labour party as the party of organized labour. This is true as far as the funding of the parties go, with the Conservative party receiving sizeable donations from business organizations while many Labour MPs are sponsored by Trades Unions. In general, the free market enterprise values of the Conservative party would appear to favour the interests of businesses, while the socialist values of the Labour party would appear to be against business interests. Historically, business has been worried at the prospect of a Labour government, as witnessed by the fall in stock market prices which has often followed a Labour party election victory. However, the United Kingdom, like many Western countries, has seen increasing levels of convergence between parties which makes business leaders very uncertain about just what makes a party's policies distinctive. For example, the UK Labour party has traditionally been opposed to privatization of public utilities, but it seems unlikely that it would ever contemplate re-nationalizing the privatized British Telecom or British Airways. Marketers in the education sector must wonder whether a Labour government could ever commit itself to abolishing grant maintained schools, a type of school that it has been opposed to, but which it knows are popular with the electorate. As political parties have targeted the crucial middle ground 'floating voter', their policies have become increasingly indistinguishable.

7.2.4   The parliamentary life cycle

Political parties typically make bold promises in their election manifestos. If elected, they may promptly enact legislation that formed the flagship of their campaign. However, after a honeymoon period, governments must set to work addressing structural issues in the economy which will take some time to make good. This may involve painful economic measures in the short term, but the payoff is improved economic performance in a few years time. With a five year election cycle for Parliament in the United Kingdom, it is often claimed that voters have short memories and will forget austere economic conditions of two or three years ago. What matters at election time is the appearance that economic conditions are getting better. Thus government economic planning may try to achieve falling unemployment, stable prices and a consumer boom just ahead of a general election. This may itself lead to structural problems which must be sorted out after the election, leading to a repeat of this cyclical process (see Figure 7.3). Cynical marketers may acknowledge this cycle by gearing up for a boom in sales just ahead of a general election.

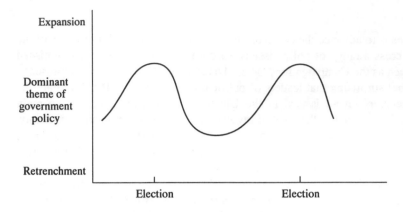

Figure 7.3   The political life cycle

7.2.5   The civil service

The civil service is the secretariat responsible for implementing government policy. In the United Kingdom, civil servants are paid officials who do not change when the government changes, adding a degree of continuity to government (although in some countries such as the United States, it is normal for senior officials to be political appointees and therefore replaced following a change of government). Although legally civil servants are servants of the Crown, they are technically employed by a separate government department and are responsible to a Minister. Each department is generally headed by a Permanent Secretary, responsible to the Public Accounts Committee of Parliament. The Permanent Secretary is a professional administrator who gives advice to his or her Minister, a political appointee who generally lacks expertise in the work of the department.

The fact that civil servants are relatively expert in their areas and generally remain in their posts for much longer than their minister has given them great power. A delicate relationship develops between the Permanent Secretary and the Minister, based on sometimes conflicting goals. The Minister may view an issue in terms of broader political opportunities while the civil servant may be more concerned about his or her status and career prospects resulting from a change affecting his or her department.

The nature of the career civil servant is changing with the emergence of agencies to take over the activities of civil service departments (see below). In theory, these new executive agencies should be much freer of ministerial control, meeting longer-term performance standards with less day-to-day ministerial intervention as to how this should be achieved.

The marketer seeking to influence government policy must recognize the power that civil servants have in advising their Minister, especially on the details of proposed legislation. Civil servants are usually involved in consultation exercises, for example on the details of proposed food regulations. In some countries, business may seek to influence the policy-making process at this stage through overt or covert bribery. This is not a feature of most mature democracies such as Britain, and business seeks to exert influence in a more mutually co-operative manner. Civil servants require information on the background to policy and need to understand its possible implications. A close dialogue between the business community and civil servants can increase the chances of civil servants' policy recommendations being based on a sound understanding of business needs, rather than ignorance.

7.2.6   The judiciary

Most democratic systems of government provide a number of checks and balances against the abuse of executive power. The judiciary is independent of government and judges in the United Kingdom are answerable to the Crown and not to politicians. Through the court system, citizens can have some redress against a legislature, executive or civil service that acts beyond its authority. For example, if complainants believe that they have suffered because a government minister did not follow statutory consultation procedures, they may apply to the courts for a judicial review of the case. A court may order that ministers reconsider the matter by following statutory procedures.

7.3   LOCAL GOVERNMENT

Local authorities in the United Kingdom are responsible for a wide range of services, from social services and education to refuse collection and street cleaning. The structure of local government which was implemented in 1974 divided the largely rural areas of England into counties ('shire counties'), each with their County Council. The chief responsibilities of these County Councils included education, social services, emergency services, highways and refuse disposal. Shire counties were further subdivided into District Councils (sometimes designated as Borough or City Councils) which had responsibilities for housing, leisure services and refuse collection. Districts in rural areas were usually further divided into parishes with a Parish Council (sometimes designated as a Town Council) responsible for local matters such as the maintenance of playing fields.

In the larger conurbations, Metropolitan District Councils had greater functions than their shire county counterparts, for example they were additionally responsible for education and social services. Following the abolition of Metropolitan County Councils in 1986, responsibility for conurbation-wide services (such as public transport and emergency services) passed to a series of joint boards governed by the District Councils. In London, the pattern of government is broadly similar to that of Metropolitan areas. In Scotland, the structure of local government has been based on a two-tier system of Regional and District Councils.

The government has been undertaking a review of the structure of local government in Britain, following dissatisfaction by many with the system established in 1974. It has been argued that the existence of two layers of local government in the shires on such issues as planning policies had become expensive and time consuming. Furthermore, arguments for large County Councils based on economies of scale and centralized provision had given way to a philosophy based on small, locally responsive units acting as an enabler for services provided by subcontracted suppliers. Even a small former county such as Rutland, it is argued, can provide many services previously considered too complex for such a small unit, by buying them in from outside suppliers.

The government has recognized that there is not necessarily one 'right' structure that should form a blueprint for the whole of Britain. It has accepted the recommendations of a Commission appointed to review local government that there should be a mixture of structures to suit local needs. In many cases, this means retaining the current two-tier structure of District and County Councils. In other cases, especially conurbations such as Leicester and Nottingham, it has allowed for the creation of 'unitary' authorities which will undertake all local government functions in their area, thereby avoiding duplication and delay where responsibilities of District and County Councils overlap. For example, the new 'unitary' authority for Leicester combines existing City Council functions of housing, refuse collection and car parking (among others) with functions transferred from Leicestershire County Council, including education, social services and highways.

7.3.1   The changing relationship between central and local government

It has been argued that local government in Britain is losing its independence from central government, despite claims by Conservative governments that it supports a philosophy of less government and decentralization of powers. There is a lot of evidence of this erosion of local autonomy:

- Over half of local government income now comes in the form of grants from the Department of the Environment.
- Local authorities have had the ability to set rates on business premises taken away from them altogether and this is now determined by central government.
- Furthermore, central government has the power to set a maximum permitted total expenditure for a local authority and to set a maximum amount for its council tax due from householders.

In addition, legislation setting performance standards in education and social services (among others) has limited the independence of local government to set locally determined standards. Local authorities now have less local discretion in determining what is an acceptable standard for services in its area and in deciding between satisfying competing priorities.

Local authorities have had increasing numbers of functions removed from their responsibility and placed with QUANGOs which are no longer answerable to the local authority. This has particularly affected education, with the former polytechnics (or 'new' universities) being transferred from local authorities to newly created Higher Education Corporations and schools being allowed to 'opt-out' of local authority control. In both cases, block grant funding comes from central government, replacing financial control that local government previously exercised over these organizations.

The process of privatization has altered the role of local authorities who are being regarded more as enablers of service provision rather than the actual provider. The Local Government Act 1988 specified a number of activities, such as refuse collection and school catering, where local authorities are required to put the provision of services out to competitive tender. Local authorities have entered the market for these services as buyers of services which were previously produced internally—sometimes they are still provided internally, but by a separately accountable section within the authority.

7.3.2   Local authorities and marketing

Many would argue that government policy towards local authorities has been guided by a perception that they have been too production oriented and consumers have been unable to exercise sufficient sovereignty over the services that they provide. The principle of opting out of local authority control which has been made to parents of school children, tenants of council-owned houses and residents of elderly people's homes, among others, gives some choice back to users of services. This has, for instance, prompted many local authority housing departments to take researching and satisfying the needs of their tenants very seriously, in the knowledge that dissatisfaction could lead tenants to vote to sack the local authority as their managers and instead to transfer control to an independent housing association.

Contracting out of services is designed to create a division between the production of services and their provision to meet users' needs. Compulsory competitive tendering (CCT), introduced by the Local Government Act 1988, requires local authorities to submit the provision of an ever-widening range of services to competitive tender, even though the services themselves may still be provided by the authority in a centrally planned manner, often at no cost to users. CCT forces local authorities to ensure that services are produced from the least-cost provider, thereby lowering the financial burden on local tax payers. Sceptics would argue that there has been too much emphasis on price and less on the quality of services provided. Many new businesses have been created to exploit opportunities presented by contracting out, although in many areas, such as the management of leisure centres, their failure rate has been high. Firms bidding for contracts have often underestimated the costs of providing services as specified and have often suffered heavy 'fines' where performance has not come up to the specified standard. Many have also argued that paperwork involved with submitting tenders is onerous for small businesses, in particular, and favours bids submitted by the existing local authority managers.

Services remaining with local authorities are becoming increasingly market oriented. Delegation of responsibilities has resulted in a clearer specification of objectives for managers which are today more likely to emphasize users' benefits. For example, managers of museums are now more likely to be given targets for visitor numbers and sales from trading activity. Marketing is increasingly being used as a tool to achieve such objectives. In some cases, delegated responsibility has led to competition between local authority units. Local management of schools has led to schools using a variety of marketing techniques to attract pupils, and the funding that follows.

COUNCIL USES MARKETING RESEARCH TO PUT ITS HOUSE IN ORDER

Attitudes towards public sector housing have often viewed tenants of council properties as fortunate people who should be happy that they have even managed to obtain a council house. So long as councils provided accommodation which was habitable, the idea of studying tenants' satisfaction with the service provided by local authority housing departments had seemed unnecessary. However, the 1988 Housing Act signalled changes in the way that tenants expected to be treated by their local authorities landlords. Previous 'right-to-buy' legislation had already depleted local authorities' stocks of housing to rent. Now there was the prospect of whole estates of residents having the right to sack their local authority landlords and have ownership and management of their houses transferred to a trust organization. Local authorities realized that they had to become more market oriented in their dealings with tenants.

One example of this new-found marketing orientation occurred in 1988 when Warwick District Council employed the market research organization MORI to undertake a 'Tenant Satisfaction Survey'. Although the Council's Housing Officers thought that they provided a first class housing service, the newly appointed Chief Housing Officer—fired by the concept of customer care and the new housing legislation—wanted to test this out by conducting independent research of the Council's users.

Undertaking research was considered to present valuable opportunities both as an input to the policy-making process and as a means of assessing the effectiveness of policy imple-

mentation. The latter was to be achieved through a follow-up survey two years later, when policy changes had been completed.

MORI, who were experienced in undertaking consumer projects on behalf of councils, were attracted by this survey. It offered the agency one of the few opportunities to use a pure unclustered random sample. As the Council has a database of all its properties, it was possible to list them in geographical order and draw a straightforward 1 in 10 sample across the key regions used by the Housing Department. The only variation from a purely random selection involved slight over-sampling in rural areas to make the sample more robust. MORI drew a sample of 1221 names from the tenant list and interviewers were sent out to conduct personal in-house interviews with the person in each household who had most dealings with the Department. The level of co-operation and the consequent response rate was very good—906 respondents in total, or a contact rate of 74.2 per cent.

The results of the survey were pleasing for the Council—the tenants were quite flattering about many aspects of the housing service. Overall, two-thirds of tenants were satisfied with the service provided and, in a comparative analysis, Warwick District Council received a higher rating than any other authority that MORI had previously studied. However, from an analysis of the data, the Council was able to identify some areas where policy measures were required. These included communications with tenants, efficiency of heating, speed and quality of repairs, consultation on proposed improvements and awareness of the legislation on tenants' choice.

The resultant policy outcome was an action plan which included:

- The introduction of a feedback instrument (a [dis]satisfaction card) for monitoring the repairs service. Tenants were unhappy with the speed and quality of the repairs service.
- A series of meetings was arranged on tenants' choice legislation to counteract the low level of awareness of the implications of the 1988 Housing Act.
- Tenant consultation was to be improved. There was also concern about the limited information provided by the Council.
- A budget was given over to the Department for the creation of a *Tenants Handbook* and *Newsletter* in response to the criticism of council communications.
- The recruitment of an additional recep-

tionist at the Housing Office and refurbishing of the waiting areas. Concern had been expressed about the speed with which enquiries were handled at the Office.

After this series of actions by the Council the survey was repeated in order to evaluate customers' reactions to the changes. The programme of initiatives was generally well received and satisfaction remained high. In particular, the new communications policy was very well received and more customers now felt that they were being kept well informed. The overall shift in emphasis towards customer care was seen to be a big improvement in the Council's marketing.

(Adapted from 'Towards an Action Plan' by D. Dyas and T. Burns, in *Research Works*, eds D. Martin and J. Goodyear, AMSO/NTC Publications, 1991.)

QUESTIONS

1. What factors might have prompted the Council to introduce a programme of marketing research?
2. Compare the benefits to the Council of quantitive and qualitative methods of research.
3. In what circumstances could the type of research undertaken be described as a failure?

7.4 QUASI-GOVERNMENTAL BODIES

The 1990s has seen significant developments in the delegation of powers from government organizations to 'arms length' executive agencies, often referred to collectively as quasi-autonomous governmental organizations (QUANGOs). In Britain, quasi-governmental bodies exist because direct involvement by a government department in a particular area of activity is considered to be inefficient or undesirable, while leaving the activity to the private sector may be inappropriate where issues of public policy are concerned. The quasi-government body thus represents a compromise between the constitutional needs of government control and the organizational needs of independence and flexibility associated with private sector organizations.

The growth of QUANGOs may seem surprising in Britain in view of earlier Conservative party pledges to sweep away the bureaucracy which they appeared to represent in the 1970s. At that stage, many, such as electricity boards and gas boards, were converted to PLC status and privatized. Yet the Conservative governments from 1979 onwards have been responsible for a significant increase in their numbers, which had reached 5500 in number by 1994 (Weir and Hall, 1994). In that year they accounted for £46.4 billion of expenditure, equivalent to about one-third of total government expenditure. Many aspects of government have been devolved to QUANGOs. These are some examples:

- National Health Service Trusts
- Registered housing associations
- Grant maintained schools
- Higher education corporations
- Training and Enterprise Councils
- Regulatory bodies (e.g. Oftel, Ofwat and Ofgas)

In addition to large spending organizations such as these, QUANGOs also cover a plethora of advisory bodies such as the Black Country Advisory Panel and the Hearing Aid Council, as well as funding bodies such as the Housing Corporation and the Funding Agency for Schools.

QUANGOs enjoy considerable autonomy from their parent department and the sponsoring Minister has no direct control over the activities of the body, other than making the appointment of the chairman. Thus, the Minister ceases to be answerable to Parliament for the day-to-day activities of a QUANGO, unlike the responsibility that a Minister has in respect of a government department. The responsibilities of QUANGOs vary from being purely advisory to making important policy decisions and allocating large amounts of expenditure. Their income can come from a combination of government grant, precepts from local authorities and charges to customers.

QUANGOS also have important responsibilities at a local level. Following the abolition of Metropolitan County Councils in 1986, residuary bodies were set up to take over some of the county-wide services such as fire and ambulance services which were not reallocated to the Borough Councils.

The main advantage of delegation to QUANGOs is that action can generally be taken much more quickly than may have been the case with a government department, where it would probably have been necessary to receive ministerial approval before action was taken. Ministers may have less time to devote to the details of policy application with which many QUANGOs are often involved, and may also be constrained to a much greater extent by broader considerations of political policy. Being relatively free of day-to-day political interference, QUANGOS are in a better position to maintain a long-term plan free of short-term diversions which may be the result of direct control by a Minister who is subject to the need for short-term political popularity.

Against the advantages of QUANGOs are a number of potential disadvantages, compared with a government department. It is often argued that QUANGOs are not sufficiently accountable to elected representatives for their actions. This can become an important issue where a QUANGO is responsible for developing policy or is a monopoly provider of an essential service. Many have also questioned the actual independence of QUANGOs from government, as many are still dependent on government funding for block grants.

The new breed of QUANGOs running government services are quite different to those that the incoming Conservative government pledged to sweep away in 1979. A major objective of delegation to QUANGOs has been to ensure that services are provided more in line with users' requirements rather than political or operational expediency. High-level appointments to QUANGOs have been made from the private sector with a view to bringing about a cultural change that develops business ethos. For the marketing services industry, the development of QUANGOs has resulted in many opportunities as they increasingly use the services of market research firms, advertising agencies and public relations consultants. However, QUANGOs can easily become unpopular with the public, especially where senior managers are seen paying themselves high salaries as they take 'business-like' decisions to cut back on services that they provide to the public.

7.5   THE EUROPEAN UNION

The European Union (EU), formerly known as the European Community (EC), has its origins in the European Coal and Steel Community. The EC was founded by the Treaty of Rome, signed in 1957 by the original six members of the ECSC—France, West Germany, Italy, Belgium, the Netherlands and Luxembourg. Britain joined the EC in 1972, together with Ireland and Denmark, to be joined by Greece in 1981, Spain and Portugal in 1986 and Austria, Finland and Sweden in 1995. The combined population of EU countries in 1994 was 368 million. Further states are expected to join.

7.5.1   Aims of the EU

The Treaty of Rome initially created a Customs Union and a Common Market. The creation of a Customs Union has involved the introduction of a common external tariff on trade with the rest of the world and the abolition of tariffs between member states. When the United Kingdom joined the EC, tariffs tended to encourage trade with Commonwealth countries at the expense of European countries. In particular, the UK had been able to obtain a source of relatively cheap agricultural produce from Commonwealth countries, but on joining the EC was forced to phase in a common tariff for agricultural products imported from outside the EC.

An important aim of the Treaty of Rome was the creation of a common market in which trade could take place between member states as if it was one country. The implication of a common market is the free movement of trade, labour and capital between member states. So far, it is in agriculture that the most genuinely common market has been created, with a system of common pricing and support payments between all countries and free movement of produce between member states. Further development of a common market has been hampered by a range of non-tariff trade barriers, such as national legislation specifying design standards, the cost and risk of currency exchange and the underlying desire of public authorities to back their own national industries. In principle, the creation of the Single European Market in January 1993 should have removed many of these barriers, but many practical barriers to trade still remain, of which differences in language and cultural traditions are probably the most intractable.

There is considerable debate about the form that future development of the EU should take and in particular, the extent to which there should be political as well as economic union. Many might have hoped that the 1993 Treaty of Maastricht would give the EU a clear sense of direction, but it has opened up a debate about the future of the EU. Recent debate has focused on the following issues:

1. The creation of a common unit of currency has been seen by many as crucial to the development of a single European market, avoiding the cost and uncertainty for business and travellers of having to change currencies for cross-border transactions. A common currency could also allow member states' central banks to reduce their holdings of foreign currency. Opposition to monetary union has been based on economic and political arguments. Economically, a common currency would deny to countries the opportunity to revalue or devalue their currency to suit the needs of their domestic economy. This lack of flexibility implies a political sacrifice, as control of currency is central to government management of the economy.

2. Argument continues about the amount of influence the EU should have in nation states' social and economic policy. For example, the Treaty of Maastricht adopted the Social Chapter which was designed to protect the employment conditions of workers. For the UK government, this would reduce the flexibility of the labour market which it had been seeking to promote and it was allowed to opt out of the provisions of this part of the treaty. The UK government has supported the idea of 'subsidiarity' whereby decisions are taken at the most localised level of government that is compatible with achieving EC objectives. Cynics have, however, pointed out that the British government has not been willing to practice this principle at home, as witnessed by the gradual erosion of the powers of local authorities in favour of central government.

3. Many additional countries have now formally or informally applied to join the EU. There is concern that the arrival of many less-developed economies (such as many Eastern European countries) could put strains on EU budgets. Many have argued that enlargement should allow the EU to become a loose federation of states, rather than a centralizing bureaucracy which many critics claim it has become.

4. The principle of free movement of people across borders remains controversial, in view of the

possibility of large numbers of refugees being admitted by one state and then being automatically allowed to migrate to other member states.

5. Member states still have difficulty formulating a coherent foreign policy for the EU as a whole, as has been seen in the fragmented approach taken towards the wars in former Yugoslavia.

7.5.2   The structure of the EU

The Treaty of Rome (as modified by the Treaty of Maastricht) developed a structure of government whose elements reflect in part the structure of the UK government. The executive (or Cabinet) is provided by the Council of Ministers, the secretariat (or Civil Service) is provided by the European Commission, while the legislature is provided by the European Parliament. The judiciary is represented by the European Court of Justice.

The Treaty of Rome places constraints upon the policies that the institutions of the EU can adopt. The European Court of Justice is able to rule that an action or decision is not in accordance with the Treaty. In some cases, such as competition policy, the Treaty is quite specific, for example Articles 85 and 86 which define the basic approach to be adopted in dealing with cartels and monopoly power. On the other hand, the Treaty says little more on transport policy than that there should be a common policy, giving the community institutions considerable power to develop policies.

The activities of the EU are now directly funded from income received from customs duties and other levies on goods entering the EU from non-member countries. In addition, a value added tax collected by member states on purchases by consumers includes an element of up to 1.45 per cent which is automatically transferred to the EU budget. More recently, a new resource transfer payment between members states and the EU has been introduced which is based on the gross domestic product of each member state. The United Kingdom remains a net contributor to the EU budget.

New legislation is increasingly the result of co-operation between the various institutions of the EC. The process of co-operation is shown in Figure 7.4 and the role of the principal institutions described below.

7.5.3   The Council of Ministers

The Council of Ministers represents the governments of member states and can be regarded as the principal lawmaker of the EU, although it can only act on proposals submitted by the Commission. It has powers to:

- Adopt legislation
- Ratify treaties after consultation with the European parliament
- Ask the commission to undertake studies and to submit legislation
- Delegate executive and legislative powers to the Commission

Each member state sends one Minister to the European Council of Ministers. Which Minister attends will depend on the subject being discussed—for example agriculture Ministers would be sent if the Common Agricultural Policy was being discussed. The Ministers of foreign affairs, of agriculture, and those with budgetary responsibilities meet more frequently, making a senior body within the Council, sometimes called the General Council. The chairmanship or presidency of the Council of Ministers rotates between countries in alphabetical order, with each period of presidency lasting for six months.

The Council of Ministers adopts new legislation either by simple majority, qualified majority or unanimity:

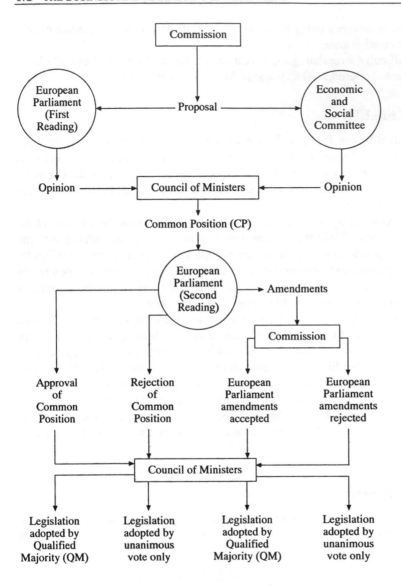

Figure 7.4   The process of co-operation in passing new European legislation

- Simple majority gives each Minister one vote and is used for proposals such as procedural rules for the convening of intergovernmental conferences.
- Qualified majority voting is based on a weighted voting system where member states' votes are roughly proportional to their size and economic strength (see Table 7.1). Qualified majority voting prevents smaller states being consistently outvoted and eliminates the risk of two of the larger member states constituting a blocking majority. A qualified majority is 62 votes out of a total of 87. A blocking minority is 26 votes. Examples of applications of this method of voting include completion of the internal market, the freedom to provide professional services across national borders and measures to free-up the movement of capital within the EU.
- Unanimity is required on issues that are fundamental to individual member states' interests, such as enlargement of the EC, harmonization of taxation and extension of EU powers.

Table 7.1 Voting rights within European Union institutions

Country	Qualified voting rights of EU Council of Ministers	Number of MEPs returned to European Parliament
Germany	10	99
Italy	10	87
United Kingdom	10	87
France	10	87
Spain	8	64
Netherlands	5	31
Belgium	5	25
Greece	5	25
Portugal	5	25
Austria	4	21
Sweden	4	22
Denmark	3	16
Finland	3	16
Ireland	3	15
Luxembourg	2	6
Total	87	626

The Council of Ministers can generally pass laws even if the European Parliament disagrees with them, unlike the practice within the UK system where Ministers must obtain approval of a majority of Members of Parliament. There are two main exceptions to this authority of the Council. Firstly, the European Parliament has power to approve or reject the EU budget (see below). Secondly, the Single European Act introduced a system of legislative co-operation between the Council and Parliament, obliging the Council and the Commission to take Parliament's amendments to proposals into consideration, although a unanimous vote by the Council of Ministers retains ultimate authority.

The Committee of Permanent Representatives (Coreper) complements the work of the Council of Ministers. Because Ministers have responsibilities to their own national governments as well as to the European Union, they cannot give a continuing presence. To make up for this, each member state sends one ambassador to the Committee, which is based in Brussels. Proposals are discussed in Coreper and its subcommittees before they reach Ministers. If Coreper reaches full agreement on the matter, it is empowered to pass it through the Council without further debate, but where disagreement occurs it is left for Ministers to discuss.

7.5.4 The European Commission

Each member state sends one Commissioner to the Commission (the larger members send two), each appointed by the member government for a renewable term of four years. They are supported in their work by a staff of about 14 000 civil servants, divided between 23 directorates-general and mainly based at the Commission's headquarters in Brussels. The Commission is headed by a President. Each Commissioner is given responsibility for a portfolio which could be for a policy area such as transport, or for administrative matters, such as the Commission's relations with the Parliament, while others are given a combination of responsibilities in their portfolio. Unlike the Council of Ministers, all members of the Commission are supposed to act primarily for the benefit of the Union as a whole, rather than the country that they represent. This is spelt out in Article 157 of the Treaty of Rome which states that Commissioners 'shall neither seek nor take instruction from any other body'.

The Commission has an initiation, mediation and implementation role. As an initiator, it is the task of the Commission to draft proposals for legislation which the Council of Ministers has to consider. If the Council does not accept a proposal, it can only alter the draft by a unanimous vote. If unanimity cannot be achieved, the proposal has to go back to the Commission for it to draft a revised proposal which will be acceptable to the Council of Ministers.

As a mediator, the Commission can intervene in disputes between member states to try and find a solution through negotiation. The Commission has frequently acted as mediator in trade disputes between members, avoiding recourse to the European Court of Justice.

As an implementer, the Commission undertakes the day-to-day administration of the EC. This involves monitoring the activities of member states to ensure that they do not conflict with community policy. In addition, the Commission implements community policies such as the Regional Development Fund and Common Agricultural Policy.

7.5.5   The European Parliament

Unlike the UK parliament, the European Parliament is primarily consultative and has relatively little power. Its main function is to monitor the activities of other EU institutions. It can give an opinion on Commission proposals but only has powers to amend, adopt or reject legislation, especially the EU budget. It also has the theoretical power to dismiss the entire Commission, for which a censure motion must be passed by a two-thirds majority of Members. Although it can dismiss the entire Commission, the Parliament has no control over the selection of new Commissioners to replace those who have been dismissed. It does not yet have the power to initiate and enact legislation.

Members of the European Parliament are now directly elected by the constituents of each country. Parliament has a total of 626 members (MEPs), of which 87 represent United Kingdom constituencies, with other countries returning members roughly in proportion to their populations, as shown in Table 7.1. The European Parliament generally meets in Strasbourg, but Parliamentary Committee meetings are held in Brussels and in Luxembourg, where the Parliament's Secretariat is mainly based. Members of the European Parliament increasingly belong to political rather than national groupings (e.g. the British Conservative MEPs sit in the European People's Party).

7.5.6   The European Court of Justice

The supreme legislative body of the EU is provided by the Court of Justice. Article 164 of the Treaty of Rome gave the Court the task of 'ensuring that the law is observed in the interpretation and implementation of the Treaty'. It is the final arbiter in all matters of interpreting Community Treaties and rules on disputes between member states, between member states and the Commission and between the Commission and business organizations, individuals or EU officials. Although the Court can condemn violations of the Treaty by member governments, it has no sanctions against them except goodwill. The European Court of Justice can investigate complaints that the Commission has acted beyond its powers and, if upheld, can annul decisions of the Commission.

The European Court of Justice is composed of 15 judges, assisted by 9 advocates-general. Each is appointed by common agreement between the 15 member states on the basis of their qualifications and impartiality, for a renewable six year term of office. Members of the Court must put European interests before national interests. The Court can be called upon to settle disputes where the persuasion and negotiations of the Commission have failed to yield results. For example, in the area of competition policy, the Commission may by decision forbid an anti-competitive practice or impose a fine. The companies concerned can appeal to the European Court of Justice for the Decision to be set aside. In one case, several dye producers appealed to the European Court of Justice against the fines imposed on them for an alleged price cartel. The Court has also been called upon to give its judgement on whether British retailers seeking to open on Sundays could claim that the Shops Act 1950 is in conflict with the Treaty of Rome by restricting trade.

7.5.7 Relationship between EU and United Kingdom government

A distinction needs to be drawn between primary and secondary legislation of the EU. Primary legislation is contained in the Treaties of Rome and Maastricht and takes precedence over national legislation, although national legislation may be required to implement it. Primary legislation can only be altered by an intergovernmental conference of all members. Secondary legislation is made by the Council of Ministers and the Commission under authority delegated to them by the Treaties. Secondary legislation affects member states in several forms.

- *Regulations* automatically form part of the law of member states and apply directly to every individual in the EU. They give rights and duties to individuals that national courts must recognize.
- *Directives* are mandatory instructions to member states who must take steps to implement them through national legislation. For example, national laws concerning vehicle safety vary from state to state and as a result trade across frontiers may be impeded. One solution has been to harmonize standards between all member states by means of a directive. The directive will require member sates to amend their national legislation governing the design of cars. Individuals will then have to obey the modified national law.
- *Decisions* of the EU are directly binding on the specific individuals or organizations to whom they are addressed, as where the Commission intervenes in a proposed merger between organizations.

7.5.8 Effects of EU membership on UK marketers

The EU is having an increasingly important effect on marketers in the United Kingdom. The relationship between the company and its customers is increasingly being influenced by EU regulations and directives, for example in the provision of safety features in cars or the labelling of foods. The influence extends to the relationship between the firm and the public at large, as where the EU passes directives affecting advertising standards and pollution controls. The marketer needs to monitor proposed EU legislation not only to spot possible changes in national legislation when it is eventually implemented in the United Kingdom, but also to lobby to bring about a desired change in EU law. To an increasing extent, lobbying of the UK parliamentary process is becoming less effective as the United Kingdom is bound to implement legislation emanating from the EU.

The extent to which the Single European market legislation (and the European Economic Area which extends this to most former European Free Trade Association (EFTA) members) will affect marketers is open to debate. The EU has already had the effect of removing tariff barriers within the Community and progress is being made on EU legislation specifying common product design standards. To be fully effective, the Single European market will need much greater harmonization of fiscal policies and monetary union. The latter cannot be brought about without a change in primary legislation. No amount of legislation is likely to overcome the hidden barriers to trade provided by language and by engrained market characteristics such as the UK practice of driving on the left and using electrical plugs that are not used elsewhere in Continental Europe.

Nevertheless, firms are increasingly seeing Europe as one market and designing standardized products which appeal to consumers in a number of EU states. Many would argue that overseas investors, especially American firms, have always regarded Europe as one market and developed products as varied as soft drinks and cars to satisfy the whole European market.

Debate continues about the effects that the UK's exemption from the Social Chapter of the Treaty of Maastricht will have on UK marketers. It has been argued that this will give British firms a competitive advantage compared to other EU firms who may be forced to pay higher levels of minimum wages. As evidence of this, many would point to a number of multinational firms who have relocated factories from mainland Europe to the United Kingdom.

7.6 SUPRANATIONAL GOVERNMENTAL ORGANIZATIONS

National governments' freedom of action is further constrained by international agreements and membership of international organizations. In general, although the Treaties of Rome and Maastricht impose duties on the UK government which it is obliged to follow, membership of other supranational organizations is voluntary and does not have binding authority on the UK government.

Probably the most important organization which affects UK government policy is the United Nations (UN). Its General and Security Councils are designed as fora in which differences between countries can be resolved through negotiation rather than force. In the field of international trade, the UN has sought to encourage freedom of trade through the United Nations Conference on Trade and Development (UNCTAD). In matters of national security, the United Kingdom is a member of the North Atlantic Treaty Organization (NATO) whose role is changing following the end of the 'Cold War'.

Because the importance to the United Kingdom of international treaties and organizations lies to such a great extent in their benefits for international trade, they are considered in more detail in Chapter 12.

7.7 INFLUENCES ON GOVERNMENT POLICY FORMATION

Political parties were described earlier as organizations that people belong to in order to influence government policy, generally over a range of issues. Political parties aim to work within the political system, for example by having members elected as MPs or local councillors. A distinction can be drawn between political parties and pressure groups or interest groups. These seek to change policy in accordance with members' interests, generally advancing a relatively narrow cause. Members of pressure groups generally work from outside the political system and do not become part of the political establishment.

7.7.1 Pressure groups

Pressure groups can be divided into a number of categories. In the first place there is a division between those who are permanently fighting for a general cause and those who are set up to achieve a specific objective and are dissolved when this objective is met—or there no longer seems any prospect of changing the situation. Pressure groups set up to fight specific new road schemes fit into this category.

Pressure groups can also be classified according to their functions. *Sectional* groups exist to promote the common interests of their members over a wide range of issues. Trades unions and employers associations fall into this category. They represent their members' views to government on diverse issues such as proposed employment legislation, import controls and vocational training. This type of pressure group frequently offers other benefits to members such as legal representation for individual members and the dissemination of information to members. *Promotional* groups, on the other hand, are established to fight for specific causes, such as nuclear disarmament which is represented by CND.

Not all pressure groups represent a widespread body of grass roots public opinion. Businesses also frequently join pressure groups as a means of influencing government legislative proposals that will affect their industry sector. An example of a powerful commercial pressure group is the British Road Federation, which represents companies with interests in road construction and lobbies government to increase expenditure on new road building.

Pressure groups can influence government policy using three main approaches.

1. The first, propaganda, can be used to create awareness of the group and its cause. This can be aimed directly at policy formers, or indirectly by appealing to the constituents of policy formers to apply direct pressure themselves. This is essentially an impersonal form of mass communication.
2. A second option is to try and represent the views of the group directly to policy formers on a one-to-one basis. Policy formers frequently welcome representations that they may see as preventing bigger problems or confrontations arising in the future. Links between pressure groups and government often become institutionalized, such as where the Department of Transport routinely seeks the views of the Automobile Association and RAC on proposals to change road traffic legislation. Where no regular contacts exist, pressure groups can be represented by giving evidence before a government appointed enquiry or by approaching sympathetic MPs or by hiring the services of a professional lobbyist.
3. A third approach used by pressure groups is to carry out research and to supply information. This has the effect of increasing public awareness of the organization and usually has a valuable propaganda function. The British Road Federation frequently supplies MPs with comparative road statistics purporting to show that the government should be spending more money on road building.

Pressure groups are most effective where they apply pressure in a low key manner, for example where they are routinely consulted for their views. Lobbying of MPs—which combines elements of all three methods described above—has become increasingly important over recent years. Yet it is not only national government to which pressure groups apply their attention—local authorities are frequently the target of pressure groups over issues of planning policy or the provision of welfare services. Increasingly, pressure is also being applied at the EU level. Again, the European Commission regularly consults some groups while other groups apply direct pressure to members of the Commission.

Marketers have achieved numerous triumphs in attempting to influence the political environment in which they operate. The pressure group representing the tobacco industry—the Tobacco Advisory Council—has had a significant effect in countering the pressure applied by the anti-tobacco lobby, represented by Action on Smoking Health. Anti-smoking legislation has been considerably watered down as a result.

Pressure groups are increasingly crossing national boundaries to reflect the influence of international governmental institutions such as the EU and the increasing influence of multinational business organizations. Both industrial and consumer pressure groups have been formed at a multinational level to counter these influences—a good example of the latter is Greenpeace.

The media   The media—press, radio and television—not only spreads awareness of political issues but also influences policy and decision making by setting the political agenda and influencing public opinion. The broadcast media in the United Kingdom must by law show balance in their coverage of political events, but the press is often more openly partisan. Campaigns undertaken by the press frequently reflect the background of their owners—the *Daily Telegraph* is more likely to support the causes of deregulation in an industry while the *Guardian* will be more likely to put forward the case for government spending on essential public services. It is often said that *The Times* and the BBC Radio 4 *Today* programme set the political agenda for the day ahead.

CASE STUDY—BUS INDUSTRY RESPONDS TO SHIFT
IN POLITICAL ENVIRONMENT

The provision of bus services in Britain has been significantly influenced by the nature of the political environment, both at a central and local government level. The bus industry can be used to illustrate many of the issues raised in this chapter, especially the changing attitude at central government level towards regulation of economic activity and at a local level to the changing role of local government. In this changing political environment, the role of marketing has been transformed. In a sense the political environment has turned full circle, from reliance on free market forces until the 1920s, strict regulation until the 1980s, followed by a return to a political obsession with competitive markets.

The early 1920s saw large numbers of small entrepreneurs operating in competition with each other, resulting in sometimes wasteful and dangerous competitive practices. The dominant political attitude shifted during the 1920s away from a pure *laissez-faire* approach to one where state intervention in the economy was becoming more acceptable. Against this changing background, government was able to recognize that public transport was an important public service and passed the Road Traffic Act 1930. This required all bus routes to be licensed; route licences were strictly limited in number and, in general, a licence would only be granted if the applicant could prove that there was unsatisfied demand for a service. Route licences gave the holder substantial monopoly power and large bus operating companies emerged during the 1930s by acquiring the licences of their smaller competitors. The companies thus acquired territorial monopolies which made it even more difficult for a small company to prove the need for a new service and thereby acquire a route licence. In these conditions, bus companies tended to be production rather than marketing led. A further recognition that public transport was an essential public service came when a large section of the bus industry was nationalized by the Labour government in 1948.

By the 1960s bus operation had ceased to be profitable outside the main corridors of movement, mainly due to increasing levels of car ownership. Faced with a deterioration in the quantity and quality of bus services, the Labour government of the late 1960s again intervened with the acquisition of the largest private sector group of companies, and the subsequent formation of the National Bus Company and Scottish Bus Group. These were given responsibility for running most of the large bus operators outside the major cities. The two companies were given strict financial rather than social objectives, although government did later intervene in a manner that appeared to make the companies an instrument of wider government policy. For example, they had been asked to keep fare increases down to help the government's anti-inflation policy.

Local authorities in a number of areas had for many years operated their own bus fleets for various reasons. Making profits to help keep the level of rates charged to ratepayers down was one objective, but, in addition, local authorities provided bus services out of civic pride and to ensure that a high standard of public service was provided. Local government legislation frequently prevented them from operating outside their own boundaries. By the 1960s, local authority bus operations had also become generally unprofitable. They were often allowed to lose money if councillors decided that the service being provided justified being subsidized out of rates income.

By the 1970s, a highly regulated system of route licensing and companies having large territorial monopolies resulted in the business environment becoming increasingly production rather than marketing orientated. Promotion was aimed almost entirely at existing users, providing basic information rather than trying to create a favourable image among potential users. Faced with an inelastic demand bus companies would set fares as high as politically possible with the regulatory Traffic Commissioners. Innovation in new products was nearly always reactive rather than proactive. Most innovation was aimed at cutting production costs, such as reducing the need to employ conductors through one-person operation, rather than meeting the needs of consumers, such as providing faster journey times or a reliable service.

At the same time as the market for scheduled bus services appeared to be going into decline, the market for contract hire by schools, factories and private groups remained buoyant. In this market there were no quantity restrictions on operators, only the quality controls that applied equally to operators of scheduled bus services. The market was dominated by a large number of small firms aggressively competing against each other on price and the quality of service provided. It would be difficult for a production-orientated company to survive in this environment for long.

By the 1980s the question was being asked whether the unregulated environment that had encouraged a marketing orientation in the contract service sector could also be applied to the scheduled services sector to achieve the same effect. The traditional argument against deregulation was that licence holders who had a territorial monopoly provided some element of social service. They used profits generated on one route or at one time of day to cross-subsidize loss-making routes or less-profitable evening and weekend Sunday services. The National Bus Company used this argument to defend itself, even though it had been given clearly defined profit rather than social goals by the government.

The political environment for bus operators changed significantly during the 1980s. The first change was brought about by the Conservative government's ideological belief that free and unregulated markets were inherently better than regulation, which was presumed to stifle innovation. The government therefore abolished the need for route licences in most parts of the country. Any company could now operate a bus service subject to satisfying quality criteria. In addition, subsidies from local authorities to provide socially necessary but unprofitable bus services were put out to competitive tendering, rather than being allocated to the existing licence holder.

The second major change brought about was the restructuring and gradual dismantling of public sector bus operations. The ideology of the time considered that the state was bad at providing marketable goods and services compared to the private sector. Where a social service was considered desirable, this should be explicitly identified by policy makers in government and satisfied by market mechanisms. The first step was the breaking up of the National Bus Company and sale to the private sector. Many of the individual companies of which it was comprised were sold on

favourable terms to their management and employees, fulfilling another wish of the Conservative government of the late 1980s— widespread capitalism. Local authorities, which had frequently operated their bus fleets as a quasi-social service, were forced to restructure their operations by forming limited companies to which a board of directors was appointed with a view to eventual sale to the private sector.

Changes in the political environment had totally transformed the market for bus services during the 1980s. Marketing tools that had been used by the fast-moving consumer goods sector for many years, but ignored by this section of the bus industry, became widely used. Tactical pricing was used aggressively to gain market share, particularly by new entrants to a route who frequently made no charge to attract initial custom. Market-led new service developments occurred, such as high-frequency minibus services. Much more attention was paid to product quality, including reliability, availability of service information, training of staff and the appearance of vehicles. Corporate identity increasingly took as its starting point the values of the target customers rather than those of management.

Local monopolies of bus services had until the 1980s been seen as beneficial by the government, recognizing the implicit public service obligations of licence holders. However, in a sudden about-turn, bus operators were now subject to the same vetting for anticompetitive practices as most other industries. The Office of Fair Trading was constantly investigating claims that companies were trying to drive their competitors off the road using practices that were reminiscent of the 1920s. The powers of the OFT were weak and investigations often took a long time, allowing competitors to be driven out of a market in the meantime.

The early years of deregulation were characterized by a lot of competition between small- and medium-sized firms. However, by the mid 1990s, consolidation of the industry was beginning to create large companies, such as Stagecoach and First Bus, which had significant local monopoly power. As numbers of passengers continued to fall and fares continued to rise, cynics argued that a publicly regulated monopoly had effectively been replaced by private unregulated monopolies.

QUESTIONS

1. Summarize the arguments for and against regulation of the bus industry.
2. To what extent has government policy towards the bus industry reflected the dominant political ideology of the time?
3. Briefly summarize the main marketing implications of a change from regulation to free competition for bus services.

REVIEW QUESTIONS

1. Against the background of a world-wide trend towards privatization and de-regulation, prepare a report for an Industry Association of your choice, assessing the potential threats and opportunities arising for your sector.
   (CIM Marketing Environment Examination, December 1994, Q.5)
2. Prepare arguments, for and against, greater control being exercised over business and marketing practices by government.
   (CIM Marketing Environment Examination, June 1995, Q.9, part i)
3. Briefly identify the main areas of attention which the Marketing Manager of a UK bicycle manufacturer is likely to give to his or her political environment.
4. For a newspaper lobbying against government proposals to impose value added tax on newspaper sales, identify the key points within the government system at which lobbying could be applied.
5. For a British manufacturing company, briefly summarize the principal problems and opportunities presented by the development of closer economic and political union within the EU.
6. What measures can a large multinational business take to monitor the political environment in its various operating areas?

REFERENCES

Weir, S. and Hall, W. (eds) (1994) 'Ego-Trip: Extra-governmental Organizations in the UK and Their Accountability', Charter 88 Trust, London.

FURTHER READING

Bryne, T. (1994) *Local Government in Britain*, 6th edn, Penguin, Harmondsworth.
Ernst, J. (1994) *Whose Utility? The Social Impact of Public Utility Privatization and Regulation in Britain*, Open University Press, Buckingham.
Farnham, D. and Morton, S. (eds) (1993) *Managing the New Public Services*, Macmillan, Basingstoke.
Fenwick, J., Shaw, K. and Foreman, A. (1994) 'Managing Competition in UK Local Government', *International Journal of Public Sector Management*, vol. 7, no. 6, pp. 4–14.
Hood, C. (1991) 'A Public Management for all Seasons', *Public Administration*, vol. 69 (Spring), pp. 3–19.
Richardson, J. J. (ed.) (1993) *Pressure Groups*, Oxford University Press, Oxford.
Shaw, K., Fenwick, J. and Foreman, A. (1993) 'Client and Contractor Roles in Local Government: Some Observations in Managing the Split', *Local Government Policy Making*, vol. 20, no. 2, pp. 22–7.
Walsh, K. and Davis, H. (1993) *Competition and Service: The Impact of the Local Government Act 1988*, Department of the Environment, HMSO, London.
Wilson, K. G. (1990) *Interest Groups*, Blackwell, Oxford.

CHAPTER EIGHT

THE SOCIAL AND DEMOGRAPHIC ENVIRONMENT

OBJECTIVES

After reading this chapter, you should understand:

● The processes by which individuals develop distinct social and cultural values
● The concepts of social class, life-styles, reference groups, family structure and culture
● The effects of changing social and cultural values on consumers' purchase decisions
● The impact of demographic change on the marketing of goods and services
● Approaches to analysing the demographic structure and trends of a population

8.1 MARKETING AND THE EFFECTS OF SOCIAL STRUCTURES

It is very easy for an individual to take for granted the way they live. Furthermore, young people may imagine that people have always lived their lives that way. Taking one year with the next, change may seem quite imperceptible, but when life today is compared with what it was like 10 years ago, noticeable changes begin to appear. If comparisons are made with 20 or 50 years ago, it may seem like two entirely different societies are being compared. Simply by looking at an old movie, big differences become apparent, such as attitudes to the family, leisure activities and the items commonly purchased by consumers.

Change in society is also brought about by changes in its composition. Much recent attention has been given in many Western European countries to the effects of an ageing population on society. Taken to an extreme, some commentators have seen major problems ahead as an increasingly large dependent population has to be kept by a proportionately smaller economically active group in society. Some see this as challenging basic attitudes that individuals have towards the community and the family. At the very least, marketers should be concerned about the effects of demographic change on patterns of demand for goods and services and the availability of a work-force to produce those goods and services.

It is bad enough not to recognize social change that has happened in the past. It is much worse to fail to read the signs about social change that is happening now and which could have profound effects on the goods and services that people will buy in the future.

This chapter begins by examining what can loosely be described as a society's social and cultural values. These are what make people in the United Kingdom different from what they were 20 years ago, or different from what people in Algeria or Indonesia are today. Social and cultural differences between countries focus on differences in attitudes, family structures and the pattern of interaction between individuals. Marketers should understand the consequences of what may appear nebulous social changes for the types of things that consumers buy.

8.1.1   Social influences on behaviour

The way an individual behaves as a consumer is a result of their unique physical and psychological make-up on the one hand, and a process of learning from experience, on the other. The debate about the relative importance of nature and nurture is familiar to social psychologists. This chapter is concerned with the effects of learned behaviour on individuals' buying behaviour.

An individual learns norms of behaviour from a number of sources (Figure 8.1):

1. The dominant cultural values of the society in which they live
2. The social class to which they belong
3. Important reference groups, in particular the family

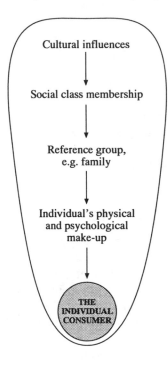

Figure 8.1   Factors affecting the socialization process

Culture can be seen as an umbrella within which social class systems exist and reference groups exert influence on individuals or groups of individuals. The following sections consider the effects of each of these influences.

8.2   THE CULTURAL ENVIRONMENT

The Oxford English Dictionary defines culture as a '… trained and refined state of understanding, manners and tastes'. Central to culture is the concept of learning and passing down of values from one generation to the next. A culture's values are expressed in a complex set of beliefs, customs and symbols which help to identify individuals as members of one particular culture rather than another. The following are typical manifestations of cultural identity:

- Shared attitudes, for example towards the role of women or children in society
- Abstract symbols and rituals, which can be seen in historic cultures by such events as harvest festivals and maypole dancing, and in more modern times by support for local football teams
- Material manifestations, for example the literature and art of a culture or, more prosaically, the style of decorations used in private houses

It is common to distinguish between 'core' and 'secondary' cultural values:

- Core cultural values tend to be very enduring over time. In Britain, for example, the acceptance of monogamy represents a core belief and one that very few people would disagree with.
- Secondary cultural values are more susceptible to change over time. While there may be a core belief in marriage, this does not prevent changes in attitudes towards the form that marriage should take, as is evident from the growing incidence of divorce and the increasing number of single parent families. It is shifts in these secondary cultural values that are particularly important for marketers to monitor.

8.2.1   Subcultures

It is difficult to talk about a uniform culture for a society, because most cultures contain distinctive subcultures. The most obvious manifestations of subcultures are based on religious and ethnic differences, so in Britain it is common to talk about distinctive subcultures associated with immigrants from Asia and Ireland, for example. Other bases for defining subcultures include age (the values of young people today are typically quite different from elderly people and from young people of 50 years ago), area of residence (e.g. many very affluent or very poor areas become associated with distinctive attitudes and patterns of behaviour) and groups who share a common role in life (e.g. distinctive subcultures for criminals and the aristocracy).

The United Kingdom is becoming an increasingly culturally diverse society. This is partly related to increasing levels of wealth which allows individuals greater freedom to choose their own life-style and means of self-expression. However, more importantly, cultural diversity arises from the growing numbers of people from overseas cultures who have settled in the country. Immigrants bring with them a distinctive set of cultural values and adapting to the values of the host country can be a difficult task for some. A lack of understanding from members of the host country may cause them to be seen as lazy, industrious or lacking in humour by the standards of the host culture, but they may nevertheless be perfectly normal by the standards of their home culture. Where members of ethnic minorities are concentrated into distinct areas (such as certain suburbs of London, Leicester and Bradford), their traditional cultural values may be strengthened and prolonged by mutual support and the presence of an infrastructure (such as places of worship and specialized shops) to support the values of the culture.

The presence of concentrations of ethnic subcultures in a town presents opportunities for businesses who cater for distinctive cultural preferences. In many towns catering for people of Asian origin, these include Halal butchers, bureaux for arranged marriages and travel agents specializing in travel to India.

Members of ethnic minorities have contributed to the diversity of goods and services available to consumers in the host country. The large number of Indian restaurants in Britain, for example, can be attributed to the entrepreneurial skills of immigrants, while many food products (such as kebabs and Chinese food) have followed the example of immigrants.

8.2.2   Effects of culture on marketing

It is crucial for marketers to fully appreciate the cultural values of a society, especially where an organization is seeking to do business in a country that is quite different from its own. The possible consequences of failing to do this can be illustrated by the following examples:

- When McDonalds entered the UK market, it initially found hostility from the British, who did not appreciate the brash, scripted 'Have a nice day' mentality of its staff. The company subsequently adapted its style of business to cater for British preferences.
- When Sock Shop opened stores in New York, it failed to appreciate the violent nature of an important subculture in the city and lost large amounts of money in armed raids
- Many UK businesses have set up operations overseas and gone about business in an open and above-board manner, only to find that corruption and the use of bribes is endemic in the local culture and essential for business success.

Cultural sensitivity affects many aspects of marketing planning, for example:

- Understanding processes of buyer behaviour (for example, the role of men in buying routine household goods varies between countries, leading sellers to adjust their product specification and promotional efforts to meet the needs of the most influential members of the buying unit).
- Some products may be unacceptable in a culture and must be adapted to be culturally acceptable (e.g. the original formulation for McDonald's 'Big Mac' is unacceptable in Moslem cultures).
- Symbols associated with products, such as the design and colour of packaging, may be unacceptable in some cultures (e.g. the colour white is associated with pureness in most West European cultures, but in others it is associated with bereavement).
- Distribution channel decisions are partly a reflection of cultural attitudes and not just economics and land use. Retailers and wholesalers may be seen as a vital part of a culture's social infrastructure. Although it may appear economically rational for shoppers to buy in bulk, small local shops opening long hours may be seen by consumers as an extension of their pantry. Individuals may feel a sense of loyalty to their suppliers. Japan, despite being an economically prosperous nation, is characterized by a complex range of small retailers and wholesalers and it is not surprising therefore that the American toy retailer 'Toys "R" Us' had difficulty breaking into the Japanese market.
- Advertising messages do not translate easily between different cultures, reflecting culturally influenced standards of what is considered decent and appropriate.
- Methods of procuring sales vary between cultures. In some Far Eastern countries, it is essential to establish a trusting relationship with a buyer before the buyer will even consider placing an order. Sometimes, it is essential to personally know the key decision maker or to offer a bribe, which is considered routine business practice in some cultures.

Even in home markets, business organizations should understand the processes of gradual cultural change and be prepared to satisfy the changing needs of consumers. The following are examples of contemporary cultural change in Western Europe and the possible responses of marketers:

- Women are increasingly being seen as equal to men in terms of employment expectations and household responsibilities. This is reflected in the observation that women made up 45 per cent of the UK paid work-force in 1994, compared with 37 per cent in 1971. Examples of marketing responses include variants of cars designed to meet women' needs and ready prepared meals which relieve working women of their traditional role in preparing household meals.
- Greater life expectancy is leading to an ageing of the population and a shift to an increasingly 'elderly' culture. This is reflected in product design which reflects durability rather than fashionability.
- Leisure is becoming an increasingly important part of many peoples' lives and marketers have responded with a wide range of leisure-related goods and services.
- Increasing concern for the environment is reflected in a variety of 'green' consumer products.

There has been much recent discussion about the concept of 'cultural convergence', referring to an apparent decline in differences between cultures. It has been argued that basic human needs are universal in nature and, in principle, capable of satisfaction with universally similar solutions. Companies have been keen to pursue this possibility in order to achieve economies of scale in producing homogeneous products for global markets. There is some evidence of firms achieving this, for example the world-wide success of Coca-Cola and MacDonalds. In the case of fast food, many Western chains have capitalized on deep-seated habits in some Far Eastern countries of eating from small hawkers' facilities by offering the same basic facility in a clean and hygienic environment.

The desire of a subculture in one country to imitate the values of those in another culture has also contributed to cultural convergence. This is nothing new. During the Second World War, many individuals in Western Europe sought to follow the American life-style, and nylon stockings from the United States became highly sought after cultural icons by some groups. The same process is at work today in many developing countries where some groups seek to identify with Western cultural values through the purchases they make. Today, however, improved media communications allow messages about cultural values to be disseminated much more rapidly. The development of satellite television and the Internet can only hasten the process of creating shared world-wide values.

It can be argued that business organizations are not only responding to cultural change, they are also significant contributors to that change. The development of global brands backed up by global advertising campaigns has contributed to an increasing uniformity in goods and services offered throughout the world. In some countries, this has been seen as a threat to the sense of local identity which culture represents. Governments have therefore taken measures in an attempt to slow down this process of cultural homogenization. This has achieved significance in France where legislation requires the use of the French language—an important means of creating identity for any culture—in packaging and advertising for products. Attempts by firms to homogenize cultural values can meet with more widespread public resistance. One of the aims of Islamic Fundamentalism is to preserve traditional values against domination by Western cultural values.

8.2.3 Social class

In most societies, divisions exist between groups of people in terms of their access to privileges and status within that society. In some social systems, such as the Hindu Caste system, the group that an individual belongs to exerts influence from birth and it is very difficult for the individual to change between groups. Western societies have class systems in which individuals are divided into one of a number of classes. Although the possibilities for individuals to move between social classes in Western countries is generally greater than the possibilities of movement open to a member of a Caste system, class values tend to be passed down through families.

While some may have visions of a 'classless' society which is devoid of divisions in status and privileges, the reality is that divisions exist in most societies and are likely to persist. It is common in Western societies to attribute individuals with belonging to groups that have been given labels such as 'working class' or 'middle class'. This emotional language of class is not particularly helpful to marketers who need a more measurable basis for describing differences within society.

Why do marketers need to know about the class to which an individual belongs? The basic idea of a classification system is to identify groups who share common attitudes and behaviour patterns and access to resources. This can translate into similar spending patterns. There are, for example, many goods and services that are most heavily bought by people who can be described as 'working class', such as Lada cars, the *Daily Star* newspaper and betting services, while others are more often associated with 'upper class' purchasers, such as Jaguar cars, the *Financial Times* and investment management services.

Marketers also need to take note of the class structure of society. As the size of each class changes, so market segments, which are made up of people who are similar in some important respects, also change. In the United Kingdom during the 1960s and 1970s it has been observed that a lot of people were moving into the 'middle classes'. The effects of taxation, the welfare state and access to education had flattened the class structure of society. Thus, in terms of selling cars, there was a very large demand for mainstream middle-of-the-road cars. However, during the 1980s, both the upper and lower classes tended to grow in what had become a more polarized society. In terms of car sales, there was a growing demand for luxury cars such as Jaguars and BMWs at one end of the market and cheaper cars such as Ladas and Skodas at the other.

It is also useful to study the extent to which individuals are able to move from one class to another. In some societies, such as those with a Caste system, it is almost impossible for an individual to change their class in society. In West European countries, there is a belief by many that people can move around the class system on the basis of their efforts. The very fact that it is seen as possible to move classes may encourage people to see the world in a different way from that which has been induced in them during their years of socialization.

8.2.4   Measuring social class

The aim of measurements of social class is to provide a measure that encapsulates differences between individuals in terms of their type of occupation, income level, educational background and attitudes to life, among other factors. There are three theoretical approaches to measuring social class:

1. *By self-measurement* Researchers could ask an individual which of a number of possible classes they belong to. This approach has a number of theoretical advantages for marketers, because how an individual actually sees him or herself is often a more important determinant of behaviour than some objective measure. If people see themselves as working class, they are probably proud of the fact and will choose products and brands that accord with their own self-image. The danger of this approach is that many people tend to self-select themselves for the middle class category. In one self-assessment study, over two-thirds of the sample described themselves as 'middle class'.
2. *By objective approaches* These involve the use of measurable indicators about a person, such as their occupation, education and spending habits, as a basis for class determination.
3. *By asking third parties* This combines the objective approach of indicators described above with a subjective assessment of an individual's behaviour and attitudes.

Social scientists have traditionally used the second of these approaches as a basis for class definition, largely on account of its objectivity and relative ease of measurement. However, marketers recognize that an individual's attitudes can be crucial in determining buying behaviour, so have been keen to introduce more subjective and self-assessed bases for classification.

One of the most frequently used objective bases for social classification is the system adopted by the Institute of Practitioners in Advertising (IPA). It uses an individual's occupation as a basis for classification, on the basis that occupation is closely associated with many aspects of a person's attitudes and behaviour. The classes defined range from A to E (Table 8.1).

Of course, any attempt to reduce the multidimensional concept of class to a single measure is bound to be an oversimplification which leads to limited usefulness of the measure for marketers. A person's occupation is not necessarily a good indicator of their buying behaviour. For example, the owner of a large scrap metal business and a bishop would probably be put in the same class group, but there are likely to be very significant differences in their spending patterns and the way they pass their leisure time. Nevertheless, the classification system described above is very widely used. Newspapers regularly analyse their readership in terms of membership of these groups and go out of their way to show how many of the highly prized A/B readers they have.

Table 8.1 IPA basis for social classification

Class category	Occupation
A	Higher managerial, administrative or professional
B	Intermediate managerial, administrative or professional
C1	Supervisory or clerical, and junior managerial, administrative or professional
C2	Skilled manual workers
D	Semi- and unskilled manual workers
E	State pensioners or widows (no other earners),casual or lower grade workers, or long-term unemployed

An alternative approach which is being adopted by many marketers is to redefine the idea of class by basing it on where an individual lives. A lot of research has shown a correlation between where a person lives and their buying behaviour. The type of house and its location says much more about an individual than occupation alone can. Income, the size of the family unit, attitudes towards city life/ country living as well as occupation are closely related to residence. The classification of individuals in this way has come to be known as geodemographic analysis. Perhaps the best-known geodemographic classification system is the ACORN system (standing for 'a classification of residential neighbourhoods') developed by CACI Systems Ltd. On the basis of postcodes, individuals are allocated to one of a number of categories. The following are examples of just three of the groups defined by ACORN:

Group	Description
A	Better-off rural areas (sometimes likened to 'Ambridge')
B	Larger houses in suburban areas (likened to 'Brookside')
C	Smaller houses in urban areas (likened to 'Coronation Street')

This is a much more scientific approach to measuring classes. By analysing a lot of sales data from people in each postcode area, it is possible to build up a good picture of the life-style associated with each classification. It is also possible to see how the distribution of the population between different classifications changes over time. For example, it has become evident that more people are moving into the B category defined above.

8.3 LIFE-STYLES AND ATTITUDES

Many marketers have argued that traditional indicators of social class are of little relevance to understanding buyer behaviour. Instead of monitoring changes in such indicators, an analysis of changing attitudes is considered to be more useful. Changes in attitudes may be behaviourally manifested by changes in life-styles.

8.3.1   Life-styles

Life-style analysis seeks to segment the population into groups based on distinctive patterns of behaviour. It is possible for two people carrying out an identical occupation to have two very different life-styles that would not be apparent if marketers segmented markets solely on the basis of occupation. Consequently, product development and marketing communications have often been designed to appeal to specific life-style groups. This type of analysis can be very subjective and quantification of numbers in each category within a population at best can only be achieved through a small sample survey. Life-style segments tend to be descriptive, which may in itself help in defining target markets. However, gaining knowledge of the current composition and geographical distribution of life-style segments is much more difficult than monitoring occupation-based segments, for which data are regularly collected by government and private sector organizations.

Because of their subjectivity, there is a wide variety of life-style segmentation models which tend to reflect the needs of the companies that created them. One model developed by Young and Rubicom talks about four life-style groups to which members of a population can be allocated:

- *Conformers*, comprising the bulk of the population who typically may live in a suburban semi-detached house, drive a Ford Escort, shop at Sainsburys and book a Thomsons package holiday.
- *Aspirers*, a smaller group who are ambitious, innovative and keen to surround themselves with the trappings of success. This group may typically live in a mews house, drive a GTI car, shop at a trendy clothes store and take adventure holidays.
- *Controllers*, by contrast, are comfortable in the knowledge that they have made it in life and do not feel the need to flaunt their success. They are more likely to live in a comfortable detached house, drive a Ford Scorpio, shop at Marks and Spencers and book their holiday through the local travel agent they trust.
- *Reformers* have a vision of how life could be improved for everybody in society. At home, they may be enthusiastic about DIY and energy conservation. They may see their car more as a means of transport than a status symbol and buy own-label brands at Sainsburys.

Of course, these are ideal types, and very few people will precisely meet these descriptions. However, they are a useful starting point for trying to understand who it is that a company is targeting. The numbers in each category have undoubtedly risen and fallen in the recent past. Aspirers seemed to appear in great numbers in Britain in the boom times of the 1980s, but have become less conspicuous since then.

Many more informal, almost tongue-in-cheek bases for segmenting life-style groups are commonly used. It is common, for example, to talk about life-styles that have been labelled Yuppies (young, upwardly mobile professionals), Dinkys (dual income, no kids yet) and Bobos (burnt out, but opulent), to name but a few. New descriptions emerge to describe new life-styles. Again, these classifications are not at all scientific, but they give marketers a chance to describe target markets.

8.3.2   Attitudes

Attitudes should be distinguished from the behaviour that may be manifested in a particular life-style. An individual may have an attitude about a subject, but people keep their thoughts to themselves, possibly in fear of the consequences if behaviour does not conform with generally accepted norms. A man may think that it should be acceptable for men to use facial cosmetics, but unwilling to be the first to actually change behaviour by using them.

It is important for marketers to study changes in social attitudes, because these may eventually be translated into changes in buying behaviour. The change may begin with a small group of social pioneers, followed by more traditional groups who may be slow to change their attitudes and more reluctant to change their behaviour. They may be prepared to change only when something has become the norm in their society.

Marketers have monitored a number of significant changes in individuals' attitudes in Western Europe, for example:

- Healthy living is considered to be increasingly important.
- Consumers have a tendency to want instant results, rather than having to wait for things.
- Attitudes are increasingly based on secular rather than religious values.

Marketers have been able to respond to these attitude changes creatively, for example:

- Demand for healthy foods and gymnasium services has increased significantly. At first, it was only a small group of people whose attitude towards health led them to buy specialist products—now it is a mainstream purchase.
- The desire for instant gratification has been translated into strategies to make stock always available, next day delivery for mail order purchases, instant credit approval and instant lottery tickets. Many people's attitudes have changed so that if an item is not instantly available, they will go elsewhere.
- Supermarkets in England have capitalized on the secularization of Sunday by opening stores and doing increasing levels of business on Sundays.

SUPERMARKETS GET READY FOR A NEW GENERATION OF 'YABs'

The grocery retail industry in the United Kingdom is dominated by a small number of very large supermarket chains operating from large superstores, with the names of Sainsbury, Tesco, ASDA, Gateway and Kwik Save being familiar to most shoppers. The high degree of concentration within the trade has not, however, influenced competition in any negative way as far as customers are concerned. The range of food and household items on sale has never been so varied and prices are very keen as the major players strive to capture further market share. However, consumer loyalty can never be guaranteed and an insight into the service requirements of shoppers may help the retailers retain their relationship with customers.

A study undertaken by the Henley Centre for Forecasting on behalf of one of the large multiples illustrates how research on the future of the market can form a basis for strategic change. In this instance the research was concerned with predicting patterns of shopping behaviour in the mid 1990s and particularly with establishing a set of market segments based on behaviour patterns.

The outcome of the Henley Centre's investigation was the identification of a number of different types of shopper based on a multivariable approach which took account of demographic factors such as age, sex and income as well as life-style, personality and finally attitude to the shopping experience. As with so many of these studies the resultant new breeds of shopper have been labelled with glib titles.

The Harried Hurrier will be the most important type of new shopper. They are typically burdened with squabbling children and crippled by a severe lack of time. Hurriers are averse to anything that eats into their precious minutes, such as having too much choice, which makes them impatient. Another large group but spending less money will be the middle-aged Young-at-Heart who in contrast to the first group have time on their hands and like to try new products. An important and growing species of grocery shopper is the Young, Affluent and Busy (or 'YABs'), for whom money is not a major constraint in their quest for convenience and more interesting products, but they do have a low boredom threshold. Two other types who are expected to grow in importance are the Fastidious, who are attracted by in-store hygiene and tidiness; and the mainly male Begrudgers who only shop out of obligation to others. At the same time the Perfect Wife and Mother who is concerned with the balanced diet would appear to be on her way out. She is likely to be more than compensated for by the Obsessive Fad-Followers whose choice of food tends to be dominated by brand image and current trends.

It is expected that the new breeds will act as a catalyst for a shopping revolution. Although the already established need for convenience will still predominate, retail analysts anticipate some significant changes such as in-store traffic-routing systems, one-way layouts, and themed food centres by nationality. There would appear to be a considerable amount to be gained from transforming the sometimes stressful encounter with the superstore into a pleasurable leisure activity.

However, balancing the needs of all these groups may prove to be a difficult task which may lead to greater specialization within the sector. For example, it is not impossible to imagine chains of speciality food retailers that act as menu stores offering the YABs the alternative of buying different dinner party food on different days, switching the emphasis from French to Italian to Indian recipes.

(Adapted from 'Keeping 'em Rolling in the Aisles', *Marketing Week*, 11 August 1989.)

QUESTIONS

1. To what extent are segment descriptions such as those used for YABs and Harried Hurriers useful to supermarkets in supermarket planning?
2. Analyse some of the implications for a supermarket of the ageing of the population.
3. How can you explain differences between countries in grocery shoppers' behaviour?

8.4   THE FAMILY

The family is an important element of the social and cultural environment which marketers must study for a number of reasons:

1. Many household goods and services are typically bought by family units, for example food and package holidays. When family structures and values change, consumption patterns may change significantly.
2. The family is crucial in giving individuals a distinctive personality. Many of the differences in attitude and behaviour between individuals can be attributed to the values that were instilled in them by their family during childhood. These differences may persist well into adult life.
3. The family has a central role as a transmitter of cultural values and norms, and can exercise a strong influence on an individual's buying behaviour.

8.4.1   Family composition

Many people still live with the idea that the typical family comprises two parents, and an average of 2.4 children. In many West European countries, this is increasingly becoming a myth with single person and single parent households becoming increasingly common. The following factors have contributed to changes in family composition:

● An increasing divorce rate, with about one third of all marriages in the United Kingdom now ending in divorce.
● The age at which individuals first get married is becoming later (for females, this has risen from 23 in 1971 to 26 in 1992 and for males from 25 to 27).

- More people are living on their own outside a family unit, either out of choice or through circumstances (e.g. divorce, widowhood).
- Family role expectations have changed with an increasing number of career-oriented wives.

Changes in family composition have led firms to develop new goods and services that meet the changing needs of families, such as creche facilities for working mothers and holidays for single parents. Advertising has increasingly moved away from portraying the traditional family group which many individuals may have difficulty in identifying with. Recent examples that have portrayed the new reality include an advertisement for MacDonalds in which a boy takes his separated father to one of the company's restaurants and one for Volkswagen in which a career-minded woman puts her car before her husband.

8.4.2   Family roles

As well as changing in composition, there is evidence of change in the way that families operate as a unit. Many household products have been traditionally considered to be dominated by either the male or female partner, but these distinctions are becoming increasingly blurred as family roles change. In the United Kingdom, *Social Trends* records some of the changes in family roles that have been occurring. For example, in family households in 1991:

- 47 per cent of household shopping was done jointly (a slight increase on 10 years ago).
- The main evening meal is made mainly by women in 39 per cent of households, having fallen from 77 per cent a decade earlier.
- Household cleaning is carried out mainly by women in 68 per cent of households (down from 72 per cent a decade earlier).

There has been much debate about the fragmentation of families into 'cellular households' in which family members essentially do their own activities independently of other members. This is reflected in individually consumed meals rather than family meals and leisure interests that are increasingly with a family member's peer groups rather than other family members. Marketers have responded to the needs of the cellular household with products such as microwave cookers and portable televisions which allow family units to function in this way. It can also be argued, however, that new product developments are actually responsible for the fragmentation of family activities. The microwave cooker and portable television may have lessened the need for families to operate as a collective unit, although these possible consequences were not immediately obvious when they were launched. The family unit can expect to come under further pressures as new products, such as on-line entertainment and information services, allow individual members to consume in accordance with their own preferences rather than the collective preferences of the family.

8.5   REFERENCE GROUPS

The family is not the only influence on an individual as they develop a view of the world. Just as individuals learn from and mimic the values of parents and close relations, so too they also learn from and mimic other people outside their immediate family. Groups that influence individuals in this way are often referred to as *reference groups*. These can be one of two types:

- Primary reference groups exist where an individual has direct face-to-face contact with members of the group.
- Secondary reference groups describe the influence of groups where there is no direct relationship, but an individual is nevertheless influenced by its values.

8.5.1   Primary reference groups

These comprise people with whom an individual has direct two-way contact, including those with whom an individual works, plays football and goes to church. In effect, the group acts as a frame of reference for the individual. Small groups of trusted colleagues have great power in passing on recommendations about goods and services, especially those where a buyer has very little other evidence on which to base a decision. For many personal services, such as hairdressing, word of mouth recommendation from a member of a peer group may be a vital method by which a company gains new business. If an individual needs to hire a builder, the first thing they are likely to do is ask friends if they can recommend a good one on the basis of their previous experience. For many items of conspicuous consumption, individuals often select specific brands in accordance with which brand carries most prestige with its primary reference group.

8.5.2   Secondary reference groups

These are groups with whom an individual has no direct contact, but which can nevertheless influence a person's attitudes, values, opinions and behaviour. Sometimes, the individual may be a member of the group and this will have a direct influence on their behaviour patterns, with the group serving as a frame of reference for the individual member. Individuals typically belong to several groups which can influence attitudes and behaviour in this way, for example university groups, trades unions and religious organizations. A member of a trade union may have little active involvement with the organization, but may nevertheless adopt the values of the union such as solidarity.

At other times, an individual may not actually be a member of a group, but may *aspire* to be a member of it. Aspirational groups can be general descriptions of the characteristics of groups of people who share attitudes and behaviour. They range from teenage 'wannabees' who idolize pop stars through to business men who want to surround themselves with the trappings of their successful business heros. It can be difficult to identify just which aspirational groups are highly sought at any one time. In the 1980s, the 'yuppie' was considered an aspirational group by many, but largely disappeared in the early 1990s. Middle-aged marketers marketing youth products may find it difficult to keep up with which pop stars and fashion models are currently in favour with teenagers.

Although a person may not be influenced by all the attitudes or behaviour patterns of a particular reference group, the fact that such influence occurs at all makes it important for marketers to try to identify the reference groups of the target markets they are selling to. The importance of secondary group influences tends to vary between products and brands. In the case of products that are consumed or used in public, group influence is likely to affect not only the choice of product but also the choice of brand. (For example, training shoes are often sold using a 'brand spokesperson' to create an image for the shoe. There are some people who are so influenced by the images developed by famous athletes wearing a particular brand that they would not want to be seen wearing anything else). For mass-market goods which are consumed less publicly (e.g. many grocery items), the effects of reference groups are usually less.

8.6   DEMOGRAPHY

Demography is the study of populations in terms of their size and characteristics. Among the topics of interest to demographers are the age structure of a country, the geographic distribution of its population, the balance between male and females and the likely future size of the population and its characteristics.

8.6.1   The importance of demographic analysis to marketers

A number of reasons can be identified why marketers can usefully study the changing demographic structure:

1. Firstly, on the demand side, demography helps to predict the size of the market that a product is likely to face. For example, demographers can predict an increase in elderly people living in the United Kingdom and the numbers living in the South West region of the country. Marketers can use this information as a basis for predicting, for example, the size of the market for retirement homes in the South West.
2. Demographic trends have supply side implications. The aim of strategic marketing management is to match the opportunities facing an organization with the resource strengths that it possesses. In many businesses, labour is a key resource and a study of demographics will indicate the human resources that an organization can expect to have available to it in future years. Thus a business that has relied on relatively low wage, young labour, such as retailing, would need to have regard to the availability of this type of worker when developing its product strategy. A retailer might decide to invest in more automated methods of processing transactions and handling customer enquiries rather than relying on a traditional but diminishing source of relatively low-cost labour.
3. The study of demographics also has implications for public sector services which are themselves becoming more marketing oriented. Changing population structures influence the community facilities which need to be provided by the government. For example, fluctuations in the number of children has affected the number of schools and teachers required, while the increasing number of elderly people will require the provision of more specialized housing and hospital facilities suitable for this group.
4. In an even wider sense, demographic change can influence the nature of family life and communities and ultimately affects the social and economic system in which organizations operate. The imbalance that is developing between a growing dependent elderly population and a diminishing population of working age could affect government fiscal policy and the way in which we care for the elderly, with major implications for marketing.

Although the study of demographics has assumed great importance in Western Europe in recent years, study of the consequences of population change dates back a considerable time. T. R. Malthus studied the effects of population changes in a paper published in 1798. He predicted that the population would continue to grow exponentially, while world food resources would grow at a slower linear rate of growth. Population growth would only be held back by 'war, pestilence and famine' until an equilibrium point was again reached at which population was just equal to the food resources available.

Malthus' model of population growth failed to predict the future accurately and this only serves to highlight the difficulty of predicting population levels, when the underlying assumptions on which predictions are based are themselves changing. Malthus failed to predict, on the one hand, the tremendous improvement in agricultural efficiency which would allow a larger population to be sustained, while, on the other hand, overlooking changes in social and cultural attitudes that were to limit family size.

8.6.2   Global population changes

Globally, population is expanding at an increasing rate. The world population level at AD 1000 has been estimated at about 300 million. Over the next 750 years, it rose at a steady rate to 728 million in 1750. Thereafter, the rate of increase became progressively more rapid, doubling in the following 150 years to 1550 million in 1900 and almost doubling again to 3000 million in the 62 years to 1962. It is

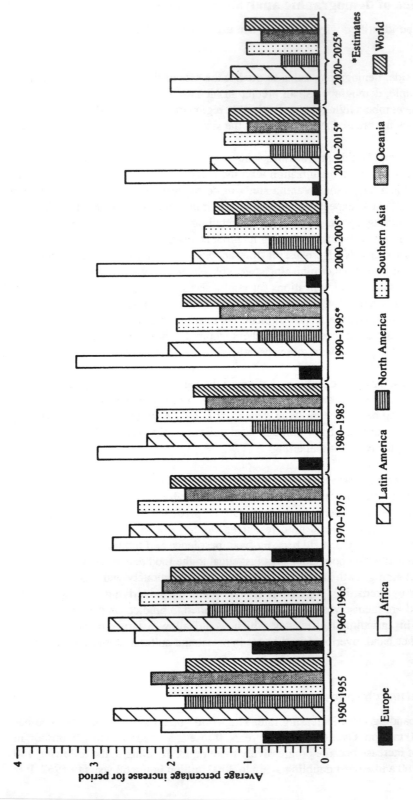

Figure 8.2 Growth in world population
Source: based on UN estimates, 1985.

predicted that world population will double again in an even shorter period—a United Nations Report has predicted that it will double again to 6000 million in just 30 years. The growth of world population has not been uniform, with recent growth being focused on Far East countries, especially Korea and China, as well as South America. By contrast, the total population levels of most Western developed countries are stable, or in some cases actually declining. An indication of the variation in population growth rates is given in Figure 8.2. It should, however, be noted that there is still considerable debate about the likely world population level at the end of the century, with many predictions being revised downwards.

A growth in the population of a country does not necessarily mean a growth in market opportunities, for the countries with the highest population growth rates also tend to be those with the lowest gross domestic product per head. Indeed, in many countries of Africa, total GDP is not keeping up with the growth in population levels, resulting in a lower GDP per head. On the other hand, the growth in population results in a large and low-cost labour force, which can help to explain the tendency for many European-based organizations to base their design capacity in Europe but relatively labour-intensive assembly operations in the Far East.

8.6.3   Changes in UK population level

The first British census was carried out in 1801 and the subsequent ten yearly census provides the basis for studying changes in the size of the British population. A summary of British population growth is shown in Table 8.3.

Table 8.2 Population growth 1801–2003

Year	Population of England, Wales and Scotland (000s)	Average increase per decade (%)
1801	10 501	13.9
1871	26 072	9.4
1911	40 891	4.5
1941	46 605	5.8
1971	54 369	0.8
1981	54 814	2.4
1993	56 559	3.0
2003	58 274 (estimated)	

Source: based on *Annual Abstract of Statistics and Population Censuses*

The fluctuation in the rate of population growth can be attributed to three main factors: the birth rate, the death rate; and the difference between inward and outward migration. The fluctuation in these rates is illustrated in Figure 8.3 These three components of population change are described in more detail below.

8.6.4   The birth rate

The birth rate is usually expressed in terms of the number of live births per 1000 population. Since the Second World War, the birth rate has shown a number of distinct cyclical tendencies. The immediate post-war years are associated with a 'baby boom', followed by a steady decrease in the number of

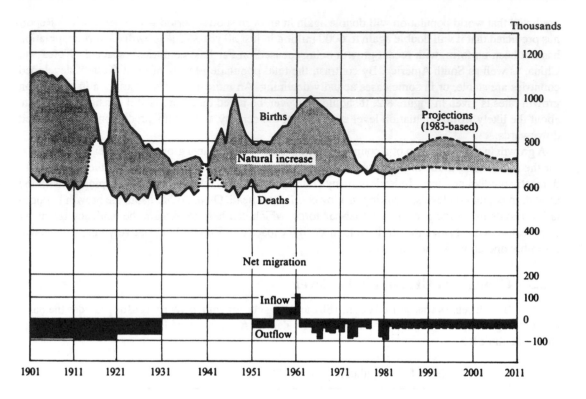

Figure 8.3   Changes in the UK birth rate, death rate and level of net migration, 1901–2011
   Source: Office of Population Censuses and Surveys, Government Actuary's Department. © Crown
   copyright.

births until 1956. Following this, the rate rose again until the mid 1960s during a second, but lesser, baby boom. The birth rate then fell until the mid 1970s, rising again in recent years.

In order to explain these trends, it is necessary to examine two key factors:

● The number of women in the population who are of child-bearing age and
● The proportion of these women who actually give birth (this is referred to as the fertility rate)

The peak in the birth rate of the early 1960s could be partly explained by the 'baby boom' children of the immediate post-war period working through to child-bearing age. Similarly, the children of this group are themselves now at child-bearing age, accounting for some of the recent increase in the birth rate. Greater doubt lies over reasons for changes in the fertility rate, usually expressed in terms of the number of births per 1000 women aged between 16 and 44. This has varied from a peak of 115 at the beginning of the century to a low point of 56.8 in 1983 (Table 8.3).

There are many possible explanations for changes in fertility rates and it is our difficulty in understanding the precise nature of these changes that makes population forecasting a difficult task. Some of the more frequently suggested causes of the declining fertility rate are listed below:

1. A large family is no longer seen as an insurance policy for future parental security. The extended family has declined in importance and state institutions have taken over many of the welfare functions towards elderly members of the family which were previously expected of children.

Furthermore, infant and child mortality has declined and consequently the need for large numbers of births has declined. Alongside this falling need for large numbers of children has come a greater ability to control the number of births.

2. Children use household resources that could otherwise be used for consumption. The cost of bringing up children has been increasing as a result of increased expectations of children and the raising of the school leaving age. Although in many Western countries this is offset by financial incentives for having children, the cost of child rearing has increased relative to consumer purchases in general.

3. In addition to diverting household resources from the consumption of other goods and services, caring for children also has the effect of reducing the earning capacity of the household. Women may also seek additional status and career progression by having fewer children or spacing them over a shorter period of time.

4. Birth rates tend to be related to current economic conditions, falling significantly in response to temporary economic recession and rising in response to a period of economic boom.

Table 8.3 General fertility rate—total births per 1000 women aged 15–44, United Kingdom

Year	Fertility rate
1900	115.0
1933	81.0
1951	73.0
1961	90.6
1971	84.3
1981	62.1
1991	64.0
1993	62.0

Source: Office of Population Censuses and Surveys.

BURTON GROUP GROWS OLDER WITH ITS CUSTOMERS

The Burton Group PLC operates many familiar High Street retail clothing stores and has built up a portfolio of brands which can meet the needs of most segments of the population. One of the bases for segmenting its markets is age, with different formats aimed at particular age segments. For the 15–24 year old segment, Burton Group has developed the Top Shop and Top Man brands; for the 24–35 year old segment Principles, Principles for Men and Burtons; while the 35+ segment is targeted with the Debenhams brand.

The response by Burton Group to demographic change has been to shift resources to those brands serving segments facing the strongest demographic growth. During the 1970s when the number of teenagers reached a peak (following the 1960s baby boom), heavy investment was made in expanding the Top Shop and Top Man brands. During the 1980s this bulge of births matured, carrying through with it new attitudes to fashion. In response to both the growing numbers of 24–35 year olds and their increasing fashion consciousness, the Burton Group channelled resources into its new Principles and Principles for Men brands, both aimed at this group. During most of the 1980s, the Debenhams brand had been the 'cash cow' of the Burton group—a relatively static business which had ceased to grow, producing steady but not spectacular profits. Its product offering was geared mainly to the older segments of the population, which had not shown the growth in spending power of younger groups. To try and bring more business back into the stores, a lot of space within Debenhams was turned into concessions for other brands within the Burton Group. This had the effect of attracting many of the younger segments into the stores.

By the end of the 1980s, however, the teenage market had gone into numerical decline, whereas the number of people aged over 50 was increasing, not only numerically, but even more so in terms of their spending power. The Burton Group responded to this in a number of ways. The Debenhams chain, which had been static during the 1980s, received new investment with a series of new store openings and refurbishments. The brand emphasized older age groups' values of quality and durability—as opposed to purely fashionability—in its product offering. The space allocated within Debenhams to the younger Top Shop and Top Man has been reduced. Meanwhile, the Dorothy Perkins brand, which had previously targeted 18–40 year old women, was refocused to meet the needs of the more discerning 30–40 year old woman.

QUESTIONS

1. Discuss methods by which Burton Group could most effectively monitor changes in its demographic environment.
2. To what extent is it appropriate to treat the growing number of elderly people in the population as a homogenous segment?
3. What other major changes in the marketing environment are likely to affect the marketing strategies of groups such as Burton over the next decade?

8.6.5 The death rate

Death rates are normally expressed as the number of people in the country that die in a year per 1000 of the population. This is sometimes called the crude death rate; the age-specific death rate takes account of the age of death and is expressed as the number of people per 1000 of a particular age group that die in a year.

In contrast to the volatility of the birth rate during the post-war period, the death rate has been relatively stable and has played a relatively small part in changing the total population level. The main feature of mortality in the United Kingdom has been a small decline in age-specific death rates, having the effect of increasing the survival chances of relatively old people. The age-specific death rate of women has fallen more significantly than men. The main reasons for the decline in age-specific death rates are improved standards of living, a better environment and better health services. While age-specific death rates have been falling in most advanced industrial countries, the United Kingdom has generally experienced a slower fall than most other EU member states.

8.6.6 Migration

If immigration is compared with emigration, a figure for net migration is obtained. During most periods of this century, the United Kingdom has experienced a net outflow of population, the main exceptions being the 1930s, caused by emigrants to the Commonwealth returning home during the depression; the 1940s when a large number of refugees entered the United Kingdom from Nazi Europe; and the late 1950s/early 1960s when the prosperity of the British economy attracted large numbers of immigrants from the new Commonwealth. Emigration has tended to peak at times of economic depression in the United Kingdom.

While migration has had only a marginal effect upon the total population level, it has had a more significant effect on the population structure. On the demand side, many immigrants have come from different cultural backgrounds and pose new opportunities and problems for segmenting markets for goods and services. Furthermore, immigrants themselves need to be segmented into various ethnic minorities, each with differing needs. Table 8.4 indicates the extent of the main ethnic minorities in the United Kingdom.

Table 8.4 United Kingdom population by ethnic group, 1986–88

	Number	*Percentage of population*
Indian	787 000	1.44
West Indian or Guyanese	495 000	0.91
Pakistani	428 000	0.78
Chinese	125 000	0.23
African	112 000	0.20
Bangladeshi	108 000	0.19
Arab	73 000	0.13
Mixed	287 000	0.53
Other	163 000	0.30
Total ethnic minorities	2 577 000	4.72
Not stated	472 000	0.86
White	51 470 000	94.40
Total population	54 519 000	100.00

Source: *Labour Force Survey*, Office of Population Censuses and Surveys.

In some cases, completely new markets have emerged specifically for ethnic minorities, such as the market for black sticking plasters. It has sometimes proved difficult for established businesses to gain access to immigrant segments. Many established companies have not adequately researched the attitudes and buying processes of these groups, with the result that in markets as diverse as vegetables, clothing and travel, ethnic minorities have supported businesses run by fellow members of their minority group. On the supply side, immigrants have tended to be of working age and have filled a vital role in providing labour for the economy. Moreover, some Asian minorities have brought vital entrepreneurial skills to the economy. Balanced against this is the fact that the emigrants that Britain has lost have tended to be highly trained and represent a loss to the economy.

8.6.7 The age structure of the population

It was noted earlier that the total population of the United Kingdom—and indeed most countries of the EU—is fairly stable. Within this stable total, there has been a more noted change in the composition of particular age groups. The changes that have affected the size of a number of young and elderly age segments over time are illustrated in Figure 8.4.

A number of bulges in the distribution are evident and these can have important marketing implications. The shortage of 8–15 year olds will in due course pose problems for organizations serving the young adult market as well as depriving organizations of a traditional source of relatively low-cost

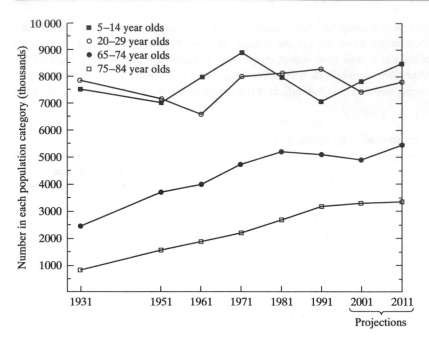

Figure 8.4 Size of selected age cohorts in United Kingdom, 1931–2001
Source: based on Population Censuses and Office of Population Censuses and Surveys estimates.

labour. The declining presence of this group may alter many of the values of our youth-orientated culture. For example, the emphasis on fashion and short-life products may give way to an emphasis on quality and durability as the growing numbers in the older age groups increasingly dominate cultural values. Another major issue that may affect the cultural environment of marketing is the growing imbalance between the size of the working population and an increasingly large dependent population. Government statistics show that between 1961 and 1991, the number of people of working age available to support the retired population decreased from 4.1 per pensioner to 3.3. This figure is expected to fall again slightly to 2020 but then fall again sharply as the baby boom generation start to become eligible for their pensions. The ratio of those contributing to the pensions that sustain the retired population is smaller still, to take account of the fact that although many people of working age are available to work, many are either unemployed or pay no taxes. By 2020, each pensioner will be supported by the contributions of two tax-paying workers. This is expected to fall to 1.6 by 2040.

8.6.8 Household structure

Reference was made earlier in this chapter to the changing role and functions of family units, and this is reflected in an analysis of household structure statistics. A number of important trends can be noted:

1. Firstly, there has been a trend for women to have fewer children. From a high point in the 1870s, the average number of children for each woman born in 1930 was 2.35, 2.2 for those born in 1945 and it is projected to be 1.97 for those born in 1965. There has also been a tendency for women to have children later in life. In the United Kingdom, the average age at which women have their first child has moved from 24 years in 1961 to 28 in 1994. There has also been an increase in the number of women having no children. According the Office of Population Census and Surveys, more than one-

fifth of women born in 1967 are expected to be childless when they reach the age of 40, compared with 13 per cent of those born in 1947.

2. Alongside a declining number of children has been a decline in the average household size. This has fallen continuously from an average of 3.1 people in 1961 to 2.4 in 1993. There has been a particular fall in the number of very large households with five or more people (down from 9 per cent of all households in 1961 to 5 per cent in 1993) and a significant increase in the number of one person households (up from 11 per cent to 27 per cent over the same period). A number of factors have contributed to the increase in one-person households, including the increase in solitary survivors, later marriage and an increased divorce rate. The marketing implications of the growth of this group are numerous, ranging from an increased demand for smaller units of housing to the types and size of groceries purchased. A single person household buying for him or herself is likely to use different types of retail outlets compared to the household buying as a unit—the single person may be more likely to use a niche retailer than the (typically) housewife buying for the whole family whose needs may be better met by a department store. A recent Mintel report showed a number of ways in which the spending patterns of single person households deviates from the average. For example, compared to the British average, a person living in a single-person household spends 49 per cent more on tobacco, 26 per cent more on household services and 23 per cent less on meat (Mintel, 1996).

3. Along with the rise in single person households has been a fall in other household types. Family households comprising one to three dependent children have fallen from 38 per cent of all households in 1961 to 25 per cent in 1993. Lone parents with childern have increased during the same period from 6 to 10 per cent of all households.

The role of the woman in the household structure has been changing, with a rising proportion having some form of employment (58 per cent in 1993). Along with this has been the emergence of a large segment of career-minded women who are cash rich but time poor. This has created new opportunities for labour-saving consumer durables in the home and for convenience foods. It has also resulted in women becoming important target markets for products that were previously considered to be male preserves, such as new cars.

8.6.9   Geographical distribution of population

The population density of the United Kingdom of 231 people per km^2 is one of the highest in the world. However, this figure hides the fact that the population is dispersed very unevenly between regions and between urban and rural areas. The distribution of population is not static.

Regional distribution   The major feature of the regional distribution of the United Kingdom population is the dominance of the South East of England with 30 per cent of the population, and the industrial regions of the West Midlands, Lancashire and Yorkshire. By contrast, the populations of Scotland, Wales and Northern Ireland account in total for only 17 per cent of the total population.

Movement between the regions tends to be a very gradual process. In an average year, about 10 per cent of the population will change address, but only about one-eighth of these will move to another region. Nevertheless, there have been a number of noticeable trends. Firstly, throughout the twentieth century there has been a general drift of population from the north to the Midlands and South. More recently, there has been a trend for population to move away from the relatively congested South East to East Anglia, the South West and Home Counties. This can be partly explained by the increased cost of industrial and residential location in the South East, the greater locational flexibility of modern industry and the desire of people for a pleasanter environment in which to live. The drift of population is illustrated in Figure 8.5.

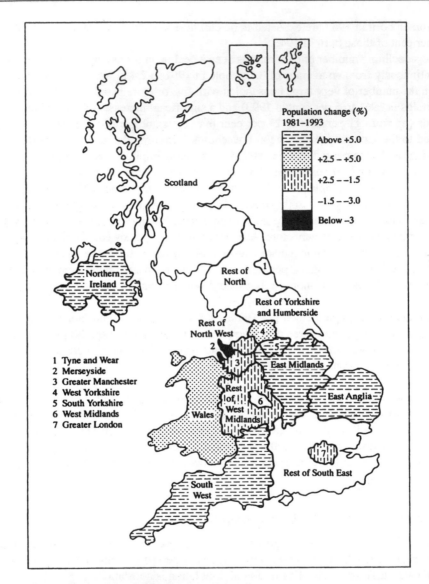

Figure 8.5   Percentage population change by region, 1981–93
Source: based on information published by the Office of Population Censuses and Surveys, General
Register Office (Scotland) and General Register Office (Northern Ireland).

Urban concentration   Another trend has been a shift in the proportion of the population living in
urban areas. Throughout most of Western Europe, the nineteenth and twentieth centuries have been
associated with a drift from rural areas to towns. In the United Kingdom, this has resulted in the urban
areas of Greater London, Greater Manchester, Merseyside, Greater Glasgow, West Midlands, West
Yorkshire and Tyneside having just one-thirtieth of the United Kingdom's surface area, but nearly
one-third of the total population. More recently, the trend towards urbanization has been partly
reversed, with many of the larger conurbations experiencing a decline in population since the 1960s,
combined with a deterioration in many inner city areas. Those moving out have tended to be the most
economically active, leaving behind a relatively elderly and poor population. Much of the movement
from the conurbations has been towards the rural areas just beyond the urban fringe. For example,

London has lost population to the Home Counties of Berkshire, Buckinghamshire, Hertfordshire and Essex. The increasingly large dormitory population of these areas remains dependent on the neighbouring conurbation. Movement from urban to rural areas has brought about a change in life-style which has implications for marketing. Higher car ownership in rural areas has led more households to make fewer shopping trips for household goods, to travel further to the shop that best suits their life-style and to spend more on each trip. In this changed shopping pattern, the decision making unit may comprise more members of the household than in an urban area where the (typically) wife may have made more frequent trips to the local supermarket by herself.

8.6.10   EU comparisons

Although the population of most EU countries is stable, a number of structural differences can be noted between member states. From Table 8.5, it can be seen that an exporter to the Irish Republic will face a much younger age structure than in the domestic UK market, and many more young people than in the former West Germany. The total population of the Irish Republic is also likely to grow the most rapidly, in contrast to Belgium and West Germany, which are expected to fall.

Table 8.5 Population structure of the EU

| | Population | Birth rate | Death rate | Percentage aged | | % increase | |
				under 15	60+	1985–90	1985–2000
UK	56.6	13.3	11.8	19	21	1.23	4.06
Belgium	9.9	11.6	11.2	19	20	–1.02	–2.06
Denmark	5.1	10.5	11.4	18	20	0.00	1.96
France	55.2	13.9	10.0	21	19	1.63	4.89
W. Germany	61.0	9.6	11.5	15	20	0.00	–0.82
Greece	9.9	11.7	9.3	21	18	1.01	4.04
Irish Republic	3.5	17.6	9.4	30	15	5.70	14.28
Italy	57.1	10.1	9.5	19	19	3.50	1.75
Luxembourg	0.4	11.2	11.3	17	18	0.00	0.00
Netherlands	14.5	12.3	8.5	19	17	2.75	7.58
Portugal	10.3	12.8	9.6	23	17	1.01	7.77
Spain	38.6	12.1	7.7	23	17	1.55	5.44

Source: Statistical Office of the European Communities.

On average, the population of Western Europe grew by 1.6 per cent during the period 1985–90, but this hides a number of differences. Western Germany, although it has a high level of GDP per capita, grew in numerical terms by only 1.04 per cent, while Belgium actually contracted during the same period (by 1 per cent). The strongest growth was shown by Italy and Ireland (3.5 and 5.7 per cent respectively).

Within these population totals, there are significant differences within the EU in the proportion of the population that is either young or elderly, with consequent implications for demand for age-related products. As an example, the proportion of the population aged 60 and above ranges from 15 per cent in the Irish Republic to 21 per cent in the United Kingdom. By contrast, the Irish Republic has the greatest proportion of under fifteens (30 per cent), compared to West Germany which has the lowest (15 per cent).

In addition, the geographical distribution of the population and structure of household units differs between EU member states. For example, EU statistics show a number of interesting contrasts in geodemographic characteristics between member states which could have implications for the marketing of goods and services:

1. Very significant differences occur in home ownership patterns, with implications for demand for a wide range of home-related services. The proportion of households living in rented accommodation ranges from 21 per cent in Spain to 53 per cent in West Germany, while the proportion with a mortgage ranges from 8 per cent in Spain to 44 per cent in the United Kingdom.
2. The proportion of the population living within metropolitan areas varies from 13 per cent in Italy to 44 per cent in France. The resulting differences in life-styles can have implications for goods and services as diverse as car repairs, entertainment and retailing.
3. The proportion of self-employed people ranges from 45 per cent in the Netherlands to 17 per cent in Italy, with implications for the sale of personal pension schemes, etc.

REVIEW QUESTIONS

1. (a) Discuss the likely impact of ageing on the labour market.
   (b) What recommendations would you make to a business currently reliant on recruiting large numbers of school leavers to meet its labour needs?
   (CIM Marketing Environment Examination, June 1995, Q.1b)
2. 'Businesses will have to cope with changes in demand patterns as older consumers become more significant in their markets and younger people less so.' Explain, with examples, some of the opportunities provided by these changing demand patterns and how the marketer should address this buyer segment.
   (CIM Marketing Environment Examination, June 1995, Q.1b)
3. 'Ageing is one of the few trends that can be forecast with confidence.' Briefly explain why this is so, and suggest two forecasting approaches, showing how they might enable the marketer to forecast the future with greater confidence.
   (CIM Marketing Environment Examination, June 1995, Q.1c)
4. In what ways do you think the different culture of a less-developed country may affect the marketing of confectionery that has previously been successfully marketed in the United Kingdom?
5. In what ways are the buying habits of a household with two adults and two children likely to change when the children leave home?
6. Critically assess some of the implications of an increasingly aged population on the demand for hotel accommodation in the United Kingdom.

REFERENCE

Mintel (1996) *Single Person Households: Getting Younger, Richer and Happier*, Mintel, London.

FURTHER READING

Bottomore, J. (1991) *Classes in Modern Society*, 2nd edn, London, Routledge, London.
Crompton, R. (1993) *Class and Stratification: An Introduction to Current Debates*, Polity, Cambridge.
Office of Population Censuses and Surveys (OPCS), *General Household Survey* (annual), HMSO, London.
Office of Population Censuses and Surveys (OPCS), *Family Spending Report* (annual), HMSO, London.
Weinstein, A. (1994) *Market Segmentation, Using Demographics, Psychographics and Other Niche Marketing Techniques to Predict and Model Customer Behaviour*, Probus Publishing, Chicago, Ill.

THE SOCIAL RESPONSIBILITY OF ORGANIZATIONS

OBJECTIVES

After reading this chapter, you should understand:

● The nature of external costs and benefits that give rise to an organization's social responsibility
● The concept of a stakeholder and identification of the principal stakeholders in a business organization
● The societal marketing concept and its applicability to commercial organizations
● Issues in organization's involvement with their ecological environment.
● Ethical issues and their effects on business practices

9.1 INTRODUCTION

In Chapter 4, the objectives of business organizations were defined primarily in terms of objectives which are set by the owners of the organization. In a perfectly functioning market, free market theorists would argue that the pursuit of individual goals by firms is the best way to maximize benefits to society. This approach is, however, flawed because of the existence of external costs and benefits (or 'externalities'). The former represent the costs of producing goods and services which are not borne by the producer but by society as a whole. Similarly, external benefits represent benefits produced by an organization which benefit society as a whole and for which the organization is not able to appropriate any payment from the recipient.

The existence of external costs and benefits results in a diverse range of individuals and organizations having an interest in the activities of a company, in addition to those groups that are most directly affected by its activities, such as customers, shareholders, employees and distributors. This broader group of people who are directly and indirectly affected by the activities of a company are often referred to as 'stakeholders' in an organization.

9.1.1 Externalities

A contemporary definition of externalities is provided by Samuelson (1992) who says that 'externalities (or spillover effects) occur where firms or people impose costs or benefits on others without those others receiving the proper payment or paying the proper costs'. Externalities represent the failure of market mechanisms to determine prices according to benefits received or costs incurred.

9.1.2 External benefits

The external benefits of a product can be direct or indirect to the recipient. Direct benefits imply a simple transmission of benefit from producer to recipient. For example, a factory keeping its boundary fences clean and tidy transmits the benefit of higher property values directly to householders living adjacent to the factory. Indirect benefits are more remote and it may not be possible to precisely identify the recipients of benefits. As an example, the invention of a new production process may result in lower prices charged to customers of other companies as well as those of the inventing company.

External benefits have a number of important characteristics:

1. It is not possible to exclude individuals from benefiting from goods or services. Thus a shop providing a clock on the outside of a building cannot exclude non-customers from benefiting from the service that the clock provides. Similarly, government provided services such as defence and street cleaning have to be made available to everybody, with little realistic possibility of exclusion.
2. External benefits usually allow one individual to consume a benefit without having to exclude other individuals from receiving benefits. For example, one individual's benefit from using a public clock to tell the time does not prevent another person also enjoying that benefit. There is said to be no rivalry in consumption.
3. It may not be practical for individuals to directly purchase benefits as discrete units. An individual cannot buy a safe road system on his or her own. The decision to invest in additional safety measures must be taken at a collective level.

External benefits can be provided by both public and private sector organizations and have been used as a rationale for government provision of goods and services. However, the rationale for public provision of services has changed through time. Nineteenth century liberal free traders saw no reason for governments to intervene in the running of the economy to provide goods and services which could adequately be provided by the private sector. Thus railways were developed almost entirely by the private sector despite the fact that their construction brought significant external benefits (and costs) to the areas where they were built. Public intervention was limited to services that were considered unmarketable. Thus collectively consumed and essential services such as defence were provided for the benefit of all. These were later supplemented by a range of services for which market mechanisms had failed. One example was public health, where market mechanisms had failed to protect society against the possibilities of epidemics. By providing healthy living conditions and medical facilities for an individual, liberal free traders recognized that it was not just the individual receiving medical treatment or vaccinations who benefited but society as a whole. Members of society could not easily buy through market mechanisms the ability to avoid catching an infectious disease.

During the inter-war and post-war periods, the concept of external benefit was recognized by governments in the context of an ever-widening range of activities that had suffered from market failure. In Chapter 6, it was noted that Keynsian economists argued for the economic benefits arising from government intervention to stimulate the national economy. Thus government spending on capital schemes such as road building and railway electrification was based on the resulting external benefits of increased employment levels. The period from the 1950s to the 1970s saw mild oscillations in political attitudes towards externalities, followed by an attempt at a significant redefinition during the 1980s. In the United Kingdom, the Thatcher government saw the concept of external benefits as a means of allowing central planners to avoid the test of consumer preference expressed through willingness to pay for goods or services.

During the 1980s, there was a trend for external benefits provided by public services to be made internal to the user. Two instruments have been employed to internalize benefits—simplification of the product and the introduction of market-mediated methods of distribution:

- Simplification of public sector services occurs where a complex offering is broken down into a series of relatively simple services. The first effect of simplification is to introduce greater service accountability. Thus the Post Office has been transformed from offering an all-embracing postal service to a series of specialized units offering a relatively simplified range of services—letter delivery, parcel delivery and retail services—each with differing environmental conditions.
- Simplification has allowed services involving high levels of externalities to be provided in a different management environment compared to those where externalities are relatively absent. While there have been many arguments about the external benefits of preserving the Royal Mail's monopoly in letter delivery (e.g. it does not discriminate against rural communities), this argument does not hold for other services such as parcel delivery which can operate as conventional profit-oriented business units.

Although external benefits are most commonly associated with the public sector, they are also commonly provided by private sector business organizations. Private sector producers could be expected to minimize the level of external benefits which they provide by charging recipients of the benefit, thus internalising the benefit. In practice, external benefits have been provided by the private sector for a number of reasons:

1. As with public sector services, it is not always possible to exclude groups from receiving benefits. Thus a company that spends money renovating the facade of its building would provide a visual benefit to customers and non-customers alike.
2. Companies who enjoy a protected market may have little incentive to try and appropriate the benefits received by non-customers as their position allows sufficient profits to be generated from their relatively captive customers.
3. Some external benefits have been provided by companies through the convictions of their owners, usually helped by a strong market position which allows such convictions to be satisfied. The external benefits provided to employees and the community by companies such as Cadbury and Rowntree often fit into this category, although philanthropy—provided independently of any marketing strategy—should be distinguished from the societal marketing concept, which has received increasing attention in recent years (see Section 9.1.5).

9.1.3   External costs

External costs are similar in principle to external benefits in that they represent a failure of market mechanisms to match the individual or organization that incurs costs with the one that receives the benefit resulting from that cost. External costs arise where the law does not recognize any proprietary interest of an individual in an asset that is consumed in a production process. Thus the law of most countries recognizes that individuals have a proprietary interest in most tangible assets which can be traded using market mechanisms. However, such rights are often not recognized with more intangible assets such as peace and quiet or access to fresh air.

Whether a cost is borne internally by a company or externally by society as a whole is very much influenced by the laws of a country. As a generalization, the more developed economies have given members of society greater levels of protection against bearing firms' costs than is typical of less developed countries. For example, manufacturing firms in developing countries are often allowed to emit pollution levels from their factories that would be illegal in developed economies. In fact, many companies choose to locate polluting factories in such countries, knowing that they will not have to bear the expensive fines and compensation costs that they would face if they caused pollution in a more developed economy. As economies develop, legislation increasingly recognizes firms' responsibilities to the community and what were previously external costs borne by societies become internal costs. As internal costs, a firm must either pay for the use of resources involved or find alternative methods of production that do not incur these costs. The following are examples of costs that have been internalized by companies in many Western countries in recent years:

- Companies have traditionally discharged waste water into rivers, but river authorities now either insist on the discharger paying for prior treatment of effluent or the river authority makes a charge for doing so itself. Similarly, extracting water from a river is often charged for, reflecting the value to the public of finite water supplies.
- Government is increasingly looking to firms to pay for services that were previously provided by government at no charge or a subsidized price. In the United Kingdom, for example, charges for firms seeking planning permission for new buildings have increased significantly.
- In the workplace, legislation is increasingly recognizing that employees have rights against certain business practices that may be beneficial to organizations but harmful to the individuals affected. Thus the law now recognizes the costs (emotional and financial) that individuals incur when they are made redundant or are discriminated against on the grounds of their gender or race.

There has been much debate about the imposition on firms of minimum levels of wages for employees. To advocates of free markets, the absence of minimum wages increases firms' competitiveness in international markets and, it is argued, increases employment prospects. Against this, it is argued that lower wages result in more individuals receiving government social security benefits to supplement their incomes to what is considered to be a reasonable level. An argument in favour of minimum wages is that government is effectively subsidizing firms who use low-wage labour by providing supplementary payments to their employees. Firms do not have to pay the external costs to society of having to support a low-paid work-force through social security payments.

9.1.4   Stakeholders in organizations

Because of the existence of external costs and benefits described above, it is wrong to assume that the only people who have an interest in the performance of an organization are its shareholders and customers. However, as employers, producers of pollutants or benefactors of charities, society as a whole can be affected by the actions of businesses. Therefore there is a move towards seeing that business organizations serve the needs of wider groups of interested parties. These groups are often referred to as 'stakeholders'. It has been argued that business organizations have a moral responsibility to take account of the interests of these stakeholders. More pragmatically, it can also be argued that a company that does not take the needs of this broader group of stakeholders into account will find it increasingly difficult to achieve its narrower commercial goals.

The following principal stakeholders in business organizations can be identified (Figure 9.1).

Customers   Conventional definitions of marketing revolve around the idea of satisfying customers' needs. However, a stakeholder approach to organization recognizes shortcomings in this simple marketing-led approach. The analysis of external costs and benefits in the previous section suggests that the provision of goods and services from a company to its customers may involve costs and benefits to other people who are not party to a sale. Strategic marketers would recognize that socially unacceptable levels of external costs may bring pressure for legislation which has the effect of raising selling prices to customers or making illegal the provision of goods demanded by customers.

There is another sense in which traditional customer-focused definitions of marketing have shortcomings. It can be argued that customers may not be aware of their true needs or may have these needs manipulated by exploitative companies. Taking a long-term and broad perspective, companies should have a duty to provide goods and services that satisfy these longer-term and broader needs rather than

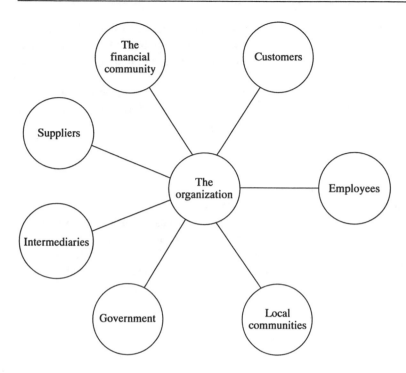

Figure 9.1   A stakeholder approach to business organizations

immediately felt needs. There have been many examples where the long-term interests of customers have been ignored by companies. Increasingly, legislation is saying that the customer is *not* always right and companies have a duty to consider the long-term interests of customers as stakeholders. This has been very clearly seen in the mis-selling of pensions in the United Kingdom during the 1980s. Private pension companies knew that many members of employers' occupational pension schemes would have undoubtedly been better off remaining in their scheme, rather than making alternative pension arrangements. Nevertheless, many employees were tempted by short-term incentives to leave their employers' scheme and to take out a private pension, leaving them very much worse off over the longer term. Regulatory authorities have recognized the wider interests of customers by requiring the pensions companies to provide compensation to customers who were sold a pension which was inappropriate to their long-term needs.

Employees   The law has increasingly recognized the social responsibility of employers towards their employees. For example, it is no longer considered acceptable for firms to dismiss long-serving employees for no good reason. Employees are considered to have some sort of proprietary interest in their jobs, reflected in legislation that gives rights to compensation for redundancy and unfair dismissal. Firms also have responsibilities in their recruitment policies, for example in the recruitment of racial minority groups.

  Firms often go way beyond satisfying the basic legal requirements of this group of stakeholders. For some businesses, getting an adequate supply of competent workers is the main constraint on growth and it would be in its interest to promote good employment practices. For example, many telemarketing bureaux rely on large numbers of relatively unskilled, part-time employees who are needed during antisocial hours. Women with children who seek part-time work to supplement their household budget have commonly been recruited by such companies who have responded by offering employment that fits around school holidays and opening times. They have also often promoted a caring image by sponsoring events likely to appeal to parents with young children, for example by giving prizes for childrens' art competitions.

Although caring for employees is often assessed by businesses in terms of the additional returns from a more productive work-force that result from such concerns, there have been many cases where businesses have taken a much more philanthropic approach towards its employees as stakeholders. Quaker companies such as Cadburys have a historic tradition of paternalism towards their staff.

Local communities   It is sometimes important for an organization to be seen as a 'good neighbour' in the local community. Therefore, the organization can enhance its image through the use of charitable contributions, sponsorship of local events and being seen to support the local environment. Again, this may be interpreted either as part of a firm's genuine concern for its local community or as a more cynical and pragmatic attempt to buy favour where its own interests are at stake. If a metal manufacturer installs improved noise installation, is it doing it to genuinely improve the lives of local residents or merely attempting to forestall prohibitive action taken by the local authority?

Government   Government represents the interests of the population at large, and can be seen as a stakeholder in business organizations. More specifically, government has a number of interests in businesses, for example:

1. Businesses provide governments with taxation revenue, so a healthy business sector is in the interests of government.
2. Government is increasingly expecting business organizations to take on more responsibility from the public sector, for example with regard to the payment of sickness and maternity benefits to employees, thereby reducing government expenditure.
3. Business organizations are important vehicles through which governments achieve their economic and social objectives, for example with respect to economic growth, skills training and the employment of disadvantaged groups of the work-force.

Intermediaries   The wholesalers, retailers and agents with whom an organization deals can claim to have a stake in that organization. These may share many of the same concerns as customers and need reassurance about the company's capabilities as a supplier who is capable of working with intermediaries to supply goods and services in an ethical manner and which customers will repeatedly buy.

Suppliers   The way in which an organization places orders for its inputs can have a significant effect on suppliers. Does a company favour domestic companies rather than possibly lower priced overseas producers? Does it divide its orders between a large number of small suppliers or place the bulk of its custom with a small handful of preferred suppliers? Does it favour new businesses or businesses representing minority interests when it places its orders?

Whatever form they take, suppliers may need assurances that the company is a credible one to deal with and that contractual obligations will be met.

The financial community   This includes financial institutions that have supported, are currently supporting or who may support the organization in the future. Shareholders—both private and institutional—form an important element of this community and must be reassured that the organization is going to achieve its stated objectives.

9.1.5   The societal marketing concept

Some marketers have argued that marketing itself cannot claim to be a discipline if it is unwilling to investigate systematically issues of social welfare and the impacts of market-based distribution systems (e.g. Anderson, 1982). The existence of external costs and benefits and the presence of multiple stakeholders in an organization serve to emphasize this point. Supporters of societal marketing point to a change of heart by companies who attach importance not just to satisfying their customers' needs but the needs of society as a whole. A distinction should be made between social philanthropy and the societal marketing concept. There have always been companies that have given to good causes quite independently of their marketing strategy.

Rising consumer incomes have resulted in the increasing importance of the augmented elements of a purchase. The external benefits provided by consumer purchases are becoming an increasingly important element of the product offering which consumers use to judge competing products in increasingly competitive markets. Fragmentation of consumer markets has resulted from a diversity in the needs that consumers seek to satisfy. To most people, goods and services no longer have to provide for the most basic level of physiological or social needs.

According to Maslow, when individuals' basic physiological and social needs are satisfied, higher order needs are developed which influence their buying behaviour. In these circumstances, consumers seek to satisfy a relatively intangible inner need for peace of mind, which may come about through knowledge that their purchase is helping to change the world in a way that they consider desirable. A century ago, a packet of washing powder would have largely satisfied a need to produce tangible cleanliness. With most of the population being able to afford cleaning powders that could produce this effect, emphasis moved to promoting washing powder on the basis of satisfying social needs. Therefore one brand was differentiated from another by signifying greater care for the family or was seen to produce results that were visibly valued by peer groups. Today, manufacturers of washing powder recognize that a significant segment seeks to buy more than the packet of washing powder— they seek also to buy a chance to change the world by reducing ecological damage caused by washing powders containing high levels of harmful phosphates.

Possible examples of societal marketing approaches adopted by firms include:

- Designing products and production processes that minimize ecological damage (e.g. using recycled paper for burger containers, rather than styrene)
- Supporting charitable causes (e.g. supermarkets giving tokens with which schools can buy computer equipment)
- Recruitment practices that favour disadvantaged groups in society such as the disabled

Critics of the societal marketing concept see it as short-term and cynical manipulation by a company of its principal stakeholders. Others have pointed out that there is not necessarily any incompatibility between traditional marketing objectives and societal objectives. For example, Arbratt and Sacks (1988) give the reminder that the societal marketing concept does not involve a company in foregoing its long-term profitability and survival objectives.

Criticisms of the societal marketing concept can take two forms—philosophical and pragmatic:

1. At a philosophical level, it has been argued by the followers of Milton Friedman that firms should concentrate on doing what they are best at—making profits for their owners. The idea of social responsibility by firms has been criticized as it would allow business organizations to become too dominant in society. It is argued that any attempt by firms to contribute to social causes is a form of taxation on the customers of the business. It would be better for firms to leave the money represented by such expenditure in the hands of customers, so that customers themselves can decide what

worthy causes they wish to support. Alternatively, donations to social causes should be handled by government which is democratically accountable, unlike business firms. There is particular strength in this argument where benefits are provided by private sector organizations who have considerable monopoly power, such as utility companies. It is probably too simplistic to say that customers voluntarily buy a company's products and therefore consent to the payment of social contributions. In reality, many markets are uncompetitive and customers may have very little choice.

2. At a more pragmatic level, it is often argued that companies support social causes because it is a cheap way of gaining attention and a unique selling proposition. In a crowded advertising market-place in which goods on offer are all broadly similar, sponsorship of a social cause may allow a company to develop a unique identity for a product using relatively unused means of promotion. Critics of the societal marketing concept argue that most external benefits provided under the guise of societal marketing are in fact rapidly internalized by their provider. Thus litter bins sponsored by a fast food restaurant, the provision of recycling points by supermarkets and donations to animal charities are not altruism—they are simply a new way of buying awareness of a company and liking of it, using values that are currently fashionable.

A further danger in expecting too much from organizations by way of societal marketing activity is that they tend to be very selective in terms of which sections of society they support. Firms have a habit of supporting causes that have popular appeal (e.g. animal charities and equipment for schools), but may fail to protect minorities in society who command very little public prestige. For example, very few organizations support activities in the fields of mental illness or freedom for political prisoners. It is argued that responsibilities for such causes cannot be given up by the public sector and handed to private sector organizations.

Taken collectively, consumers represent the same constituency of interest as the electorate. Electors have always expected government to act in the best public interest, otherwise—in the extreme—the government will not be elected. Consumers are developing similar expectations towards the suppliers of private sector goods. If they do not feel the company is acting in the public interest, their goods will not be purchased. In taking on this role, some have suggested that private sector companies are becoming more important than the government in setting the agenda for ecological reform. For example, the development of organically produced vegetables and the replacement of CFCs in aerosols are developments that originated primarily with the private sector rather than the government.

9.2   THE ECOLOGICAL ENVIRONMENT

Business organizations operate in a physical environment that provides them with raw material inputs and also provides space to receive their waste materials, either directly from the organization's production processes or indirectly after consumption. Growing concern with what has come to be known generally as 'the environment' has resulted from two principal factors:

- Growing pressure on natural resources, which is evidenced by the extinction of species of animals and the disappearance of agricultural land to housing and industrial development
- Increasing awareness of environmental issues by the public and, more importantly, a greater willingness and ability to spend money to alleviate the problems associated with ecologically harmful practices

There is argument about whether ecological problems are *actually* worse today than they were a century ago, or whether it is mainly our perceptions of problems that have changed. Certainly, comparing stories of manufacturing industry in Victorian England with industry today will probably leave the impression that environmental issues are lessening in their technical importance. Supporters of this view will point to rivers in England, such as the River Thames, which only a couple of decades previously supported very little marine life but now support extensive fish stocks.

Support for the ecological environment has sometimes been seen as a 'luxury' which societies cannot afford as they struggle to satisfy the essentials of life. As these necessities are satisfied, individuals, and society collectively, can move on to satisfy higher-order needs to protect what are seen as aesthetic benefits such as fresh air and a rich flora and fauna. The idea of environmentalism being a luxury is supported by the observation that countries with the strongest environmental movements, such as the United States and Western Germany, tend also to be the richest. Developing countries often see attempts by developed nations to impose world-wide controls on the environment as a means of constraining their economic development. Tolerance of poor environmental conditions by many developing countries results in relatively little environmental protection legislation, which in turn attracts manufacturing organizations who have become uncompetitive because of increasing levels of regulation in their home countries.

9.2.1   Assessing ecological impacts

It can be difficult for an organization to know just what is meant by the idea of being friendly to the ecological environment. Consumers may be confounded by alternative arguments about the consequences of their purchases decisions, with goods that were once considered to be environmentally 'friendly' becoming seen as 'unfriendly' in a new conventional wisdom. The public are not generally technical experts to judge ecological arguments and only larger businesses generally have employees who can understand such arguments at a technical level. The following are recent examples to illustrate how technical evaluations of products in terms of their ecological credentials have changed over a short space of time:

- In the 1980s, diesel was seen as a relatively clean fuel because it produced less greenhouse gases and diesel engines were more efficient than petrol engines. By the 1990s, particulates released into the environment by diesel engines had become linked with increasing levels of asthma and the environmental credentials of diesel were downgraded.
- Similarly, much of the shine was taken off unleaded petrol when studies began showing that an additive of unleaded petrol—benzine—was carcinogenic.
- Considerable technical debate about ecological impacts surrounded the decision by the Shell Oil Company to dump its redundant Brent Spar oil platform at sea rather than to dismantle it on land.
- Both the supporters and opponents of proposals to build bypasses around towns use environmental arguments to support their arguments. Opponents argue that a new road in itself will create more road traffic which is environmentally harmful, while supporters argue that environmental damage will be lessened by moving traffic out of town where it causes less harm.

In view of the controversial nature of the ecological impacts of many products, non-technical members of the public may be easily swayed by what appears to be the most compelling arguments, put forward most vociferously by individuals or organizations that hold most influence with the public in general and legislators in particular. In the case of the Brent Spar oil platform described above, government and the scientific community appeared to agree that environmental risks would be minimized by dumping the platform in deep water. Considerable risks would result from breaking it up on land, removing toxic materials and dumping the remains in landfill sites. Despite the backing that Shell received from the UK government and members of the scientific community, the public sympathy was with Greenpeace, which mounted a campaign against Shell. The public appeared to trust Greenpeace rather than a multinational oil company. Damage to the marine environment was easier for the public to conceptualize and become emotional about, compared to unrecognized risks on land which would occur 'somewhere else'. Because of the mounting damage to the reputation of Shell, the company was forced to back down and settle for dismantling its platform on land.

Taken to its logical extreme, consumption of the vast majority of goods and services can itself result in ecological harm. For example, the most environmentally friendly means of transport is to avoid the need for transport in the first place. The most environmentally friendly holiday is for an individual to stay at home. Individuals with a true concern for preserving their ecological environment would choose to reduce their consumption of goods and services in total. At the moment, such attitudes are held by only a small minority in Western societies, but the development of a widespread anticonsumption mentality would have major implications for marketers.

9.2.2   Benefits to businesses of being 'green'

Rather than seeing environmentalism as a means of adding to an organization's costs, many have turned environmentalism into an opportunity to reduce costs. Being pro-active to environmentalism can bring a number of benefits to companies, as well as improving their image with the public:

1. Being 'green' may actually save a company money (see the case study). Often, changing existing environmentally harmful practices primarily involves overcoming traditional mind sets about how things should be done.
2. In Western developed economies, legislation to enforce environmentally sensitive methods of production is increasing. A company that adopts environmentally sensitive production methods ahead of compulsion can gain experience to competitive advantage ahead of other companies.
3. The use of environmental impact assessments may prevent a company gaining planning permission for expansion of production facilities unless it has fully thought through the environmental impacts of its actions. At best, a failure to recognize environmental issues will result in increased cost and delay to a planning application.

TESCO STORES MOVES INTO RECYCLING

The grocery retailer Tesco developed an early lead over its main competitors in identifying with environmental causes. It was a leader in promoting the sale of unleaded petrol through its petrol stations and most of its stores had recycling facilities where the store's customers could deposit their old newspapers and bottles for recycling.

In 1995, the company made a significant step in applying environmental principles to its own operations by opening the first of a series of recycling centres. The company's plans envisaged opening nine centres throughout the country which would collect hundreds of thousands of tonnes of cardboard and plastic waste from its 500 plus stores. The company sought to prove that being 'green' was not a luxury for business, but a means of saving money while meeting the growing ecological expectations of its customers and society in general.

The first recycling unit was opened in Middleton, Greater Manchester, and is operated on behalf of Tesco by Christian Salvesen. Each unit will be capable of recycling 160 000 tonnes of cardboard and 10 000 tonnes of plastic shrink-wrap every year from the group's stores. There is also the possibility of earning additional income by taking in waste materials from other companies.

The main saving to Tesco results from lower charges for dumping its waste. The company expected to save £12 million a year by not having to incur costs for dumping waste cardboard and shrink-wrap materials in landfill sites. Not using landfill sites will itself produce environmental benefit, as there has been considerable attention given to the problems of effluent leaking out of such sites and polluting water courses. It may be that government objectives to increase the amount of waste that is recycled may lead to policy implementation which increasingly penalizes companies who are responsible for producing waste. By having experience of recycling, Tesco can hope to have an early competitive advantage in such an eventuality.

Tesco's attempts to save money by being 'green' did not end with its recycling centres. A further 50 000 tonnes a year of cardboard waste will be saved through the use of new plastic trays which will be washed and re-used.

However, critics continued to argue that all was not environmentally friendly at Tesco. Superstores themselves had a tendency to be inaccessible by public transport, therefore forcing people to travel by car rather than public transport. The great success of superstores had forced many small community stores to close. However, Tesco, like other large retailers has partly addressed this issue by opening smaller 'Metro' and 'Express' stores in town centres and suburbs. Critics also point to the volume of goods transported by road which Tesco generates. Tesco's distribution system has become very efficient by operating a few very large warehouses, but this requires goods to travel long distances between the source of supply, the warehouse and then on to the store. In some cases, a product would travel several hundreds of miles to end up on a shelf just a few miles from where it was produced. Worse still, the need for consistency in its supply chain has led the company to transport many of its products from overseas sources, when alternative, but less predictable, sources are available at home. Overcoming these issues are challenges that Tesco will doubtless rise to. After all, the idea of saving money by recycling might have seemed absurd just a couple of decades ago.

QUESTIONS

1. What problems are inherent in relying on firms to voluntarily develop environmentally sensitive methods of production, rather than bringing forward legislation?
2. Suggest methods by which customers of supermarkets can be segmented according to their concerns for environmental issues.
3. Suggest further ways in which the retailing sector can fully embrace concepts of environmental responsibility.

9.2.3 Role of environmental pressure groups

Although it is often true that firms take on social responsibilities because it is commercially sensible for them to do so, there are many more cases where some form of pressure is needed to encourage them to become socially responsible. Two of the most important means by which firms can be influenced are through pressure groups and the media. In both cases, the pressure to become more socially conscious can come about either as a direct effect of these influences or indirectly as a result of pressure to change the law within which a firm operates.

Environmental pressure groups generally exist to promote a single cause related to environmentalism. These can be general environmental issues (such as Friends of the Earth and Greenpeace) or more specific (such as campaigns for or against specific road-building schemes). Sometimes, environmental groups have been accused of having a hidden agenda for their members in the form of social reform. It is often suggested that environmental pressure groups attract individuals who see environmental issues as part of a broader class struggle between the interests of those who own the means of production and those who feel disenfranchised from society.

Groups can seek to alter the behaviour of firms either directly or indirectly. Direct intervention entails making direct representations to firms whose behaviour is seen as socially unacceptable. Alternatively, pressure groups can act indirectly either by persuading customers to boycott such firms or by persuading government to pass legislation that will make antisocial behaviour by firms an offence. These are some approaches commonly used by pressure groups:

- Propaganda is a basic tool used by environmental groups to create awareness of the group and its cause. This can be aimed directly at policy formers in government or by appealing indirectly to the constituents of such policy formers who can apply direct pressure themselves.
- Pressure groups often seek to represent the views of the group directly to business organizations on a one-to-one basis. Many enlightened companies welcome representations which they consider could prevent bigger problems or confrontations arising in the future. Some environmental charities have developed a profitable business activity by selling advice to companies who might otherwise have been ignorant about how they could have saved money while at the same time operating in a more environmentally friendly way. For example, the charity Green Flag International earns money by advising tour operators that being 'green' can actually save them money.
- A third approach used by pressure groups is to carry out research and to supply information with the aim of increasing public awareness of environmental issues. An example is provided by health campaign groups which provide information on the nutritional content of food.
- Where low-key activities have failed, pressure groups may resort to more high-profile campaigns. Customer boycotts have proved on many occasions to be effective in influencing business policy. Following its decision to dump the Brent Spar oil platform at sea, Greenpeace mounted a boycott of Shell petrol stations throughout Europe, which, combined with other action by Greenpeace, posed too high a cost for Shell (directly in terms of lost sales and indirectly in terms of damage to its reputation). It decided that, given such opposition, it was not worth fighting for its principle.
- Demonstrations at key places and events (such as new product launches and official visits by key personnel) serve to draw negative media attention to a company and to embarrass its officials.
- Increasingly, members of pressure groups are buying shares in companies that are the target of their opposition. This gives them a right to attend the company's annual general meeting and to ask awkward questions directly to the directors of the company. Again, the main effect is to create media attention to such shareholders' actions.
- Some factions of pressure groups are not satisfied by peaceful means of protest and resort to direct action against companies. For example, extreme animal rights groups have targeted butchers and fur traders with arson attacks and product tampering.

Pressure groups have achieved numerous triumphs in attempting to influence business policy through the medium of new legislation. It is largely through campaigning groups' intervention at the political level that restrictions on tobacco advertising have become increasingly strict in Britain, for example. During the 1980s, the activities of the pressure group CLEAR (Campaign for Clear Air) were instrumental in developing government policy which eventually resulted in the take-up of unleaded petrol in a way which the oil companies had been reluctant to develop solely on the basis of direct pressure from groups such as CLEAR.

Pressure groups are increasingly crossing national boundaries to reflect the influence of international governmental institutions such as the European Union and the increasing influence of multinational business organizations. Both industrial and consumer pressure groups have been formed at a multinational level to counter these influences—a good example of the latter is Greenpeace.

9.2.4   Business response to pressure groups

Pressure groups can undoubtedly have significant effects on businesses that may have initially underestimated the response of such groups to their actions. Successful companies therefore seek to anticipate such problems before they occur. This can be facilitated by maintaining a dialogue with pressure groups, although there is a danger that mainstream pressure groups may not be able to convey the attitudes or control the actions of extremist members of their group.

Firms involved in environmentally sensitive business practices often go on the offensive in justifying their practices. For example, most people have an underlying suspicion about nuclear power and could probably be swayed by environmentalists' arguments about its dangers. However, this has not stopped the UK's Nuclear Electric Generating Company from mounting a comprehensive campaign to put the possible problems associated with nuclear energy in a very favourable light compared to the environmental harm caused by generating electricity from non-renewable fossil fuels and emitting harmful greenhouse gases from coal-fired power stations. In addition to press and television advertising, the company has been active in public relations. This has included opening its power stations to the public, providing educational materials for schools and maintaining mutually beneficial relationships with the media.

Where an apparently irreconcilable conflict occurs, firms must balance the costs of fighting a pressure group against the cost of pulling out from a particular market. For single-product companies who have no desire to diversify into unrelated business areas, there may be little alternative to fighting a pressure group with counter arguments and, where necessary, appropriate security measures. Where a company comes under direct attack by pressure groups and has a good case to make for its practices, it may be able to capitalize on public sympathy for its position.

9.2.5 The media and environmental issues

The media often acts as an important change agent on business practices. It not only spreads awareness of social issues but also influences business policy and decision making by setting the political agenda and influencing public opinion.

At national and local levels, the media has adopted social issues and campaigned in pursuit of goals with which their readers can identify. Recent examples include:

- Campaigns by local newspapers to prevent the development of open cast mining which will create noise and dust pollution for local residents
- Television programmes that have drawn attention to problems caused by excessive dumping of waste into the North Sea
- Press and television coverage of threats to the rain forests in tropical areas

Pressure groups appreciate the power of the media to influence public opinion and generally go to great lengths to present their case to media correspondents. Where companies refuse to talk to the media about environmentally sensitive issues, victory in the media can go to pressure groups by default. It was claimed in the Brent Spar dispute that the broadcast media, including the BBC, gave undue emphasis to the arguments of Greenpeace, at the expense of those advanced by Shell. The BBC in particular was accused of showing film taken by Greenpeace without making much attempt to obtain footage putting forward an opposite view. An emotive story and an opponent who is reluctant to talk can leave media editors welcoming film from pressure groups with open arms. Many organizations realize that good public relations is about more than dampening down crises once they have broken out: it is about developing an ongoing programme of mutual understanding between themselves and their publics, including the media in particular.

9.3 BUSINESS ETHICS

The law provides substantial regulation of the dealings between individuals and organizations, for example in the form of the law of contract and the law of tort. However, law cannot cover every aspect of dealings between individuals, so people are guided in their actions by a formal or informal set of rules in society. Members of the society recognize that everybody will be better off if they adhere to a moral code of governance.

Ethics are a moral code of what is right and wrong. The difficulty comes in trying to decide what is right and wrong. No two people have precisely the same opinions, so critics would argue that ethical considerations are of little interest to business. It is sometimes difficult to distinguish between ethics and legality. For example, it may not be strictly illegal to exploit the gullibility of children in advertisements, but it may nevertheless be unethical.

Ethics are very much culturally bound and what is considered unethical in one society may be considered perfectly acceptable in another. In Western societies, ethical considerations confront marketers on many occasions. For example:

1. A company may advertise a product and provide information that is technically correct, but omit to provide vital information about side effects associated with using the product. Should a marketing manager be required to spell out the drawbacks of using their products, as well as the benefits?
2. An estate agent may not disclose a personal financial interest he has to a customer whose property he is handling. An estate agent may try to convince a seller of a house to accept a low price for the sale of their house, when the agent has not disclosed that his friend is interested in buying it. Should disclosure be required?
3. A dentist is short of money and diagnoses fillings that may need renewing. How does he reconcile his need to maximize his earning potential with the need to provide what is best for his patient?
4. In order to secure a major new construction contract, a sales person must entertain the client's buying manager with a weekend all-expenses paid holiday. Should this be considered acceptable business practice in Britain? Or in South America?

It is suggested that society is becoming increasingly concerned about the ethical values adopted by its business organizations. With increasing levels of media availability and an increasingly intelligent audience, it is becoming easier to expose examples of unethical business practice. To give one example, the Hoover Company has been highlighted in a number of television programmes and newspaper articles for the unethical way in which it tried to talk people out of using 'free' air tickets which they had earned from a sales promotion run by the company.

Firms are responding to increasing levels of ethical awareness by trying to put their own house in order. These are some examples of how firms have gone about the task:

1. Greater attention to training can make clear to staff just what is expected of them, for example that it is unethical (and in the long run harmful to the business) for a financial services company's sales personnel to try and sell a policy to a person that really does not suit their needs. Training may emphasize the need to spend a lot of time finding out just what the true needs of the customer are.
2. More effective control and reward systems can help to reduce unethical practices within an organization. For example, sales personnel employed by a financial services company on a commission-only basis are more likely to try and sell a policy to a customer regardless of their needs compared to a salaried employee who can take a longer term view of the relationship between the company and its clients.
3. A company may be able to identify segments of the population who are prepared to pay a premium to buy a product that has been produced in an ethical manner or from a company that has adopted ethical practices. Many people would consider certain treatment of cattle grown for meat to be inhuman and unethical and would be happy to buy from a supplier who they knew acted ethically in the manner in which the cattle were raised and slaughtered. Similarly, many people who invest money are concerned not just about the return that they will get but the way in which that return will be earned. This explains the increasing popularity of ethical investment funds that avoid investing in companies that are considered to be of a socially dubious nature.

Acting ethically need not add a burden to organization's production costs, but can lead to improved financial performance. For example, good safety standards and employment policies can improve productivity. In the United Kingdom, the DIY retailer B&Q has reduced discrimination against older workers by employing predominantly older people in one of its stores. It is claimed that this store has become one of the firm's most profitable.

It has been argued that society is moving away from one in which relationships between individuals are governed by moral values towards one that is based on contractual governance (Gundlach and Murphy, 1993). The proliferation of regulations affecting the financial services industry, for example, is evidence of the trend to prevent the abuse of power where suppliers who are put in a position of trust act unethically in abusing that trust.

Some segments of consumers have become increasingly selective about who they make their purchases from, basing their decision on the environmental and ethical credentials of a supplier. An individual may, for example, favour a company that has refused to purchase supplies from countries with oppressive governments. There have been a number of well-documented cases of goods manufacturers who have sold socially harmful goods and faced boycotts from consumer groups. The Nestle Company's exploitation of the market for dried milk products in underdeveloped countries, for example, saw many Western consumers boycotting the company's products on principle.

Many goods and services organizations are keen to link themselves to good social causes—the Tesco supermarket group's support for recycling schemes and the purchase of computers for schools helped to give it a distinctive positioning as a socially aware store during the late 1980s. The opposite—linking a corporate brand to a bad cause—can have long-term harmful effects on an organization, for example the association of Barclays Bank with an oppressive government in South Africa during the 1970s.

9.3.1 Good corporate governance

Recognition that companies should be answerable to more stakeholders than just their shareholders has led to many prescriptions for corporate governance to be raised to a moral plane. Recent examples of poor corporate governance, where highly paid directors have undertaken financial transactions of dubious value to shareholders, have served to strengthen the need for a code by which directors run a business.

In the United Kingdom, a number of attempts to develop blueprints for corporate governance have been developed (e.g. those by the Cadbury and Greenbury Committees). 'Good practice' in corporate governance is increasingly being defined in terms of:

1. Having in place internal control systems which prevent the type of abuse of directors' power that occurred in the former Maxwell group of companies.
2. Having an appropriate structure for the board of directors which combines full-time executive directors with non-executive directors brought in from outside.
3. Striking a balance when remunerating senior directors and employees between the reassurance of a long-term salary and performance for results. During the 1980s, many critics had drawn attention to the abuse of three year 'rolling contracts' which effectively gave directors and senior staff three years notice of their termination of employment. Shareholders began to wonder how an entrepreneurial individual could be taken on at a high performance-related salary, but end up with three years payment as compensation if he or she failed and was dismissed. Good corporate governance has tended to favour shorter contracts.
4. Directors' pay has received considerable adverse attention in the popular press, and good governance should ensure that such pay is determined in a manner that is fair to shareholders and is not part of an incestuous circle of pay review bodies.

5. Employees are recognized as increasingly important stakeholders in organizations and there have been many initiatives, such as 'investors in people', to promote the training and development of an organization's work-force.

Corporate governance debates that have been taking place throughout the world over the past few years have focused on national issues, but to companies operating in overseas countries the international dimension can be crucial. Ideas about appropriate corporate governance are deeply rooted in national cultures, reflecting economic, political, social and legal traditions in each country. Despite convergence, differences still predominate, for example in attitudes towards the disclosure of directors' salaries.

MIS-SELLING OF FINANCIAL SERVICES

The early 1990s was a bad time for the life insurance and pensions industry. Deregulation of financial services markets and weak policing of regulations governing the industry had finally caused major casualties among firms and customers alike.

One major area of controversy had focused on the manner in which pensions policies had been sold. Most people in full-time jobs in the United Kingdom belong to an occupational pension scheme in which they and their employer pay a proportion of their monthly salary into a scheme and draw a pension based on their final salary when they retire. However, during the 1980s, the government had introduced legislation that made it much easier for individuals to create their own personal pension, as an alternative to belonging to their employees' scheme. The government also offered incentives to individuals who wished to switch to such schemes, in the form of rebates of National Insurance premiums.

The short-term incentives on offer from the government were a carrot that commission-hungry pensions sales personnel used to dangle in front of potential customers, who by and large had very little understanding of the complexities of pension policies. The imbalance in knowledge gave the pension sales person considerable power over their potential customers, who could much more easily grasp the short-term benefits of National Insurance benefits, but fail to fully appreciate the long-term disadvantages of switching to a private pension scheme.

Following a period of steady sales of personal pension schemes during the late 1980s, the bubble burst in the early 1990s when many groups, such as nurses and teachers, found that they had transferred out of a very good employer-funded scheme into one that was offering much lower returns. Worse still, customers had often not appreciated the very high costs of switching out of personal pensions schemes part-way during their term, should they subsequently change their mind.

In the controversy that followed, the industry regulator LAUTRO investigated the behaviour of pension companies' sales personnel and found that their training and control frequently allowed unethical behaviour on their part. Commission-hungry sales staff often had too much need for income and too little training to allow them to assess customers' true financial needs. Consequently, many customers who would have been much better off by staying in a company pension scheme were talked into taking out a personal pension scheme. LAUTRO recognized that this was unethical behaviour and fined a number of companies, including Norwich Union, while ordering others to retrain their work-force.

QUESTIONS

1. From a broad perspective, identify the principal stakeholders in a pension company such as Norwich Union.
2. How could a company like Norwich Union improve the ethical manner in which it conducts its business?
3. What role do you think pressure groups could play in bringing about more ethical behaviour by pensions companies?

REVIEW QUESTIONS

1. Giving examples, explain what is meant by the term 'environmental lobbies'. Provide a résumé of the tactics you would advise a high profile company to use in managing relations with special interest groups.
   (CIM Marketing Environment Examination, December 1994, Q.1(d))
2. (a) Identify *two* stakeholder groups and briefly assess the nature and terms of their stake in the organization.
   (b) Prepare a brief for your marketing director outlining the concept of social responsibility and indicating how this might be applied to your customers and how it might be of overall benefit.
   (CIM Marketing Environment Examination, December 1994, Q.2)
3. For what reasons might a tour operating company choose to adopt the societal marketing concept? By adopting the concept, is it really changing the way it does business?
4. Explain the reasons why good corporate governance has become an important issue in many countries.
5. For a multinational company operating in many different cultures, is it possible to define an ethical code of conduct?
6. What approach should businesses take in response to pressure groups' claims that their activities are causing ecological damage?

REFERENCES

Anderson, P. (1982) 'Marketing, Strategic Planning and Theory', *Journal of Marketing*, Spring, pp. 15–26.

Arbratt, R. and Sacks, D. (1988) 'Perceptions of the Societal Marketing Concept', *European Journal of Marketing*, vol. 22, pp. 25–33.

Gundlach, Gregory T. and Murphy, Patrick E. (1993). 'Ethical and Legal Foundations of Relational Marketing Exchange', *Journal of Marketing*, vol. 57 (October), pp. 35–46.

Samuelson, P.A. (1992) *Economics*, 14th edn, McGraw-Hill, New York.

FURTHER READING

Bromley, D. (ed.) (1995) *The Handbook of Environmental Economics*, Blackwell, Oxford.

Cairncross, F. (1991) *Costing the Earth*, Harvard Business School Press, Boston, Mass.

Ferrell, O. C. and Gresham, L. (1985) 'A Contingency Framework for Understanding Ethical Decision Making in Marketing', *Journal of Marketing*, vol. 49 (Summer), pp. 87–96.

Frederick, W. C., Post, J. E. and Davis, K. (1992) 'Business and Society: Corporate Strategy, Public Policy and Ethics', in *Business Ethics: A European Casebook*, ed. J. Donaldson, 7th edn, Academic Press, London.

Harvey, B. (1994) *Business Ethics: A European Approach*, Prentice-Hall, Englewood Cliffs, N.J.

Hoffman, M. and Frederick, R. E. (eds) (1995) *Business Ethics: Readings and Cases in Corporate Morality*, 3rd edn, McGraw-Hill, New York.

Robin, D. P. and Reidenbach, E. E. (1987). 'Social Responsibility, Ethics and Marketing Strategy: Closing the Gap between Concept and Application', *Journal of Marketing*, vol. 51 (January), pp. 44–58.

Solomon, R. C. (1992) *Ethics and Excellence*, Oxford University Press, Oxford.

THE LEGAL ENVIRONMENT

OBJECTIVES

After reading this chapter, you should understand:

- The principal sources of law and their impact upon marketing activities.
- Legal remedies and processes available to a firm's customers.
- Voluntary codes of conduct as an alternative to law.

10.1 INTRODUCTION

The legal environment impinges on the marketing activities of a business organization at various levels:

- The nature of the relationship between the organization and its customers is influenced by the prevailing law. At one time, the two parties were considered to be equal partners, both being able to look after their affairs by their own means. Over time, however, there has been a tendency for the law to give additional rights to the buyer of goods and additional duties to the seller, especially in the case of transactions between businesses and private individuals. Whereas the nineteenth-century entrepreneur in Britain would have had almost complete freedom to dictate the terms of the relationship with its customers, developments in statute law and common law now require, for example, the supplier to ensure that the goods are of satisfactory quality and that no misleading description of them is made.

  Furthermore, the expectations of an organization's customers have changed over time. Whereas previous generations may have resigned themselves to suffering injustice in their dealings with a business, today the expectation is increasingly for perfection every time. Greater awareness of the law on the part of consumers has produced an increasingly litigious society.

- In addition to the direct relationship that a company has with its customers, the law also influences the relationship that it has with other members of the general public. The law may, for example, prevent a firm having access to certain sectors of the market, as where children are prohibited by law from buying cigarettes or drinking in public houses. Also, the messages that a company sends out in its advertising are likely to be picked up by members of the general public, and the law has intervened to protect the public interest where these messages could cause offence—adverts that are racially prejudicial, for example. The law is imposing increasing duties on businesses in their dealings with the general public.

- The legal environment influences the relationship between business enterprises themselves, not only in terms of contracts for transactions between them, but also in the way they relate to each other in a competitive environment. The law has increasingly prevented companies from joining together in anticompetitive practices, such as legislation that regulates the activities of monopoly providers of public utilities.

● Companies need to develop new products, yet the rewards of undertaking new product development are influenced by the law. The laws of copyright and patent protect a firm's investment in fruitful research.

● From a wider perspective, the legal environment influences the production possibilities of an enterprise and hence the products that can be offered to consumers. These can have a direct effect—as in the case of regulations stipulating car safety design requirements—or an indirect effect—as where legislation to reduce pollution increases the manufacturing costs of a product, or prevents its manufacture completely.

The legal environment of marketing is very closely related to the political environment. Law derives from two sources. The common law develops on the basis of judgments in the courts: a case may set a precedent for all subsequent cases to follow; the judiciary is independent of government; and the general direction of precedents tends gradually to reflect changing attitudes in society. Statute law, on the other hand, is passed by Parliament and to a much greater extent reflects the prevailing political ideology of the government.

The law is a very complex area of the marketing environment. Most marketers would call upon expert members of the legal profession to interpret and act upon some of the more complex elements of the law. The purpose of this chapter is not to give definitive answers on aspects of the law as it affects marketers—this would be impossible and dangerous in such a short space. Instead, the aim is to raise the marketer's awareness of legal issues so that he or she can recognize in general terms the opportunities and restrictions that the law poses for them and the areas in which they may need to seek the specialized advice of a legal professional.

10.2 THE LAW OF CONTRACT

The first area to consider in examining the legal environment is the nature of the contract governing the relationship between the business organization and its customers.

There can be no direct legal relationship between a company and customers unless it can be proved that a contract exists. An advertisement on its own only very rarely creates a legal relationship. The elements of a contract comprise: offer, acceptance, intention to create legal relations, consideration and capacity.

10.2.1 Offer

An offer is a declaration by which the offeror intends to be legally bound on the terms stated in the offer if it is accepted by the offeree. The offer may be oral, in writing or by conduct between the parties, and must be clear and unambiguous. It may be made to a particular person or to the whole world. It is extremely important that it be distinguished from an 'invitation to treat', which can be defined as an invitation to make offers. Normally, all advertisements are regarded as invitations to treat, as is illustrated in a case in which a man was charged with offering for sale live birds, bramble finches (*Partridge* v. *Crittendon* [1968] 1 WLR 286). A person reading the advert wrote, enclosing the money for the bird which was duly sent. The advertiser was charged with the offence of offering wild birds for sale, but it was held that the advertisement was not an offer but an invitation to treat and therefore he escaped the charge.

Of importance to the consumer is the rule that priced goods on display in supermarkets and shops are not offers but invitations to treat. Therefore, if a leather jacket is priced at £20 (through error) in the shop widow, it is not possible to demand the garment at that price: as the display is an invitation to treat, it is the consumer who is making the offer which the shopkeeper may accept or reject as he wishes.

10.2.2 Acceptance

Acceptance may be made only by the person(s) to whom the offer was made, and it must be absolute and unqualified; i.e. it must not add any new terms or conditions, for to do so would have the effect of revoking the original offer. Acceptance must be communicated to the offeror unless it can be implied by conduct. In the case of *Carlill* v. *Carbolic Smoke Ball Co.* ([1893] 1 QB 256 CA), the defendants were the makers of a smoke ball which was purported to prevent influenza. The advertisement stated that £100 would be given to any person catching influenza after having sniffed their smoke ball in accordance with the instructions given. The manufacturers deposited £1000 at a bank to show that their claim was sincere. Mrs Carlill bought a smoke ball in response to the advertisement, complied with the instructions but still caught influenza.

In Mrs Carlill's case, her purchase implied her acceptance, for this was an offer to the world at large and it was not therefore necessary to communicate her acceptance in person to the offeror. She sued for the £100 and was successful. It was argued by the defence that the advertisement was an invitation to treat, but in this rare instance it was held to be an offer.

10.2.3 Intention to create legal relations

The above case turned on the third element of a contract—the intention to create legal relations. It was held that, because the company had deposited the £1000 in the bank, this was evidence of its intention to be legally bound and therefore here the advertisement constituted an offer. Generally, in all commercial agreements it is accepted that both parties intend to make a legally binding contract and therefore it is unnecessary to include terms to this effect.

10.2.4 Consideration

This factor is essential in all contracts unless they are made 'under seal'. Consideration has been defined as some right, interest, profit or benefit accruing to one part or some forebearance, detriment, loss or responsibility given, suffered or undertaken by the other—i.e. some benefit accruing to one part or a detriment suffered by the other. In commercial contracts generally, the consideration takes the form of a cash payment. However, in contracts of barter, which are common with Eastern bloc countries, goods are often exchanged for goods.

10.2.5 Capacity

The final element is that of capacity. Generally, any persons may enter into an agreement which may be enforced against them. Exceptions include minors, drunks and mental patients; for this reason, companies usually exclude people under 18 from offers of goods to be supplied on credit.

An offer may be revoked at any time prior to acceptance. However, if postal acceptance is an acceptable means of communication between the parties, then acceptance is effective as soon as it is posted, provided it is correctly addressed and stamped.

10.3 STATUTORY INTERVENTION

Prior to 1968, there was very little statutory intervention in the relationship between the business organization and its customers, with a few exceptions such as those that came within the scope of the Food and Drugs Act 1955.

Every advertisement is now governed by the Trade Descriptions Act 1968 and 1972, which make it an offence for a person to make a false or misleading trade description.

10.3.1 Trade Descriptions Act 1968

The Trade Descriptions Act 1968 imposes an obligation on local authorities for enforcement and creates three principal offences.

A false trade description to goods Under s. 1, this states that 'a person who, in the course of business, applies false trade descriptions to goods or suppliers or offers to supply goods to which a false description has been applied is guilty of an offence'. Section 2 defines a false trade description as including 'any indication of any physical characteristics such as quantity, size, method of manufacture, composition and fitness for purpose'.

A description is regarded as false when it is false or, by s. 3(2), misleading to a material degree. In one case it was held that to describe as 'new' a car that had sustained damage while in the manufacturer's compound was not an offence because of the excellent repair work carried out on the car which rendered the vehicle 'good as new' (*R. v. Ford Motor Co. Ltd* [1947] 3 All ER 489).

In some cases consumers are misled by advertisements that are economical with the truth. A car was advertised as having one previous 'owner'. Strictly this was true, but it had been owned by a leasing company who had leased it to five different buyers. The divisional court held this was misleading and caught by s. 3(2) of the Trade Descriptions Act (*R. v. South Western Justices* ex parte *London Borough of Wandsworth, Times* [20 January, 1983]).

A false statement of price Section 11 makes a false statement as to the price of an offence. If a trader claims that his prices are reduced, he is guilty of an offence unless he can show that the goods have been on sale at the higher price during the preceding six months for a consecutive period of 28 days.

A false trade description of services Section 14 states that it is an offence to make false or misleading statements as to services. An example of this is illustrated in the case of a store that advertised 'folding doors and folding door *gear*—carriage free'. This statement was intended to convey to the consumer that only the folding door gear would be sent carriage-free on purchase of the folding doors. It was held that the advert was misleading and that it was irrelevant that it was not intended to be misleading (*MFI Warehouses Ltd. v. Nattrass* [1973] 1 All ER 762).

Defences under the Trade Descriptions Act are set out in s. 24(i):

(a) that the commission of the offence was due to a mistake or to reliance on information supplied to him or to the act or default of another person, an accident or some other cause beyond his control; *and*
(b) that he took all reasonable precautions and exercised all due diligence to avoid the commission of such an offence by himself or any person under his control.

For the defence to succeed, it is necessary to show that both subsections apply.

In a case concerning a leading supermarket, a brand of washing powder was advertised as being 5p less than the price marked in the store. The defendants said that it was the fault of the store manager who had failed to go through the system laid down for checking shelves. The court held that the defence applied; the store manager was another person (s. 24(i)(*a*)) and the store had taken reasonable precautions to prevent commission of the offence (*Tesco Supermarkets Ltd v. Nattrass* [1971] 2 All ER 127).

10.3.2 Sale of Goods Act 1979

What rights has the consumer if on purchase he discovers that the goods are faulty or are different from those ordered? The Sale of Goods Act (SOGA) contains implied terms specifically to protect the consumer. A party deals as a consumer according to s. 12 of the Unfair Contract Terms Act 1977 if:

(a) he neither makes the contract in the course of a business nor holds himself out as doing so; and

(b) the other party does make the contract in the course of a business; and

(c) in the case of a contract governed by the law of sale of goods or hire purchase …. The goods passing under … the contracts are of a type ordinarily supplied for private use or consumption.

Section 13 of the Sale of Goods Act 1979 states that 'Where there is a contract for the sale of goods by description there is an implied condition that the goods will correspond with the description.' The sale is not prevented from being a sale by description even if the goods are on display and selected by the buyer. It is important to note that s. 13 applies to sales by private individuals and businesses.

In a case concerning a 1961 Triumph Herald, advertised for sale in the paper, it was discovered that the car was made up of two halves of different Triumph Heralds, only one of which was a 1961 model, and in the Court of Appeal the plaintiff's claim for damages was upheld (*Beale* v. *Taylor* [1967] 1 WLR 1993).

The goods must, for example, be as described on the package. If a customer purchases a blue long-sleeved shirt and on opening the box discovers that it is a red short-sleeved shirt, then he is entitled to a return of the price for breach of an implied condition of the contract.

A recent example that illustrates the operation of s. 13 is a case concerning the sale by one art dealer to another of a painting that both assumed genuine. It later transpired that the painting was a forgery. The buyer brought an action relying on a breach of s. 13(1) and s. 14(2) of SOGA. It was, however, held that the contract was not one for the sale of goods by description within s. 13(1) because the description of the painting as regards its author did not become a term of the contract. It was clearly fit for the purpose for which art is commonly bought and therefore of merchantable quality. In this case, 'by description [it] was held to imply that the description must have been so important a factor in the sale to become a condition of the contract' (*Harlingdon & Leinster Enterprises Ltd* v. *Christopher Hull/Fine Art Ltd* [1990] 1 All ER 737).

Section 14(2) as amended by the Sale and Supply of Goods Act 1994 states:

Where the seller sells goods in the course of a business, there is an implied term that the goods supplied under the contract are of satisfactory quality.

Section 14(2A) gives a definition of satisfactory quality which now replaces the term 'merchantable quality':

For the purposes of this Act goods are of satisfactory quality if they meet the standard that a reasonable person would regard as satisfactory, taking account of any description of the goods, the price (if relevant) and all other relevant circumstances.

This definition is further expanded by s. 14(2B) as follows:

For the purposes of this Act, the quality of goods includes their state and condition and the following (among others) are in appropriate cases aspects of the quality of the goods:

(a) fitness for all the purposes for which goods of the kind in question are commonly supplied,

(b) appearance and finish,

(c) freedom from minor defects,

(d) safety, and

(e) durability.

Section 14(2C) states:

The term implied by subsection (2) above does not extend to any matter making the quality of goods unsatisfactory:

(a) which is specifically drawn to the buyer's attention before the contract is made,
(b) where the buyer examines the goods before the contract is made, which that examination ought to reveal, or
(c) in the case of a sale by sample, which would have been apparent on a reasonable examination of the sample.

(The moral for the consumer is therefore: examine thoroughly or not at all.)

The implied term of unsatisfactory quality applies to sale goods and second-hand goods, but clearly the consumer would not have such high expectations of second-hand goods. For example, a clutch fault in a new car would make it unsatisfactory, but not so if the car were second-hand. In a second-hand car—again, depending on all the circumstances—a fault would have to be major to render the car unsatisfactory. Thus, the question to be asked is, 'Are the goods satisfactory in the light of the contract description and all the circumstances of the case?'

It is often asked for how long the goods should remain merchantable. It is perhaps implicit that the goods remain merchantable for a length of time reasonable in the circumstances of the case and the nature of the goods. If a good becomes defective within a very short time, this is evidence that there was possibly a latent defect at the time of the sale.

In one case, a new car which on delivery had a minor defect that was likely to, and subsequently did, cause the engine to seize up while the car was being driven was neither of merchantable quality nor reasonably fit for its purpose under s. 14. The purchaser could not, however, rescind the contract and recover the price because it was held that he had retained the car 'after the lapse of a reasonable time' without intimating to the seller that he had rejected it even though the defect had not at that time become obvious (*Berstein* v. *Pampson Motors (Golders Green) Ltd* [1987] 2 All ER 220 N3). It was held that s. 35(1) of SOGA did not refer to a reasonable time to discover a particular defect: rather, it meant a reasonable time to inspect the goods and try them out generally. Thus, the owner, having been deemed to have accepted the car, was entitled to damages to compensate him for the cost of getting home, the loss of a tank of petrol and the inconvenience of being without a car while it was being repaired. Had there been any evidence that the car's value had been reduced as a result of the defect, he would obviously have been entitled to damages for that too. The moral here is to examine thoroughly immediately on purchase.

Under s. 14(3), there is an implied condition that goods are fit for a particular purpose:

> Where the seller sells goods in the course of a business and the buyer, expressly or by implication, makes known to the seller ... any particular purpose for which the goods are being bought, there is an implied condition that the goods ... are reasonably fit for that purpose, whether or not it is a purpose for which goods are commonly supplied, except where the circumstances show that the buyer does not rely, or that it is unreasonable for him to rely, on the skill or judgment of the seller.

Thus, if a seller, on request, confirms suitability for a particular purpose and the product proves unsuitable, there would be a breach of s. 14(3); if the product is also unsuitable for its normal purposes, then s. 14(2) would also be breached. If the seller disclaims any knowledge of the product's suitability for the particular purpose and the consumer takes a chance and purchases it, then if it proves unsuitable for its particular purpose there is no breach of s. 14(3). The only circumstance in which a breach may occur is, again, if it were unsuitable for its normal purposes under s. 14(2).

In business contracts, implied terms in ss. 13–15 of the Sale of Goods Act 1979 can be excluded. Such exclusion clauses, purporting, for example, to exclude a term for reasonable fitness for goods (s. 14), are valid subject to the test of reasonableness provided that the term is incorporated into the contract (i.e. that the buyer is or ought reasonably to be aware of the term).

Where consumer contracts are concerned, then such clauses that purport to limit or exclude liability are void under s. 6(2) of the Unfair Contract Terms Act 1977. Obviously, the goods purchased must come within the scope of consumer goods, and thus items such as lorries or machinery would take the transaction outside the scope of a consumer sale.

The case of *R & B Customs Brokers Co Ltd* v. *United Dominions Trust Ltd* ([1988] I All ER 847) is of some importance to the business world. Here, a company operating as shipping brokers and freight forwarding agents purchased a car for use by a director in the business. The sale was held to be a consumer sale within the meaning of s. 12 of the Unfair Contract Terms Act 1977 (UCTA); therefore a term for reasonable fitness for purposes under s. 14 of SOGA 1979 could not be excluded from the contract of sale (s. 6(2) of UCTA). The Court of Appeal followed the decision in a Trade Descriptions Act case in which a self-employed courier traded in his old car in part-exchange for a new car. The mileometer registered 18 100 miles, but it was evident that the true mileage was 118 000 miles. The owner was therefore prosecuted for having applied a false trade description to the car and was convicted by the magistrate's court. The division court allowed the appeal on the grounds that the vehicle was not disposed of in the course of a business—the point on which the prosecution turned. Lord Keith held that the expression 'in the course of a trade or business' in the context of an Act having consumer protection as its primary purpose conveys the concept of some degree of regularity. He said that the requisite degree of regularity had not been established here because a normal practice of buying and disposing of cars had not been established at the time of the alleged offence in the case. From this it follows that, had R & B Custom Brokers been dealing in cars, then the purchase of a director's car would not have been a consumer purchase. It is clear then that the self-employed—the sole traders—who no doubt assume that they are dealing in the course of a business are extremely well protected under the Sale of Goods Act and the Trade Descriptions Act. How anomalous it is when one considers that R & B Customs Brokers would no doubt be horrified if the Inland Revenue held that they were not operating in the course of a business and refused capital allowances on the director's car.

Where the buyer is dealing otherwise than as a consumer, any exclusion or limitation clause will be valid subject to the tests of reasonableness contained in s. 11 and schedule II of the Unfair contract Terms Act 1977.

The Supply of Goods and Services Act 1982 (SGSA) offers almost identical protection where goods are passed under a Supply of Goods and Services contact in s. 3 (which corresponds to s. 13 of SOGA) and s. 4 (which corresponds to s. 14 of SOGA). Where exclusion clauses are incorporated that relate to the supply of goods, then s. 7 of the Unfair Contract Terms Act replaces s. 6, previously discussed.

Section 13 of SGSA provides that, where the supplier of a service under a contract is acting in the course of a business, there is an implied term that the supplier will carry out the service with reasonable care and skill. Reasonable care and skill may be defined as 'the ordinary skill of an ordinary competent man exercising that particular act'. Much will depend on the circumstances of the case and the nature of the trade or profession.

10.4   MISREPRESENTATION

If a consumer cannot find a remedy under statute, there is a possibility that in certain circumstances he or she may be able to rescind the contract or claim damages arising from misrepresentation. Even though the essential elements of a contract are present, the contract may still fail to be given full effect.

Generally it is assumed that statements which are made at the formation of a contract are terms of that contract, but many statements made during the course of negotiations are mere representations. If the statement is a term, the injured party may sue for breach of contract and will normally obtain damages that are deemed to put him or her in the position they would have been in if the statement had been true. If the statement is a mere representation, it may be possible to avoid the contract by obtaining an order—known as rescission—which puts the parties back in the position they were in prior to the formation of the contract.

Statements of opinion and mere 'puffs' (e.g. advertising jargon) are not statements of fact and consequently are not actionable. For a long time estate agents have been free to describe houses for sale in unjustifiably glowing terms without fear of redress as the terms were mere puffs. However, as a result of growing pressure from the public, in March 1991 the House of Commons debated a Private Members' Bill to make misleading property particulars illegal. The Bill, which has the support of both the Consumers Association and the government, could signal the end of such gems as 'easily managed garden' (meaning a 2 ft × 2 ft yard at the back) and 'in need of some restoration' (meaning derelict). The most common complaints from estate agents' descriptions include incorrect room sizes, misleading photographs and deceptive descriptions of local amenities in the area—in one case the agents blocked out in the photograph an ugly gasworks which overshadowed a house they were trying to sell.

Once it has been established that the statement in question is a representation and not a term of the contract, it is necessary to consider whether it is actionable. An actionable misrepresentation may be defined as 'a false statement of existing or past fact made by one party to the other before or at the time of making the contract, which is intended to, and does, induce the other party to enter into the contract'.

A representation has no effect on a contract unless it was intended to cause and has caused the representee to make the contract.

10.4.1   Remedies for misrepresentation

The main remedy for all types of misrepresentation is the equitable remedy of rescission. Obviously it is not always possible to make rescission. It cannot occur where the plaintiff has by his or her actions affirmed that he or she is continuing with the contract, where restitution is impossible, where there are supervening third-party rights or where there is a lapse of time without any step towards repudiation being taken. In these cases, damages form the principle remedy.

When considering the availability of damages for misrepresentation, it is necessary to distinguish between the position before and after the Misrepresentation Act 1967. Prior to the Act there were two types of misrepresentation: fraudulent and innocent.

Fraudulent misrepresentation could be defined as a statement made knowingly, or without belief in its truth, or recklessly, i.e. careless as to whether it was true or false. If the representee could prove fraud, then in addition to rescission damages could also be claimed.

Innocent misrepresentation was any misrepresentation prior to the 1967 Act for which fraud could not be proved, and there was no remedy in damages for innocent misrepresentation. Since the 1967 Act, however, it has been necessary to maintain a clear distinction between negligent misrepresentation and wholly innocent misrepresentation.

Section 2(1) states:

Where a person has entered into a contract after a misrepresentation has been made to him by another party and as a result has suffered loss, then, if the person making the representation would be liable to damages in respect thereof had the misrepresentation been made fraudulently, that person shall be so liable not withstanding that the misrepresentation was not made fraudulently, unless he pleads that he had reasonable grounds to believe and did believe up to the time the contract was made that the facts represented were true.

Section 2(2) states:

Where a person has entered into a contract after a misrepresentation has been made to him otherwise than fraudulently, and he would be entitled, by reason of the misrepresentation, to rescind the contract, then if it is claimed, in any proceedings arising out of the contract, that the contract ought to be or has been rescinded, the court or arbitrator may declare the contract subsisting and award damages in lieu of rescission, if of the opinion that it would be equitable to do so having regard to the nature of the misrepresentation and the loss that would be caused by it if the contract were upheld, as well as to the loss that rescission would cause to the other party.

The 1967 Act introduced a different type of misrepresentation (negligence under s. 2(i), but this is misleading because negligence does not have to be proved, as Bridge LJ held in *Howard Marine and Dredging Co Ltd* v. *Ogden and Sons* (*Excavations*) Ltd:

The liability of the representor does not depend on his being under a duty of care the extent of which may vary according to the circumstances in which the representation is made. In the course of negotiations leading to a contract the 1967 Act imposes an absolute obligation not to state facts which he cannot prove he had reasonable grounds to believe.

Section 2(2) empowers the court to refuse rescission or to reconstitute a rescinded contract and award damages in lieu.

To sum up, rescission is a remedy for all three types of misrepresentation. In addition to rescission for fraudulent misrepresentation, damages may be awarded under the tort of fraud, and in respect of negligent misrepresentation damages may be awarded under s. 2(1) of the 1967 Act. Under s. 2(2) damages may also be awarded at the discretion of the court, but, if so, these are in lieu of rescission.

10.5   NON-CONTRACTUAL LIABILITY

Consider now the situation where the consumer discovers that goods are defective in some way but is unable to sue the retailer because the consumer is not a party to the contract. The only possible course of action was to sue the manufacturer. This situation was illustrated in 1932 in the case of *Donaghue* v. *Stevenson*, where a man bought a bottle of ginger beer manufactured by the defendant. The man gave the bottle to his female companion, who became ill from drinking the contents as the bottle (which was opaque) contained the decomposing remains of a snail. The consumer sued the manufacturer and won. The House of Lords held that on the facts outlined there was remedy in the tort of negligence.

To prove negligence, there are three elements that must be shown:

1. That the defendant was under a duty of care to the plaintiff.
2. That there had been a breach of that duty.
3. That there is damage to the plaintiff as a result of the breach which is not too remote a consequence.

In the case, Lord Atkin defined a duty of care thus:

> A manufacturer of products, which he sells in such a form as to show that he intends them to reach the ultimate consumer in the form in which they left him with no reasonable possibility of intermediate examination, and with the knowledge that the absence of reasonable care in the preparation or putting up of the products will result in an injury to the consumer's life or property, owes a duty to the consumer to take reasonable care. ...
>
> You must take reasonable care to avoid acts or omissions which you can reasonable foresee would be likely to injure your neighbour. Who then is my neighbour? The answer seems to be persons who are so closely and directly affected by my act that I ought reasonably to have them in contemplation as being so affected when I am directing my mind to the acts or omissions which are called in question.

The law of negligence is founded almost entirely on decided cases, and the approach adopted by the courts is one that affords flexibility in response to the changing patterns of practical problems. Unfortunately, it is unavoidable that with flexibility comes an element of uncertainty. Whether or not liability will arise in a particular set of circumstances appears to be heavily governed by public policy, and it is not clear exactly when a duty of care will arise. At present, the principles or alternatively the questions to be asked in attempting to determine whether a duty exists are:

● Is there foreseeability of harm, and if so,
● Is there proximity—a close and direct relationship—and if so,
● Is it fair and reasonable for there to be a duty in these circumstances?

Having established in certain circumstances that a duty of care exists, defendants will be in breach of that duty if they have not acted reasonably. The question is, What standard of care does the law require? The standard of care required is that of an ordinary prudent man in the circumstances pertaining to the case. For example, in one case it was held that an employee owed a higher standard of care to a one-eyed motor mechanic and was therefore obliged to provide protective goggles—not because the likelihood of damage was greater, but because the consequences of an eye-injury were more serious (*Paris* v. *Stepney BC* (1951)). Similarly, a higher standard of care would be expected from a drug manufacturer than from a greetings cards manufacture because the consequences of defective products would be far more serious in the former case.

Where a person is regarded as a professional—i.e. where people set themselves up as possessing a particular skill, such as a plumber, solicitor, surgeon—then they must display the type of skill required in carrying out that particular profession or trade.

With a liability based on fault, the defendant can only be liable for damages caused by him or her. The test adopted is whether the damage is of a type or kind that ought reasonably to have been foreseen even though the extent need not have been envisaged. The main duty is that of the manufacturer, but cases have shown that almost any party who is responsible for the marketing of goods may be held liable.

The onus of proving negligence is on the plaintiff. Of importance in this area is s. 2(1) of the Unfair Contract Terms Act 1977, which states: 'a person cannot by reference to any contract term or notice exclude or restrict his liability for death or personal injury resulting from negligence', and s. 2(2): 'in the case of other loss or damage, a person cannot so exclude or restrict his liability for negligence except in so far as the contract term or notice satisfies the test of reasonableness'. Thus, all clauses that purport to exclude liability in respect of negligence resulting in death or personal injuries are void, and other clauses, e.g. 'goods accepted at owner's risk', must satisfy the test of reasonableness.

10.6 THE CONSUMER PROTECTION ACT 1987

The Consumer Protection Act 1987 came into force in March 1988 as a result of the government's obligation to implement an EC directive and provides a remedy in damages for anyone who suffers personal injury or damage to property as a result of a defective product. The effect is to impose a *strict* (i.e. whereby it is unnecessary to prove negligence) tortious liability on producers of defective goods. The Act supplements the existing law; thus, a consumer may well have a remedy in contract, in the tort of negligence or under the Act if he or she has suffered loss caused by a defective product.

A product is defined in s. 12 as 'any goods or electricity'; s. 45(1) defines goods as including substances (natural or artificial, in solid, liquid or gaseous form), growing crops, things compressed in land by virtue of being attached to it, ships, aircraft and vehicles.

The producer will be liable if the consumer can establish that the product is defective and that it caused a loss. There is a defect if the safety of the goods does not conform to general expectations with reference to the risk of damage to property or risk of death or personal injury. The general expectations will differ depending on the particular circumstances, but points to be taken into account include the product's instructions, warnings and the time elapsed since supply, the latter point to determine the possibility of the defect being due to wear and tear.

The onus is on the plaintiff to prove that loss was caused by the defect. A claim may be made by anyone, whether death, personal injury or damage to property has occurred. However, where damage to property is concerned, the damage is confined to property ordinarily intended for private use or consumption and acquired by the person mainly for his or her own use or consumption, thus excluding commercial goods and property. Damage caused to private property must exceed £275 for claims to be considered. It is not possible to exclude liability under the Consumer Protection Act.

The Act is intended to place liability on the producer of defective goods. In some cases the company may not manufacture but may still be liable, as follows:

1. Anyone carrying out an 'industrial or other process' to goods that have been manufactured by someone else will be treated as the producer where 'essential characteristics' are attributable to that process. Essential characteristics are nowhere defined in the Act, but processes that modify the goods may well be within the scope. It is important to note there that defects in the goods are not limited to those caused by the modifications, but encompasses any defects in the product.
2. If a company puts its own brand on goods that have been manufactured on its behalf, thus holding itself out to be the producer, that company will be liable for any defects in the branded goods.
3. Any importer who imports goods from outside EC countries will likewise be liable for defects in the imported goods. This is an extremely beneficial move for the consumer.

The Act is also instrumental in providing a remedy against suppliers who are unable to identify the importee or the previous supplier to him. If the supplier fails or cannot identify the manufacturer's importee or previous supplier, then the supplier is liable.

It should be noted that if the product itself is defective the remedy lies in contract (usually SOGA 1979).

LEGISLATION STRENGTHENED IN A BID TO END 'NIGHTMARE' HOLIDAYS

Tour operators have probably felt more keenly than most businesses the effects of new legislation to protect consumers. Because holidays are essentially intangible, it is very difficult for a potential customer to check out claims made by tour operators' advertising until the holiday is underway, when it may be too late to do anything to prevent a ruined holiday. Traditional attitudes of 'let the buyer beware' can be of little use to holidaymakers who have little tangible evidence on which to base their decision when they book a holiday.

Consumers have traditionally had very little comeback against tour operators who fail to provide a holiday that is in line with the expectations held out in their brochure. Their brochures have frequently been accused of misleading customers, for example by showing pictures of hotels which conveniently omit the adjacent airport runway or sewerage works. The freedom of tour operators to produce fanciful brochures was limited by the Consumer Protection Act 1987. Part III of the Act holds that any person who, in the course of a business, gives (by any means whatsoever) to any consumer an indication that is misleading as to the price at which any goods, services, accommodation or facilities are available shall be guilty of an offence. These provisions of the Act forced tour operators to end such practices as promoting very low priced holidays that in reality were never available when customers enquired about them—only higher priced holidays were offered. Supplements for additional items such as regional airport departures could no longer be hidden away in small print.

Tour operators see themselves as arrangers of holidays who buy in services from hotels, airlines and bus companies, among others, over whom they have no effective management control. It was therefore quite usual for tour operators to include in their booking conditions an exclusion clause absolving themselves of any liability arising from the faults of its subcontractors. If a passenger was injured by a faulty lift in a Spanish hotel, a tour operator would deny any responsibility for the injury and could only advise the holidaymaker to sue the Spanish hotel themselves. For some time, the courts in England recognized that it would be unreasonable to expect UK tour operators to be liable for actions that were effectively beyond their management control. However, an EU directive of 1993 (implemented in England by the Unfair Terms in Consumer Contracts Regulations 1994) sought to redress the balance by providing greater protection for customers of tour operators. The directive, when implemented in national legislation throughout the EU, makes all tour operators liable for the actions of their subcontractors. In cases that have been brought before courts in England, tour operators have been held liable for illness caused by food poisoning at a hotel and loss of enjoyment caused by noisy building work. To emphasize the effects of the directive, one British tour operator was even ordered to compensate a holidaymaker in respect of claims that she had been harassed by a waiter at a hotel that had been contracted by the tour operator.

Before the Unfair Terms in Consumer Contracts Regulations 1994 had been enacted, anyone who had felt unfairly treated by a tour operator had to take the offending company to court personally, often at great expense and inconvenience to themselves. The new regulation, however, allows anyone to ask the Office of Fair Trading (OFT) to take up a case on their behalf and either to persuade the company voluntarily to remove the offending clause or to obtain an injunction removing the words from all future booking conditions. In principle, this move should be more proactive in preventing complaints by customers being brought in the first place, although doubts have been raised about the ability or willingness of the OFT to act as a consumer champion, given its reluctance in the past to bring prosecutions against traders.

In the space of less than a decade, the UK tour operating industry has been transformed from relying on exclusion clauses and seeking to rely on voluntary codes of conduct (especially the code of the Association of British Travel Agents (ABTA)) in providing fair treatment for consumers. Many would argue that voluntary regulation had failed to protect consumers in accordance with their rising expectations. Legislation, while it was initially resisted by tour operators, has undoubtedly increased consumers' confidence in buying package holidays and lessened the chances of them buying a holiday from a rogue company, and thereby harming the reputation of the industry as a whole.

QUESTIONS

1. What factors could explain the increasing amount of legislation that now faces tour operators?
2. Summarize the main consequences of the EU directive referred to above on the marketing of package holidays in the United Kingdom.
3. Is there still a role for voluntary codes of conduct in preference to legislation as a means of regulating the relationship between a tour operator and its customers?

10.7   CONSUMER CREDIT

Obviously, in paying for goods there are several methods of payment apart from a direct settlement. Nowadays a common method of payment is hire purchase, now regulated by the Consumer Credit Act 1974, which is a consumer protection measure to protect the public from, among other things, extortionate credit agreements and high-pressure selling off trade premises. The Act became fully operational in May 1985, and much of the protection afforded to those affecting hire purchase transactions is extended to those obtaining goods and services through consumer credit transactions. It is important to note that contract law governs the formation of agreements coming within the scope of the Consumer Credit Act. Also, the Act is applicable only to credit agreements not exceeding £15 000 or where the debtor is not a corporate body.

10.7.1   Consumer credit agreements

Section 8(1) states: 'A personal credit agreement is an agreement between an individual ('the debtor') and any other person ('the creditor') by which the creditor provides the debtor with credit of any amount.'

Section 8(2) defines a consumer credit agreement as a personal credit providing the debtor with credit not exceeding £15 000.

Section 9 defines credit as a cash loan and any form of financial accommodation. There are two types of credit. The first is a running account credit (s. 10(a)), whereby the debtor is enabled to receive from time to time, from the creditor or a third party, cash, goods and services to an amount or value such that, taking into account payments made by or to the credit of the debtor, the credit limit (if any) is not at any time exceeded. Thus, running account credit is revolving credit, where the debtor can keep taking credit when he or she wants it subject to a credit limit. Any example of this would be a Visa or Mastercard.

The second type is fixed-sum credit, defined in s. 10(b) as any other facility under a personal credit agreement whereby the debtor is enabled to receive credit. An example here would be a bank loan.

The Act then covers hire purchase agreements (s. 189), which are agreements under which goods are bailed or hired in return for periodical payments by the person to whom they are bailed or hired and where the property in the goods will pass to that person if the terms of the agreement are complied with and one or more of the following occurs:

- The exercise of an option to purchase by that person
- The doing of any other specified act by any party to the agreement
- The happening of any other specified event.

In simple terms, a hire purchase agreement is a contract of hire which gives the hirer the option to purchase the goods. The hirer does not own the goods until the option is exercised.

In addition to hire purchase agreements, also within the scope of the Act are conditional sale agreements for the sale of goods or land, in respect of which the price is payable by instalments and the property (i.e. ownership) remains with the seller until any conditions set out in the contract are fulfilled, and credit sale agreements, where the property (ownership) passes to the buyer when the sale is effected.

10.7.2 Restricted use and unrestricted use credit

Unrestricted use credit is where the money is paid to the debtor direct and the debtor is left free to use the money as he or she wishes. Restricted use credit is where the money is paid direct to a third party (usually the seller), e.g. via Barclaycard or Access.

10.7.3 Debtor–creditor and debtor–creditor supplier agreements

Every agreement regulated by the Act must be either a debtor–creditor or debtor–creditor supplier agreement. The latter relates to the situation where there is a business connection between creditor and supplier—i.e. a pre-existing arrangement—or where the creditor and the supplier are the same person.

Formalities   Section 55 and ss. 60–65 deal with formalities of the contract, their aim being that the debtor be made fully aware of the nature and the cost of the transaction and his or her rights and liabilities under it. The Act requires that certain information must be disclosed to the debtor before the contract is made. This includes total charge for credit, and the annual rate of the total charge for credit which the debtor will have to pay expressed as a percentage. All regulated agreements must comply with the formality procedures and must contain:

- Names and addresses of the parties to the agreement
- Amount of payments due and to whom payable
- Total charge for credit
- Annual rate of charge expressed as a percentage
- Debtor's right to pay off early

- All the terms of the agreement
- The debtor's right to cancel (if applicable)

All further copies of the agreement must contain the same, and the debtor and creditor must then sign. Sections 62 and 63 provide for the debtor and the hirer to receive a copy or copies of the agreement. The consumer should always receive one copy when the agreement is signed. A second copy must be sent if the agreement was not actually made on the occasion on which it was signed.

If the consumer credit agreement is drawn up off business premises, then it is a cancellable agreement designed to counteract high-pressure doorstep salesmen. If an agreement is cancellable, the debtor is entitled to a cooling-off period, i.e. to the close of the fifth day following the date the second copy of the agreement is received. If the debtor then cancels in writing, the agreement and any linked transaction is cancelled. Any sums paid are recoverable, and the debtor has a lien on any goods in his or her possession until repayment is made.

10.8 CODES OF PRACTICE

Codes of practice do not in themselves have the force of law. They can, however, be of great importance to marketers. In the first place, they can help to raise the standards of an industry by imposing a discipline on their members not to indulge in dubious marketing practices, which—although legal— act against the long-term interests of the industry and its customers. Secondly, voluntary codes of practice can offer a cheaper and quicker means of resolving grievances between the two parties compared with more formal legal channels. For example, the holiday industry has its own arbitration facilities which avoid the cost of taking many cases through to the courts. Thirdly, business organizations are often happy to accept restrictions imposed by codes of practice as these are seen as preferable to restrictions being imposed by laws. The tobacco industry has more influence over restrictions on tobacco advertising if they are based on a voluntary code rather than imposed by law.

The post of Director General of Fair Trading was established by the Fair Trading Act 1973 and is instrumental in encouraging trade associations to adopt codes of practice. An early example of a voluntary code is provided by the Motor Trade Association. On advertising, the code prohibits misleading comparisons of models and fuel consumption. Any statement must be substantiated by reference to the methods of testing and statements as to price must show clearly what is or is not incorporated in the figure. The code insists that unexpired warranties must be transferable and repair work must be capable of being carried out by any franchised dealer—not solely the dealer from whom the car was purchased. Similar criteria apply to used cars. Here the code states that mileage must be verified or the customer made aware. In the event of a dispute between a customer and a member of the Association, a conciliation service is available which reduces the need to resort to legal remedies.

A HOUSE FULL OF VOLUNTARY CODES

Many purchases of household durables are covered by a voluntary code of one form or another. The following examples serve to illustrate.

Home improvements
The Glass and Glazing Federation's Code of Ethical Practice was established in 1981. It provides that products and installations must comply with BSI Codes of Practice. It lays down rules regarding delivery and completion dates, and where the customer has stated time to be of the essence (i.e. where the customer has specified a date by which the work must be completed) then any work that remains uncompleted after six weeks may be cancelled without the consumer incurring any penalty.

Furniture

This code of practice was established in August 1978 and covers the manufacture and selling of furniture. The code ensures that full information regarding price, measurements and cleaning is available with each product. It also provides realistic dates for delivery to customers and gives details of a conciliation scheme with a testing service. The fee for this independent service will be returned where any complaint is upheld.

Association of Manufacturers of Domestic Electrical Appliances

The code here requires that calls regarding servicing should be responded to within three days and that 80 per cent of servicing should be completed on the first visit, the balance to be finally completed within 15 days. Manufacturers are expected to carry a comprehensive supply of spare parts and to ensure that the spare parts are available up to a minimum specified period after the particular models are no longer produced.

Useful leaflets published by the Office of Fair Trading giving information regarding codes of practice can be obtained free of charge from local Consumer Advice Bureaux.

10.9   CONTROLS ON ADVERTISING

There are a number of laws that influence the content of advertisements in Britain. For example, the Trade Descriptions Act makes false statements in an advertisement an offence, while the Consumer Credit Act lays down quite precise rules about the way in which credit can be advertised. However, it could be argued that the content of advertisements is influenced just as much by voluntary codes as by legislation. Contrary to popular belief, there is no law stating that cigarettes should not be advertised on television or that health warnings should be printed on all newspaper advertisements for cigarettes. Both of these are examples of restrictions imposed on advertisers by a voluntary code.

For printed media, the Advertising Standards Authority (ASA) oversees the British Code of Advertising Practice which states that all advertisements appearing in members' publications should be legal, honest, decent and truthful. Thus, an advertisement by a building society offering 'free' weekend breaks was deemed to have broken the code by not stating in the advertisement that a compulsory charge was made for meals during the weekend. An advert by the fashion retailer H & M Hennes depicting a reclining female model dressed in underwear with the caption 'Last time we ran an ad for Swedish lingerie 78 women complained—no men' was held to be offensive, inaccurate and sexist. The penalty for breaching the ASA code is the adverse publicity that follows, and ultimately the Authority could ban a business from advertising in all members' publications.

A stronger voluntary code is provided by the Independent Television Commission, which governs all terrestrial television broadcasting. Although the ITC is a statutory body, the Broadcasting Acts have devolved to the Commission the task of developing a code for advertisers. Like the ASA code, it too is continually evolving to meet the changing attitudes and expectations of the public. Thus, on some products restrictions have been tightened up—cigarette advertising is now completely banned on television, and loopholes have been closed which allowed tobacco brand names to be used to promote non-tobacco products offered by the manufacturers, such as sportswear and overseas holidays. Restrictions on alcohol advertising have also been tightened up, for example by insisting that young actors are not portrayed in advertisements and by not showing them when children are likely to be watching. On the other hand, advertising restrictions for some products have been relaxed in response to changing public attitudes. Adverts for condoms have moved from being completely banned to being allowed, but only in very abstract form, to the present situation where the product itself can be mentioned using actors in life-like situations. Similarly, restrictions on adverts for women's sanitary products have been relaxed, although, as for condoms, the ITC code stipulates that adverts should not be shown when children are likely to be viewing.

Numerous other forms of voluntary controls exist. As mentioned previously, many trade associations have codes which impose restrictions on how they can advertise. Solicitors, for example, were previously not allowed to advertise at all, but now can now do so within limits defined by the Law Society. The health warnings that appear on packets of cigarettes are the result of a voluntary agreement between the government and the tobacco industry. The latter illustrates an important reason for the existence of many voluntary codes—namely, that an industry would prefer a code over which it has some influence rather than a law over which it has none. Government is saved the task of passing legislation and policing the law, while knowing that if the voluntary code fails to work it could still step in to pass legislation. In the field of advertising, the EU is currently proposing directives that will ultimately have the effect of giving legal effect to many of the voluntary codes that currently exist.

ASA CODE FOR PRINTED MEDIA ADVERTISING TIGHTENED UP

Contrary to popular belief, advertising in the United Kingdom is not primarily constrained by the law. Instead, advertisers are restricted by quasi-legal codes of conduct. Although failure to comply with such codes of conduct does not bring with it the threat of punishment by the courts, non-compliance can nevertheless cause problems for a business. The Advertising Standards Authority is an industry body that regulates all print and non-broadcast advertisements. During 1995, it completed the first major review of its codes since 1988 to take account of changing attitudes in society.

The revised code built on the previous requirement for all advertisements to be legal, decent, honest and truthful by spelling out clearly to advertisers their responsibilities. The following are examples of new requirements that were added to reflect changing public attitudes:

1. On decency, the code requires advertisements to contain nothing that is likely to cause serious or widespread offence, particularly on grounds of race, religion, sex, sexual orientation or disability.
2. To reduce problems of under-age drinking, the code bans alcohol advertisements in publications or on poster sites where more than 25 per cent of the potential audience is aged under 18. Advertisements should include a warning on the dangers of drinking and driving.
3. Advertising for slimming products aimed at children or adolescents was banned by the code, as is any suggestion that it is desirable to be underweight.
4. To further protect childrens' health, the code requires that no advertisement should encourage them to eat or drink near bed time, to eat frequently throughout the day or to replace main meals with confectionery or snack foods.
5. Claims such as 'environmentally friendly' will not be allowed without convincing proof that a product causes no environmental damage.
6. Car manufactures are not allowed to make speed or acceleration the predominant message in their advertisement.

The ASA code is subscribed to by most organizations involved in advertising, including the Advertising Association, the Institute of Practitioners in Advertising and the associations representing publishers of newspapers and magazines, the outdoor advertising industry and direct marketing. The primary role of the ASA code is to give guidance to advertisers which can be helpful in preventing advertisements being produced that are perceived by the public as inappropriate. Inevitably, however, some individual advertisers break the code where they feel unduly constrained by its provisions. Action against such advertisers can take a number of forms:

1. The advertiser can be asked to withdraw an advertisement which is in breach of the code.
2. The ASA regularly publishes details of cases that it has investigated. Where complaints by members of the public are upheld, the ASA circulates details of its ruling to interested media in the hope that the bad publicity which this generates will

prevent the offender breaching the code in future.

3. Where an advertiser refuses to withdraw its advertisement, the ASA can request its media members to refuse to publish an advertisement or to refuse all advertising from an advertiser for a specified period of time.

In general, the system of voluntary regulation of advertising has worked well in the United Kingdom. For advertisers, voluntary codes can allow more flexibility and opportunities to have an input to the code. For the public, a code can be updated in a less bureaucratic manner than may be necessary with new legislation or statutory regulations. However, the law still protects the public from wholly untruthful advertising. For example, it remains an offence under the Consumer Protection Act 1987 for advertisers to give a false description of a product, while the Consumer Credit Act 1974 specifies quite clearly constraints on advertisers of credit facilities.

The question remains as to how much responsibility for the social and cultural content of advertising should be given to industry-led voluntary bodies rather than being decided by government. While some European countries such as France have incorporated social and cultural factors into their legislation on advertising (e.g. in respect of the use of the French language), deciding what is socially acceptable in the United Kingdom has been largely left to voluntary codes. The question arises as to whether voluntary codes unduly reflect the narrow financial interests of advertisers rather than the broader interests of the public at large. Doubtless, advertisers realize that if they do not develop a code that is socially acceptable, the task will be taken away from them and carried out by government in a process where they will have less influence.

QUESTIONS

1. Summarize the main advantages and disadvantages for the public of relying on voluntary codes rather than law to regulate advertising.
2. Why is it important for advertisers to seek to comply with the ASA code?
3. Is it right for government to delegate the task of deciding on decency in advertising to an industry-led regulatory body?

10.10   PROTECTION OF A COMPANY'S INTANGIBLE ASSETS

The value of a business enterprise can be measured not only by the value of its physical assets such as land and building: increasingly, the value of a business reflects its investment in new product development and strong brand images. To protect the company from imitators reaping the benefits of this investment but bearing none of its cost, a number of legal protections are available.

10.10.1   Patents

A patent is a right given to an inventor which allows him or her exclusively to reap the benefits from the invention over a specified period.

To obtain a patent, application must be made to the Patent Office in accordance with the procedure set out in the Patents Act 1977. To qualify for a patent, the invention must have certain characteristics laid down—it must be covered by the Act, it must be novel and it must include an inventive step.

Nowhere does the Act define what is patentable, but it does specify what is not under s. 1:

- s. 1(2)(a)—discoveries, scientific theories or mathematical methods
- s. 1(2)(b)—literacy, dramatic, musical or artistic works or any other aesthetic creations (obviously, works such as these are protected by copyright)

- s. 1(2)(*c*)—schemes, rules or methods for performing a mental act, playing a game, doing business; or a program for a computer
- s. 1(2)(*d*)—the presentation of information

Obviously, to qualify for a patent the invention must be novel in that it does not form part of the state of the art at the priority date (i.e. the date of filing for a patent, not the date of invention).

State of the art (s. 2(2)) comprises all matter that has at any time before that date been made available to the public anywhere in the world by written or oral description, by use or in any other way.

An inventive step (s. 3) is apparent if it is not obvious to a person skilled in the art having regard to the prior art other than co-pending patent applications which are deemed to be prior art for the purpose of testing for novelty only.

The effect of the Patents Act 1977 has only been to bring UK patent law more into line with that of the EU in accordance with the provisions of the European Patent Convention.

As a result of the implementation of the Convention, there are almost uniform criteria in the establishment of a patent in Austria, Belgium, Switzerland, Germany, France, the United Kingdom, Italy, Liechtenstein, Luxembourg, the Netherlands and Sweden. A European Patent Office has been set up in Munich which provides a cheaper method to obtain a patent in three or more countries, but it should be noted that, if the patent fails as a result of an application to the European Patent Office, the rejection applies to all member states unless there is contrary domestic legislation which covers this part.

10.10.2 Trade marks

The Trade Marks Act 1938 provides protection for trade marks. (They are also protected under the common law of passing off.) The Act gives the owner of the mark exclusive rights to its use. A trade mark can be defined as words or symbols used to signify a connection in the course of trade between the owner of the mark and the goods imprinted with the mark. It is possible to register only marks used in connection with goods (s. 68).

The Trade Marks Register consists of two parts. Registration under Part A applies to marks 'adapted to distinguish goods or services with which the proprietor is connected from those with which he is not'. It is easier to obtain registration under Part B but the protection afforded is less. To obtain registration under Part A, the trade mark must conform to at least one of the criteria set out in s. 9 as follows. It must contain:

- s. 9(i)(*a*)—the name of a company's individual or firm, represented in a special or particular manner
- s. 9(i)(*b*)—the signature of the applicant for registration or of some predecessor of his or her in business
- s. 9(i)(*c*)—a word or words having no direct reference to the character or quality of the goods, and not being according to its ordinary meaning, a geographical name or surname
- s. 9(i)(*e*)—any other distinctive mark; however, a name, signature or word other than those covered by ss. 9(*a*)–(*d*) above is not registerable except on evidence of distinctiveness

If the trade mark is infringed in any way, a successful plaintiff will be entitled to an injunction and to damages.

10.11 LAW IN ACTION

It has frequently been suggested that as a society develops economically, its citizens have a tendency to become increasingly litigious. Whereas less-developed societies may rely to a large extent on a moral code to govern relationships between members of the society, those that are more developed tend to rely increasingly on a codification of morals expressed in legal rights and responsibilities. Moral governance can work effectively where moral values are shared widely and social pressures alone can often keep a sense of order between individuals. Governance on the basis of law, on the other hand, requires a more formal system of justice to resolve disputes. It is not only changes in the law itself that should be of concern to marketers but also the ease of access to legal processes.

In England, a number of courts of law operate with distinct functional and hierarchical roles:

- The Magistrates Court deals primarily with criminal matters, where it handles approximately 97 per cent of the work load. It is responsible for handling prosecutions of companies for breaches of legislation under the Trade Descriptions and the Consumer Protection Acts. More serious criminal matters are 'committed' up to the Crown Court for trial.
- The Crown Court handles the more serious cases that have been committed to it for trial on 'indictment'. In addition, it also hears defendants' appeals as to sentence or conviction from the Magistrates Court.
- The High Court is responsible for hearing appeals by way of 'case stated' from the Magistrates Court or occasionally the Crown Court. The lower court whose decision is being challenged prepares papers (the case) and seeks the opinion of the High Court.
- The Court of Appeal deals primarily with appeals from trials on indictment in the Crown Court. It may review either sentence or conviction.
- County Courts are for almost all purposes the courts of first instance in civil matters (contract and tort). Generally, where the amount claimed is less than £25 000, this court will have instant jurisdiction, but between £25 000 and £50 000, the case may be heard here, or be directed to the High Court, depending on its complexity.
- When larger amounts are being litigated, the High Court will have jurisdiction at first instance. There is a commercial court within the structure which is designed to be a quicker and generally more suitable court for commercial matters. Only bankruptcy appeals from the County Court are heard here.
- Cases worth less than £3000 are referred by the County Court to its 'Small Claims' division, where the case will be heard informally under arbitration and costs normally limited to the value of the issue of the summons. The object of the Small Claims Court is to remove the disincentive to litigate due to the fear of High Court costs.
- The Court of Appeals' Civil Division hears civil appeals from the County Court and the High Court.
- The House of Lords is the ultimate appeal court for both criminal and domestic matters. However, where there is a European Issue, the European Court of Justice is the final court.

In addition to the court structure, there are numerous quasi-judicial tribunals which exist to reconcile disagreeing parties. Examples include Rent Tribunals (for agreeing property rents) and Valuation Tribunals (for agreeing property values).

Despite the existence of legal rights, the cost to an individual or a firm of enforcing its rights can be prohibitive, especially where there is no certainty that a party taking action will be able to recover its legal costs. For a typical intercompany dispute over a debt of £50 000, the party suing the debtor can easily incur legal expenses of several thousand pounds, not counting the cost of its employees' time. Where a case goes to the Court of Appeal, a company could be involved in inestimable costs. The legal process can also be very slow. In the case of an intercompany debt claim, a case may take up to 10 years between the first issue of a writ and compensation being finally received.

Numerous attempts have been made to make the legal system more widely accessible, such as the small claims section of County Courts which handle claims of up to £3000 in a less formal and costly manner than a normal County Court claim. There have also been attempts to reduce the risks by allowing, in certain circumstances, solicitors to charge their clients by results obtained in Court. There is a strong feeling that costs of running the courts system could be greatly reduced by reducing many bureaucratic and restrictive practices within the legal profession.

Despite moves to make legal remedies more widely available, access to the law remains unequal. Among commercial organizations, a small under-resourced firm may be unable to put money up-front to pursue a case against a larger company which could defend itself with an army of retained lawyers. Similarly, private consumers are unequal in their access to the law. It has often been suggested that easy access to the law is afforded to the very rich (who can afford it) and the very poor (who receive legal aid). An apparent paradox of attempts to make the law more accessible is that these attempts may themselves overwhelm courts with cases with which they are unable to cope. Recent restrictions on funding for legal aid reflect the fact that there can be almost unlimited demand for legal remedies, but finite judicial capacity.

Central and local government is increasingly being given power to act as a consumer champion and to bring cases before the courts which are in the interest of consumers in general. Bodies that pursue actions in this way include:

- Trading Standards Departments which are operated by County Councils (by Borough Councils in Metropolitan areas). They have powers to investigate complaints about false or misleading descriptions of prices, inaccurate weights and measures, consumer credit and the safety of consumer legislation. Consumers' knowledge of their rights has often stretched the resources of Trading Standards Departments so that, at best, they can only selectively take action against bad practice.
- Environmental Health Departments of local authorities deal with health matters such as unfit food and dirty shops and restaurants. A consumer who suspects that they have suffered food poisoning as a result of eating unfit food at a restaurant may lodge a complaint with the local Environmental Health Department, which may collate similar complaints and use this evidence to prosecute the offending restaurant, or take steps to have it closed down.
- Utility regulators have powers to bring action against companies who are in breach of their licence conditions.

10.12   THE LAW AND PRODUCTION PROCESSES

Finally, although most of this chapter has been concerned with the law as it affects relationships between businesses and their customers, it must not be forgotten that the law also influences the production possibilities of firms. This in turn affects the range of goods and services that firms can make available to their customers.

As economies develop, there is a tendency for societies to raise their expectations about firms' behaviour, particularly where they are responsible for significant external costs (see Chapter 9). The result has been increasing levels of legislation which constrain the activities of firms in meeting buyers' needs. Some of the more important constraints that affect marketing decisions are described below :

- Most developed countries recognize that individuals have a proprietary interest in their employment, and have passed legislation protecting employees from unfair dismissal or redundancy. In the United Kingdom, the proposed Employment Rights Act 1996 normally provides compensation for employees who have been employed for 2 years or more and are dismissed for reasons other than redundancy and those specified in the Act. The same Act also provides compensation for employees of over 2 years standing whose job becomes redundant. The Act specifies procedures by which large employers should consult employees over planned redundancies and failure to do so may render the redundancy unfair. Many countries extend protection to employees beyond the limits available in the United Kingdom. For example, many countries limit the use that can made of temporary or seasonal contracts of employment. The Treaty of Maastricht has pledged member states of the European Union who signed the Social Chapter to further improve the rights of employees, for example in relation to employee consultation and minimum wage levels.

- The rights of employees to enjoy safe working conditions has become increasingly enshrined in law as a country develops. In the United Kingdom, the Health and Safety at Work Act 1974 provides for large fines and, in extreme cases, imprisonment of company directors for failing to provide a safe working environment. Definitions of what constitutes an acceptable level of risk for employees to face change over time. As well as obvious serious physical injury, the courts in England now recognize a responsibility of firms to protect their employees against more subtle dangers such as repetitive strain injury. There has also been debate in cases brought before courts as to whether a firm should be responsible for mental illness caused by excessive stress in a job, and the courts have held that companies should be liable if the employee has suffered stress in the past which the company was aware of.

- Companies sometimes find themselves being required to recruit their second choice of staff in order to comply with legislation against racial and sexual discrimination. For example, one UK airline found through its research that the majority of its customers preferred its cabin crew to be female and subsequently recruited predominantly female staff for this role. The airline was fined for unlawful discrimination against men, even though it had been innovative in appointing women to the traditional male job of pilot.

- Pollution of the natural environment is an external cost which governments seek to limit through legislation such as the Environmental Protection Act 1990, the Environment Act 1990 and the Water Resources Act 1991. Examples of impacts on firms include requirements for additional noise insulation and investment in equipment to purify discharges into watercourses and the atmosphere. These have often added to a firm's total production costs, thereby putting it at a competitive disadvantage, or made plans to increase production capacity uneconomic when faced with competition from companies in countries who have less demanding requirements for environmental protection.

- In many cases it is not sufficient to rely on law to protect customers from faulty outcomes of a firm's production. It is also necessary to legislate in respect of the quality of the processes of production. This is important where buyers are unable to fully evaluate a product without a guarantee that the method of producing it has been in accordance with acceptable criteria. An example of this is the Food Safety Act 1990 which imposes requirements on all firms who manufacture or handle food products to ensure that they cannot become contaminated (e.g. by being kept at too high a temperature during transport). Many small- to medium-sized food manufacturers have closed down, claiming that they cannot justify the cost of upgrading premises. Laws governing production processes are also important in the case of intangible services where customers may have little opportunity for evaluating the credentials of one service against another. For example, to protect the public against unethical behaviour by unscrupulous sales personnel, the Financial Services Act 1986 lays down procedures for regulating business practices within the sector.

The traditional view of legislation on production is that the mounting weight of legislation puts domestic firms at a cost disadvantage to those operating in relatively unregulated environments overseas. Critics of over-regulation point to Britain and the United States as two economies that have priced themselves out of many international markets.

Against this, it is argued that as the economy of a country develops, economic gains should be enjoyed by all stakeholders of business, including employees and the local communities in which a business operates. There are also many persuasive arguments why increasing regulation of production processes may not be incompatible with greater business prosperity:

1. Attempts to deregulate conditions of employment may allow firms to be more flexible in their production methods and thereby reduce their costs. However, there is evidence that a casualized work-force becomes increasingly reluctant to make major purchases, thereby reducing the level of activity in the domestic economy. In the United Kingdom, recent moves to free employers of many of their responsibilities to employees have resulted in a large number of casual workers who are reluctant or unable to buy houses, resulting in a knock-on effect on supplies of home-related goods and services.
2. There is similarly much evidence that a healthy and safe working environment is likely to be associated with high levels of commitment by employees and a high standard of output quality. The law should represent no more than a codification of good practice by firms.
3. Environmental protection and cost reduction may not be mutually incompatible, as the case study in Chapter 9 demonstrates.

During the early 1990s, the United Kingdom and other EU member states appeared to be diverging in terms of legislation affecting business processes. While the Treaty of Maastricht has undoubtedly led to some short-term gains in employment for the United Kingdom, the long-term effect is more open to question. Supporters of greater legislative constraints on businesses see no incompatibility with economic growth.

REVIEW QUESTIONS

1. Briefly identify the main ways in which the legal environment impacts on the activities of the sales and marketing function.   (10 marks)
   Giving examples, evaluate the criticism that government legislation primarily impacts on those firms who can least afford to pay for it, mainly the small and the competitively vulnerable.   (10 marks)
   (CIM Marketing Environment Examination, December 1994, Q.8)
2. In the light of recent legislation in your own country, assess the extent to which the position of consumers compared to business has improved.   (12 marks)
   Provide a checklist for your brand manager to ensure that a new product complies with the main consumer legislation in force.   (8 marks)
   (CIM Marketing Environment Examination, June 1995, Q.5)
3. Using an appropriate example, evaluate the virtues and drawbacks of using voluntary codes of practice to regulate business activity.
   (CIM Marketing Environment Examination, June 1995, Q.9, part ii)
4. Philip, shopping at a large department store, sees a colourful spinning top which he buys for his grandson Harry. While purchasing the toy, he sees a prominent notice in the store which states: 'This store will not be held responsible for any defects in the toys sold.' The box containing the spinning top carries the description 'Ideal for children over 12 months, safe and non-toxic.' (Harry is 15 months old.) Within four weeks the spinning top has split into two parts, each with a jagged edge, and Harry has suffered an illness as a result of sucking the paint. Philip has complained vociferously to the store, which merely pointed to the prominent notice disclaiming liability. Philip has now informed the store that he intends to take legal action against it.
   Draft a report to the Managing Director setting out the legal liability of the store.
5. Zak runs his own painting and decorating business and has been engaged to decorate Rebecca's lounge. Whilst burning off layers of paint from the door with his blowtorch, Zak's attention is diverted by the barking of Camilla's Yorkshire terrier and as he turned round, the flame catches a cushion on the settee. Within seconds the room is filled with acrid smoke. Both the carpet and settee are damaged beyond repair and the dog, terrified, rushes into the road, where it is run over by a car. Consider Zak's legal liability.
6. Sharon visits Betterbuy supermarket with her children Wayne and Kylie. Consider the following scenarios:
   (a) Wayne, aged 3 years, takes some sweets from the low-level display by the check-out and puts them in his mother's basket. Sharon replaces the sweets on the display. The manager tells her she must pay for them as she put them in her basket.
   (b) Sharon chooses a large packet of washing powder marked 'Bargain offer—only 45p'. When she goes to the check-out the cashier tells her that it costs £1.45. Can Sharon demand that it be sold to her for 45p?

FURTHER READING

Bradgate, J. R. and Savage, N. (1995) *Commercial Law*, 2nd edn, Butterworth, London.

Davies, F. R. (1995) *Davies on Contract*, 7th edn, Sweet and Maxwell, London.

Goode, R. M. (1995) *Commercial Law*, 2nd edn, Penguin, Harmondsworth.

Gundlach, Gregory T. and Murphy, Patrick E. (1993) 'Ethical and Legal Foundations of Relational Marketing Exchange', *Journal of Marketing*, vol. 57 (October), pp. 35–46.

Harvey, B. W. and Parry, D. L. (1992) *Law of Consumer Protection and Fair Trading*, 4th edn, Butterworths, London.

Phillips, J. (1994) *Introduction to Intellectual Property*, 2nd edn, Butterworths, London.

Treitel, G. H. (1995) *The law of Contract*, 5th edn, Sweet and Maxwell, London.

ELEVEN

THE TECHNOLOGICAL ENVIRONMENT

OBJECTIVES

After reading this chapter, you should understand:

- The impact of technological change on a firm's product, promotion and distribution decisions.
- The important contribution of research and development to sustainable competitive advantage.
- The role of information technology in facilitating communication between a firm and its customers and suppliers.

11.1 INTRODUCTION

The aim of this chapter is to explain how changes in the technological environment influence marketing decisions. The word 'technology' can be easily misunderstood as simply being about computers and hi-tech industries such as aerospace. In fact, technology has a much broader meaning and influences our everyday lives. It impacts on the frying pan (Teflon-coated for non-stick), the programmable central heating timer, cavity wall insulation, the television, video, washing machine, car—in fact, just about everything in the home. The impact at work can be even greater, as technology changes the nature of people's jobs, creating new jobs and making others redundant. It influences the way we shop, our entertainment and leisure, and the treatment we receive in hospital. Marketing managers and other executives who fail to evaluate technological progress and assess the potential impact on their industry, company and products may find that the competition has gained a competitive advantage.

11.2 WHAT IS TECHNOLOGY?

Technology is defined in the Longman *Modern English Dictionary* as 'the science of technical processes in a wide, though related, field of knowledge'. Dibb *et al.* (1994) define technology 'as the knowledge of how to accomplish tasks and goals'. Technology therefore embraces mechanics, electrics, electronics, physics, chemistry and biology and all the derivatives and combinations of them. The technological fusion and interaction of these sciences is what drives the frontiers of achievement forward. It is the continuing development, combination and application of these disciplines that give rise to new processes materials, manufacturing systems, products and ways of storing, processing and communicating data. The fusion and interaction of knowledge and experience from different sciences is what sustains the 'Technological Revolution' (see Figure 11.1).

Kotler (1991) uses the 'demand–technology life cycle' to help explain the relevance to marketing of technological advances. Products are produced and marketed to meet some basic underlying need of

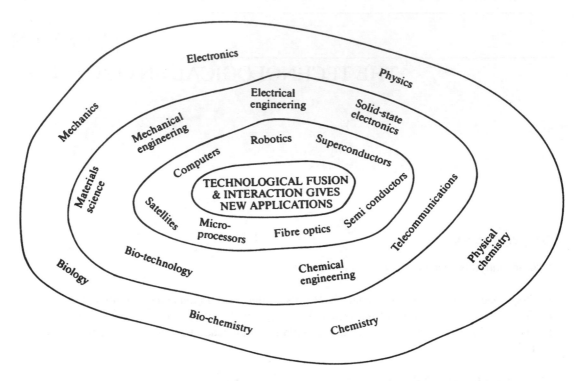

Figure 11.1   Technological fusion and interaction

individuals. An individual product or group of products may be only one way of meeting this need, however, and indeed is likely to be only a temporary means of marketing this need. The way in which the need is met at any period is dependent on the level of technology prevailing at that time. Kotler cites the need of the human race for calculating power. The need has grown over the centuries with the growth of trade and the increasing complexity of life. This is depicted by the 'demand life cycle' in Figure 11.2, which runs through the stages of emergence (E), accelerating growth (G_1), decelerating growth (G_2), maturity (M) and decline (D).

Over the centuries, the need for calculating power has been met by finger-counting, abacuses, ready-reckoners, slide rules, mechanical adding machines (as big as an office desk), electrical adding machines (half the size of an office desk), electric calculators (half the size of a typewriter), battery-

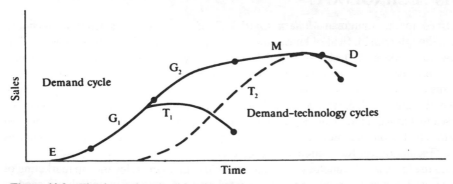

Figure 11.2   The demand–technology life cycle

powered hand calculators and now pocket-sized computers. Kotler suggests that 'each new technology normally satisfies the need in a superior way'. Each technology has its own 'demand–technology life cycle', shown in Figure 11.2 as T_1 and T_2, which serves the demand cycle for a period of time. Each demand–technology life cycle will have a history of emergence, rapid growth, slower growth, maturity and decline, but over a shorter period than the more sustainable demand cycle.

Marketing managers and other executives need to watch closely not only their immediate competitors but also emerging technologies. Should the demand technology on which their product is based be undermined by a new demand technology, the consequences may be dire. If the emerging demand technology is not recognized until the new and superior products are on the market, there may be insufficient time and money available for the firm to develop its own products using the competing technology. Companies making mechanical typewriters, slide rules, gas lights and radio valves all had to adjust rapidly or go out of business. One way executives can scan the technological environment in order to spot changes and future trends is to study technology transfer.

The term 'technology transfer' can be used in a number of contexts. It is used to refer to the transfer of technology from research establishments and universities to commercial applications. It may also be used in the context of transfers from one country to another, usually from advanced to less well advanced economies. Transfers also occur from one industry to another; technology then permeates through the international economy from research into commercial applications in industries that can sustain the initially high development and production costs. As the costs of the new technology fall, new applications become possible. Thus, the technology permeates through different industries and countries. Applications of technology first developed for the US space programme, for example, may now be found in many domestic and industrial situations. NASA (the National Aeronautics and Space Administration) established nine application centres in the United States to help in transferring the technology that was developed for space exploration to other applications (Kotler and Armstrong, 1996).

The rate at which technology is being enhanced and the rate at which it permeates through the world economy is of importance to the marketing manager. Product life cycles are typically becoming shorter. Expertise in a particular technology may no longer be a barrier preventing competitors from entering an industry. New entrants into an industry may benefit from the falling costs of technology or may be able to bypass the traditional technology by using some new and alternative technology.

The marketing manager should be interested in the degree to which technology influences his or her business. As we have all learned, the environment is always changing and throwing up new challenges. Bic produces a disposable plastic razor to challenge Wilkinson and Gillette, Imperial Typewriters are not longer in business but Olivetti, once a typewriter manufacturer, now produces computers, and so on. The fountain pen is challenged by the ball-point, and in turn the ball-point is challenged by the fibre-tip. Failure to identify changes in technology soon enough may cause severe and sometimes terminal problems for companies. Although there can be sudden changes in technology that impact on an industry, it is the gradual changes that creep through the industry that may be harder to detect. Companies that anticipate, identify and successfully invest in emerging technologies should be able to develop a strategic advantage over the competition. As the demand–technology cycle goes through the stage of rapid growth, they will grow with it. As growth slows and the cycle matures, competitors will find it increasingly hard to gain a foothold in the new and by now dominant technology.

11.3   EXPENDITURE ON RESEARCH AND DEVELOPMENT

According to the Organization for Economic Cooperation and Development (OECD) the UK's expenditure on Research and Development (R&D) between 1981 and 1992 declined from 2.4 per cent of gross domestic expenditure (GDE) to 2.22 per cent (Young, 1993; OECD, 1995). The United

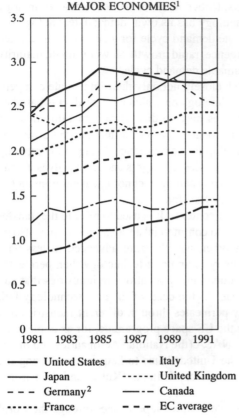

MAJOR ECONOMIES[1]

United States
Japan
Germany[2]
France
Italy
United Kingdom
Canada
EC average

Notes:
[1] Ranked by 1991 GDP in purchasing power parities.
[2] Reunified Germany in 1991.

Figure 11.3   Gross domestic expenditure on R&D as a percentage of GDP
Source: *The OECD Observer*, No. 183, August–September 1993, modified to include 1992 figures
from OECD in Figures 1995 edition, published with *The OECD Observer*, no. 194, June–July
1995.

Kingdom's ranking against other major industrial nations (Group of Seven or G7 nations) has now
slipped to fifth (Figure 11.3). In addition, the figures for the number of researchers employed per
10 000 of the labour force show the United Kingdom in a disappointing position by comparison with
the G7 leading industrial nations (Table 11.1).

In real terms the UK's R&D expenditure declined in mechanical engineering, electronics, electrical
engineering, motor vehicles and aerospace (Table 11.2). Increases in expenditure were only recorded
in chemicals, other manufactured products and non-manufactured products, thus reflecting the serious
decline of UK manufacturing industry.

International comparisons of R&D expenditure should be used with caution. According to Young
(1993) these difficulties in comparing statistics stem from:

● The basic definitions of R&D and the boundaries between R&D and education, training, related
  scientific expenditure and administration costs.

Table 11.1 R&D expenditure and numbers of researchers employed by G7 nations 1992[a]

| Country | Gross domestic expenditure on R&D (GERD) | | | | | Researchers (national totals) | |
| | Million current PPP $[b] | Percentage of GDP | Percentage financed by | | Per capita current PPP $[b] | Full-time equivalent | Per 10 000 of labour force |
			Government	Industry			
Canada	8 128.8	1.51	44.1	41.0	286	65 209[c]	47[c]
France	25 571.6	2.40	44.3	45.7	446	138 087	55
Germany	36 240.8	2.50	36.5	60.8	450	176 401[d]	59[d]
Italy	13 146.3	1.31	44.7	51.5	231	74 422	30
Japan	73 085.2[e]	3.00[e]	19.4	71.1	588[e]	622 410[e]	95[e]
United Kingdom	20 872.7	2.22	34.5	50.6	360	134 708	48
United States	167 010.0[f]	2.81[f]	38.8[f]	59.1[f]	653[f]	949 300[d]	76[d]
OECD median	**g	1.5	44.5	50.25	286	**g	47

[a] 1992 figures unless otherwise specified; some national or OECD estimates.
[b] Conversion to $ using Purchasing Power Parities (PPP).
[c] 1991.
[d] 1989.
[e] Overestimated.
[f] Excludes most or all capital expenditures.
[g] Not available.

Source: adapted from OECD Figures 1995 Edition, published with *The OECD Observer*, no. 194, June–July 1995.

Table 11.2 UK expenditure on R&D by industry group based on 1985 prices

	1985	1989	Change (%)
	(£ million)		
All product groups	5122	5664	10.6
All manufactured products	4673	4774	2.2
Chemicals	942	1326	40.2
Mechanical engineering	263	157	−40.3
Electronics	1759	1662	−5.5
Electrical engineering	126	77	−38.9
Motor vehicles	372	365	−1.9
Aerospace	818	655	−20.0
Other manufactured products	395	502	27.0
Non-manufactured products	448	920	105.4

Source: *Business Bulletin*, 28 February 1991 (CSO). Reproduced with permission of the Controller of HMSO.

- Classification by type of research: basic, applied and experimental.
  - (a) Basic or fundamental research is work undertaken primarily for the advancement of scientific knowledge without a specific application in view.
  - (b) Applied research is work undertaken with either a general or specific application in mind.
  - (c) Experimental development is the development of fundamental or applied research with a view to introduction of new, or the improvement of existing, materials, processes, products, devices and systems.
- Classification by sector, e.g. public or private, and by type of industry. The International Standard Industrial Classification Code (ISIC) is used.
- Numbers employed in R&D; e.g. definitions of full-time/part-time, directly or indirectly employed, qualifications and occupation.
- Source and destination of funds; e.g. private and commercial organizations receive some public funds, but public bodies also receive some funding from private sources. This makes it difficult to calculate the proportion of R&D expenditure financed by governments as compared to that financed by the private sector. University expenditure is typically a mix of the two, for instance.
- Distinguishing the R&D element of large-scale defence programmes. According to Young the UK Government has revised downwards the R&D expenditure in defence establishments.
- Assessment of R&D funds flowing between countries, 'particularly between the components of multinational firms' (Young, 1993). The consolidated accounts of a multinational may show R&D expenditure, but in which country was it spent?
- When to include expenditure on software development as R&D. Again according to Young, in Canada, 'software R&D is roughly a quarter of all industrial R&D and is spread across a wide range of industries'.

In order to overcome these difficulties the economists at the OECD issue guidelines in the form of the *Frascati Manual* for use by government statisticians. This helps to ensure that statistics are collected by each country on a similar basis which then aids international comparison. The Frascati standards have now spread to most industrialized countries in the world, thus improving the reliability of comparable statistics. The manual is also updated regularly to take account of new issues, such as software R&D expenditure, for example.

These internationally agreed definitions aid comparison between nations, although caution still needs to be exercised when using international statistics. The variations in the exchange rate, purchasing power of the currency in the domestic market, and the reliability and comparability of the statistics all give grounds for caution.

These figures do not make happy reading for UK industrialists and politicians. The figures for the UK's R&D expenditure in manufacturing are particularly bad with a decline in expenditure in almost every sector. The United Kingdom is well down the international league table on expenditure and on the numbers employed in R&D. Our main international competitors are well ahead in this area. Add to this the controversy surrounding cuts in academic research budgets affecting British universities and the picture looks even worse. Research and development is the seed corn for the new technologies, processes, materials and products of the future. Failure in this area is likely to mean that UK companies are less competitive in the future. Larry Elliott (1991), writing in the *Guardian*, sums up the picture nicely: 'Five Japanese companies—Toyota, NEC, Matsushita, Hitachi, and Toshiba—spent more money on civil research and development last year (1990) than the whole of British Industry.'

Having taken the broad macroview of technology thus far, the rest of this chapter looks more specifically at how technology impacts on a business and where it may be applied to improve marketing and business operations. These are: product design, manufacturing and processing systems, storage and distribution, order and payment processing, materials handling, document handling, computerized information and communications, and the individual's office (see Figure 11.4).

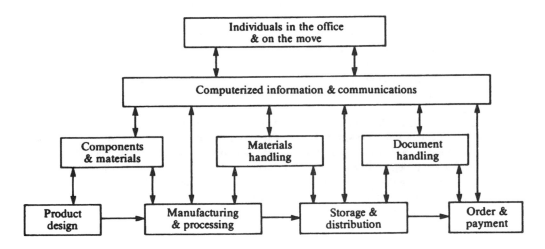

Figure 11.4   Impact of technological change on company operations

CORDLESS PHONE SERVICE LAUNCH ENDS IN A TANGLE

The launch of a series of low-cost portable telephone services in the United Kingdom during 1989 generated much interest, but their general failure to attract the expected custom illustrates the hazards of introducing a new service.

Since the initial UK launch of cellular telephone networks in the early 1980s by Cellnet and Vodaphone, the advantages of being able to make calls from any point had proved popular with the self-employed, travelling sales personnel and business executives, among others. Beyond these segments, the service remained too expensive, and possibly overspecified for more casual users.

In January 1989, the government issued

licences to four companies—Zonephone (owned by Ferranti), Callpoint (owned by a consortium of Mercury Telecommunications, Motorola and Shaye), Phonepoint (British Telecom, STC, France Telecom, Deutsche Bundespost and Nynex) and Hutchison Telecom—to operate a network of low-cost mobile phones aimed at the mass market, known as the 'Telepoint' system. These would allow callers to use a compact handset to make outgoing calls only, when they were within 150 metres of a base station, these being located in public places such as railway stations, shops, petrol stations, etc.

As in the case of many new markets that suddenly emerge, operators saw advantages of having an early market share lead. Customers who perceived that one network was more readily available than any other would—all other things being equal—be more likely to subscribe to that network. Thus operators saw that a bandwagon effect could be set up. To gain entry to the market at a later stage could become a much more expensive market-challenger exercise. With relatively low costs involved in setting up a Telepoint network, three of the four licensed operators rushed into the market, signing up outlets for terminals as well as new customers.

Such was the speed of development that the concept was not rigorously test-marketed. To many, the development was too much product-led, with insufficient understanding of buyer behaviour and competitive pressures. Each of the four companies forced through their own technologies, with little inclination or time available to discuss industry standard handsets which could eventually have caused the market to grow at a faster rate and allowed the operators to cut their costs.

Rather than thoroughly test out customer reaction to Telepoint in a small test market (as French Telecom had done with its Pointel system in Strasbourg prior to its full national launch), the operators sought to develop national coverage overnight. This was inevitably very patchy, with no outlets in some areas and heavy congestion in a few key sites. There were also the inevitable teething problems in getting the equipment to function correctly.

Worse still for the Telepoint operators, the nature of the competition had been poorly judged. Originally, a major benefit of Telepoint had been seen as removing the need to find a working telephone kiosk from which to make an outgoing call. In fact, the unreliability of public kiosks on which demand was based receded as British Telecom dramatically improved reliability, as well as increasing their availability at a number of key sites. Competition from Mercury had itself increased the number of kiosks available to users. At the top end of the Telepoint target market, the two established cellular operators had revised their pricing structure which made them more attractive for the occasional user.

The final straw for Telepoint operators came with the announcement by the government of its proposal to issue licences for a new generation of personal communications networks. Based on digital technology, this was to encourage the development of very small lightweight personal phones. These would have the additional benefit of allowing both incoming and outgoing calls, and would not be tied to a limited base station range. While this in itself might not have put people off buying new Telepoint equipment, it did have the effect of bringing new investment in Telepoint networks to a halt, leaving the existing networks in a state of limbo.

Faced with the apparent failure of their new service development strategies, the Telepoint operators looked for ways of re-launching their services by refocusing their benefits to new target markets. Now that the initial target of street-based outgoing callers had all but disappeared, new ideas were developed. Hutchison Telecom, for instance, combined an outgoing handset with a paging device which would allow business executives and self-employed people to keep in touch with base—the service was in effect being positioned as a cheap alternative to the two cellular networks. Similarly, the relaunch of Phonepoint focused on meeting the needs of three key targets—small businesses, mobile professionals and commuters. Furthermore, the company aimed to achieve excellence within the London area—where a network of 2000 base stations was planned—rather than spreading its resources thinly throughout the country. Other targets had been identified for Telepoint technology. Office networks, for example, offered the chance for employees within an organisation to keep in touch, without the need to be near a wired phone.

Two years after its initial launch, it had been estimated that no more than 5,000 subscribers in total had been signed up for Telepoint, or roughly one per base station, instead of the hundreds which were needed for viability. With hindsight, it could be argued that the launch might have been more successful had the service been more rigorously tested and developed before launch and if target markets had been more carefully selected. Moreover, many of the competitors might probably have wished that they had carried out a more rigorous environmental analysis, in which case they might have been less enthusiastic about launching in the first place.

QUESTIONS

1. Identify the environmental forces impacting on the telephone market in the United Kingdom (or your own country) during the late 1980s and early 1990s.
2. Why were so many companies in such a rush to establish themselves in this market?
3. What factors contributed to the failure of the Telepoint system? What steps could the companies have taken to evaluate the risks more thoroughly than they appeared to do?

11.4   PRODUCT DESIGN

The design of a product is influenced by its components and materials, their price and availability. Components and materials incorporating new technology may be more expensive than older components or traditional materials. They may also be in short supply. Using new components or materials may involve increased risks or delay the product launch because of more extensive testing. Products should be designed with a view to keeping material, manufacturing, handling and storage costs to a minimum. These issues should be considered at the outset of the design brief and not as an afterthought. Reducing product costs by 5 or 10 per cent can mean huge savings over the life of a product. In many industries computer-aided design (CAD) gives more flexibility and a speedier response to customer needs. As production methods may now give greater flexibility, it is possible to produce a wider variety of styles, colours and features based on a basic product. These planned variations should be designed in at the initial design stages, even though they may not be incorporated until much later.

It is argued that the life expectancy of products has generally tended to shorten as technology has advanced. The product life cycle (PLC) is a means of plotting sales and profits over time (see Figure 11.5) in such a way that different stages in the life cycle can be identified and appropriate marketing strategies thus applied.

Five stages in the product life cycle can be identified:

1. *Product development prior to launch*   At this point, sales are zero and development and investment costs are rising.
2. *Introduction of the product into the market*   This means expensive launch costs and promotion. Profitable sales may take some time to develop.
3. *Growth stage*   This is when the product is fully accepted into the market and healthy profits begin to materialize on the strength of increasing sales.
4. *Maturity*   This refers to the period over which sales growth begins to slow and eventually stop. Profits may begin to decline as increasing competition puts pressure on prices and forces up promotional expenses to defend the market share.
5. *Decline*   At this point sales begin to fall off and profits decline due to a lower volume of production.

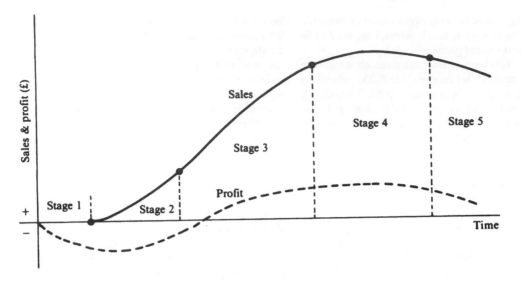

Figure 11.5 The product life cycle

Kotler (1991) makes a useful distinction between product category (say typewriters), product forms (e.g. manual, electric and electronic) and brands (individual product brands offered by particular manufacturers). According to him, product categories tend to have the longest PLCs and to stay in the mature stage for very long periods. They may begin to decline only with significant and fundamental changes in technology (as when typewriters come to be replaced by personal computers) or shifts in consumer preferences (away from smoking, for example). Product forms tend to show a more classical PLC, with each subsequent form showing a similar history to the previous one. For example, manual typewriters move through the stages of introduction, growth and maturity, and enter decline as electric typewriters are introduced. These then follow a similar history until they begin to decline as electronic typewriters are introduced. The whole product category is now entering a decline stage as the new product category of personal computers has come well into the growth stage. Individual brands follow the shortest PLC, as companies are constantly attempting to update their products to keep abreast of changes in technology, fashion, customer preferences and competitors' offerings.

Rapid advances in technology may mean shortening product life cycles in some industries. In consumer electronics, for example, advances in technology have allowed manufacturers to add more and more product features and reduce prices as costs have fallen. Brands in this product category may have a life expectancy of only 18 months before they are withdrawn and replaced.

11.5 MANUFACTURING AND PROCESSING

Technology impacts on manufacturing or processing systems, particularly in computerized numerical control (CNC) machine tools, computer-aided manufacturing (CAM), integrated manufacturing systems (IMS) and just-in-time (JIT) systems. With CNC, the machine tool is directly linked to a microprocessor so that the instructions can be created and stored. This gives greater reliability and quicker change-over times. Previously the machine would have been controlled by punch cards or cassette tapes. CAM involves linking computers to a number of machine tools and assembly robots which are interfaced with computer-controlled material handling systems. Sections of the manufacturing process are thus integrated into the same production control system. CAD/CAM (computer-aided design/computer-aided manufacturing) is where parts designed on the computer can be programmed directly into the machine tool via the same computer system. These systems can save hundreds of hours over previous methods involving the separate activities of design, building models and prototypes and then programming separate machines for production.

Integrated manufacturing systems (IMS) enable a number of CAM subsystems to be integrated together within a larger computer-controlled system. A number of manufacturers are attempting to integrate the total manufacturing process. This, however, is very difficult to do in practice, as plant and equipment are often of different ages, were designed by different companies and use different control systems. While it is possible to design a total IMS from scratch, the investment costs are likely to be prohibitive for most companies. JIT systems are designed to limit stockholding and handling costs. A supplier is expected to deliver components to the right delivery bay, at a specific day and time. There may be heavy penalties for failing to deliver on time. Components can then be moved directly on to the production floor ready for use on the line. This requires close co-operation between the manufacturer and supplier and usually is made possible only by the use of computerized information systems and data links.

These developments in technology impact on small companies and large, and on traditional industries such as textiles and shoes as well as on new ones. Generally speaking, modern manufacturing systems allow production lines to be run with greater flexibility and higher quality, making it easier to produce product variations and allowing a speedier change-over between products thus minimizing down-time.

At first sight, it may not be obvious why marketing managers should be interested in these developments in production technology. However, such developments present companies with a number of opportunities for gaining a competitive advantage. Firstly, developments in these areas are likely to contribute to a reduction in costs. Aiming to be a low-cost manufacturer should help in achieving a higher return on investment by allowing a higher margin and/or a higher volume of sales at lower prices. Secondly, modern manufacturing techniques allow for greater flexibility in production; thus, a wider variety of product variations may be produced without incurring onerous cost penalties. Thirdly, lead times between orders and delivery can be improved. Finally, it is possible to ensure that the quality of the products is more consistent and of a higher standard if desired. Recent advances in integrated manufacturing systems using computer-controlled industrial robots has meant that some Japanese car markers, for example, can produce totally different models on the same production line. Thus, low-volume/high-value cars can be produced more cheaply by utilizing an automated line set up for the high-volume output of another model. The company can take a higher profit margin or pass on lower prices to its customer, or a combination of both.

11.6 STORAGE AND DISTRIBUTION

The storage and distribution of goods has also benefited from advances in technology. In particular, the increased capacity and reliability of computerized data-processing and storage combined with improved data transmission and computer-controlled physical handling systems have led to reductions in costs and improvements in service. It is now possible to hold less stock at all stages in the distribution chain for a given product variety. From the retailer's perspective they can reduce the amount of stock on the sales floor and in the back room.

These developments would not have been possible, however, without a great deal of co-operation and the integration of other technologies. The systems developed depend on each individual product having a unique code number and the equipment at the point of sale being able to read that number. Manufacturers, retailers and other interested parties co-operated under the auspices of the Article Number Association (ANA) to devise a numbering system, allocate numbers and set standards for the use of what have become known as 'barcodes'. Each product item is allocated a unique number so that each product variation by size and colour can be identified by the manufacturer. In the words of the

Article Number Association, 'a 430 g can of peas, for example, has a different number from a 300 g can. A tin of blue paint has a different number from the same size can of red paint.' Membership of the ANA now totals over 7000 firms, and it is estimated that there are over 4000 scanning stores in the United Kingdom. According to the ANA, nearly 100 per cent of grocery products now carry a barcode on the packaging, and over 50 per cent of general merchandise.

At first, these barcodes were read by light pens and were only suitable for outlets with a medium volume of daily sales such as clothing retailers. Very high-volume outlets such as supermarkets had to wait for the development of the laser scanner, which can now be seen in most modern grocery stores. The product is simply passed over the scanner at the check-out so that the computerized till can read the barcode. It is these systems that provide itemized till receipts.

For a national clothing retailer, the improved service and reduction in costs are achieved by linking computerized tills to a central computer and stock control system which connects all stores and warehouses (Figure 11.6). In some cases large suppliers maybe linked directly into the system. Items purchased are read with a light pen or laser scanner at the till, which in addition to logging the price identifies the item. At the end of the day's trading, or periodically during the day, the central computer checks on the sales through each till. Replacement orders can then be placed with the nearest warehouse by the computer, and if necessary the warehouse stock will be replenished by calling off further orders from the supplier.

In the warehouse, orders can be processed overnight or the next day and delivered the following evening or early the next morning. On delivery to the store, most of the items will be placed directly on to the rack on the sales floor, thus considerably reducing the need for back-room storage. This allows for a greater range of items to be stocked in a given floor space as the stock on the rack for each item is reduced; the space previously given over to back-room storage (up to a third of the total space in a High Street store) can now be opened up as part of the sales floor. Thus, the total selling space is increased, sales turnover per square metre is increased and the range of items carried is increased. There is less overstocking, fewer out-of-stock situations and less shrinkage. Immediate price changes can be introduced and there is generally tighter price control. The tighter financial control, higher sales turnover and increased profits may help pay for the investment in computers, new out-of-town warehousing, transport and physical handling systems. The systems that are dependent on these computerized tills are known as EPOS (electronic point of sale), and are discussed further in Section 11.7.1.

Other benefits to these systems are obtained from the sales information collected and stored by the

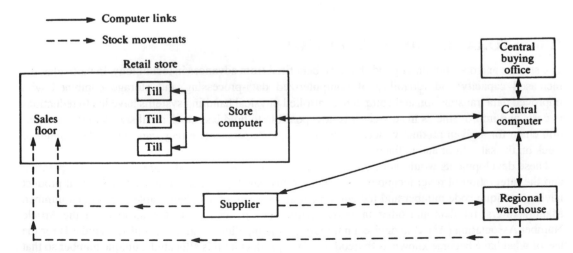

Figure 11.6 Systems linking the retail store, warehouse and head office

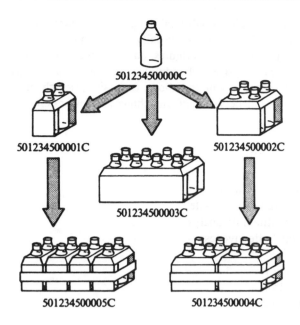

Figure 11.7   Article numbering for traded units
Source: used with permission of the Article Number Association.

computer. Sales of individual product items can be analysed. For fast-moving fashion items, this is vital information. In the past, a whole season's estimated sales had to be ordered in advance from the supplier—a risky business in the fashion world. Now initial orders from the supplier may be kept relatively low. Fast-selling lines can be identified using the computerized information and projections of sales made; further orders can then be placed with the supplier. This may be based on the first few days of a line being placed on sale. The whole process of business is thus speeded up. The links between store, warehouse, buying office and supplier become much more dynamic. Stockholding by the individual store may be as low as two days' sales, compared with a week in the late 1970s.

Barcode scanning systems are also used throughout the distribution chain. Outer cases are referred to as 'traded units' and can include pallets. The ANA co-ordinates the allocation of numbers that are used for traded units as well as consumer units. These barcodes for the 'traded units' are also machine-readable, so the outer case can be controlled more effectively at every stage in the distribution channel, from the manufacturer to the retailer or customer. According to the Article Number Association, 'Every traded unit which differs by the nature or quantity of its contents must have a different number' (Figure 11.7).

11.7   ORDER AND PAYMENT PROCESSING

11.7.1   Technology at the point of sale

In the previous section we considered the impact of computer systems and data links on storage and distribution. The combination of barcodes, laser scanners, computerized tills, data links and powerful computers with remote terminals has much improved the control of stock. Systems are constantly being improved, as is the reliability and speed with which the systems operate. These systems are also expensive to install and run. However, as the technology improves and competition increases between suppliers of systems, we can expect the costs to come down.

EPOS (electronic point of sale) systems means that each till will total the goods purchased by the individual and record the transaction in the normal way. In addition to the daily cash analysis, however, EPOS systems may provide stock reports and an analysis of sales figures, and improve control over each till and the staff using it. The retailer no longer has to price each individual item, as the price only needs to be displayed on the shelf or the rack. This saves labour and allows for easier price changes. The customer benefits from itemized till receipts, a faster check-out, greater choice and fewer items out of stock (Table 11.3).

Table 11.3 Benefits of EPOS

Improved management information
    Store-by-store comparison of sale
    Direct product profitability analysis
    Sales-promotional effectiveness

Operational efficiency
    Better stock control
    Quicker stocktaking
    Reduced shrinkage
    No item pricing
    Faster price changes

Improved customer service
    Faster check-out throughput
    Fewer queues
    Itemized sales receipts
    Reduced operator error

Source: Fletcher (1995), p. 367.

EFTPOS (electronic funds transfer at point of sale) has all the benefits of EPOS plus electronic funds transfer. This means that the computerized till is now fitted with a card reader, and data links into the banking system can transfer funds electronically. The customer's credit card such as Mastercard (e.g. Access) and Visa (e.g. Barclaycard) or debit card (e.g. Switch and Delta) is presented in the normal way, the cashier swipes this through the card reader, the till prints out the slip for signature and the customer retains the top copy. The customer's credit card company or current account (depending on the card used) is debited with the sale and the retailer's account is credited. The convenience for customers and retailers is enhanced, the accuracy of transactions is increased, cash handling is reduced and the costs of processing the sale are also significantly reduced (Table 11.4). These systems have now been applied to many types of retailing operations, including, for example, supermarkets, DIY superstores, clothing retailers, petrol stations, book shops and hotels. Such systems are set to expand rapidly in the retailing industry during the next decade. Changes are also impacting on business-to-business transactions in a similar way with electronic data interchange (EDI).

11.7.2 Business-to-business sales

In business-to-business transactions the speed at which orders can be captured and processed by the companies' systems denotes the speed at which orders and invoices can be dispatched and payment

Table 11.4 Benefits of EFTPOS

Benefits to retailers
 Reduced paperwork
 Single system for all cards
 Reduction in volume and cost of cash handling
 Reduced security risk
 Reduction in fraud
 Faster check-out time
 Faster payment into retailers account

Benefits to customers
 Less need to carry large amounts of cash
 More choice in methods of payment
 No £50 limit as with cheques
 Itemized receipts and statements easy to check
 Faster check-out time

Source: adapted from Fletcher (1995).

collected. Closely associated and inseparable from the system is the document handling, which includes orders, manufacturing dockets, picking notes, dispatch/delivery notes, invoices and statements. Advances in technology will continue to influence all these aspects of the business. Two examples illustrate what is possible with 1990s technology.

The first is provided by Golden Wonder Crisps, a UK manufacturer of crisps and snacks. The van sales representative takes the order from the local shop and drops off the goods. The order is entered in the van sales representative's portable computer, which will then print out a delivery note to leave with the buyer. In the evening the sales representative phones through to the head office mainframe computer and couples the portable computer to the phone. The mainframe draws out the sales data and passes back any messages. Next day the invoice is raised and posted so as to arrive the third day after delivery.

When these systems were first developed in the early 1980s, it would take up to 20 minutes to download these data. Today it takes only a few minutes with new portable computers, and the data transmission is much more of a two-way process. It is possible for the mainframe to input into the representative's portable the sales journey cycles for the coming weeks, relevant customer information, update on products and prices, notes on special promotional deals and messages from the manager.

This system is now being used for the direct sales force serving the larger retailers and cash-and-carries. Orders received one day are down-loaded to the mainframe the same evening. Overnight or the next day (day 2), the mainframe raises the picking and dispatch notes. On day 3 the order is dispatched, and the invoice is printed and posted. In the late 1970s this whole process would have taken between seven and ten days.

The second example comes from RS Components, a UK-based company with international operations. In the UK market the company is the largest distributor of electronic and electrical components and associated products. Its products are sold via a catalogue to industrial, educational, research and public sector organizations. Its particular unique selling proposition is the range of products stocked and the speed of delivery.

This is how it works. Regular customers have their own customer number. The customer phones RS and the call should be answered instantaneously. With 20 phone lines and a computer-controlled exchange which places the call to one of the telesales staff, the call should not ring more than three times. The customer gives a customer number, order number, part numbers of products ordered and quantity ordered—that is all. This information is typed directly into the computer by the telesales person. The total call should not take more than a few seconds. The computerized telephone system handles 7500 calls per day. The computer prints out the invoice/order picking document. The order picking document starts its run through a part-computerized warehouse with its bin. A barcode is attached to the front of the bin which directs it along a conveyor system only to those bays holding stock for that order. The order is packed and shipped the same day, and the invoice, folded and placed in an envelope by document-handling equipment, is also posted the same day. Express delivery companies are used to ensure next-day delivery. The speed and efficiency of a system such as this which can handle 10 000 separate orders per day with same-day dispatch of goods and invoices is staggering. It was simply not possible ten years ago.

11.7.3   Electronic data interchange (EDI) transactions

A huge volume of transactions taking place daily between businesses in the United Kingdom has prompted a number of companies to encourage the development and use of electronic transactions. A number of systems are now in place. Previously the limitations of telecommunications, the problems of incompatible computers and their software, and the lack of legal status for electronic documents prevented business-to-business communication via computers and electronic mail. These technical and legal problems are now behind us, and the Article Number Association (ANA), along with the support of a number of leading organizations, has set standards for and promoted the use of electronic communication. TRADACOMS (Trading Data Communications) is the term used to cover the standards developed by the ANA.

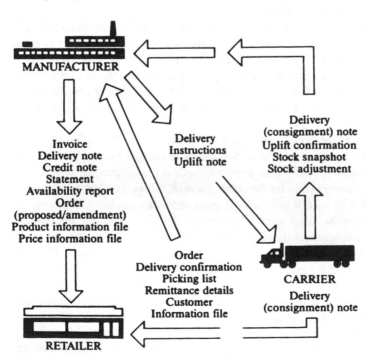

Figure 11.8   Electronic data transmission of trading documents
Source: used with permission of the Article Number Association.

Standards ares set at two levels. Firstly, common standards are applied to all the paper documents in terms of layout, which ensure clarity and improved efficiency. Secondly, the way in which these paper documents are configured electronically into computerized documents is standardized. This allows electronic data interchange (EDI), which means that data can be transmitted directly between one company's computer system and another's for automatic processing. This computer-to-computer communication improves speed, accuracy and efficiency of document transmission between manufacturers and their customers and the carriers (Figure 11.8). Documents and data that can be transmitted directly from computer to computer include orders, packing instructions, invoices, credit notes, delivery notes, statements, general text, availability reports, remittance advice, stock adjustments, product information, prices and customer details.

Major computer and telecommunication companies are involved in providing the system interchange services. These allow direct computer-to-computer communications (even between different hardware and software) via the telecommunications system. TRADANET is one such system (Figure 11.9). Companies can transmit or collect data from this electronic mailbox at any time. Transmissions to any number of receivers need only be input into the system once, leaving the TRADANET service to route and distribute the data quickly and in absolute security to each recipient's electronic mail box.

There are a number of such systems operating in the United Kingdom and throughout Europe. In addition to the well-established TRADACOMS standard and the TRADANET network, which

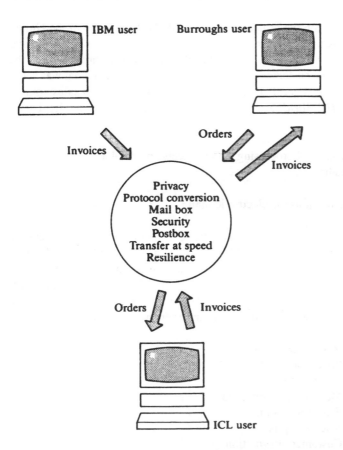

Figure 11.9   How TRADANET works
Source: used with permission of the Article Number Association.

provide a general service, there is ODETTE (Organization for Data Exchange by Teletransmissions in Europe), which provides a European service (Fletcher, 1995). Various systems have been designed to serve specific industries such as motor manufacturing, pharmaceuticals, electronics and chemicals. These services are set to expand rapidly in the 1990s and will help simplify domestic and international trade.

11.8   COMPUTERIZED INFORMATION AND COMMUNICATION SYSTEMS

Developments in these areas will influence manufacturing, processing, distribution, sales and order payment systems. The examples already discussed illustrate some of the links between computer systems used for processing and storing data and those used for communicating within and between different sites via telecommunications. The power of computers continues to increase and their size and price continues to reduce. Developments in satellites, optic fibre cable, exchanges and the miniaturizing of electronic components have given us satellite television, fax machines, the car phone, the mobile phone and the notebook computer. Telecommunication networks have had to be increased in capacity to deal with huge volumes of electronic data generated by computers. Hewlett-Packard provides an example of what is now possible with improved information and communication systems (*HP World*, March 1988).

Hewlett-Packard (HP) has been working on the project since the mid 1980s, initially in the United States and more recently in the United Kingdom, to increase the productivity of the sales force and improve the service to the customer. As is often the case with field sales, only a small proportion of the representative's total time was spent with the customer—in HP's case, 26 per cent. The goal was set to increase this by 25 per cent, and from this it was calculated that a 5 per cent increase in sales volume would pay for the system. According to *HP World* (March 1988), research showed that the field sales representatives required:

- Personal productivity solutions such as word processing, spreadsheets and databases
- Price and product availability information
- Order status reports
- Access to HP company-wide communications via electronic mail

Sales representatives were issued with a portable computer with modem and printer so as to access the company database from home or the customer's office. This first stage, a pilot involving 104 representatives in the United States, was claimed to be a great success with the computerized representatives, increasing the time spent with the customer from 26 to 35 per cent (an increase of 30 per cent) (*HP World*, March 1988). By 1987 the entire US sales force of 2100 sales representatives had been converted to the system at a cost of $6 million. The system was further enhanced to provide:

Personal tools
- Word processing
- Memo maker
- Spreadsheet
- Electronic mail
- Budgetary quotes
- Proposal generation
- Printer

Access to information
- Price availability
- Order status
- Marketing information
- Sales forecasting
- Sales analysis
- Customer information
- Lead distribution and tracking

These developments in the field would not have been possible without enhancement of the company's customer databases and the reorganization of the marketing support operation. Two new support centres were established. The installed base centre (IBC) holds the records of all existing customers and their systems. The field sales personnel can access this through their portable PCs. In addition to providing information, it is used as a resource for telemarketing and for screening customer enquiries to see if a personal call by the sales representative is really necessary. The main benefits claimed by HP for this centre are: field sales call per order down 25 per cent, costs per order down 10 per cent and sales volume up 15 per cent.

The second support centre is the customer information centre (CIC), which is used to manage new enquiries resulting from marketing activities such as mailings, seminars and exhibitions. HP in the USA receives a total of 500 000 enquiries annually by phone and mail. These need to be screened before a sales representative is dispatched, to establish whether a personal visit is necessary and whether the call will be viable. According to HP, the volume of sales leads being passed to field sales has been reduced to 5 per cent of enquiries with this new system. The quality of the leads is much higher, and the speed at which they are passed on is much faster, down from weeks to days. The CIC uses a closed-loop system to handle this huge volume of enquiries. Figure 11.10 shows how the qualified leads resulting from the marketing activity and screening by the customer information centre are passed electronically to the field sales representative's portable computer via the 'funnel management account book'. The lead cannot be removed from the file by the representative without the result first being passed back to the CIC database. The result win/loss and new contacts is used to update the database files—promotion analysis, win/lost analysis, forecasting, market analysis and list management.

The advances in technology are therefore allowing companies to manage huge volumes of information in databases that can be accessed easily and speedily by non-technical personnel from locations

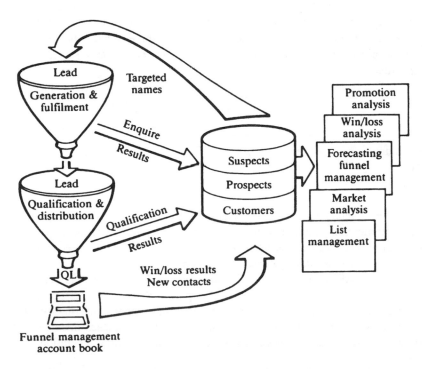

Figure 11.10   Field sales and marketing closed-loop information system
Source: *HP World* (March 1988), used with permission of Hewlett-Packard.

outside the office. The sales representative is better informed about the customer, the company's products, prices, quotations, orders, delivery lead times, competitors and market conditions. Personnel efficiency is increased and sales productivity is up as is sales volume and profit. These customer contact management systems are no longer the sole preserve of large organizations. There are many software packages available for personal computer LANs (local area networks) and lap-top computers. These packages use relational databases and communication software and are specifically designed for sales and customer contact management. Prices start from as low as £300.

The power of computers to store and manipulate huge volumes of information in databases and the ability to transmit this to people remote from the office presents marketing managers with a new marketing tool. As can be seen from the examples provided above, the potential uses for the database far exceed those of direct mail. Database marketing will be a major growth area in the next ten years.

11.9 DATABASE MARKETING (DBM)

During the 1990s a whole new industry has emerged. As yet it is so new and still changing so rapidly that it is difficult to define precisely. The terms used by industry and academics alike are still to be standardized. Direct response marketing (DRM) is a term that is now used to encompass marketing activities that are designed to induce a direct response from mail order, direct mail, direct response advertising and telemarketing. These activities developed rapidly in the 1980s and have been reliant on the production of mailing lists. As the use of computers has expanded so has the production, sale and purchase of lists multiplied. The capture of personal data and its subsequent use, including the sale of the lists for mailing purposes, has provoked a number of governments to introduce legislation to protect the individual's rights. In the United Kingdom the Data Protection Act 1984 was introduced, which requires organizations holding personal data to register and abide by the act.

It is useful to draw a distinction between direct response marketing (DRM) and database marketing (DBM), and for students studying marketing the following explanation may be helpful. Think of 'database marketing' (DBM) as being the broader of the functions and having three subactivities of direct response marketing, computer-aided sales support and customer information and service. The following then becomes apparent:

- *Database marketing* (DBM) is an interactive approach to marketing communications relying on the maintenance of accurate customer and potential customer information, competitor information and internal company information. The database is used in field sales support, for direct response marketing and to provide customer information and service systems.
- *Computer-aided sales support* (CASS) requires the field sales team, sales support team and telemarketing team to have direct access to the database via desk-top or portable computers, to access customer/potential customer information, competitor information and company information. The system is also likely to be used for internal electronic communication to aid sales management. Personal tools such as memo writing, spreadsheets, records, proposal/quotation generation, etc., would also be available.
- *Direct response marketing* (DRM) involves the use of the database in addressable communications (such as direct mail, mail order, and telemarketing), targeted at existing and potential customers,

and direct response advertising, the purpose being to stimulate a response from the consumer such as an order, request for information or a visit, or provision of information for market research purposes.

● *Customer information and service* (CIS) allows customers to contact the organization quickly and easily, possibly using a toll free number. The reasons for the contact may include: bill query, warranty claim, technical problem, product/service information or service required.

All of these systems will be anchored to the database (Figure 11.11) and will allow the organization to integrate its customer contact activities in order to build better and longer lasting relationships with its customers. The term 'relationship marketing' is often used to describe the strategy.

Figure 11.11   The components of database marketing and customer contact management

11.9.1   Computer-aided sales support

A number of marketers and writers still tend to take a narrow view of DBM as being wholly about direct response marketing. However, as can be seen by the examples of Hewlett-Packard and Golden Wonder given earlier in this chapter, when the database is made accessible to the sales teams, it has the potential to enhance their performances substantially. Thus, DBM is relevant both to business-to-business marketing and to the marketing of consumer products and services.

For companies producing products and services for other businesses, the database may hold company information such as product listings, specifications, part numbers, availability and lead times as well as pricing details. Customer and potential customer details may also be made available, such as buyer details, contract details, quotations outstanding, order status, previous purchases, installed equipment and competitor purchases. It is also possible to store competitor information on the database, thus making it directly accessible to the field sales force where it is most needed, rather than being hidden away in inaccessible files. As in the case with Hewlett Packard, if this database is made readily accessible to the field sales force by telecommunications, modems and portable personal computers, then productivity and effectiveness can be seen to rise. Such databases may also be used to improve the quality of the leads generated by direct response marketing, thus supplementing leads generated from more traditional means such as exhibitions and advertising in trade journals.

11.9.2 Direct response marketing

Direct response marketing includes such activities as direct mail, mail order, telemarketing and direct response advertising. Direct mail is targeted at a specific address and delivered by the public postal system. It is likely to include a letter, usually addressed to a named individual, a leaflet or brochure, and some response mechanism such as a coupon or order form and envelope. Mail order relies on the use of the database to identify specific target customers who would find the particular mailing of interest. The 1980s saw a huge growth in the distribution of slim, specialist catalogues aimed at very specific target groups, while the traditional full shopping catalogues aimed at the C2 and D social groups were experiencing sluggish sales. The mail order business was reshaped in the 1980s as the very powerful databases were developed. Telemarketing involves the use of the database and modern specialist telephone exchanges linked to computers which can automatically dial numbers and record the results. The term 'telemarketing' is used as it encompasses sales activity and market research. Direct response advertising uses the print or television media in the usual way, but the customer is asked to order direct from the supplier via the telephone or coupon. Information gained from customers and enquirers in this way can then be used to update the database.

The company's database is likely to be constructed from a number of sources including its own trading records, bought-in lists and bought-in database services from very specialized companies. The company then purges and merges the lists to form its own database. This last activity is most important, as it removes duplicate names and those who do not want to be or should not be contacted. Fletcher (1995) cites the Neilson Clearing House as an example of a specialist service company which has constructed a database from respondents to sales promotion offers found on grocery products; this would be of interest, then, to manufacturers of fast-moving consumer goods (FMCGs). Other specialist companies operating in the United Kingdom include International Communications and Data PLC, which operates the National Consumer Database (NCD). This database is compiled from:

- The Electoral Roll, listing 42 million adults
- Investor data from 630 company share registers, comprising 8.5 million individuals
- Life-style data from the company's Facts of Living Survey Programme, which establishes life-style and product purchasing data and holds one million records
- Home data, including details on 350 000 properties such as value, location, size, etc.
- Telephone data, matching telephone numbers and addresses for 14 million individuals.

A wide number of services are offered to clients from this database. For instance, a client may have a need for a profile analysis. The client provides a profile of current customers or enquirers which is then matched against the National Consumer Database. According to the company, a number of reports can then be produced, showing the quality of the client's file (from the accuracy of postcoding to the level of 'gone always'), the penetration of the client file into its target markets and a new target mailing list.

A growing number of companies now offer such services in the United Kingdom. As is often the case with retail audits, data can be purchased in such a way that it can be input directly into the client's own computerized marketing information system.

A good example of a company using database marketing to help build customer loyalty and aid customer retention is Tesco, who launched their Clubcard in 1995, the intention being to build and reward customer loyalty. The company can now mail special promotional offers and customer information direct to members. By December 1995 there were 6 million members (*Independent*, 2 December 1995) and those with sufficient points were rewarded with vouchers.

11.9.3 Customer information and service (CIS)

There are many reasons why customers and potential customers may wish to contact the manufacturer or supplier of services direct. Consumer product and service companies may need to respond to enquiries about the bill (public utilities), statements (banks), amount outstanding on a loan (finance company), adjusting monthly investment (pension company), technical questions (electrical products), warranty cover (household products), availability (children's electronic games), schedules (flights) or delivery (furniture). For industrial products and services customers are interested in availability, maintenance, servicing, parts, installation and technical support.

Provision of advice and information is now expected immediately either via the phone, fax, E-mail or EDI. The customer expects the supplier to have all the information available at one contact point. Customers no longer expect to be passed around from department to department and from one nameless person to another only to be left with a vague promise of a call back. See the references earlier in this chapter to Golden Wonder, Hewlett-Packard and RS Components for examples of how some companies are using the latest technology to serve the customer.

The customer help-line is now an important feature offered by a growing band of companies. The database and computerized telephone systems now provide the opportunity for companies to deal directly with their customers in a speedy and informed manner. For example, American Airlines is to locate its new European reservation centre in Ireland which will result in savings of £20 million as it phases out five older offices in Europe (*Sunday Independent*, Dublin, 19 November 1995). The new teleservicing centre will be one of the largest in Europe and is expected to handle 2.5 million calls a year and employ 220 multilingual staff.

11.10 CONCLUSIONS

This chapter has considered technological change from the macroperspective and examined the impact of technology on different aspects of the business at the microlevel. In both cases the relevance of technological change to marketing has been stressed. Marketing managers, however, are not the only executives who need to anticipate, identify and evaluate the impact of technological change.

At the macro level of technological change, the key points to remember concern the demand–technology life cycle. This will be influenced by the level of research and development expenditure, not only in a particular industry but also in related and sometimes unrelated industries. The fusion and interaction of different technologies result in new applications and processes which eventually may give rise to whole new industrials. Technology permeates through from academic and research institutions into industry, from one industry to another, and from one economy to another. However, if the UK manufacturing sector has become a follower rather than a leader, then it will have lost a much-needed competitive advantage in world markets. Marketing managers should be just as concerned with the long-term prospects of their company as with yesterday's sales. Research and development is too important to be left to the technical boffins. Production, finance and marketing people need to be involved in the R&D process along with the scientists and development engineers. The board of directors needs to show serious interest and should be seen to be giving it the priority it requires.

At the micro level, the chapter has considered the impact of technology on the company's products and operations; product design, manufacturing and processing; storage and distribution; order and payment processing; information and communication systems; and database marketing. With regard to the specific areas of marketing and company operations referred to throughout the chapter, marketing managers and other executives may look to the medium-term horizon for planning purposes. The aim is not only to improve efficiency of the business operations but also to ensure that the benefits are passed on to the customer.

These customer benefits may include better pre-order services such as product availability and specification information, faster quotations and quicker design customizing. Improved post-order services may include shorter delivery times, delivery to just-in-time (JIT) requirements, installation, training, electronic data interchange (EDI) and itemized till receipts.

Overall, the reduction of costs and the move to low-cost production relative to the competition will benefit shareholders and customers alike. The opportunity to increase the efficiency of operations such as materials handling and distribution is there. Marketing activities such as direct response marketing and computer-aided sales support have much room for future development. A more knowledgeable sales force with easy access to the right information and the modern tools to do the job will be a more productive and cost-efficient sales force.

The technological environment is a constantly changing environment. In many industries during the 1990s and beyond, change will be the norm rather than the exception. Companies that adhere to the marketing concept and that focus on customer needs, competitor activity and technological developments, rather than simply aiming to sell what the factory makes, are more likely to succeed.

ELECTRON BEAM METALLIZING

This case study illustrates the opportunities of new technology and the way a British company evaluated the market potential.

What is metallizing?
Metallizing is the popular term for vacuum coating under very high temperatures, a process used to apply ultra-thin coatings (thinner than a human hair) to a variety of materials. The coating material—in this case metallic aluminium—is vaporized in a vacuum and condensed on to a film made from another material, in this case plastic film. Aluminium imparts a bright finish but also gives plastic film a good barrier to light, oxygen, moisture and odours. Not only does packaging look good on the shelves, but it extends the shelf life of the product. In addition to the packaging industry, uses include bottle tops, gift wrappings, car trims and insulation.

Packaging is the largest single market in tonnage. The required combinations of attractiveness and effectiveness mean that the metallized film is especially of interest to firms in the fast-moving consumer goods (FMCG) industries, which are often looking for new ideas. Metallized packaging film has become more popular in recent years, particularly in the food industry, where it is now used, for example, on biscuits, tea bags and crisps. These customers, however, are price-sensitive, as a small rise in packing costs can have a significant impact on selling price.

Metallizing at Bonar Teich
Bonar Teich Flexibles, of Derby, part of the Low and Bonar Group, has been producing metallized plastic films for packaging since 1983. In 1987 it was producing to capacity, its products were well established and the company was considering further investment in metallizing. Market research was undertaken, and the size and growth rates of the European market were established. Research from a number of sources showed:

Market size
- The overall market size for metallized plastic film in Western Europe in 1986 was 21 000–23 000 tonnes.
- Packaging accounted for approximately 50 per cent.
- Growth was estimated to be 13 per cent per annum.
- Some products were expected to grow by up to 40 per cent per annum.

Market shares

Company	United Kingdom (%)	Western Europe (%)
Camvac (UK)	50	30
Converted (UK)	20	10
Bonar Teich (UK)	10	3
MF & P (UK)	10	3
Others (European)	10	54

Source: Bonar Teich.

The company was aware that, if it were to extend its applications into more price-sensitive sectors, such as packaging for grocery products, then prices and therefore costs would have to be lower. Alternative technologies for metallizing were investigated. A new machine was available, but the technology was new and not in commercial production and thus presented some development risks. Close co-operation with the suppliers of the machine dependent on the new technology would be required. Teething problems could be expected. Development and commissioning trials using the new technology could be expected to take longer than with the proven technology. Once the new machine was in commercial production, there was the risk that its performance might never quite match the initial expectations or claims of the manufacturer.

The estimated performance of the new technology then had to be matched against the proven reliability and performance of the conventional machines. Financial projections had to be made on the basis of this technical judgement. A summary of the competing technologies follows.

The metallizing process: conventional technology versus new technology
All commercial metallizing is done on a batch process as rolls of material are loaded on to the machine for processing. However, there are some important differences between the conventional process and the new technology (see Figure 11.12). With the conventional method of 'resistance-heated evaporation', the roll of material is loaded into the processing

chamber and the vacuum pumped down. The vacuum reduces the evaporation temperature of the coating material and prevents oxidation. The material is processed by unwinding the material in such a way that it passes over the aluminium which is vaporized at a very high temperature. This process coats the plastic film with the aluminium, and the now metallized material is received on to the rewind drum. The vacuum is then broken so that the finished product can be removed from within the machine. The efficiency of the process, i.e. the actual running time of the machine to total time from start to finish of the operation is 50 per cent. This is because of the time taken to load the machine and then pump down the vacuum at the start, and to allow cooling at the end before the roll of metallized material can be removed. The actual speed at which the machine can process the material is 450 metres per minute. The machine can use only aluminium as a coating material as the maximum temperature at the source of evaporation is 1500°C. The consumable costs are 0.235 pence per square metre. The machine is mechanically complex but of proven technology with a known reliability.

The new technology uses an 'electron beam evaporation' process. The principles by which the machine works are the same as with the conventional machine. The roll of material is unwound and passed over a heat source where the coating material is vaporized. The now metallized material is then received on to the rewind drum. There are a number of important differences, however. Firstly, the roll of material and the rewind drum are located outside the vacuum chamber, so there is no need for waiting time to break the vacuum and allow for cooling. The evaporation energy is provided by two electron beams which can give a higher operating temperature, up to 2200 °C. This means that other materials, in addition to aluminium, can be used in the metallizing process if desired. The machine can operate up to speeds of 600 metres per minute. Very thick coatings can be applied at full speed if desired.

Financial estimates
The parent company of Bonar Teich was prepared to invest in its packaging business if projects gave a worthwhile return. The finan-

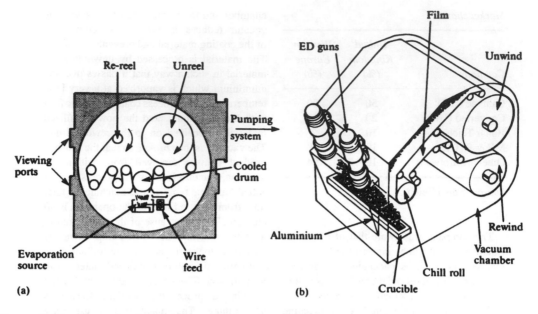

Figure 11.12   Conventional versus new technology in metallizing
(a)   Resistance heated evaporation (conventional)
(b)   Election beam evaporation (new technology)
Source: Bonar Teich.

cial estimates for the investment are shown in Table 11.5. No sales for years 1 and 2 were assumed, and sales of £1.75 million were judged to be the electron beam's maximum capacity on five-day working. The same figure was used for the conventional machine, but an element of overtime was assumed. The capital cost of the new technology was £1.60 million and of the conventional machine £1.45 million. Profit and return on capital employed (ROCE) was projected as shown in Table 11.5 For reasons of confidentiality, the profit is shown as a percentage based on the conventional machine with year 3 being the base of 100 per cent. Both machines showed a satisfactory return, with payback periods of less than four years of operation and an increase in manning of ten.

Table 11.5 Financial projections for investment in new metallizing plant

	Year 3	Year 4	Year 5	Year 6
Sales (£'000)	820	1315	1750	1750
Profit (%)				
Electron beam	120	234	328	328
Conventional	100	200	283	283
ROCE (%)				
Electron beam	13.0	26.5	34.5	38.5
Conventional	12.0	25.5	32.5	36.5

QUESTION

1. What would you do? Would you invest in another conventional machine staying with the proven technology or risk investing in the new, but commercially untried, electron beam machine with its claimed superior performance? You will find it useful to assess the technology balance by summarizing the key characteristics of the competing technologies, before comparing the financial figures.

REVIEW QUESTIONS

1. Should the United Kingdom be concerned about its relatively poor showing (compared with its main competitor countries) in research and development?
2. Should marketing managers be involved in the R&D process, and if so what should their role be?
3. Can you identify any product class that has been recently affected by changes in the demand–technology life cycle and, if so, what has been the impact of the change?
4. Identify some recent technological developments and discuss the benefits these have brought to the consumer.
5. How have recent advances in technology helped companies improve their marketing operations?
6. What are the ingredients that led to the successful development and implementation of 'article numbering' in the United Kingdom?

NOTE

1. The Article Numbers Association (UK) Ltd, 6 Catherine Street, London WC2B 5JJ.

REFERENCES

Dibb, S., Simkin, L., Pride, W. M. and Ferrell, O. C. (1994) *Marketing: Concepts and Strategies* 2nd European edn, Houghton Mifflin, Boston, Mass.

Elliott, L. (1991) 'Lesson for Britain as Sun Rises on Ideas in Japan', *Guardian*, 20 April 1991, p. 14.

Fairlie, R. (1990) *A Marketing Person's Guide to Database Marketing and Direct Mail*, Exely Publications, Watford, Herts.

Fletcher, K. (1995) *Marketing Management and Information Technology*, 2nd edn, Prentice-Hall International, London.

Kotler, P. (1991) *Marketing Management: Analysis. Planning, Implementation, and Control*, 7th edn, Prentice-Hall, Englewood Cliffs, NJ.

Kotler, P. and Armstrong, G. (1996) *Principles of Marketing*, 7th edn, Prentice-Hall, Englewood Cliffs, NJ.

OECD in Figures 1995 Edition, Published with *The OECD Observer*, No. 194, June–July 1995.

Young, A. (1993) 'What Goes into R&D?', *The OECD Observer*, no.183, August–September 1983.

TWELVE

THE INTERNATIONAL MARKETING ENVIRONMENT

OBJECTIVES

After reading this chapter, you should understand:

● The theory underlying international trade
● The role of currency exchange mechanisms in international trade
● Reasons why barriers to trade occur and the methods taken to encourage free trade
● Methods of researching the overseas marketing environment, including secondary research, primary research and the use of specialist research agencies
● Methods used by companies to adapt their products to the needs of overseas markets
● Alternative market entry strategies that address the management of risk, including exporting, direct investment, licensing/ franchising, joint ventures and management contracting

12.1   REASONS FOR INTERNATIONAL TRADE

Success in international trade can help to explain the emergence and growth of many of the countries that have achieved economic pre-eminence in the world, during both modern and ancient history. The Venetians, Spaniards and later the British, Americans and Japanese all saw periods of rapid domestic growth coincide with the growth of their trade with the rest of the world.

At some point, many organizations recognize that their growth can only continue if they exploit overseas markets. A company that has successfully developed its marketing strategy in its domestic market should be well placed to extend this into overseas markets. Many of the fundamental principles of marketing management that have been applied to the domestic market will be of relevance in an international setting. The processes of identifying market opportunities, selecting strategies, implementing those strategies and monitoring performance involve fundamentally similar principles as those that apply within the domestic market. The major challenge to companies seeking to expand overseas lies in sensitively adapting marketing strategies that have worked at home to the needs of overseas markets whose environments may be totally different to anything previously experienced.

International trade is becoming increasingly important, representing not only opportunities for domestic producers to earn revenue from overseas but also threats to domestic producers from overseas competition. The international trade of a nation is made up of the sum total of the efforts of its individual producers and consumers who decide to buy or sell abroad rather than at home. To gain a general overview of the reasons why trade between countries takes place, explanations can be found at two levels:

- At a microlevel, individual firms are motivated to trade overseas.
- At a macrolevel, the structure of an economy and the world trading system can either inhibit or encourage international trade.

12.1.1   Firms' reasons for entering international trade

For an individual company, exporting to overseas markets can be attractive for a number of reasons. These can be analysed in terms of 'pull' factors which derive from the attractiveness of a potential overseas market and 'push' factors which make an organization's domestic market appear less attractive.

1. For firms seeking growth, overseas markets represent new market segments which they may be able to serve with their existing range of products. In this way, a company can stick to producing products that it is good at. Finding new overseas markets for existing or slightly modified products does not expose a company to the risks of expanding both its product range and its market coverage simultaneously.
2. Saturation of its domestic market can force an organization to seek overseas markets. Saturation can come about where a product reaches the maturity stage of its life cycle in the domestic market, while being at a much earlier stage of the cycle in less-developed overseas markets. While the market for fast-food restaurants may be approaching saturation in a number of Western markets—especially the United States—they represent a new opportunity in the early stages of development in many Eastern European countries.
3. As part of its portfolio management, an organization may wish to reduce its dependence upon one geographical market. The attractiveness of individual national markets can change in a manner that is unrelated to other national markets. For example, costly competition can develop in one national market but not others, world economic cycles show lagged effects between different economies, and government policies—through specific regulation or general economic management—can have counterbalancing effects on market prospects.
4. The nature of a firm's product may require an organization to become active in an overseas market. This particularly affects transport-related services such as scheduled airline services and courier services. For example, a UK scheduled airline flying between London and Paris would most likely try to exploit the non-domestic market at the Paris end of its route.
5. Commercial buyers of products operating in a number of overseas countries may require their suppliers to be able to cater for their needs across national boundaries. As an example, a company may wish to engage accountants who are able to provide auditing and management accounting services in its overseas subsidiaries. For this, the firm of accountants would probably need to have created an operational base overseas. Similarly, firms selling in a number of overseas markets may wish to engage an advertising agency which can organize a global campaign in a number of overseas markets.
6. Similarly, there are many cases where private consumers demand goods and services that are internationally available. An example is the car hire business where customers frequently need to be able to book a hire car in one country for collection and use in another. To succeed in attracting these customers, car hire companies need to operate internationally.
7. Some goods and services are highly specialized and the domestic market is too small to allow economies of scale to be exploited. Overseas markets must be exploited in order to achieve a critical mass which allows a competitive price to be reached. Specialized aircraft engineering services and oil exploration services fall into this category.
8. Economies of scale also result from extending the use of brands in overseas markets. Expenditure by a fast food company on promoting its brand to UK residents is wasted when those citizens travel abroad and cannot find the brand that they have come to value. Newly created overseas outlets will enjoy the benefit of promotion to overseas visitors at little additional cost.

In addition to gaining access to new markets, individual firms may enter international trade to secure resource inputs. The benefits of buying overseas can include lower prices, greater consistency of supply, higher quality, or taking advantage of export subsidies available to overseas suppliers. In the case of raw materials that are not available in the domestic market, a firm may have little choice in its decision to buy from overseas.

12.1.2 Macroenvironmental reasons for international trade

From the perspective of national economies, a number of reasons can be identified for the increasing importance of international trade:

1. Goods and services are traded between economies in order to exploit the concept of comparative cost advantage. This holds that an economy will export those goods and services that it is particularly well suited to producing and import those where another country has an advantage. The principles of comparative cost advantage are discussed more fully in Section 12.2.1.
2. The removal of many restrictions on international trade (such as the creation of the Single European Market) has allowed countries to exploit their comparative cost advantages. Nevertheless, restrictions on trade remain, especially for trade in services.
3. Increasing household disposable incomes results in greater consumption of many categories of luxuries, such as overseas travel, which can only be provided by overseas suppliers. Against this, economic development within an economy can result in many specialized goods and services which were previously bought in from overseas being provided by local suppliers. Many developing countries, for example, seek to reduce their dependence on overseas banking and insurance organizations by encouraging the development of a domestic banking sector.
4. Cultural convergence which has resulted from improved communications and increasing levels of overseas travel has led to a homogenization of international market segments. Combined with the decline in trade barriers, convergence of cultural attitude allows many organizations to regard parts of their overseas markets as though they are part of their domestic market.

12.2 THE THEORY OF INTERNATIONAL TRADE

Today, the United Kingdom, like most industrialized countries, is dependent on international trade to maintain its standard of living. Some products that buyers have become accustomed to, such as tropical fruits and gold, would be almost impossible to produce at home. For products such as these, the UK economy could overcome this lack of availability in three possible ways:

1. By using alternative products (which can be produced at home) in place of those that cannot be produced domestically. For example, faced with a domestic shortage of aluminium, many users could switch to domestically produced steel.
2. The domestic economy could try to produce the product at home. This is often impossible where key elements of production are missing (e.g. uranium cannot be produced in the United Kingdom because it is not a naturally occurring substance). In other cases, such as the production of tropical fruits, domestic production can be achieved, but only at a very high cost.
3. The third alternative is to import the goods from a country which is able to produce it.

A similar analysis could be made of the options facing all other countries, not just the United Kingdom. Rather than producers in the United Kngdom growing bananas at great expense for domestic consumption, while a tropical company attempted to grow temperate fruits, both could benefit by specializing in what they are good at and exchanging their output. This is the basis for the theory of comparative cost advantage.

12.2.1 Comparative cost advantage

The theory of comparative cost advantage can be traced back to the work of Adam Smith in the late eighteenth century and broadly states that the world economy—and hence the economies of individual nations—will benefit if all countries:

- Concentrate on producing what they are good at and export the surplus
- Import from other countries those goods that other countries are better able to produce than themselves.

The principles of comparative cost advantage can be illustrated with an example. For simplicity, the following example will assume that there are only two countries in the world—Britain and the 'rest of the world'. A second assumption is that only two products are made in the world—food and coal.

It is possible to draw up a table showing the hypothetical food and coal production possibilities of the two countries:

1. If Britain used all of its natural resources to produce coal, then it could produce 40 tons per year, but no food. It could, on the other hand, use all of its resources to produce 40 tons of food per year, but no coal.
2. By contrast, the rest of the world could produce 160 tons of food a year or 40 tons of coal. The different ratios reflect the fact that Britain and the rest of the world possess different combinations of resources.
3. The maximum possible world output of food is therefore 200 tons or of coal 80 tons.

This can be summarized in a production possibility table (Table 12.1).

Table 12.1 Production possibility table: food and coal

	Food	*or*	*Coal*
Britain	40	or	40
Rest of world	160	or	40
World production total	200	or	80

Neither country is likely to produce solely coal or food. For Britain to give up 1 ton of coal production will result in an increase in food production of 1 ton. However, if the rest of the world gives up 1 ton of coal production, it can increase food production by 4 tons. In this example, Britain should continue to produce coal, because the comparative cost of giving up land for food is lower than the rest of the world. For Britain, the cost of 1 ton of food is 1 ton of coal. For the rest of the world, the cost of 1 ton of coal is 4 tons of food foregone. The rest of the world has a comparative cost advantage in the production of food (because the 'opportunity cost' of the resources used is lower than in Britain).

The next stage of analysing comparative cost advantages is to consider how production of coal and food may actually be divided between Britain and the rest of the world, and, from this, the pattern of trade that could take place. It is again assumed that there are only two countries in the world, that these are the only two goods traded and that total world production equals total consumption (i.e. stocks are not allowed to accumulate). An additional assumption will be made here that coal is more valuable than food. For the moment, it is assumed that 1 ton of coal is worth 5 tons of food.

Table 12.2 shows two situations:

- Where both countries divide their resources equally between food and coal production, without engaging in trade, and
- A revised trade pattern where each country specializes in the product for which it has a comparative cost advantage

Table 12.2 Effects on a national economy of specialization based on comparative cost advantage

	Original production pattern—no trade		Revised production pattern—specialisation	
	Food	Coal	Food	Coal
Britain	20	20	0	40
Rest of world	80	20	160	0
World production total	100	40	160	40
Value of 1 ton of food = 1 unit 1 ton of coal = 5 units				
	100	200	160	200
Total wealth	300 units		360 units	

On the basis of the assumptions made, Table 12.2 indicates that the world as a whole is better off as a result of the two countries specializing in doing what they are good at. Total wealth has gone up from 300 units to 360 units.

This pattern would hold so long as the relative costs of production and the terms of trade remained the same. Of course, both of these could, in practice, change. Increased costs in Britain could change its comparative cost in producing food compared to the rest of the world. The pattern would also change if the value of coal went down in relation to the value of food, for example if 1 ton of coal was worth only half a ton of food, and not 5 as in this example.

Of course, this has been a very simple example using quite unrealistic assumptions. However, it does show how international trade can benefit all nations. In reality, substitutions take place between large numbers of countries and an almost infinite range of products. Nevertheless, the underlying principles of exporting what a country is good at and importing those products that can be made more cheaply elsewhere still hold true. To give modern examples of what this actually means for the UK economy, Britain is good at producing pharmaceuticals which are sold abroad in large volume. It is not so good at producing labour-intensive textiles which are imported in large amounts from the relatively low wage countries of the Far East.

Although the concept of comparative cost advantage was developed to explain the benefits to total world wealth resulting from each country exploiting its comparative cost advantages with regard to access to raw materials and energy supplies, it can also have application to the services sector. In this way, a favourable climate or outstanding scenery can give a country an advantage in selling tourism services to overseas customers, a point that has not been lost to tourism operators in the Canary Islands and Switzerland respectively. Another basis for comparative cost advantage for services can be found in the availability of low cost or highly trained personnel (cheap labour for the shipping industry and trained computer software experts for computer consultancy respectively). Sometimes the government of a country can itself directly create comparative cost advantages for a service sector, as where it reduces regulations and controls on an industry, allowing that industry to produce services for export at a lower cost than its more regulated competitors (e.g. many 'offshore' financial services centres impose lower standards of regulation and taxation than their mainstream competitors).

12.2.2   Limitations to the principle of comparative cost advantage

Unfortunately, the principles of comparative cost advantage may sound fine in theory, but it can be difficult to achieve the benefits in practice. In reality, the global ideals described above can become obscured by narrower national interests. Consequently, the full benefits of comparative cost advantage may not be achieved:

1. Imports can be seen as a threat to established domestic firms. Short-term political pressure to preserve jobs may restrict the ability of firms and individuals to import from the country that is best placed to produce specific products.
2. Governments seek to pursue a portfolio of activities within their economies in order to maintain a balanced economy. Also, governments may protect industries in order to create greater employment opportunities for particular social or regional groups of the population.
3. Governments may seek to temporarily protect fledgling new industries during their development stage in the hope that they will eventually be able to become strong enough to compete effectively in world markets. Competition early on could kill such infant industries before they are able to develop.
4. Trade may not take place in some products—or may be made more difficult—because the requirements of different markets vary. National regulations on matters such as food purity and electrical safety may make it uneconomic to produce special versions of a product for an overseas market.
5. Transport costs act as a deterrent to international trade. Although it may be cheaper to produce building materials in Southern Europe than in the United Kingdom, the very high transport costs of getting them to the UK market will limit the amount that actually enters international trade.
6. National governments often artificially stimulate exports by giving export subsidies, allowing domestic producers to compete in world markets against more efficient producers. The European Union, for example, has frequently been accused of subsidizing the export of agricultural products such as grain and meat to protect European farmers against competition from more efficient and less subsidized American and Australian farmers.
7. International politics may severely limit the trade that a country has with the rest of the world. Although the trade barriers that existed between Eastern and Western European trading blocks are now disappearing, there is increasing concern that the creation of the European Single Market and other trading blocs, such as the North Atlantic Free Trade Area, will have the effect of reducing trade between Europe and the rest of the world.
8. Sometimes governments have defence considerations in mind in restricting international trade. This is reflected, for example, in regulations that make it very difficult for foreign companies to acquire domestic airlines.
9. Imports may represent a threat to the culture of a country and governments seek to prevent their import. This particularly affects films and publications (e.g. the governments of many Muslim countries make it difficult for films made in the West to be imported).

Despite a plethora of international agreements to facilitate trade between nations, minor, and sometimes major, trade disputes occur between nations. The countries involved may agree that the benefits of open markets and comparative cost advantage leading to benefits to all are fine in theory, but the actual short-term implications for them are too harmful. It could be that the government in one country is facing an election and restrictions on imports could gain rapid approval for the government. However, if one country is tempted to introduce some sort of control on imports from another country, it will almost inevitably result in retaliation by the other country. This can spiral, resulting in progressively declining world trade levels. The precise methods by which trade is restricted can take a number of forms:

1. The extreme form of import control is for a country to ban imports of a product or class of products from one or more countries.
2. A tariff can be imposed on goods of a specified type. Governments have imposed tariffs on imports where they believed the product was being 'dumped' by the exporting country at below its production cost, thereby threatening domestic producers with unfair competition. As an example, this was the reason given by the EU in 1995 for the imposition of tariffs ranging from 13 per cent to 48 per cent on bicycles imported from Indonesia, Malaysia and Thailand.
3. A quota on the volume of imports of a particular product can be imposed—imports of cars to the United Kingdom from Japan have been restricted on the basis of a voluntarily agreed quota.
4. Governments sometimes impose covert controls as an alternative to more formal controls, in order to try and diffuse attention and avoid retaliation. A country may unreasonably claim that an exporting nation's products do not meet quality or safety standards imposed by that country. This type of argument was used by Germany when it banned imports of beef from the United Kingdom, claiming that outbreaks of the cattle disease BSE made meat from the United Kingdom potentially unsafe. Sometimes, import documentation and procedures are made so complex that they act to increase the costs of importers relative to domestic producers.

12.2.3 Exchange rates

Nation states generally have their own currency system which may be quite different to the currency of an international trading partner. It follows therefore that the currency which a buyer wants to use as payment may not be the currency that a seller wants to receive as payment for goods or services. If a British customer buys a Japanese built car, they would expect to pay for their car in pounds sterling, and not Japanese yen. So the Japanese manufacturer must become involved in foreign exchange transactions by converting the sterling which it has received back into yen which it will need in order to buy components and to pay its work-force. The fact that different countries have their own currencies makes life for an exporter more complex and risky than for a company that just serves its domestic market.

Probably the biggest problem arising from the use of multiple currencies for trade is that their value in relation to each other fluctuates through time. The value of one currency in terms of another currency is known as its exchange rate. The exchange of the yen to sterling will determine how many yen the Japanese car maker will receive for the sterling that it has received from its customers.

Currencies are just like any other commodity which is traded in a market. If the demand for a currency is great relative to its supply, then its 'price' (or exchange rate) will rise. The opposite will happen if there is excess supply of that currency. The principles of exchange rate determination are illustrated in Figure 12.1.

Changes in the supply of, or demand for, a currency can come about for a number of reasons:

1. Changes in demand for a nation's currency can result from a significant change in exports from that country. If UK exports to Japan suddenly increase, UK firms would be left holding large volumes of yen from its Japanese customers. When the UK exporting company went to the currency markets to exchange its yen for sterling, its demand for sterling would have the effect of pushing up the price of sterling in terms of yen.

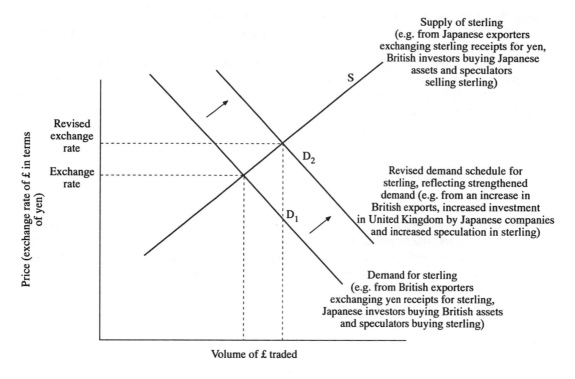

Figure 12.1 Market mechanisms and exchange rate determination

2. An increase in imports by UK firms from Japan would have an opposite effect. Japanese firms would seek to change the sterling payments they have received into yen. Their supply of sterling will increase relative to demand for it and its price will fall. Of course, in this and the previous example, the actual transactions would normally be handled routinely by the companies' bankers and most trading firms' transactions would be too small on their own to significantly affect exchange rates. Large overseas orders or the collective effects of many buyers and sellers could, however, have a significant effect on exchange rates.

3. Demand for foreign currencies can similarly arise from transactions involving the purchase of assets overseas and the remission of profits and dividends overseas.

4. As in many commodity markets, demand for a currency at any given time is influenced by individuals' *expectations* about future price levels for a currency. Traders in currencies may use their reserves to buy currencies that they consider are likely to rise and sell those that they expect to fall. Expectations about changes in currency values can be based on factors such as the inflation rate in a country (which has the effect of reducing the purchasing power of its currency); growing imbalances between a country's imports and exports; and general government macroeconomic policy.

5. Intervention by government can affect the supply of, and demand for, its currency. For example, if a government seeks to raise the value of its currency in terms of other currencies (or at least prevent it falling), it can use its gold and foreign currency reserves to buy up its own currency, thereby raising its exchange rate.

From an importer's or exporter's point of view, fluctuations in exchange rates cause considerable uncertainty. Companies selling goods or services abroad may not be certain what revenue they will actually receive if they invoice in a foreign currency, since a change in the exchange rate—between agreeing the price and receiving payment—can earn them more or less than anticipated. Where imports are priced in a producer's currency, importers of goods or services may be uncertain about the final price of their purchases.

From a national government's perspective, a falling exchange rate creates inflationary pressures, since imports become relatively expensive (i.e. it takes more pounds to buy any given yen's worth of imported products). A falling exchange rate helps exporters to achieve overseas sales, because their products effectively become cheaper overseas. It also has the effect of making imports more expensive. Through both of these effects, employment opportunities in the domestic economy are enhanced by a relatively low exchange rate. Governments must balance the stimulus to companies that a low exchange rate brings with the inflationary pressure that it generally entails.

Individual companies can minimize their exposure to risks arising from exchange rate fluctuation in a number of ways:

1. Where it is important for a firm to be certain of the future cost of materials imported from overseas, it can buy contracts which provide it with a specified amount of foreign currency at an agreed time in the future, at an agreed exchange rate. So even if the value of a currency changes in the meantime, a company can buy its materials from overseas at its budgeted price, using an overseas currency whose value was fixed during its budgeting process.
2. Where the buyer's or seller's currency has a history of volatility, they may decide to use a third currency which is regarded as a relatively stable or 'hard' currency. Many sectors of international trade, such as oil and civil aviation, are routinely priced in US dollars, regardless of the nationality of the buyer and seller.
3. The impact of currency fluctuations on large multinational companies can be reduced by trying to plan for expenditure (on components, etc.) in one currency to roughly equal the revenue it expects to earn in that currency. Any change in exchange rates therefore has an overall broadly neutral effect on the organization.
4. Fluctuating exchange rates can become an opportunity to companies who can rapidly shift their resources to take advantage of imports from countries that have suddenly become advantageous. Commodity traders operating in 'spot' markets may be able to switch supply sources according to changes in exchange rates.

12.2.4   Fixed exchange rates

An alternative to market-based fluctuating exchange rates is a fixed exchange rate system. Here, countries agree to maintain the value of each others' currency, or at least to keep fluctuations within a very narrow range. Where necessary, governments take action to maintain the agreed rates of exchange.

The Exchange Rate Mechanism (ERM) of the European Union's European Monetary System (EMS) is an example of a fixed exchange rate system. Each currency in the system is given a fixed value against the European Currency Unit (ecu) and hence, a fixed value against all other ERM member currencies. The value of ERM currencies in terms of the Ecu is shown in Table 12.3, together with the margin within which the value of a currency is allowed to fluctuate.

Countries must keep their exchange rates within their agreed level. They seek to achieve this by a variety of policy measures, such as increasing interest rates (which in the short term can attract 'hot money' into a currency, thereby pushing up its value); open market operations where the government uses gold and foreign currency reserves to buy up its own currency; and by generally increasing speculators' confidence in its economy (e.g. by reducing inflation or a balance of payments deficit).

Each member state of the EMS has agreed to place 20 per cent of its gold and dollar reserves in a

Table 12.3 European Currency Unit (ecu) central exchange rates for ERM member currencies.

	Ecu central rate	Permitted range around central rate (%)
Austria (Sch)	13.438	15
Belgium (BFr)	39.396	15
Denmark(DKr)	7.285	15
France (FFr)	6.406	15
Germany (DM)	1.910	2.5
Ireland (I£)	0.792	15
Netherlands (F1)	2.152	2.5
Portugal (Es)	195.792	15
Spain (Pta)	162.493	15

(*Note*: Central rates correct at 12/3/96)

central fund which provides short- to medium-term finance for member states to use when their currency has fallen as a result of speculation or some other short-term pressure.

Fixed exchange rates cannot over-ride market forces over the longer term. While short-term problems with a currency may be capable of resolution by government action, longer-term problems may only be resolved by a restructuring of the fixed exchange relationships. Tensions exist within the EMS between strong currencies such as the German deutschmark which has a tendency to exceed its permitted value and weaker currencies such as the Italian lire which has drifted to its lower permitted level. In both cases, the change in the underlying market value of each currency reflects changes in the underlying strength of their respective economies. Fixed exchange rates alone cannot overcome these underlying problems. It is therefore necessary on occasions to re-set the value of currencies in terms of the ecu.

Fixed exchange rates can undoubtedly make planning more predictable for business. It is also argued that a fixed set of exchange rates can help a country lower its inflation and interest rates as a result of the disciplines imposed by the ERM. However, against this, the short-term costs of adapting to fixed exchange rates can be very great for governments and firms alike. The need to keep fixed exchange rates prevents governments taking unilateral action to change their exchange rates as a means of restructuring their national economies. If an exchange rate is fixed at too high a level, exporters will suffer from the double effects of their exports being overpriced and competitors' imports being underpriced. A major consequence of this for governments is rising levels of unemployment. An exchange rate which is fixed at too low a level can create inflationary pressure for firms and the economy in general, as the cost of imported materials is forced up.

The United Kingdom entered the ERM in October 1990, but left two years later when the short-term cost to the economy of maintaining its fixed parity with other European countries became too great. The high fixed value of sterling had caused interest rates to rise to very high levels (to support sterling) and had made exporters uncompetitive in overseas markets. At the same time, consumers enjoyed low prices for imports, exacerbating unemployment problems in the domestic economy.

12.2.5   European Monetary Union (EMU)

In theory, problems of fluctuating exchange rates should be overcome if all countries in a trading bloc use the same currency. Advocates of a single currency for Europe point to the strength that the United States of America gained from having a single currency from a very early stage in the country's development.

The Treaty of Maastricht envisaged a single currency for the whole of the European Union by 1999. As well as having a political objective of uniting Europe, advocates of EMU pointed to numerous economic benefits, in particular the reduction in transaction costs of cross-border trade within Europe, greater certainty for businesses and the creation of one strong world currency to replace several weaker ones and provide a strong alternative to dominance of the US dollar. EMU has similar effects to the Exchange Rate Mechanism in terms of its ability to limit member states' economic freedom of action. For EMU to work without undue short-term harm to national economies, it has been recognized that a convergence of national economies is a prerequisite. The Treaty of Maastricht therefore set a series of targets for member states' budget deficits, inflation and public sector borrowing, which must be met before national currencies can effectively be merged. Severe doubts have been expressed about whether such convergence is achievable. Without convergence, the short-term costs of EMU may be politically unacceptable.

12.3   OVERSEAS TRADE PATTERNS

The existence of comparative cost advantages and variations between countries in the types of goods and services demanded results in each country having its own distinctive pattern of overseas trade. The nature of a country's overseas trade can be described with respect to:

- The items that it imports and exports and
- The countries it trades with

Trade patterns throughout the world change in response to changes in the economic, political, technological and social environments. For example, the rising GDP per capita of many Far Eastern countries has resulted in members of those countries purchasing increasing numbers of overseas holidays. At the same time, growing environmental protection legislation has resulted in many production processes being transferred from Western developed countries to less developed ones where regulations are relatively lax, leading to new export trade.

12.3.1   Measuring overseas trade

The difference between what a country receives from overseas and the amount it spends overseas is referred to as a country's balance of payments. Countries differ in the way in which they break down their overall balance of payments, but these can broadly divided into:

- The purchase and sale of goods and services (usually described as current account transactions) and
- The acquisition and disposal of assets and liabilities abroad (referred to as capital account transactions)

Although it is common to talk about a country's overall balance of payments being in surplus or deficit, they must technically be balanced (Figure 12.2). If, for example, a country has a deficit in its current account, this has to be made up by running down one of its assets (e.g. by using holdings of foreign

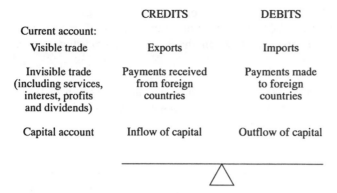

	CREDITS	DEBITS
Current account:		
Visible trade	Exports	Imports
Invisible trade (including services, interest, profits and dividends)	Payments received from foreign countries	Payments made to foreign countries
Capital account	Inflow of capital	Outflow of capital

Figure 12.2   Components of a country's balance of payments

currencies to reduce a capital asset or borrowing from overseas and thereby increasing a capital liability). The opposite would be true if a country produced a current account surplus (holdings of foreign assets would increase or foreign liabilities would reduce).

Media headlines which describe a 'trade deficit' or 'surplus' generally refer to the current account element of the balance of payments. The components of the current and capital account elements are described below:

- The *current account* is generally further divided into two components: a visible trade balance and an invisible trade balance. Visible trade includes transactions in manufactured goods, raw materials and fuel products. Invisibles comprise intangible sales and purchases overseas. Invisible trade is made up of services (e.g. tourism, insurance and shipping), including government services (e.g. payments to overseas armed forces and diplomatic missions), and interest, profit and dividends receivable from or payable abroad.
- The *capital account* records outward and inward flows of capital for investment purposes (i.e. it excludes routine trading transactions). It includes payments made for long-term investment in tangible assets (e.g. new factories and equipment) and intangible assets (such as the purchase of shares in an overseas company). It also includes short-term movements of money between traders in the money markets (sometimes referred to as 'hot money').

12.3.2   Measuring overseas transactions

Traditionally, the value of manufactured goods has been measured as they pass through Customs, and from this information, the total value of imports and exports has been calculated. In the case of capital transactions, governments generally make provisions for large transactions to be reported (e.g. many countries restrict the free movement of capital to a specified maximum amount per transaction). However, it is becoming increasingly difficult to measure the value and volume of overseas trade.

- It is very difficult to accurately measure trade in services, which are transacted through a variety of means (e.g. the sale of insurance and banking services using postal and telecommunication methods). In the case of earnings and expenditure on tourism, it can be difficult to measure the total expenditure of tourists whose spending can be dispersed through a variety of business sectors. Governments estimate such figures using various survey techniques. However, initial estimates frequently have to be subsequently revised.

● With the advent of the Single European Market, border controls on trade within the EU have been largely removed, so it is very difficult to get an accurate indication of the volume of imports and exports between EU member states. Again, overseas trade within the EU is measured using various survey techniques.

Having made these caveats, recent trends in the UK overseas current account are shown in Table 12.4. The years for which data is shown correspond roughly to turning points in world-wide business cycles.

Table 12.4 UK overseas current account (£000,000)

| Year | Visible trade | | | Services balance | Current account surplus/deficit |
	Exports	Imports	Balance		
1984	70 265	75 601	−5336	4205	1482
1986	72 627	82 186	−9559	6223	−864
1988	80 346	101 826	−21 480	3957	−16 475
1990	101 718	120 527	−18 809	3689	−19 293
1992	107 343	120 447	−13 104	5051	−9468
1994	134 465	145 059	−10 594	3790	−1684

Source: based on Annual Abstract of Statistics.

12.3.3   Trends in UK overseas trade

A number of immediate observations can be made about the changing pattern of UK overseas trade:

1. During the recent past, the United Kingdom has run a deficit in its visible balance, but partly made up for this by having a surplus in invisibles. Although the visible trade balance has deteriorated in recent years, growth in the invisible balance has not been sufficient to counteract the decline in visible exports.
2. Overall, the UK current account has tended to be in deficit in recent years (i.e. although there has been a surplus in invisibles, these have not been sufficient to counteract a deficit in the visible balance).
3. The development of North Sea oil has made the visible balance of trade very dependent on world oil prices. The high visible trade surpluses of the early 1980s can be partly explained by the very high level of world oil prices, which benefited Britain as a net oil exporter. The world oil price had fallen by the end of the 1980s, accounting for some of the deterioration in the visible trade balance.

The overseas trade balance of a nation is very much influenced by the structure of the domestic economy. For the UK economy, the deterioration of the visible balance is symptomatic of the declining competitiveness of its manufacturing industries. Indices of competitiveness reached a low point during the late 1980s as many markets became dominated by products from low-cost producers, especially those in the Far Fast, which had more flexible labour markets and had invested in new productive capacity. More recently, however, there are signs that the United Kingdom has regained some of its competitiveness. This is manifested in the growing number of Far Eastern manufacturers who have located factories in the United Kingdom. While part of the reason for their UK investment is the avoidance of EU external tariff barriers, their decisions also reflect the attractiveness of an increasingly flexible UK labour market and an exchange rate that gives competitive advantage to goods made in the United Kingdom, rather than Far Eastern countries with strong currencies (especially Japan).

Some indication of the importance of international trade in services for the United Kingdom can be seen by examining trade statistics. In 1993, the United Kingdom earned £116 billion from selling services overseas, compared to £121 billion from selling goods. More importantly, the United Kingdom had a small surplus (£2.9 billion) in services, compared with a growing deficit in goods (£13.2 billion). A closer examination of trade statistics indicates the relative importance of the main service sectors. The most important in terms of overseas sales continues to be financial services, with credits ('exports') of £18.2 billion in 1993, set against debits ('imports') of £7.3 billion, although the export/import ratio has deteriorated in favour of imports during recent years. Travel-related sectors were the next most significant group recorded by national statistics, although in this area the United Kingdom is now a net importer of services (with debits of £12.3 billion, against credits of £9.0 billion) and the trade balance has been steadily deteriorating.

The year-to-year pattern of overseas trade is influenced by business cycles at a national and international level. The world business cycle has the effect of reducing the total value of world trade (or at least slowing down its rate of growth). The business cycles of individual countries may lead or lag the general cycle, or various local reasons may mean that a country is not significantly affected by the world-wide business cycle. A consumer boom in a domestic economy often has the effect of sucking in manufactured imports. The economic boom in the United Kingdom during the mid to late 1980s, coupled with a high exchange rate, resulted in a very large increase in manufactured imports. At the same time, the domestic manufacturing sector was becoming increasingly uncompetitive, leading to a capacity reduction which limited its opportunities for exports. This contributed to the record visible trade deficits of the early 1990s, which were only corrected as the economic recession caused a reduction in consumer goods imports and falling production costs once more stimulated exports of manufactured goods. During 1995, UK consumer expenditure remained fairly depressed, but exporters were able to seize opportunities in overseas markets which emerged from the recessionary cycle ahead of the United Kingdom.

An indication of the changing relative competitiveness of UK business sectors can be found by examining ratios of:

- Imports as a proportion of home demand and
- Exports as a proportion of manufacturers' sales

Department of Trade and Industry statistics indicate varying industrial performance. In the case of the former, the most recent figures indicate a particular weakness in office machinery and data processing equipment and instrument engineering and relatively limited penetration in the case of food, drink and mineral products. For exports, transport equipment and chemicals performed strongly, while furniture, timber and paper products achieved low proportions of exports.

Trade patterns can also be analysed in terms of the origin and destination of a country's transactions. Recent years have witnessed a number of changes in the pattern of the UK's trading partners:

1. UK trade has become increasingly focused on the EU, accounting for 52 per cent of all imports to the United Kingdom in 1992 and 55 per cent of exports.
2. An increasing proportion of the UK's international trade is with developed economies, accounting in 1993 for over 80 per cent of total trade. The share of trade with developing economies has fallen, reflecting a growing self-sufficiency on the part of the latter.
3. After strong growth, imports from Japan accounted for 5.9 per cent of the UK's total imports in 1993, although only 2.0 per cent of exports were destined for Japan. There is evidence of a reversal of this trend, as a strong yen makes Japanese imports to the United Kingdom uncompetitive, while

at the same time even making it economical for Japanese companies to assemble goods in the United Kingdom and ship them to the Japanese market.

4. Trade with the United States has gradually become a smaller proportion of the UK's international trade, accounting for about 11 per cent of exports and imports in 1993.

5. The share of imports accounted for by oil-exporting countries has fallen with the development of North Sea oil reserves.

12.3.4 Prospects for UK international trade

The post-war years have been generally disappointing for the UK's balance of trade, with a worsening deficit in visible trade being only partly offset by surpluses in services and North Sea oil. In view of its extensive ownership of overseas assets, the United Kingdom can afford to continue running a moderate trade deficit, but governments have sought to keep deficits within tolerable limits. Very high deficits are likely to lead to a fall in the value of sterling, which itself would be inflationary and may lead to an increase in interest rates. Governments would prefer to avoid the social, economic and political consequences of a large trade deficit.

A league table of international competitiveness published in 1995 showed the United Kingdom slipping to eighteenth place, having fallen behind the 'tiger' economies of the Far East. Prescriptions for the UK's prosperity in international trade have focused on a number of issues, including the following:

1. Continuing to improve the cost structure of UK industry, particularly through deregulation of the economy and improvements in the flexibility of labour.

2. Exploiting service sector competitive advantages, especially within the fields of banking and insurance. However, although the United Kingdom has historically achieved surpluses in these fields, competition from newly developed countries has intensified. Many commentators have predicted that if the United Kingdom does not join the European Monetary Union, its role as a financial centre of Europe will be further weakened.

3. Many have pointed to the valuable role played by governments, such as the Japanese, in promoting a country's exports. In the United Kingdom, the emphasis of government policy has been in improving supply side efficiency rather than promoting specific sectors overseas.

4. It is argued that many UK companies have failed to invest in new capacity during periods of recession in order to meet an upturn in the world economy. The consumer boom of the 1980s resulted in imports of goods such as agricultural equipment for which domestic production capacity had been cut during the previous recession and not subsequently replaced.

5. The proportion of GDP spent by the United Kingdom on research and development has been falling, placing doubts on the ability of its manufacturers to become world leaders in new product fields.

6. Finally, many commentators have pointed to the poor training in marketing and management skills of UK managers, which leaves them badly placed to aggressively tackle overseas markets, or even to protect their domestic markets from import competition. It has been pointed out that improvements in service levels have often been led by overseas companies (e.g. many overseas car manufacturers have gained market share in the United Kingdom by offering superior back-up services for their cars).

It must not be forgotten that market mechanisms in themselves have a tendency to correct trade imbalances, at least in theory. A country with long-term trade deficits based on structural weaknesses in its economy will experience a weakening in the value of its currency, which will have the effect of making exports cheaper and imports dearer. Through a substitution effect in its domestic markets, domestic manufacturers will gain competitive advantage over importers, thereby reducing a trade deficit. Similarly, exports will become cheaper in overseas markets, again reducing a trade deficit. For countries which run continuing trade surpluses (e.g. Japan), market forces will tend to reduce the surplus. Continuing surpluses will cause a rise in the value of a country's currency, making exports expensive and imports cheaper. Eventually, exports may become so expensive (when priced in buyers' currencies) that the country's exporters will establish factories overseas, and may even find it cheaper to assemble products overseas for import to its domestic market.

12.4   INTERNATIONAL TRADE INSTITUTIONS AND AGREEMENTS

The exploitation of comparative cost advantages through free trade may sound fine in theory, but is often difficult to achieve in practice, for the reasons described earlier in this chapter. There have therefore been many attempts to develop international agreements for the free movement of trade.

At their simplest, international trade agreements comprise bilateral agreements between two countries to open up trade between the two. Sometimes, groups of countries join together to form *trading blocs* in which trade between member states is encouraged at the expense of trade with non-bloc members. There are also multilateral agreements between nations to develop free trade. Some of the more important are described below.

12.4.1   The Single European Market

A principal aim of the European Community has been the removal of barriers to trade between member states. The most significant step towards this was achieved through the EU's Single European Market programme, which since 1993 has been progressively easing trade between EU member states. These are some of the benefits that a Single European Market have brought to cross-border trade:

● The removal or reduction of institutional barriers to trade (e.g. reduced import/export documentation), thereby reducing travel times
● The technical harmonization of product standards, allowing for greater economies of scale
● The ability for companies with licences to operate in their home market to be able to extend these rights to other EU markets
● The liberalization of capital movements
● The removal of discriminatory public purchasing policies

It has been estimated that the effects of the Single Market after five years of operation will be to increase EU output as a whole by 7 per cent, for prices to fall by up to 6 per cent in real terms and for EU-wide employment to increase by 1.8 millions. These benefits will be achieved through a combination of reduced costs and increased competition which will have the effect of reducing local national monopoly power enjoyed by some suppliers. A number of UK sectors have been identified as likely beneficiaries of more open markets, able to exploit their comparative cost advantages. These include pharmaceuticals, the food and drink industry, insurance and civil aviation.

Despite the efforts of the Single European Market programme, a number of barriers to trade within the EU remain:

● There is debate about the extent to which cultural variations within Europe will eventually be homogenized. Some of these variations are based on geographical factors (e.g. life-styles and attitudes of the hot southern climates differ markedly from those of northern countries) and may be difficult to change.
● Although harmonization of product standards has proceeded a long way, some problems remain. For example, the UK's non-standard design of electrical plugs or its practice of driving on the left may never be harmonized to a European standard.

- It is still often necessary for individuals or firms to obtain licences before they can operate in another member state. Although removal of such barriers is on the EU agenda for reform, free trade in services has generally been harder to open up to cross-border trade than dealings in manufactured goods.
- The absence of a single European currency remains a barrier to cross-border trade and doubts persist about whether full monetary union can ever be achieved.

Nevertheless, the Single European Market has become a major trading bloc which has made trade within the bloc easier, while creating common policies with respect to trade with the rest of the world. It is set to expand further with the development of the European Economic Area, which extends the principles of the single market to include most members of the European Free Trade Area (EFTA).

12.4.2   Other regional trading blocs

A number of other trading blocs exist in the world with aims which are similar to those of the Single European Market. These include the North America Free Trade Area (NAFTA), the Gulf Co-operation Council (GCC) and the Association of South East Asian Nations (ASEAN). In the case of NAFTA, the United States, Canada and Mexico have sought to reduce barriers to trade between their countries so that each can exploit its comparative cost advantage. Some measures are already in place, but the creation of the single market will have increasing effect during the 1990s. Inevitably, while trade is made easier within the free trade area, there is a danger of other outside countries being disadvantaged.

12.4.3   Organisation for Economic Co-operation and Development (OECD)

The OECD was originally set up in 1947 to administer America's Marshall Aid programme in Europe, but subsequently turned increasing attention to the developing world. The OECD now has 21 members which include most European countries, the United States, Canada and Japan. It works by trying to co-ordinate the economic policies of members, to co-ordinate programmes of economic aid and by providing specialized services, especially information.

12.4.4   The World Bank

The World Bank (officially known as the International Bank for Reconstruction and Development) acts as an adviser to governments in the provision of international finance. The main role of the World Bank is to provide capital on favourable terms to aid the economic reconstruction of countries. In cases where it advances loans to overseas governments, it may require its advice to be incorporated into government policy as a condition of its loan.

12.4.5   The International Monetary Fund (IMF)

The IMF shared its origins with the OECD and World Bank in that all three institutions were created in the immediate post Second World War period and were seen as a means towards world economic regeneration. The IMF is essentially a world forum for international negotiations on governments' fiscal policies. Its original aims of regulating and stabilizing exchange rates have been somewhat undermined by the ability of traders and multinational companies to influence exchange rates, often having a bigger impact on markets than policies agreed by the IMF.

12.4.6   The World Trade Organization (WTO)

The WTO has its origins in the General Agreement on Tariffs and Trade (GATT) of the early post-war period. The signatories to the agreement sought to achieve greater international economic prosperity by exploiting fully the comparative cost advantages of nations by reducing the barriers that inhibited international trade. All the signatories agreed not to increase tariffs on imported goods beyond their existing levels and to work towards the abolition of quotas which restricted the volume of imports.

WTO has proceeded to reduce tariffs and quotas through several negotiating 'rounds', the most recent of which—the Uruguay round—has sought to reduce barriers to international trade in services. It has also tried to redress the distortion to world trade and the unfair competitive advantage given to subsidized exporters of agricultural products.

12.4.7 Other international agreements and institutions

A wide range of other agreements and institutions affect international trading companies. Some of these will be very general in nature and affect a wide range of businesses. An example in this category is the agreement to set up a European Bank for Reconstruction and Development, aimed at helping the restructuring of the emerging East European economies. Improved access to loans may help a wide range of exporters of capital equipment. Another example is where business in general—especially multinational companies—can be affected by bilateral agreements between countries on the treatment of profit taxes.

There are also very many agreements and institutions covering specific industries. An example of an institution that has a direct effect on an industry is the International Civil Aviation Organization (ICAO) to which most countries belong and which has agreed international safety standards for civil aviation. In other cases, agreements between countries can have an indirect effect on a market, as with the international agreement signed in 1990 to restrict international trade in ivory.

12.5 EVALUATING OVERSEAS MARKETING OPPORTUNITIES

Overseas markets can represent very different opportunities and threats compared to those that an organization has been used to in its domestic market. Before a detailed market analysis is undertaken, an organization should consider in general terms whether the environment of a market is likely to be attractive. By considering in general terms such matters as political stability or cultural attitudes, an organization may screen out potential markets for which it considers further analysis cannot be justified by the likelihood of success. Where an exploratory analysis of an overseas marketing environment appears to indicate some opportunities, a more thorough analysis might suggest important modifications to a product format which would need to be made before it could be successfully offered to the market.

This section firstly identifies some general questions which need to be asked in assessing the marketing environment of overseas countries and then considers specific aspects of researching such markets.

12.5.1 The overseas marketing environment

The combination of environmental factors that contributed to success within an organization's domestic market may be absent in an overseas market, resulting in the failure of export attempts. In this section, questions to be asked in analysing an overseas marketing environment are examined under the overlapping headings of the political, economic, social and technological environments.

The political environment At a national level, individual governments can influence market attractiveness in a number of ways:

1. At the most general level, the stability of the political system affects the attractiveness of a particular national market. While radical change rarely results from political upheaval in most Western countries, the instability of many Eastern European governments leads to uncertainty about the economic and legislative framework in which goods and services will be traded.
2. Licensing systems may be applied by governments in an attempt to protect domestic producers. Licences can be used to restrict individuals practising a particular profession (e.g. licensing requirements for accountants or solicitors may not recognize experience and licences obtained overseas) or they can be used to restrict foreign owners setting up an overseas operation (e.g. the UK government does not allow overseas investors to own more than 25 per cent of the shares in UK scheduled airlines).
3. Regulations governing product standards may require an organization to expensively re-configure its products offer to meet local regulations, or may prohibit their sale completely.
4. Controls can be used to restrict the import of manufactured goods, requiring a company to create a local source of supply, leading to possible problems in maintaining consistent quality standards and also possibly losing economies of scale.
5. Production possibilities can be influenced by government policies. Minimum wage levels and conditions of service can be important in determining the viability of an overseas operation. For example, many countries restrict the manner in which temporary or seasonal staff can be employed. This could make the operation of a seasonal holiday hotel inflexible and uneconomic.
6. Restrictions on currency movements may make it difficult to repatriate profits earned from an overseas operation.
7. Governments are major procurers of goods and services and may formally or informally give preference in awarding contracts to locally owned organizations.
8. Legislation protecting trade marks varies between companies. In some countries, such as Greece and Thailand, the owner may find it relatively hard to legally protect itself from imitators.

Beyond the nation state, companies increasingly look towards the free trading agreements that one country has with others as a means of gaining access to the largest possible market. Many companies have invested in manufacturing capacity in the United Kingdom not just because of the attractiveness of the UK market, but also because of the access that it will offer to the wider EU market.

The economic environment   A generally accepted measure of the economic attractiveness of an overseas market is the level of GDP per capita. The demand for most products increases as this figure increases. However, organizations seeking to sell goods and services overseas should also consider the distribution of income within a country which may identify valuable niche markets. For example, the relatively low GDP per head of South Korea still allows a small and relatively affluent group to create a market for high-value overseas holidays.

An organization assessing an overseas market should place great emphasis on future economic performance and the stage that a country has reached in its economic development. While many Western developed economies face saturated markets for a number of products, less developed economies may be just moving on to that part of their growth curve where a product begins to appeal to large groups of people.

A crucial part of the analysis of an overseas market focuses on the level of competition within that market. This can be related to the level of economic development achieved within a country. In general, as an economy develops, its markets become more saturated. This is true, for example, of the market for household insurance which is mature and highly competitive in North America and most Western European countries, but is relatively new and less competitive in many developing economies of the Pacific Rim, allowing better margins to be achieved.

The level of competitive pressure within a market is also a reflection of government policy towards the regulation of monopolies and the ease with which it allows new entrants to enter a market. The government of a country can significantly affect the competitive pressure within a market by legislation aimed at reducing anticompetitive practices.

The social and cultural environment   An understanding of cultural differences between markets is very important for marketers. Individuals from different cultures not only buy different products but may also respond in different ways to similar products. Examples of differing cultural attitudes and their effects on international trade in goods and services include the following:

- Buying processes vary between different cultures. For example, the role of women in selecting a product may differ in an overseas market compared to the domestic market, thereby possibly requiring a different approach to product design and promotion.
- Some categories of goods and services may be rendered obsolete by certain types of social structure. For example, extended family structures common in some countries have the ability to produce a wide range of services within the family unit, including caring for children and elderly members.
- A product that is taken for granted in the domestic market may be seen as socially unacceptable in an overseas market. Frequently encountered examples include pork products in Muslim countries and beef in Hindu countries.
- Attitudes towards promotional programmes differ between cultures. The choice of colours in advertising or sales outlets needs to be made with care because of symbolic associations (e.g. the colour associated with bereavement varies between cultures).
- What is deemed to be acceptable activity in procuring sales varies between cultures. In Middle Eastern markets, for example, a bribe to a public official may be considered essential, whereas it is unacceptable in most Western countries.

The technological environment   An analysis of the technological environment of an overseas market is important for organizations who require the use of a well-developed technical infrastructure and a work-force that is able to use technology. Communications are an important element of the technological infrastructure—poorly developed telephone and postal communications may inhibit attempts to make credit cards more widely available, for instance.

12.6   SOURCES OF INFORMATION ON OVERSEAS MARKETS

The methods used to research a potential overseas market are in principle similar to those that would be used to research a domestic market. Companies would normally begin by using secondary data about a potential overseas market which is available to them at home. Sources that are readily available through specialized libraries, government organizations and specialist research organizations include Department of Trade and Industry information for exporters, reports of international agencies such as the Organisation for Economic Co-operation and Development (OECD), Chambers of Commerce and private sources of information such as that provided by banks. Details of some specific sources are shown in Table 12.5.

Initial desk research at home will identify those markets that show greatest potential for development. A company will then often follow this up with further desk research of materials available locally within the short-listed markets, often carried out by appointing a local research agency. This may include a review of reports published by the target market's own government and specialist locally based market research agencies.

Just as in home markets, secondary data have limitations in assessing market attractiveness. Problems in overseas markets are compounded by the greater difficulty in gaining access to data, possible language differences and problems of definition which may differ from those with which an

Table 12.5 Sources of secondary information on overseas markets

Government agencies
  Department of Trade and Industry sources (e.g. DTI Market Information Enquiry Service)
  Overseas governments (e.g. US Department of Commerce)
  Overseas national and local development agencies

International agencies
  European Union (Eurostat, etc.)
  Organisation for Economic Co-operation and Development (OECD)
  World Trade Organization
  United Nations
  International Monetary Fund
  World Health Organization

Research organizations
  Economist Intelligence Unit
  Dun and Bradstreet International
  Market research firms

Publications
  Financial Times country surveys
  International Trade Reporter
  Banks' export reviews

Trade associations
  Chambers of Commerce Export Marketing Research Scheme
  Industry-specific associations (e.g. International Air Transport Association)

organization is familiar. In the case of products that are a new concept in an overseas market, information on current usage and attitudes to the product may be completely lacking. For this reason, it would be difficult to use secondary data to try and assess the likely response from consumers to large out-of-town superstores in many Eastern European countries.

Primary research is used to overcome shortcomings in secondary data. Its most important use is to identify cultural factors which may require a product format to be modified or abandoned altogether. A company seeking to undertake primary research in a new proposed overseas market would almost certainly use a local specialist research agency. Apart from overcoming possible language barriers, a local agency would better understand attitudes towards privacy and the level of literacy that might affect response rates for different forms of research. However, the problem of comparability between markets remains. For example, when a Japanese respondent claims to 'like' a product, the result may be comparable to a German consumer who claims to 'quite like' the product. It would be wrong to assume on the basis of this research that the product is better liked by Japanese consumers than German consumers.

Primary research is generally undertaken overseas when a company has become happy about the general potential of a market, but is unsure of a number of factors that would be critical for success, for example whether intermediaries would be willing and able to handle their product or whether traditional cultural attitudes will present an insurmountable obstacle for a product not previously available in that market. Prior to commissioning its own specific research, a company may go for the lower cost but less specific route of undertaking research through an omnibus survey. These are surveys regularly undertaken among a panel of consumers in overseas markets (e.g. the Gallup European Omnibus) which carry questions on behalf of a number of organizations.

12.7 ADAPTING THE MARKETING MIX FOR OVERSEAS ENVIRONMENTS

Having analysed an overseas market and decided to enter it, an organization must make marketing mix decisions that will allow it to successfully penetrate that market. Marketing mix decisions focus on the extent to which the organization will adapt its product offering to the needs of the local market, as opposed to the development of a uniform marketing mix that is globally applicable in all of its markets.

12.7.1 Product decisions

Sometimes, products can be exported to overseas markets with little need for adaptation to local needs. Improved communications and greater opportunities for travel have helped create much more uniform world-wide demand for products. For example, McDonald's and Coca-Cola now appeal to people from Boston to Beijing and from Manchester to Moscow (although in both of these examples, the company's products have been subtly adapted to local markets). Products often need to be adapted for a number of reasons:

1. The law of an overseas country may set differing product standards. For example, legislation specifying vehicle lighting means that cars often have to be re-specified for overseas markets. Within the EU, harmonization of product standards is making this task much simpler for traders operating within the EU.
2. Despite convergence of cultural values, inertia often results from centuries of tradition. It has taken time, for example, for the idea of fast food to take hold in France where the culture stresses eating as a pleasurable social experience. Tastes may take time to change, which helps to explain why McDonald's restaurants offer different menus in many of the markets that it serves.
3. There are often good geographical reasons why products would need to be adapted. The hotter climates of Southern Europe result in different patterns of demand for ice cream, car design and clothing, for example.
4. Socioeconomic factors may call for product reformulation. For example, high incomes and low petrol prices combine with long travel distances to boost demand in the United States of America for large, well specified cars, at the expense of small hatchbacks which are popular in the United Kingdom.

Standardization of the product can also yield benefits of economies of scale which include economies in market research and large-scale, centralized production methods. The use of a common brand name in overseas markets also yields benefits from economies of scale in promotion.

In the case of transport services which operate between different markets, it may not be feasible to adapt the service offering to each of the local markets served, and either a compromise must be reached or the needs of the most important market given precedence. Airlines flying between two countries may find the pricing of in-flight services, the decor of the aircraft and catering having to satisfy very different market needs at either end of the route.

Markets may emerge overseas for which a domestic company has no product offering that can be easily adapted. In the field of financial services, the absence in some overseas countries of state provision for certain key welfare services may create a market for insurance-related products (e.g. dental health insurance cover) which is largely absent in the domestic UK market, where the Welfare State is relatively comprehensive. Similarly, the social and economic structure of a country can result in quite different products being required. For example, the pattern of property ownership in Malaysia has given rise to a novel two-generation property mortgage not generally found in Western European markets.

12.7.2 Promotion decisions

A promotional programme that has worked at home may fail miserably in an overseas market. Usually, this is a result of the overseas country's differing cultural values, although legislation can additionally call for a reformulation of promotion. These are a few of the reasons why promotion reformulation may be needed:

1. The law on promoting goods and services that are considered socially harmful varies between countries. For this reason, television advertising may not be available in some countries for promoting some medicines, alcohol and children's products.
2. The availability of promotional media varies between countries. While television advertising is widely used in the United Kingdom, the low levels of television ownership in many countries may limit the potential for this form of communication.
3. Different cultures respond to promotional messages in different ways, reflecting different attitudes towards hard-sell, brash and seductive approaches, for example.
4. Certain objects and symbols used to promote a product might have the opposite effect to that which might be expected at home (e.g. animals that are used effectively to promote a product at home may be viewed with disgust in some markets).
5. Sometimes, the brand name to be promoted will not work in the overseas market, so it may be changed. There are many examples of brand names that fail overseas. For example the Spanish brand of 'Bum' snacks would probably not sell well in English-speaking countries and McDonald's 'Big Mac' translates in French as 'the big pimp'.
6. There can also be problems where legislation prevents an international slogan being used. In France, for example, law no. 75-1349 of 1975 makes the use of the French language compulsory in all advertising for goods and services—this also applies to associated packaging and instructions, etc.

In practice, a combination of product and promotion modification is needed in order to meet both differing local needs and differences in local sensitivity to advertising.

12.7.3 Pricing decisions

A common global pricing policy will help to project a company as a global brand. However, the reality is that a variety of factors cause global organizations to charge different prices in the different markets in which they operate. There is usually no reason to assume that the pricing policies adopted in the domestic market will prove to be equally effective in an overseas market. Furthermore, it may be of no great importance to customers that comparability between different markets is maintained.

There are a number of factors which affect price decisions overseas:

1. Competitive pressure varies between markets, reflecting the stage of market development that a service has reached and the impact of regulations against anticompetitive practices.
2. The cost of producing a product may be significantly different in overseas markets. For services that employ people-intensive production methods, variations in wage levels between countries will have a significant effect on total costs. Personnel costs may also be affected by differences in welfare

provisions that employers are required to pay for. Other significant cost elements which often vary between markets include the level of property prices or rental costs. The cost of acquiring space for a retail outlet in Britain, for example, is usually significantly more than in Southern or Eastern Europe.

3. Taxes vary between different markets. For example, the rate of value added tax (or its equivalent sales tax) can be as high as 38 per cent in Italy compared to 17½ per cent in the United Kingdom. There are also differences between markets in the manner in which sales taxes are expressed. In most markets, these are fully incorporated into price schedules, although on other occasions (such as in Singapore) it is more usual to price a service exclusive of taxes.

4. Local customs influence customers' expectations of the way in which they are charged for a product. While customers in the domestic market might expect to pay for bundles of goods and services, in an overseas market consumers might expect to pay a separate price for each component of the bundle. For example, UK buyers of new cars expect features such as audio equipment to be included in the basic price of a car, whereas buyers in many Continental European countries expect to buy these as separate items.

5. For some service industries, it is customary in many countries to expect customers to pay a tip to the front-line person providing a service, as part of the overall price of the service.

6. Formal price lists for a service may be expected in some markets, but in others the prevalence of bartering may put an operator who sticks to a fixed price list at a competitive disadvantage.

7. Government regulations can limit price freedom in overseas markets. In addition to controls over prices charged by public utilities, many governments require 'fair' prices to be charged in certain sectors and for the prices charged to be clearly publicized.

8. A product that is considered quite ordinary in its domestic market may be perceived as exclusive in an overseas market and therefore it will adopt a higher price position. For example, the price position of the retailer Marks and Spencers is middle market in its domestic UK base, but the company has positioned its stores in Indonesia as up-market with a high price position relative to local competitors. By contrast, a company with a strong brand in its home market may have to adopt (initially at least) a lower price position when it launches into a competitive overseas market. For example, airlines developing new foreign routes may have to offer price discounts in an overseas market where it is unknown, compared to the domestic market where its established brand reputation allows it to charge a price premium.

12.7.4   Distribution decisions

Distribution decisions can be crucial to the success of an exporter and are a focus for market entry strategies (discussed below in Section 12.8):

1. Consumers' attitudes towards intermediaries may differ significantly in overseas markets. What is a widely accepted outlet in one country may be regarded with suspicion in another. For example, the idea of buying cosmetics from a grocery store may be viewed with suspicion in many countries, although it is now accepted in most Western European countries.

2. The extensiveness of outlet networks will be influenced by customers' expectations about ease of access, which in turn may be based on social, economic and technological factors. The proliferation of many small-scale distributors in less-developed economies, for example, can be partly explained by the lack of domestic refrigeration, which may favour frequent replenishment of household supplies from a local store rather than less frequent bulk buying from a large centralized store.

3. Differences in the social, economic and technological environments of a market can be manifested in the existence of different patterns of intermediaries. As an example, the interrelatedness of wholesalers and retailers in Japan can make it much more difficult for an overseas retailer to get into

that market compared to other overseas opportunities. In some markets, there may be no direct equivalent of a type of intermediary found in the domestic market—estate agents on the UK model are often not found in many markets where the work of transferring property is handled entirely by a solicitor.

4. The technological environment can also affect distribution decisions. The relatively under-developed postal and telecommunications services of many Eastern European countries makes direct availability of goods and services to consumers relatively difficult.

5. What is a legal method of distributing goods and services in the domestic market may be against the law of an overseas country. Countries may restrict the sale of financial services, holidays and gambling services—among others—to a much narrower set of possible intermediaries than is the case in the domestic market.

12.7.5   People decisions

'People' decisions are an important element of the overseas marketing for services in particular. Where goods or services produced overseas involve direct producer-consumer interaction, a decision must be made on whether to employ local or expatriate staff. The latter may be preferable where a service is highly specialized and may be useful in adding to the global uniformity of the service offering. In some circumstances, the presence of front-line expatriate serving staff can add to the appeal of a service. For example, a chain of traditional English pubs established on the Continent may add to their appeal by employing authentic English staff.

For relatively straightforward goods and services, a large proportion of staff would be recruited locally, leaving just senior management posts filled by expatriates. Sometimes, an extensive staff development programme may be required to ensure that locally recruited staff perform in a manner that is consistent with the company's global image. This can in some circumstances be quite a difficult task—a fast food operator may have difficulty developing values of speed and efficiency among its staff in countries where the pace of life is relatively slow.

Where staff are recruited locally, employment legislation can affect the short- and long-term flexi-bility of production. This can affect the ease with which staff can be laid off or dismissed in response to changes in demand from customers. For example, in Germany, the Dismissals Protection Law (Kundigungsschutzgesetz) gives considerable protection to salaried staff who have been in their job for more than six months, allowing dismissal only for a 'socially justified' reason. There are also differ-ences between countries in the extent to which an employer can prevent an employee with valuable trade secrets leaving their employment to work for a competitor. In Germany, a 'non-competition' clause can be expressly agreed for a maximum of two years after termination of employment, but only under a number of conditions.

12.8   MARKET ENTRY STRATEGIES

A new overseas market represents both a potential opportunity and a risk to an organization. A company's market entry strategy should aim to balance these two elements.

The least risky method of developing an overseas market is to supply that market from a domestic base. This is often not a cost-effective method of serving a market, and may not be possible in the case of some inseparable services where producer and consumer must interact. Where an exporter needs to set up production facilities overseas, risk can be minimized by gradually committing more resources to a market, based on experience to date. Temporary facilities could be established that have low start-up and close-down costs and where the principal physical and human assets can be transferred to another location. A good example of risk reduction through the use of temporary facilities is found in the pattern of retail development in East Germany following reunification. West German retailers who initially entered East Germany in large numbers were reluctant to commit themselves to building stores in specific locations in a part of the country that was still economically unstable and where patterns of land use were rapidly changing. The solution adopted by many companies was to offer branches of their chain in temporary marquees or from mobile vehicles—these could move in response to the changing pattern of demand. While the location of retail outlets remained risky, this did not prevent retailers from establishing their networks of distribution warehouses which were considered to be more flexible in the manner in which they could respond to changing consumer spending patterns.

Market entry risk reduction strategies also have a time dimension. While there may be long-term benefits arising from being the first company to develop a new product field in an overseas market, there are also risks. If development is hurried and launched before consistent quality can be guaranteed to live up to an organization's international standards, the company's long-term image can be damaged, both in the new overseas market and in its wider world market. In the turbulent marketing environment of Eastern Europe in the late 1980s, two of the world's principal fast food retailers—McDonald's and Burger King—pursued quite different strategies. The former waited until political, economic, social and technological conditions were capable of allowing it to launch a restaurant that met its global standards. In the case of Burger King, its desire to be first in the market led it to offer a substandard service, giving it an image from which it will probably take a long while to recover.

An assessment of risk is required in deciding whether an organization should enter an overseas market on its own or in association with another organization. The former maximizes the strategic and operational control that the organization has over its overseas operations, but it exposes it to the greatest risk where the overseas market is relatively poorly understood. A range of entry possibilities are considered below.

12.8.1 Exporting

It is often possible for a company to gain a feel for a market by exporting to an overseas market from its home base. Where economies of scale in production are high and transport costs are low, this is often a very cost-effective solution. To minimize risks associated with an unknown market, an exporter would often employ an export agent at home or an import agent in the overseas target market. The use of an agent may also be more cost-effective for the company than creating its own overseas sales force. If initial export attempts succeed, a company may then consider setting up its own production base overseas. As an example of this strategy of gradual commitment, the Müller yoghurt company initially exported its premium yoghurts from Germany to the United Kingdom, until its market had grown to such an extent that it felt confident about committing resources to a new UK production centre.

Exporting is likely to be the less satisfactory option for manufacturers who produce high-volume, low-value products for which transport costs could put them at a competitive disadvantage in overseas markets. Exporting is often not possible in the case of services that demand a high level of interaction between a company and its customers at the latter's home base (e.g. high contact services such as street cleaning subcontracting cannot be very easily exported without creating an overseas base).

Although the use of export/import agents may initially minimize risks for an exporter, their use also brings potential problems. Where an import agent acquires exclusive rights to market a product in a country, conflict can occur between the agent and exporter on marketing policy issues (e.g. in the early 1990s there was an acrimonious disagreement on policy between Nissan and its UK sole importer AFG).

12.8.2 Direct investment in overseas subsidiary

This option gives an organization maximum control over its overseas operations, but can expose it to a high level of risk on account of the poor understanding that it may have of the overseas market. A company can either set up its own overseas subsidiary from scratch (as many UK hotel companies have done to develop hotels in overseas markets), or it can acquire control of a company that is already trading (such as the acquisition by Marks and Spencers of the American-based Brooks Brothers store group).

Where the nature of the product offer differs relatively little between national markets or where it appeals to an international market (e.g. hotels), the risks from creating a new subsidiary are reduced. Where there are barriers to entry and the product is aimed at an essentially local market with a different culture to the domestic market, the acquisition of an established subsidiary may be the preferred course of action. Even the latter course of action is not risk free, as was illustrated by the problems encountered by Midland Bank following its acquisition of a substantial interest in the American-based Crocker Bank during the 1980s.

Direct investment in an overseas subsidiary may also be made difficult by legislation restricting ownership in certain sectors by foreigners. Civil aviation is a good example, where many countries prevent foreigners owning a controlling interest in a domestic airline.

12.8.3   Management contracting

Rather than setting up its own operations overseas, a company with a proven track record in a product area may pursue the option of running other companies' businesses for them. This is particularly important for services-based organizations. For a fee, an overseas organization which seeks to develop a new service would contract a team to set up and run the facility. In some cases, the intention may be that the management team should get the project started and gradually hand over the running of the facility to local management. This type of arrangement is useful for an expanding overseas organization where the required management and technical skills are difficult to obtain locally. In countries where the educational infrastructure offers less opportunity for management and technical training, a company (or in many cases, overseas governments) can buy in state-of-the-art management skills.

For the company supplying management skills under such contracts, the benefits are numerous. Risks are kept to a minimum as the company generally does not need to invest its own capital in the project. The company gathers overseas market knowledge which it may be able to use to its own advantage if it plans similar ventures of its own in other countries. For staff employed by the company, the challenge of working on an overseas project can offer career opportunities outside the mainstream domestic management route.

Management contracting has found many applications in the service sector. For UK companies, the demise of the British empire resulted in most newly independent colonies seeking to establish their own service organizations, for which they were ill-equipped to manage themselves. Most countries immediately set up their own airline, making use of management expertise bought in from BOAC—the forerunner of British Airways. More recently, developments in Eastern Europe have resulted in many opportunities for UK-based service companies, including the management of hotels, airlines and educational establishments (e.g. the hotel group Forte has been contracted to set up and operate a number of hotels in Eastern Europe and the University of Strathclyde has been contracted to set up and run a Business School in Poland).

12.8.4   Licensing/franchsing

Rather than setting up its own operations in an overseas market, a company can license a local company to manufacture and sell a product in the local market. This is commonly used, for example, by soft drinks manufacturers who sell the right to overseas companies to market a branded product overseas. The licensee must usually agree to follow a product formulation closely and to maintain consistent standards of quality and brand image.

In the service sector, it can be difficult to define when a licence becomes a franchise. The inseparability of service offers makes service producers an integral part of a service, requiring greater control over the whole process by which an overseas business operates. Therefore, while exporters of manufactured goods frequently licence an overseas producer to manufacture and sell their products, a company developing a service overseas is more likely to establish a franchise relationship with its overseas producers, which gives it greater control over the whole service production process.

As with the development of a domestic franchise service network, franchising can allow an organization to expand rapidly overseas with relatively low capital requirements. While a clearly defined business format and method of conducting business is critical to the success of an overseas franchise, things can still go wrong for a number of reasons. The service format could be poorly proven in the home market, making overseas expansion particularly difficult. Unrealistic expectations may be held about the amount of human and financial resources that need to be devoted to the operation of an overseas franchise. Problems in interpreting the spirit and letter of contractual agreements between the franchisee and franchisor can result in acrimonious misunderstanding. A good example of an overseas franchise failure is the breakdown of the agreement made in the 1970s between McDonald's and its Paris franchisee, which resulted in McDonald's successfully pursuing legal proceedings against the latter for failing to maintain standards as specified.

CHOICE OF INTERNATIONAL MARKET ENTRY OPTIONS

While franchising is no stranger to the service sector, the hotel industry in particular has been quick to recognize its advantages. A franchised hotel chain with a proven business format and favourable customer recognition is able to grow quite rapidly using capital introduced by its franchisees. Furthermore, in an industry that involves a lot of client contact and attention to detail, it can be easier to motivate relatively small scale franchisees compared to salaried managers of a large corporation.

The existence of internationally branded chains can in itself offer many advantages over independent stand-alone hotels. For international travellers, brands allow rapid recognition of the standards of service that a hotel is likely to offer. A chain is also better able to support a world-wide sales operation than a single hotel, making the onward reservation of accommodation relatively easy for travellers. Hotel chains have achieved such significance that by the early 1990s, it has been estimated that about 70 per cent of 50+ bedroom 2 to 4 star hotels in the United States belonged to some form of chain, the majority as franchise operations. The comparable figure for the United Kingdom was just 15 per cent.

International expansion by hotel operators has often been achieved through franchising. This was the route chosen by Choice Hotels International, the largest hotel operator in the world (when measured by hotel numbers rather than rooms). The American-based company operates over 2300 hotels in 29 countries and of its 250 000 bedrooms, all but 5000 are operated on a franchise basis, the latter comprising a small number of company operated or managed hotels. Its hotel chains are highly segmented with Econo Lodge and Friendship Inns providing basic facilities at the lower end of the market and its Clarion and Quality brands providing more up-market chains.

An analysis of Choice Hotels' European development strategy indicates some of the opportunities as well as the possible pitfalls of international franchising. Its strategic plan for Europe, developed during the late 1980s, envisaged having 300 hotels operating under the Choice umbrella by 1997 and 500 by 2000.

One of Choice's first moves into the UK market was to sign a franchise agreement with Scandic Crown Hotels UK, a small chain of five hotels. In return for paying franchise fees, the owners of Scandic Crown Hotels were able to benefit from the world-wide marketing effort of Choice Hotels. The chain was to operate under the brand name of Clarion—one of Choice Hotels' more up-market brands. However, on the point of developing an internationally recognized brand, this initial venture into UK franchising encountered a number of problems. While Choice sought to develop a strong brand which would stand for internationally consistent attributes, it came up against the loyalty of franchisees to their existing names. The latter insisted on giving primary emphasis to their own name and only secondary emphasis to the Clarion brand name, to the point where one typical hotel became known confusingly as the 'Clarion Scandic Crown Nelson Dock'. Choice hotels also became mindful of the variable efforts made by its franchisees in implementing service quality standards which the Clarion brand stood for.

Faced with the problem of establishing values for its franchisees to follow, the company resorted to developing its own small chain of branded hotels to hold up as an example to franchisees of the standards that were expected of the brand. In this way, Quality Hotels Europe was founded with the aim of creating a chain of 30 Quality Hotel or Comfort Inn branded hotels throughout Europe, using $200 million of capital provided by the American parent company.

In seeking to expand into Europe, the company was careful not to Americanize the European hotel scene, but to incorporate the local character and operating style of hotels to suit the needs of both domestic and international customers. For this reason, it initially decided not to bring the American style Econo Lodge, Rodeway and Friendship brands to Europe, opting instead to develop the Clarion, Quality, Comfort and Sleep Inn brands. Of the latter, Quality and Comfort Inns formed the focus of the company's effort.

In the case of the Sleep Inn brand, Choice sold a franchise for exclusive UK development rights to an organization called Budgotel. Its first hotel opened at Nottingham in 1990, with planned openings soon following on new sites at Hull and Chesterfield. Meanwhile, the European subsidiary established by Choice continued to sell franchises for the Quality and Comfort brands. Unlike the completely new build which characterized new Sleep Inn open-

ings, 75 per cent of Quality and Comfort franchises were conversions from existing hotels. Franchise fees typically worked out at an initial one-off fee of £120 per bedroom, a 1 per cent payment on sales turnover and reservation fees paid to Choice of £3.50 per booking. Franchise agreements were normally for an initial term of 20 years, with mutual rights to terminate after three, six, ten and fifteen year periods.

The initial poor performance of its European operations led Choice to impose much more stringent strictures on its franchisees with regard to branding. Existing franchisees were no longer allowed to use the corporate brand as secondary to its own name while new franchisees were required to be fully branded from the outset. Any hotel owners who failed to brand their hotels in this manner would lose their franchise. Plans to extend the range of Choice brands available in Europe for franchise were limited to the four core brands of Comfort, Quality, Sleep and Clarion.

For the longer term, the company recognized that opportunities existed in the more up-market luxury hotel sector which it currently did not adequately serve. In addition to the possibility of developing franchise links with existing well-respected hotel names, it has also investigated the possibility of acquiring an up-market European brand which already has a strong position in the luxury hotel sector. Such a move might make a lot of sense for Choice, allowing its bed space to be sold through its world-wide sales network. The development of an additional brand for the European market in addition to its highly segmented range of American brands can be seen as a recognition of the need to adapt brands to meet the needs of overseas markets.

QUESTIONS

1. What environmental considerations are crucial to an American hotel chain such as Choice in its assessment of European business opportunities?
2. For Choice Hotels International, compare the advantages and disadvantages of franchising with those of managing its own hotels in Europe.
3. What alternative strategies for overseas development are open to Choice?

12.8.5   Joint ventures

An international joint venture is a partnership between a domestic company and an overseas company or government. A joint venture can take a number of forms and is particularly attractive to a domestic firm seeking entry to an overseas market where:

- The initial capital requirement threshold is high, resulting in a high level of risk.
- Overseas governments restrict the rights of foreign companies to set up business on their account, making a partnership with a local company—possibly involving a minority shareholding—the only means of entering the market.
- There may be significant barriers to entry which a company already based in the overseas market could help to overcome. An important barrier is often posed by the availability of intermediaries. As an example, the UK mortgage market is dominated by banks and building societies, largely selling their own mortgages, and a number of foreign banks have taken the view that their best market entry strategy would be to work in partnership with a smaller building society, providing them with funds and allowing them to sell the mortgages under their own name through their established network of branches.
- There may be reluctance of consumers to deal with what appears to be a foreign company. A joint venture can allow the operation to be fronted by a domestic producer with whom customers can be familiar, while allowing the overseas partner to provide capital and management expertise.
- A good understanding of local market conditions is essential for success in an overseas market. It was noted above that the task of obtaining marketing research information can be significantly more difficult abroad as compared to an organization's domestic market. A joint venture with an organization already based in the proposed overseas market makes the task of collecting information about a market, and responding sensitively to it, relatively easy.
- Taxation of company profits may favour a joint venture rather than owning an overseas subsidiary outright.

A distinction can be made between equity and non-equity joint ventures. The former involves two or more organizations joining together to invest in a 'child' organization which has its own separate identity. A non-equity joint venture involves agreement between partners on such matters as marketing research, new service development, promotion and distribution, without any agreement to jointly provide capital for a new organization. Some recent examples of joint ventures are shown in Table 12.6.

Strategic alliances—whether or not involving joint equity—are becoming increasingly important. These are agreements between two or more organizations where each partner seeks to add to its competencies by combining its resources with those of a partner. A strategic alliance generally involves co-operation between partners rather than joint ownership of a subsidiary setup for a specific purpose, although it may include agreement for collaborators to purchase shares in the businesses of other members of the alliance.

Strategic alliances are frequently used to allow individual companies to build upon the relationship that they have developed with their clients by allowing them to sell on services that they do not produce themselves, but are produced by another member of the alliance. This arrangement is reciprocated between members of the alliance. Strategic alliances have assumed great importance within the airline industry, where a domestic operator and an international operator can join together to offer new travel possibilities for their respective customers.

International strategic alliances can involve one organization nominating a supplier in related product fields as a preferred supplier at its outlets world-wide. This strategy has been used by car rental companies to secure a link-up with other transport principals, to offer what the latter sees as a value-added service. An example is the agreement between Hertz Car Rental and Eurotunnel to provide a new facility for customers of each company called 'Le Swap'. By the agreement, customers are able to rent a right-hand-drive car in the United Kingdom, travel through the tunnel by train and swap to a left-hand-drive car at the other end, and vice versa.

Table 12.6 Examples of the involvement of UK financial service organizations in overseas joint ventures

Venture partners	Holding %	Subsidiary/purpose
Equity joint ventures		
Lombard North Central	50	Creation of Lombard Orient Leasing to develop lease
Orient Leasing (Japan)	50	business for Japanese office automation equipment in the United Kingdom
Prudential	50	Creation of Prudential Assicurazione to provide insur-
Inholding (Italy)	50	ance services in Italy
Abbey National	92	Creation of Abbey National Mutui to offer mortgages in
Diners Club (Italy)	0	Italy
Winterthur (Switzerland)	8	
Gerard and National	33	Creation of Trifutures to offer brokerage services on
Caisse des Depots et		Paris futures exchange
Consignations (France)	33	
Banque d'Escompte (France)	33	
Non-equity joint ventures		
Commercial Union		Agreement for CI to sell and distribute CU's life and non-
Credito Italiano (Italy)		life insurance policies in Italy
Hambros Merchant Bank		Co-operation agreement in cross-frontier merger and
Bayerische Vereinsbank (West Germany)		acquisition finance
Barclays Bank		Agreement gave Barclays Bank a banking licence to
Tokyo Trust (Japan)		operate in Japan to provide trust management and securities handling in collaboration with its partner

BRITISH AIRWAYS AND US AIR TO FORM WORLD'S LARGEST AIRLINE ALLIANCE

It is not economically feasible for airlines to operate direct flights between all airports which they serve, just as a telephone company doesn't run cable from each telephone to every other telephone in its network. During the 1970s and 1980s, airlines therefore developed a series of 'hubs'—airports where passengers could fly in on one route (a 'spoke') and make a connection on to another route. The development of hub-and-spoke systems potentially allows an enormous range of origin-destination possibilities.

Against the improved journey possibilities which the development of a hub-and-spoke system brings, making connections at a hub airport can result in problems for transferring passengers. If the two connecting services are operated by completely independent carriers, it may be necessary to purchase two separate tickets and the passenger would have to transfer their own baggage rather than checking it in through to their final destination. Should the incoming flight be delayed, the second carrier may show little sympathy in rescheduling a ticket on account of delay caused by another airline.

Because of these operational problems, competitive advantage at hub airports is gained by airlines that can offer the most comprehensive and integrated network of services. This can either be achieved by being very large or by forming strategic alliances with other airlines. The latter approach can make sense where a domestic operator with an intensive network of local routes from its hub and an overseas carrier operating into that hub come to an agreement for the through ticketing of passengers between national and international routes. The benefit for passengers would be a 'seamless' journey, free of the dual ticketing and transfer problems described above. For the airlines, a strategic alliance brings mutual benefits—the domestic operator feeds passengers into its partner's international services, while the latter provides its partner with additional domestic business.

During the late 1980s, British Airways had been watching with concern the growth of very large American carriers such as American, Delta and United who were capable of offering a very comprehensive network of services. These were putting British Airways at a competitive disadvantage. For a number of years, British Airways had been seeking a strategic alliance with an airline which would allow it to compete with these large carriers by being able to provide 'seamless' transatlantic travel to a comprehensive range of American destinations. Discussions had been taking place with United Airlines to form a strategic alliance, but these broke down. British Airways then pursued an alliance with the Dutch airline KLM, hoping that the alliance might have included the Dutch airline's stake in Northwest Airlines. Again, discussions broke down.

In July 1992, British Airways (BA) announced that it had reached agreement to buy 21 per cent of the voting shares in US Air for $750 million, creating an airline with a combined annual turnover of $16 billion. Due to statutory restrictions on the level of voting power that could be held by non-American citizens in American airlines, BA would only be able to cast 25 per cent of the votes at US Air shareholders' meetings, despite agreeing to purchase 44 per cent of the total shares. Nevertheless, its American competitors pointed out that the structure of the deal would give BA effective control over a number of crucial issues. As a result of strong lobbying by the large American airlines—who wanted permission for the takeover to be made conditional upon American airlines gaining greater access to the UK market—BA's attempted strategic alliance was initially blocked by the American government.

BA was anxious not to let the proposed alliance be lost and lobbied hard to win approval, both directly to the American government and indirectly through the UK government. Eventually, in March 1993, a modified strategic alliance was approved by the American government with a number of awkward caveats which prevented BA taking too much control too quickly. Crucial to BA was approval of a 'code sharing' agreement which allowed international flights to appear in US Air schedules as US Air operated flights, but in BA's schedules as BA flights. The agreement with US Air meant that British Airways would be able to feed passengers from its transatlantic route network into US Air's hub airports for onward movement by the latter's network. Similarly, US Air's loyal clientele using its transatlantic services would be fed into British Airway's European hub airports for onward connections. Both airlines would be able to significantly increase the range of 'seamless' journeys possible within their networks.

BA claimed that the alliance with US Air was a major step towards achieving its policy of globalization, paving the way for a comprehensive global airline group. Progress towards globalization had already been made by an agreement in 1990 with the Russian airline Aeroflot to form a new international airline 'Air Russia' and with a German regional airline to form Deutsch BA.

QUESTIONS

1. Why have international strategic alliances become so important in the marketing of airline services?

2. In their analysis of the business environment, what possible problems with such an alliance might have been envisaged by British Airways?
3. What public policy issues are raised by this alliance?

REVIEW QUESTIONS

1. What are the nature of the gains arising from trade liberalization and why is it such a painful process?
   (CIM Marketing Environment Examination, December 1994, Q.1 (b))
2. Explain who will be the winners and losers of trade liberalization in your own country. Summarize what advice you would give any company to ensure it ends up on the winning side.
   (CIM Marketing Environment Examination, December 1994, Q.1 (c))
3. (a) Your consultancy firm has decided to produce a brief booklet, in bullet point format, to provide advice to marketing clients who are considering establishing overseas operations.
   (b) Using relevant headings and points, produce an outline draft for this booklet, including a bibliography and useful sources of information.
   (CIM Marketing Environment Examination, June 1995, Q.6)
4. Summarize the advantages and disadvantages to a British capital goods manufacturer resulting from full European Monetary Union.
5. Suggest how the UK insurance industry can avoid going the same way as the motorcycle industry and losing out to overseas competition.
6. What cultural differences might cause problems for a hotel chain developing a location in India?

FURTHER READING

Mayes, D. G. (ed.) (1995) *The European Challenge: Industry's Response to the 1992 Programme*, Harvester Wheatsheaf, London.

McDonald, F. and Dearden, S. (eds) (1994) *European Economic Integration*, 2nd edn, Longman, Harlow.

Ohmae,K. (1989) 'The Global Logic of Strategic Alliances', *Harvard Business Review*, March–April, pp. 143–54.

Paliwoda, S. J. (1993) *International Marketing*, 2nd edn, Heinemann, Oxford.

Phillips, C., Doole, I. and Lowe, R. (1994) *International Marketing Strategy, Analysis, Development and Implementation*, Routledge, London.

Spencer, J. (1994) *Principles of International Marketing*, Blackwell, Oxford.

Walsh, L. S. (1995) *International Marketing*, 3rd edn, Pitman, London.

ANALYSING THE MARKETING ENVIRONMENT

OBJECTIVES

After reading this chapter, you should understand:

● Frameworks within which to understand the marketing environment.
● The importance of information for planning and controlling marketing activities.
● Techniques for predicting future environmental change.
● Methods of minimizing exposure to risk from environmental change.

13.1 INTRODUCTION

The purpose of this chapter is to examine how business organizations can interpret the marketing environment and develop frameworks within which decisions on future courses of action can be made. The aim is to progress from perceiving how a company can have a general understanding of the environment to how it can use specific methods of assessment. The emphasis will be on methods of predicting environmental change and of their impact on an enterprise, rather than on assessing the internal rate of return of a project to a business.

13.2 THE MARKETING AUDIT

It has been customary for business organizations to undertake financial audits to check on their financial health. Increasingly, the principles of the independent and objective audit are being applied to the marketing function of companies. The following definition of a marketing audit is given by Kotler (1991):

A marketing audit is a comprehensive, systematic, independent and periodic examination of a company's—or business unit's—marketing environment, objectives, strategies and activities with a view to determining problem areas and opportunities and recommending a plan of action to improve the company's marketing performance.

The marketing audit is not itself a framework for decisions: it is essentially a set of procedures by which an organization explicitly asks questions about the internal and external environments in which marketing operates, as well as the performance of the marketing functions themselves (such as the firm's distribution and pricing effectiveness). The process begins by the appointment of an independent person to undertake the audit. This could be a consultant from outside the organization, or somebody from another position within the firm, either sideways or above the function being audited. A self-audit could be undertaken, but at the risk of a loss of objectivity. However, a number of books containing check-lists and questions are published which will aid objectivity.

A large part of the audit is devoted to an objective analysis of the micro- and macro-environment. In the case of the macro-environment the audit would independently verify or challenge any assumptions that the company had been making—for instance about the likely rate of economic growth or the speed of change in the technological environment. In the case of the micro-environment, the person undertaking an audit of the distribution environment could proceed by asking retailers themselves about how they perceive the company's products and future trends in retailing for that type of product.

The marketing audit would also look inwardly to examine the relationships within the marketing function and between it and other functional areas of the firm. Organizational structures and decision-making procedures would be objectively assessed for effectiveness.

13.3   MARKETING INFORMATION SYSTEMS

Some of the elements of marketing research were examined in Chapter 1. Information is of such importance to marketing management that its collection and dissemination needs to be undertaken in a systematic way. It has been suggested by Christopher, McDonald and Wills (1980) that: 'Good information is a facilitator of successful marketing and indeed, seen in this light, marketing management becomes first and foremost an information processing activity.'

Piercy (1985) has argued that processing information should be regarded as the fifth P of the marketing mix. Information represents a bridge between the business organization and its environment and is the means by which a picture of the changing environment is built up within the company. Marketing management is responsible for turning information into specific marketing plans.

A marketing information system is a subsystem of a company's management information system; other systems are concerned with production, finance, personnel, etc. An important requirement for an effective marketing information system is that all the elements of it are driven by meeting decision-makers' needs, rather than the needs of people producing information. Clear aims must be set; these might include the need for information on the size and characteristics of markets, customer attitudes and awareness of brand names and the effectiveness of the firm's pricing and distribution policies, to name but a few. Aims should specify the frequency with which information is to be collected, the speed with which it is to be transmitted, the level of accuracy required, whom it is to be given to and who is responsible for acting on the information.

The marketing information system could have a number of possible functions covering the planning, implementation and control of marketing programmes. A practical problem for environmental analysis is that information is typically much more difficult to obtain to meet strategic planning needs than it is to meet operational and control needs. There can be a danger of the marketing information system being focused too heavily on information that is easily available and quantifiable at the expense of that which is needed. At an operational level, the system might, for example, monitor the performance of individual sales personnel or brand awareness levels among a company's target market. These are not the direct concern of this chapter as far as marketing information systems are concerned—rather, the emphasis is on turning observations about the marketing environment into information that management can act upon. It is not easy to identify, format, store and distribute intangible and non-quantified information concerning the future of the external environment.

The complexity of the task of gathering information about the marketing environment will vary between individual firms. Ansoff (1984) attributes this variation to two principal factors. Firstly, firms will perceive varying levels of uncertainty in the environment as measured by the rate of environmental change. Secondly, the extent of complexity will also be affected by the range of activities the company is either involved in or likely to be involved in in the future.

The information collection exercise can be seen as comprising four main elements which make up a

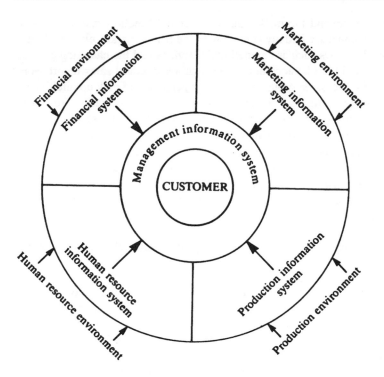

Figure 13.1   The marketing information system

company's marketing information system: a marketing research system, an internal reporting system, an intelligence gathering system and an analytic market modelling system (Figure 13.1).

The internal reporting system is concerned primarily with the reporting of operational and control matters rather than the changing state of the marketing environment. The tools of the marketing research system were described in some detail in Chapter 1, where it was noted that they could be used to provide both routine information about marketing effectiveness—such as brand awareness levels or delivery performance—and external environmental information—such as changing attitudes towards diet or the pattern of income distribution. The latter could be collected either routinely or as a series of discrete exercises, through both primary and secondary data collection.

The intelligence gathering system comprises the procedures and sources used by marketing managers to obtain pertinent information about developments in their marketing environment. It complements the marketing research system, for, whereas the latter tends to focus on structured and largely quantifiable data collection procedures, the intelligence gathering system concentrates on picking up relatively intangible ideas and trends. Marketing management can gather this intelligence from the following sources:

● Where no specific information is sought, intelligence can be acquired through exposure to general sources of information (such as daily newspapers and television news programmes).
● Selected sources may be recognized as being particularly valuable for throwing up information highly pertinent to the firm's environment. Marketing management may arrange for these to be scanned routinely and for news cuttings of new developments to be fed into the marketing information system. Trade journals fit into this category of intelligence; exhibitions and conferences are also recognized as a valuable method of collecting intelligence.

- People employed in the company beyond the marketing management function may be valuable sources of intelligence. Sales personnel are in daily contact with the firm's market-place and are in a good position to pick up valuable news such as competitors' activities and the changing attitudes of customers—information that could not be accommodated within a standard sales report. Some businesses have used unstructured discussion groups among sales personnel to pick up intelligence.
- In a similar manner, a company may formalize procedures for collecting information from firms within its immediate external environment, especially distributors and suppliers. Many manufacturers arrange seminars for their distributors which have the function not only of selling the product range, but also of picking up comments about the market-place in general.
- The business organization may require intelligence on a specific subject about which its routine intelligence gathering system described above has provided insufficient information. It may then enter into a more formal search, either by referring to specialized publications or by employing a consultant to provide the required information.

For those enterprises that have set up marketing intelligence systems, their effectiveness will be determined by three factors:

1. *The accurate description of the information needs of the enterprise* Needs can themselves be difficult to identify, and it can be very difficult to identify the boundaries of the firm's environments and to separate relevance from irrelevance. This is a particular problem for large multiproduct firms. The mission statement of the business may give some indication of the boundaries for environmental search—the TSB Bank, for example, has a mission statement which includes an aim for it to be the dominant provider of financial services in the United Kingdom. The information needs therefore include anything related to the broader environment of financial services rather than the narrower field of banking.
2. *The extensiveness of the search for intelligence* A balance has to be struck between the need for information and the cost of collecting it. The most critical elements of the marketing environment must be identified and the cost of collecting intelligence on that element weighed against the cost of an inaccurate forecast. (See the following section on probability assessment.)
3. *Speed of communication* The marketing intelligence system will be effective only if information is communicated quickly and to the appropriate people. Deciding which information to withhold from an individual and concisely reporting relevant information can be as important as deciding what information to include if information overload is to be avoided.

The fourth element making up a company's market information—the analytic marketing modelling system—is discussed below.

13.4 FRAMEWORKS FOR ANALYSING THE MARKETING ENVIRONMENT

There are two aspects to be considered when describing an analytic framework:

1. A definition of the elements that are to be included in the analysis
2. The choice of methods by which these input elements are to be used in predicting outcomes

The nature of the framework used bears a relation to the nature of the dominant business environment at the time. In the relatively stable environment that existed during the early years of this century, management could control its destiny by controlling current performance. In the the turbulent environment of the 1990s, control becomes dependent upon management's ability to predict the future and respond to change.

Diffenbach (1983) has argued that detailed environmental analysis became important only in the mid-1960s. Prior to that, the marketing environment was analysed primarily for the purpose of making short-term economic forecasts. The developments to include a longer-term appreciation of the wider economic, technological, demographic and cultural elements of the environment came about in three stages:

1. An increased appreciation of environmental analysis was encouraged by the emergence of professional and academic interest in the subject.
2. Awareness of the concepts of environmental analysis led to academic analysis of the subject.
3. Eventually, the concepts that had been vindicated by subsequent academic analysis were taken on board by business organizations and used as a tool for strategic decision making.

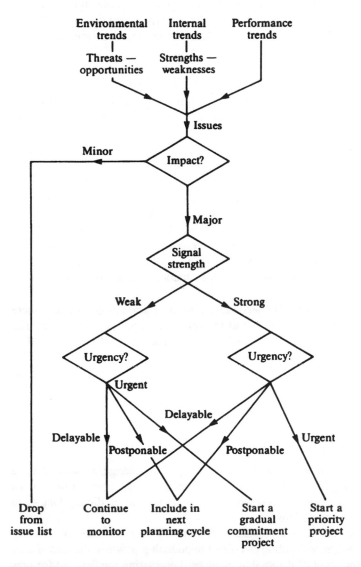

Figure 13.2   Ansoff's model of strategic issue analysis
   Source: based on H. I. Ansoff (1985) *Marketing Strategy and Management*. Reproduced by permission of Macmillan Ltd. © H. I. Ansoff 1979.

As frameworks for analysis have developed in sophistication, so has the paradox that, by the time sufficient information has been gathered and analysed, it may be too late for the firm to do anything about the opportunities or threats with which it is faced. Ansoff (1984) has put forward a framework that helps to overcome this decision-making dilemma. His model allows the firm to respond rapidly to problems whose precise details are a surprise, but whose general nature could have been predicted. Ansoff's model of strategic issue analysis is shown in Figure 13.2. The central feature of the model is the continuing monitoring of the firm's external and internal environments for indicators of the emergence of potentially strategic issues which may significantly influence the firms operations in future. The focal point for Ansoff's analysis is the *issue*—such as the emergence of environmentalism—rather than the conventional headings of the economic, technological environments, etc. The model allows for a graduated response: as soon as weak signals are picked up, steps are taken to allow for the possibility of these issues developing further. Responses become more precise as the signals become more amplified over time. In other words, Ansoff's model avoids the need for a firm to wait until it has sufficient information before taking a decision—it responds gradually as information emerges.

13.4.1   Choice of framework

A wide range of analytic frameworks are available for companies to use in analysing their marketing environment and making strategic marketing decisions. The choice of framework will depend upon four factors.

Firstly, the *level of turbulence* in the marketing environment will vary between firms operating in different markets. For example, the marketing environment of an undertaker has not been—and in future is even less likely to be—as turbulent as that of a brewery. An extrapolation of recent trends might be adequate for the former type of business, but the latter must seek to understand a diverse range of changing forces if it is to be able to accurately predict future demand for its products.

Secondly, the *cost* associated with an inaccurate forecast will reflect the capital commitment to a project. A clothing manufacturer can afford to trust his or her judgement in running off a small batch of jackets—the cost of making a mistake will probably be bearable, unlike the cost of building a chemical refinery on the basis of an inaccurate forecast. The latter situation calls for relatively sophisticated analytic techniques.

Thirdly, more sophisticated *analytic techniques* are needed for long-time-scale projects where there is a long time lag between the planning of the project and the time it comes into production. The problem of inaccurate forecasting will be even more acute where an asset has a long lifespan with few alternate uses.

Finally, *qualitative* and *quantitative* techniques may be used as appropriate. In looking at the future, facts are hard to come by. What matters is that senior management must be in the position to make better informed judgements about the future in order to aid decision making and planning.

13.4.2 Trend extrapolation

At its simplest level, a firm identifies an historic and consistent long-term change in demand for a product over time. Demand forecasting then takes the form of multiplying current sales by an historic growth factor. In most markets, this can at best work effectively only in predicting long-term sales growth at the expense of short-term variations.

Trend extrapolation methods can be refined to recognize a relationship between sales and one key environmental variable. An example might be an observed direct relationship between the sale of new cars to the private buyer sector and the level of disposable incomes. Forecasting the demand for new cars then becomes a problem of forecasting what will happen to disposable incomes during the planning period. In practice, the task of extrapolation cannot usually be reduced to a single dependent and independent variable. The car manufacturer would also have to consider the relationship between sales and consumer confidence, the level of competition in its environment and the varying rate of government taxation.

While multiple regression techniques can be used to identify the significance of historical relationships between a number of variables, extrapolation methods suffer from a number of shortcomings. Firstly, one variable is seldom adequate to predict future demand for a product, yet it can be difficult to identify the full set of variables that have an influence. Secondly, there can be no certainty that the trends identified from historic patterns are likely to continue in the future. Trend extrapolation takes no account of discontinuous environmental change, as was brought about by the sudden increase in oil prices in 1973. Thirdly, it can be difficult to gather information on which to base an analysis of trends—indeed, a large part of the problem in designing a marketing information system lies in identifying the type of information that may be of relevance at some time in the future. Fourthly, trend extrapolation is of diminishing value as the length of time used to forecast extends: the longer the time horizon, the more chance there is of historic relationships changing and new variables emerging.

Trend extrapolation as applied by most business organizations is a method of linking a simple cause with a simple effect. As such, it does nothing to try to understand or predict the underlying variables, unless extrapolation is applied to these variables too.

At best, trend extrapolation can be used where planning horizons are short, the number of variables relatively limited and the risk level relatively low. A retailer may use extrapolation to forecast how much ice cream will be demanded in summer. An historic relationship between the weather (quantified in terms of sunshine hours or average daily temperatures) may have been identified, on to which a long-term relationship between household disposable income and the domestic freezer population has been added. The level of demand for ice cream during the following month could be predicted with reasonable accuracy with input from the Meteorological Office on the weather forecast, from the Treasury or *Economist*'s forecast of household disposal incomes (relatively easy to obtain if the forecast period is only one month) and from statistics showing recent trends in household freezer ownership (available from the Annual General Household Survey).

13.4.3 Expert opinion

Trend analysis is commonly used to predict demand where the state of the causative variables is known. In practice, it can be very difficult to predict what will happen to the causative variables themselves. One solution is to consult expert opinion to obtain the best possible forecast of what will happen to these variables.

In Diffenbach's (1983) study of American corporations, 86 per cent of all firms said they used expert opinion as an input to their planning process. Expert opinion can vary in the level of specialty, from an economist being consulted for a general forecast about the state of the national economy to industry-specific experts. An example of the latter are the fashion consultants who study trends at the major international fashion shows and provide a valuable source of expert opinion to clothing manufacturers seeking to know which types of fabric to order, ahead of a fashion trend.

Expert opinion may be unstructured and come either from a few individuals inside the organization, or from external advisers or consultants. The most senior managers in companies of reasonable size tend to keep in touch with developments by various means. Paid and unpaid advisers may be used to keep abreast of a whole range of issues such as technological developments, animal rights campaigners, environmental issues, government thinking and intended legislation. Large companies may employ MPs or MEPs (Members of the European Parliament) as advisers as well as retired civil servants. Consultancy firms may be employed to brief the company on specific issues or monitor the environment on a more general basis.

In today's modern economy, it is essential that businesses monitor not only the domestic environment but also the European Union and the international environment. Today as much legislation affecting companies comes from the EU as from the UK government. Legislation passed in the United States can have an indirect affect on UK companies, even though their products may not be intended for sale in America. What is happening in America today may be happening in Europe next year.

Relying on individuals may give an incomplete or distorted picture of the future. There are, however, more structured methods of gaining expert opinion. One of the best known is probably the Delphi method. This involves a number of experts, usually from outside the organization, who (preferably) do not know each other and who do not meet or confer while the process is in play. A scenario or scenarios about the future are drawn up by the company. These are then posted out to the experts. Comments are returned and the scenario(s) modified according to the comments received. The process is run through a number of times with the scenario being amended on each occasion. Eventually a consensus of the most likely scenario is arrived at. It is believed that this is more accurate than relying on any one individual, because it involves the collected wisdom of a number of experts who have not been influenced by dominant personalities.

13.4.4   Scenario building

Scenario building is an attempt to paint a picture of the future. It may be possible to build a small number of alternative scenarios based on differing assumptions. This qualitative approach is a means of handling environmental issues which are hard to quantify because they are less structured, more uncertain and may involve very complex relationships.

Often the most senior managers in a company may hold no common view about the future. The individuals themselves are likely to be scanning the environment in an informal way, through conversations with colleagues and subordinates within the organization and through business acquaintances and friends outside. The general media and business and technical publications will also shape a person's 'view' of the future. Individuals will vary in their sensitivity to the environment. Such views may never be harnessed in any formal way, but they may be influencing decisions taken by these individuals. Yet the views each person holds may never have been exposed to debate or challenge in a way that would allow the individual to moderate or change his or her view.

Scenario building among senior management will help individuals to confirm or moderate their views. A new perspective may be taken on issues or forthcoming events. A wider perspective may be taken by individuals who may become more sensitive to the environment and the impact it can have on business. A more cohesive view may be adopted by senior management which may help strategy formulation and planning. The scenarios may be built up over a number of meetings which may be either totally unstructured or semi-structured, with each meeting focusing on different aspects of the environment. The approach may be used at different levels of management in a large organization; a multinational company may build scenarios at the global, regional and country level. For example, Johnson and Scholes (1984) cite the example of Shell UK Ltd which has used this approach on a number of occasions. In the early 1980s it was used as part of the company's methodology for attempting to assess the demand for oil depending on a number of alternative scenarios (see the case study of the Shell Oil Company below).

SHELL OIL COMPANY USES SCENARIOS TO PLAN FOR THE FUTURE

The Shell Oil Company is a multinational organization with business interests in all geographic areas of the world, ranging from the exploration of energy resources through to the downstream marketing of energy and chem- ical-related products to groups that include private consumers, industry, agriculture and governments. Shell has a history of being one of the world's most profitable companies. The company illustrates how traditional demand forecasting methods are being replaced by methods that take into consideration a much closer examination of environmental change.

The traditional approach used by Shell planners to forecast the amount of refinery capacity it would need to meet consumer demand for refined oil-based products was to extrapolate from recent patterns of demand, on the assumption that recent trends would by and large continue. Like most oil companies, Shell had been caught largely unaware in 1973 by the actions of OPEC, a cartel which had used its monopoly power to increase crude oil prices threefold. This represented a very severe discontinuity in recent trends, and left most oil companies facing much lower levels of demand than they had previously planned for. Most oil companies were not much better prepared for the second sudden OPEC price rise which occurred in 1979.

Today, Shell tries to manage its future by developing a range of possible scenarios of future business environments. From these scenarios, managers can develop plans of action to meet each eventuality that can be envisaged. Identifying the nature of scenarios can be a challenge to managements' creativity.

One example quoted by Shell to justify its scenario-based approach to planning is the oil price collapse that occurred in 1986. In 1984 crude oil prices stood at $28 a barrel. Other oil companies using trend extrapolation predicted that oil prices would rise over the next two years to the $25–$30 a barrel level. The prospect of it falling to $15 may have seemed far-fetched to many planners, yet in February 1986 the world market price of oil fell first to $17 a barrel and then drifted down to a low point of $10 two months later.

Shell claimed it was much better prepared for this price collapse, as it had envisaged a scenario in which this occurred and had developed a contingency plan of action in the event of its taking place. This covered, for example, alternative plans for investment in new energy sources and renewal plans for its shipping fleet. For most of its activities, Shell was trading in commodity markets in which product differentiation was either very difficult or impossible. The ability to learn and react rapidly to environmental change gave Shell its only major advantage over its competitors.

More recently, Shell's approach to scenario building demonstrated its value during the Gulf War. Although Shell had not foreseen the details of the conflict that followed the invasion of Kuwait by Iraq, it had envisaged a scenario in which there was a serious disruption to oil supplies in the Gulf region, whether this arose from war, accident or something else. Contingency plans allowed the company to rapidly replace oil supplies from alternative sources and to redeploy its tanker fleet. The speed with which the company could adjust the forecourt price of petrol to the consumer in response to volatile spot market prices had been increased with improved internal communications.

For the future, Shell feels that attitudes towards the environment represent an opportunity for alternative scenario building. The company has developed two scenarios. In the first, the world moves towards sustainable growth, with a change in attitudes towards consumption among consumers throughout the world and increasing controls on pollution-creating processes. The second scenario envisages a drop in environmentalism as an issue, with increasing emphasis on the need to generate economic wealth; at a national level, governments may seek to stimulate employment even if this results in greater environmental damage, while concern for world-wide approaches to the control of pollution may give way to increasing trade barriers as countries struggle for short-term economic survival. The marketing contingency plan for the former eventuality might include shifting resources to increase the production of wind-generated electricity or biodegradable packaging.

The development of scenario building methods has seen the increasing importance attributed within Shell to the forecasting of business environments. It has attributed its high and stable level of profits to this approach. The first business environment planners at Shell were regarded as eccentric mavericks whose conclusions were seen as relatively marginal to achieving the short-term aims of most managers. Today, the findings of the business environment planners at Shell are communicated within the organization more effectively and managers attach much more significance to the scenarios presented by drawing up their own response plans.

QUESTIONS

1. What are the benefits to Shell of business environment planning?
2. Does such planning always work and if not, why not?

13.4.5 Influence diagrams and impact grids

A more applied approach is to assess the likely impact of specific aspects of environmental change on the business. One method is to construct *influence diagrams* (Narchal *et al.*, 1987), so that a better understanding of the relationships between environmental forces can be obtained. If the price a company has to pay for raw materials is a critical factor, then the forces that influence the price of raw materials will be of interest to it; by monitoring these it will have an earlier warning about price rises than if it were to wait until its supplier told it of the price increase. In the influence diagram (Figure 13.3), a positive relationship means that if the value of one force rises then the pressure on the dependent factor will be in the same direction. A negative relationship means that if the value of the environmental force rises then the pressure on the dependent factor is the opposite direction—downwards.

A number of specific influence diagrams may be used to improve the understanding of how forces in the environment may influence particular aspects of the business. To gain a broader view, *impact grids* can be constructed. Specific environmental forces or events are identified and their impact on particular aspects of the business are assessed (see Jenster, 1987). Weighting the assessment on a simple scale—say 1 equals no effect and 10 equals substantial or critical impact—will help decision making. A simple grid can then be constructed as in Figure 13.4.

For those companies that wish to structure the environmental analysis in a more detailed way, there are two different but complementary methods of impact analysis. The simplest is trend impact analysis

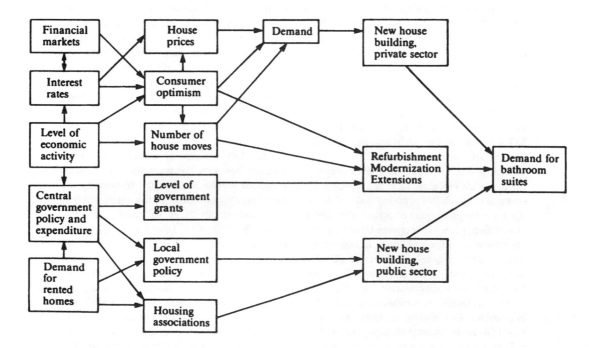

Figure 13.3   Influence diagram

Impact on UK car market \ Environment change	UK Government raises VAT	EU directive to limit exhaust emissions	EU announces plans for single currency	Japanese car makers abandon voluntary limits on imports to Europe	Technological breakthrough for battery cars
UK demand	8				
EU demand	0				
UK production levels	4				
Prices	8				
Production costs					
Marketing costs					

Figure 13.4   Environmental impact grid: 0 = no effect; 10 = substantial or critical impact

(TIA), where the movements in a particular variable are plotted over time and the projected value is assessed (Figure 13.5).

Cross-impact analysis (CIA) is used in an attempt to assess the impact of changes in one variable on other variables. This is much more difficult to do but at the minimum it will help mangers to understand the possible relationships between forces in the environment. At best, it will provide key information in order to aid strategic decision making (see Figure 13.6). According to Glueck (1980), the General Electric Company (USA) uses these impact grids as an aid to writing scenarios.

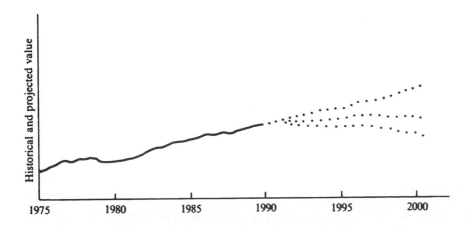

Figure 13.5   Trend impact analysis

Wild cards \ Possible events	OPEC force price of oil to $30/barrel	OPEC fall out: oil drops to $12/barrel with over-supply	Economic downturn becomes recession and lasts 5 years	Government increases car and petrol taxes	
Clean-burn petrol engine developed					
Japanese launch first mass-produced battery-powered car					
Environment deteriorates suddenly; car drivers in Western world limited to 30 miles per day					

Figure 13.6   Cross-impact analysis

Probability of success

	High	Low	
	1	2	High
	3	4	Low

Attractiveness

Figure 13.7   Opportunity matrix
1. Attractive opportunity which fits well with company's capabilities
2. Attractive opportunity but low probability of success; poor fit with company's capabilities
3. High probability of success if company takes this opportunity, but not an attractive market
4. Let's forget this one

A scenario for the late 1990s may be that the use of personal phones is set to grow very rapidly as the technology improves and prices continue to fall. Will young single professional people decide that they do not need a traditional fixed phone in their apartment? One mobile phone is all they need. Newly married couples may decide to have his and her personal phones rather than install a fixed phone in the home. A cross-impact study undertaken by British Telecom may reveal a serious threat to their traditional domestic fixed line business. What is more, it is likely that the high-income, high-use customers will be the first to desert.

13.4.6   Environmental threat and opportunity profile (ETOP)

Kotler (1991) defines a marketing opportunity as 'an attractive arena for company marketing action in which the company would enjoy a competitive advantage'. He suggests that opportunities should be assessed for their attractiveness and success probability. *Attractiveness* can be assessed in terms of potential market size, growth rates, profit margins, competitiveness and distribution channels; other factors may be technological requirements, degree of government interference, environmental concerns and energy requirements. Set against the measure of attractiveness is the *probability of success*. This depends on the company's strengths and competitive advantage—such issues as access to cash, lines of credit or capital to finance new developments. Technological and productive expertise, marketing skills, distribution channels and managerial competence will all need to be taken into account. A simple matrix (Figure 13.7) can be constructed to show the relationship between attractiveness and success probability.

In 1991 a new opportunity arose in the United Kingdom for companies to bid for commercial television breakfast franchises issued periodically by the government. Since the last issue in 1981 the government had changed the regulations (Broadcasting Act) for commercial television and the criteria by which bidders for the franchise would be judged. In short, the government's intention was to create more competition in the bidding to raise revenue and to curtail broadcasting monopolies. The franchise would now go to the highest bidder subject to a minimum 'quality threshold'. According to the *Observer* (Twisk and Brooks, 1991), a number of new bidders were attempting to take the franchise away from TV AM—in particular, a consortium called Daybreak, whose partners included ITN, the *Daily Telegraph*, MAI (an advertising group), Carlton Communications, NBC (American TV network) and Taylor Woodrow (a construction company). With the experience held by consortium members, it saw an opportunity for which there was a high probability of success. Among other bidders were a consortium that included London Weekend Television, STV (Southern Television) and Broadcast Communications (owned by the *Guardian* newspaper and Disney).

Kotler describes an environmental threat as 'a challenge posed by an unfavourable trend or development in the environment that would lead, in the absence of purposeful marketing action, to the erosion of the company's or industry's position'. In this case the threats should be assessed according to their seriousness and the probability of occurrence. A threat matrix can then be constructed (Figure 13.8).

Again, using the example of an existing TV franchise holder, a number of threats developed in the late 1980s. The Broadcasting Act meant that the next time the franchise came up for renewal the bidding would be much more competitive. Advertising revenues have been under pressure because of stagnant advertising spending resulting from the recession. The government has awarded a franchise for another new channel, Channel 5. There is pressure from some quarters for the BBC to be allowed to carry advertising so as to reduce its dependence on the public purse. Satellite TV and cable are well established and gaining in popularity. Production costs continue to rise. Sponsorship of programmes has been slow to take off.

In order for the environmental analysis to have a useful input into the marketing planning process, a wide range of information and opinions needs to be summarized in a meaningful way. This is parti-

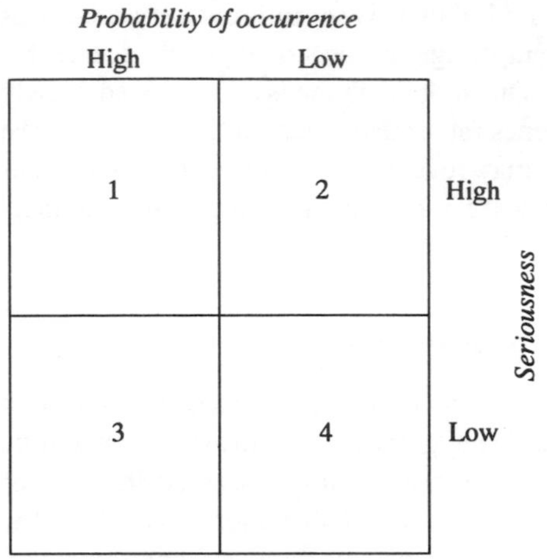

Probability of occurrence

High	Low	
1	2	High
3	4	Low

Seriousness

Figure 13.8   Threat matrix
1. Competitor launches superior product
2. Pound sterling rises to $3
3. Higher costs of raw materials
4. Legislation to cover 'environment friendly' claims on labels

Factor	Major opportunity	Minor opportunity	Neutral	Minor threat	Major threat	Probability
Economic						
Interest rates rise to 15%					✓	0.8
£ falls to $1.40	✓					0.4
Disposable incomes do not rise for 5 years				✓		0.3
Political						
Change of political party—more spending on education and public transport			✓			0.9
Legal						
EU bans flavouring additives in snacks				✓		0.1
Market						
Competitor launches major TV campaign				✓		0.5

Figure 13.9   Environmental threat and opportunity profile (ETOP): probability scale from 0.1 (very unlikely to happen) to 0.9 (very likely to happen)

cularly so if a number of the techniques described in this chapter have been used in a wide-ranging analysis. The information collated from the detailed analysis needs to be simplified and summarized for planning purposes. The environmental threat and opportunity profile (ETOP) provides a summary of the environmental factors that are most critical to the company (Figure 13.9). These provide a useful report to stimulate debate among senior management about the future of the business. Some authors suggest trying to weight these factors according to their importance and then rating them for their impact on the organization.

Marketing and business texts often refer to the SWOT analysis, which refers to strengths, weaknesses, opportunities and threats. As with ETOP, it is used to summarize the main environmental issues in the form of opportunities and threats facing the organization. With this technique, though, these are specifically listed alongside the strengths and weaknesses of the organization. The strengths and weaknesses are internal to the organization and the technique is used to put realism into the opportunities and threats. For example, the environment may be assessed as giving rise to a number of possible opportunities, but if the company is not capable of exploiting these because of internal weaknesses, then perhaps they should be left alone. Kotler (1991) suggests that these strengths and weaknesses be grouped under marketing, financial, manufacturing and organizational factors. The marketing audit discussed earlier in this chapter is one systematic method of assessing the internal strengths and weaknesses of the company.

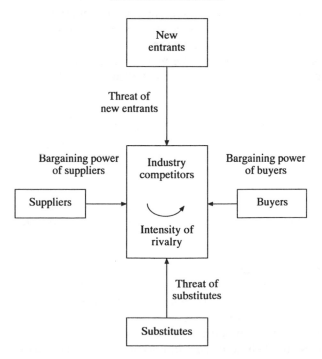

Figure 13.10   Industry competitiveness
Source: based on M. E. Porter (1985) *Competitive Advantage.*

13.4.7   Porter's five forces model of industry competitiveness

Porter's model helps managers identify the factors that affect the intensity of competition within a particular industry. The model illustrates the relationship between different players and potential players in the industry. The five forces requiring evaluation are: the power of suppliers, the power of buyers, the threat of new entrants, the threat of substitute products and the intensity of rivalry between competing firms (Figure 13.10).

The power of suppliers   The power of suppliers is likely to be high if the number of suppliers are few and/or the materials, components and services are in short supply. The suppliers of microprocessor silicone chips and compact discs have held a powerful market position due to their dominance of technology and high demand for their products.

The power of buyers   Buyer power is likely to be high if there are relatively few buyers, if there are alternative sources of supply and if the buyer has low switching costs. During the 1980s and 1990s Britain's grocery retailing has become increasingly dominated by seven very large organizations. According to the Nielsen Grocery Service (Nielsen, 1994) Asda, Co-operative, Iceland, Safeway, Sainsbury, Somerfield and Tesco held 72 per cent market share by turnover in 1992. Thus the power in the market-place has shifted away from the manufacturers of grocery products to the retailers.

The threat of new entrants   The threat of new entrants will be higher if there are low barriers to entry. New entrants may already be in the industry in another country but decide to move into your geographic market. A number of South Korean car manufacturers, including Hyundai and Daewoo, have moved into the UK and other European markets during the 1980s and 1990s. Some Indian motor cycle and scooter manufacturers (who have a very strong home market and low costs of production) are beginning to show interest in European markets. Alternatively, new entrants may arrive from outside the industry. BIC, whose technology base was plastic moulding, made disposable ball-point pens. Some years ago they were able to successfully diversify into the wet shave razor market with plastic disposable razors, thus challenging established market leaders such as Gillette and Wilkinson in their core business.

The threat of substitute products   Substitute products are likely to emerge from alternative technologies, particularly as the economics of production change. Initially the new technology may have high costs associated with it. However, as the technology and experience develops, the level of investment rises and production volumes increase, then costs of production will fall with economies of scale. Manufacturers will then look for more and more applications. Artificial sweeteners for sugar, lighters for matches, plastic containers for glass, polyester for cotton and personal computers for typewriters are obvious examples. These substitutes may change the whole economics of an industry and threaten the survival of the traditional product providers.

Intensity of rivalry between competing firms   The intensity of rivalry may be high if two or more firms are fighting for dominance in a fast growing market. For example, this occurred in the UK's personal phone market during the mid 1990s and in the fight to establish the dominant format for the domestic VCR player during the early 1980s between three competing technologies, VHS (the UK winner), Betamax and U-matic. The need is to become established as the dominant technology or brand before the industry matures. Companies are likely to engage heavily in promotional activity involving advertising and promotional incentives to buy. In a mature industry, particularly if it is characterized by high fixed costs and excess capacity, the intensity of competitive rivalry may be very high. This is because manufacturers (e.g. cars) or service providers (e.g. airlines) need to operate at near

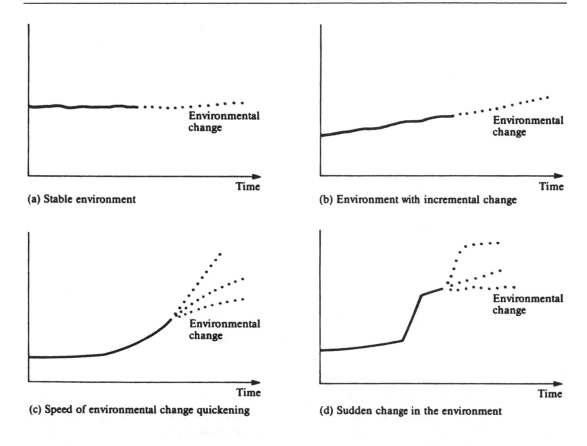

Figure 13.11 Four patterns of environmental change: — past trend, … future trend

maximum capacity to cover overhead costs. As the industry matures or at times of cyclical down-turn, or when a number of companies have invested in new capacity, firms fight to maintain their maximum level of sales. Price cuts and discounting may become commonplace and profits will be eroded. Low-cost procedures with high brand loyalty have the best chance of survival.

Porter's five forces model of industry competitiveness helps understanding of the microenvironment. Monitoring these forces will provide managers with some insight into the competitive rivalry that characterizes their industry.

13.5 FORMING A VIEW OF ENVIRONMENTAL INFLUENCE

The pace at which senior managers believe the environment is changing and the nature of that change is likely to influence their decision making and planning. Four broad patterns of environmental change may be considered, as shown in Figure 13.11. In part (a) of the figure senior management believes that there is a stable environment with little change; in part (b) senior management believes that there is incremental change at a known and predictable pace; in part (c) the pace of change is quickening and becoming harder to anticipate; in part (d) the environment may be subject to sudden change as a major factor has a dramatic impact on other environmental forces—for example sudden steep increases in oil prices.

	Stable	Dynamic
Complex	Difficult to handle but little change	Very uncertain, high risk
Simple	Predictable	Fast-moving but predictable

Figure 13.12   Simple/complex and stable/dynamic environments

Other considerations for senior management are whether the environment is simple or complex and stable or dynamic (Figure 13.12). Here it is the relationship between the company and its environment that is in question and whether this is changing. Is the environment moving from being simple to becoming more complex, for example? Or is it moving from a period of stability into one of dynamism? The same environmental change may be seen as an opportunity by one company and a threat by another. The view taken will be influenced by the analysis undertaken, the views of senior management and the ability of the company to respond.

Chapter 2 introduced readers to the three basic components of the marketing environment, which were the organization's internal environment and the external environment comprising the micro-environment and the macroenvironment. The organization's internal environment refers to the structure, processes and activities of the marketing department itself and its relationship to other business functions and activities. This is the controllable environment. The external environment is the uncontrollable element and has two components. The microenvironment is composed of all organizations and individuals who directly or indirectly affect the activities of the organization. This is sometimes referred to as the industry or task environment. It is thus necessary for the organization to track the behaviour of the market, its competitors, customers, channel members and suppliers. The macroenvironment is composed of those forces that influence the international and domestic economy and society as a whole. These forces are sometimes summarized as sociological, technological, economic and political and are often abbreviated to STEP, or PEST to aid memory.

Having completed an analysis of the business and marketing environment, ideally by means of a marketing audit, the information needs to be distilled into a SWOT summary (Figure 13.13). The strengths and weaknesses are in respect of the organization's internal environment and the opportunities and threats come from the external environment. Management needs to be able to answer the questions 'Where are we now?' and 'Where are we likely to go?', given the present performance and future environment. The SWOT summary, then, provides a key input to the planning process. If we assume that we are preparing a marketing plan for a strategic business unit (an SBU may be a subsidiary or division of a larger organization), then the chief executive officer (CEO) has to set the business objectives for the coming financial year. In arriving at a decision the CEO has to balance a number of conflicting demands. The parent organization and the board of directors will have expectations regarding the performance of the SBU. These will be expressed in financial terms such as return on capital employed (ROCE), sales revenue, profit as a percentage of sales and rate of growth, etc. The chief executive of the SBU is involved in negotiations during the setting of these objectives. During the process the CEO is conscious of the recent performance of the business (from the internal audit) and

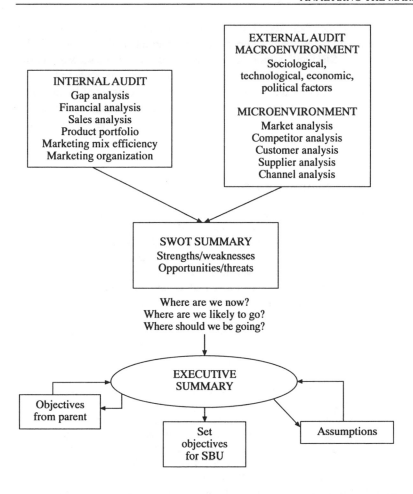

Figure 13.13   Links between environmental analysis and planning

the threats and opportunities presented from the external audit. In accepting the financial objectives from the parent organization the CEO needs to ensure that they are realistic and achievable, given the current and future environment. This may seem obvious but remember that the parent organization may be a multinational with a head office in another country or continent. The environmental forces to which the head office managers and directors are exposed may be quite different from those influencing the local SBU.

In negotiating the objectives with the parent and in setting the SBU objectives it is beneficial to state explicitly the key assumptions made. Therefore, if the growth rate of the economy will directly influence your business it is necessary to state what level you have assumed over the planning period. Likewise for interest rates, levels of disposable income, business confidence indices and exchange rates. These would all be primary assumptions. If your business is dependent on others then some secondary or derived assumptions may need to be stated. If 80 per cent of your business is sales to the automotive industry then specifying the assumed level of car sales would be important. Likewise, if you manufacture bathroom suites and fittings your business is directly dependent on the sales of new housing and the refurbishment of existing housing stock, both of which are influenced by the level of interest rates (Figure 13.3).

Planning in larger businesses is a complex activity. Once the business operates over a number of product groups, industries and international markets, then an environmental analysis needs to be conducted at the local level as well as the SBU and corporate level. Forming a cohesive view about the environment becomes much more difficult. In managing a business senior executives have to balance the immediate requirements of existing operations against the longer-term requirements of shaping and developing the future business. Where does the organization wish to be in five and ten years time? Since the organization cannot change the business environment it would be wise to attempt to monitor and predict it and then to shape the business to maximize the opportunities and minimize the threats.

TV SHAKE-UP

The UK television industry is set for another shake-up and shake-out over the next few years. Mrs Bottomley, the Government Minister responsible for the media, published a new Broadcasting Bill in December 1995 (*The Times* 1995). Given a smooth passage through Parliament it should come into force during 1997.

Background

During the early 1980s TV manufacturers found themselves in a depressed market. There had been little to excite the industry since the introduction of colour in the late 1960s. In a mature market where virtually every home had one, and without the elements of fashion or new technology to drive consumer purchases, TV sales were flat. The growth of the small-screen TV for supplementary use in other rooms of the home was the only bright spot. Large multiproduct electronic companies were able to use their resources to develop offerings in new product categories, such as the video recorder. These circumstances generated intense competition in the TV market with little product differentiation, weak prices and very low profits. Many smaller companies went bankrupt and larger companies closed factories or withdrew from the TV market altogether.

During the 1980s and early 1990s things were to change, slowly at first but then with increasing speed. In the early 1980s the UK government licensed a new commercial channel, CH4, and allowed a new franchise for Breakfast TV. By the end of the decade Satellite TV and multichannel cable TV were both developing due to the new technology and changes in government regulations. In the United Kingdom two satellite companies became operational in the 1980s offering more

choice—for a price. This was soon to be reduced to one as SKY took over the struggling BSB to become B-SKY-B. Cable companies were able to take advantage of two developments. The first was fibre optic cable which allowed multichannel delivery of a very high quality. The problem was the need to lay sufficient cable quickly. The second development was the source of programmes that could now be provided to cable companies via satellite services.

The UK population which had been used to only three channels in 1980 found themselves with a bewildering choice by 1990. However, consumers had been too used to virtually free TV. The commercial TV stations were paid for from advertising revenues and the government-controlled BBC was financed via the annual licence fee. In 1995 the BBC licence fee was still under £90 per year compared to the cost of cable or satellite of between £11 and £25 per month, which was in addition to the BBC fee. The satellite and cable services also have additional equipment and connection costs.

In addition to all the technological changes the government has had to re-evaluate its procedures for issuing licences to TV providers and the rules by which the franchise holders should operate. In the early days of commercial TV the government issued franchises to regional TV companies. These regional companies had agreements and procedures which enabled them to supply programmes to the national network. This gave the appearance of a national TV service with local ownership and some local programming. Because of rules against monopoly providers and cross-media ownership the TV service provider industry remained small scale by international comparisons.

The New Broadcasting Bill

In controlled industries affected by rapid technological change governments have difficulty keeping up with appropriate legislation and rules. The government introduced the Cable and Broadcasting Act 1984 and the Broadcasting Act as recently as 1990 and yet the government was back in 1995 with new proposals and aiming to have them on the statute book by 1997. According to Frean reporting in *The Times* (1995), some of the main proposals of the new Bill are:

- Relaxation of the tight restrictions on cross-media ownership of newspapers and television.
- Newspaper publishers controlling less than 20 per cent of the national market will be able to buy TV companies outright and radio stations.
- Scrapping of the restriction which limits ownership to two TV licences.
- New monopoly controls limiting licence holders to controlling 15 per cent of the total audience.
- New licences for digital terrestrial TV and radio services. Licences for up to 18 new terrestrial TV stations may be on offer.

Digital TV, according to a *Times* reporter will 'offer the opportunity of high definition pictures and near CD quality sound, but to receive it viewers will need to purchase a set top digital decoder box costing between £300 and £500'. All existing terrestrial broadcasters will be offered digital channels enabling them to duplicate their existing analogue services as well as providing new pay and view services. New providers will be encouraged to enter the market for the remaining licences. In order to encourage the development of the new technology and services, the government has said that there will be no licence fee payable during the first franchise period of 12 years. Also proposed is that the licence can be 'rolled over' into a second period subject to conditions. It appears that once this new technology becomes established the government may wish to 'clear the (old) analogue spectrum quickly to free it for lucrative commercial use such as telecommunications'.

The new bill has had an immediate impact on the share prices of some TV licence holders and newspaper groups as speculation mounts over mergers and takeovers. According to Mrs Bottomley reported in *The Times*, 'Our proposals will liberate British broadcasters to become world leaders.' The creation of British owned multimedia conglomerates is now a real possibility. However, in a week when the BBC lost another international sporting event to B-SKY-B, concerns have been raised in Parliament. These multimedia multinationals will be able to outbid any domestic provider for world interest and domestic interest programmes. These will then be screened over premium priced pay channels which restrict access. Other concerns are over the potential loss of regional programming, and not just UK regions such as Scotland or Anglia or the South West. Some national governments are concerned about the invasion of American programmes and the dominance of the English language. They fear not only for the survival of their domestic TV service providers and programme makers but for the dilution of their language and culture. This makes the provision of European Union legislation and regulation particularly difficult to achieve.

With differing national legislation and regulations covering so many providers—satellite, cable, terrestrial broadcasters, digital frequencies, programme makers, programme owners and advertisers—it is difficult to have a fair and level playing field in regulatory terms. The issues are compounded by ownership and corporate objectives—foreign-owned multinational corporations providing services by satellite, competing in the same market against public-owned broadcasters with a public duty to educate and inform as well as entertain, and local ITV companies who won their franchise partly on the amount paid to the government in fees and partly on a quality threshold based on their proposed programme schedules. The blend of commercial forces, quality criteria and public duty makes for a unique industry.

QUESTIONS

1. Identify the types of organizations that provide products and services to the TV industry and those that are involved in its regulation.
2. Identify the environmental forces impacting on the UK TV industry during the mid 1990s.
3. Why are governments so concerned about the media and so heavily involved in its regulation?
4. You are an advisor to the BBC. Using an appropriate tool such as an impact grid or ETOP (environmental threat and opportunity profile) prepare a report for senior management on the business environment.
5. You are an advisor to a small regional ITV company with five years remaining of your licence. Conduct an environmental analysis and produce a SWOT summary.

REVIEW QUESTIONS

1. What factors make an organization's environment so complex?   (6 marks)
   Using an industry example, suggest relevant sources of information it might access to help it understand its complexity.   (14 marks)
   (CIM Marketing Environment Examination, December 1994, Q.6)
2. Your government has approached an independent group of economic forecasters to undertake a 'SWOT' analysis of the national economy. Prepare a short series of relevant slides to support the forthcoming presentation of this analysis.
   (CIM Marketing Environment Examination, June 1995, Q.7)
3. All the industries listed below experienced a turbulent business environment during the early 1990s. Select one of these industries (or any other industry with which you are familiar) and identify the changes encountered.
   Telephones, TV, hospitals, electricity, defence, computing, retailing
4. Choose an industry and look ahead about three to five years and build a scenario for the future.
5. Construct an influence diagram (see Figure 13.3) for a product category of your choosing. Some ideas are:
   (a) Retirement apartments (private sector for sale or rent)
   (b) Children's bikes
   (c) Conservatories
   (d) Fabric material (used for curtaining and furniture coverings)
   (e) Computer-controlled document handling machinery (for handling, collating and folding documents or leaflets and stuffing envelopes).
6. For those of you in work attempt to construct an 'environmental impact grid' for your business.

REFERENCES

Ansoff, H. I. (1984) *Implementing Strategic Management*, Prentice-Hall, Englewood Cliffs, NJ.
Christopher, M., McDonald, M. and Wills, G. (1980) *Introducing Marketing*, Pan, London.
Diffenbach, J. (1983) 'Corporate Environmental Analysis in US Corporations', *Long Range Planning*, vol. 16, no. 3, pp. 107–16.
Frean, A. (1995) 'Bottomley eases restrictions on TV ownership', *The Times*, 16 December 1995, p. 4.
Glueck, W. F. (1980) Business Policy and Strategic Management, 3rd edn, McGraw-Hill, New York.
Jenster, P. V. (1987) 'Using Critical Success Factors in Planning', Long Range Planning, vol. 20, no. 4, pp. 102–9.
Johnson, G. and Scholes, K. (1984) *Exploring Corporate Strategy*, Prentice-Hall International, Hemel Hempstead.
Kotler, P. (1991) *Marketing Management: Analysis, Planning, Implementation and Control*, 7th edn, Prentice-Hall International, Hemel Hempstead.
Narchal, R. M., *et al.* (1987) 'An Environmental Scanning System for Business Planning', *Long Range Planning*, vol. 20, no. 6, pp. 96–105.
Nielsen (1994) *The Retail Pocket Book 1995*, NTC Publications Ltd.
Piercy, N. (1985) *Marketing Organization: An Analysis of Information Processing, Power and Politics*, Allen and Unwin, London.
Porter, M. E. (1985) *Competitive Advantage*, Free Press, New York.
Twisk, R. and Brooks, R. (1991) 'Ex-BBC chief spearheads breakfast bid with blast at "Terrible TV-am" ', *The Observer*, 28 April 1991, p. 1.

GLOSSARY

Accelerator effect   The idea that a small increase in consumer expenditure can lead to a very large increase in investment in capital equipment.

Aggregate demand   The total expenditure on goods and services in an economy.

Balance of payments   A record of all transactions between domestic consumers and firms and those based overseas.

Branding   The process of creating a distinctive identity for a product which differentiates it from its competitors.

Business cycle   Fluctuations in the level of activity in an economy, commonly measured by employment levels and aggregate demand.

Cartel   An association of suppliers which seeks to restrict costly competition between its members.

Competitive advantage   A firm has a marketing mix that the target market sees as meeting its needs better than the mix of competing firms.

Cost-push inflation   Price inflation that results from an increase in the cost of producing goods and services.

Cross-elasticity of demand   A measure of the responsiveness of demand for one good or service to changes in the price of another good or service.

Culture   The whole set of beliefs, attitudes and ways of behaving shared by a group of people.

Customers   People who buy a firm's products. (*Note*: customers may not be the actual *consumers* of the product.)

Demand-pull inflation   Price inflation which results from excessive demand for goods and services relative to their supply.

Demography   The study of population characteristics.

Devaluation   A reduction in the value of one currency in relation to other currencies.

Direct marketing   Direct communication between a seller and individual customers using a promotion method other than face-to-face selling.

Discriminatory pricing   Selling a product at two or more prices, where the difference in prices is not based on differences in costs.

Ecu   The European Currency Unit, not familiar to most private consumers, but frequently used in interorganizational and intergovernmental transactions in Europe.

Entrepreneur   An individual who takes risks to profitably exploit business opportunities.

Environment   Everything that exists outside the boundaries of a system.

Environmental set   The elements within an organization's environment which are currently of major concern to it.

EU   The European Union, formerly known as the European Community (EC).

Exchange rate   The price of one currency expressed in terms of another currency.

Exclusion clause   A clause in a contract which excludes or restricts liability of one party to the other.

External benefits   Product benefits for which the producer cannot appropriate value from recipients.

External costs   Production costs which are borne by individuals or firms who are not compensated for the costs they incur.

Factors of production   The inputs to a value creation process, commonly defined as land, labour and capital (entrepreneurship is often included).

Fiscal policy   Government policy on public borrowing, spending and taxation.

Five forces   Porter's model of the competitive environment of any firm, which comprises the threat of new entrants and substitute products, the bargaining powers of customers and suppliers, and competition among current competitors.

Franchise   An agreement where a franchisor develops a good service format and marketing strategy and sells the right for other individuals or organizations ('franchisees') to use that format.

Gross Domestic Product (GDP)   A measure of the value of goods and services produced in an economy during a specified period.

Gross National Product (GNP)   Similar to GDP, but with the addition of net income earned from overseas investments (after deducting investments remitted overseas).

Horizontal integration   Merging of firms' activities at a similar point in a value chain.

Human resource management   Management activity related to the effective and efficient recruitment, training, motivation, reward and control of an organization's employees.

Imperfect market   A market in which the assumptions of perfect competition are violated.

Implied term   A term in a contract which is understood by the parties, but not explicitly written into it.

Income elasticity of demand   A measure of the responsiveness of demand for a product to changes in household incomes.

Inflation   A rise in the general level of prices of goods and services.

Intermediaries   Individuals or organizations who are involved in transferring goods and services from the producer to the final consumer.

Internal marketing   The application of the principles and practices of marketing to an organization's dealings with its employees.

Investment   Expenditure on products which are not consumed immediately, but which will yield further economic benefits in the future.

Invisible trade   Overseas trade in services, as distinct from 'visible' goods.

Joint venture   An agreement between two or more firms to exploit a business opportunity, in which capital funding, profits, risk and core competencies are shared.

Just-in-time delivery   Reliably getting products to customers just before customers need them.

Macroeconomics   The study of the working of large scale economic systems.

Marginal cost   The addition to total cost resulting from the production of one additional unit of output.

Market   A group of potential customers with similar needs who are willing to exchange something of value with sellers offering products that satisfy their needs.

Market economy   An economy which distributes goods and services on the basis of consumers' decisions rather than centrally planned allocation.

Market failure   A situation where the assumptions underlying competitive markets break down, resulting in inefficient and ineffective distribution of goods and services.

Market segmentation   A process of identifying groups of customers within a broad product market who share similar needs and respond similarly to a given marketing mix formulation.

Marketing   The management process which identifies, anticipates and supplies customer requirements efficiently and profitable (CIM definition).

Marketing audit A systematic review of a company's marketing activities and of its marketing environment.

Marketing mix The aspects of marketing strategy and tactics that marketing management use to gain a competitive advantage over its competitors. A conceptual framework which usually includes elements labelled product, price, promotion, place, people, physical evidence and processes.

Matrix organization An organization structure which relies on coordination of management functions, rather than a strict hierarchical functional control.

Merger The amalgamation of two or more organizations.

Microeconomics The study of the behaviour of individual economic units (e.g. consumers and firms).

Misrepresentation A false statement made by one party in a contract.

Mission statement A means of reminding everyone within an organization of the essential purpose of the organization.

Monetarism A view of the national economy which attributes instability in the economy to issues of money supply.

Money supply The amount of money in an economy.

Monopoly A market in which there is only one supplier. Rarely achieved in practice, as most products have some form of substitute.

Multiplier effect The addition to total income and expenditure within an economy resulting from an initial injection of expenditure.

Needs The underlying forces that drive an individual to make a purchase and thereby satisfy that individual's needs.

Oligopoly A market dominated by a few interdependent suppliers.

Perfect competition A market in which there are no barriers to entry, no one firm can dominate the market, there is full information available to all buyers and sellers, and all sellers sell an undifferentiated product.

Positioning Developing a marketing mix which gives an organization a competitive advantage within its chosen target market.

Pressure group A group which is formed to promote a particular cause.

Price elasticity of demand A measure of the responsiveness of demand for a product to change in the price of the product.

Privatization Government policy to transfer economic activity from the public to the private sector.

Product mix The total range of goods and services offered by an organization.

Productivity The efficiency with which inputs are turned into outputs.

Profit The excess of revenue over costs (although it can be difficult to calculate costs, and therefore profit).

Quality The standard of delivery of goods or services, often expressed in terms of the extent to which they meet customers' expectations.

Relationship marketing A means by which organizations seek to maintain an ongoing relationship between itself and its customers, based on continuous patterns of service delivery, rather than isolated and discrete transactions.

Social responsibility Accepting corporate responsibilities to customers and non-customers which go beyond legal or contractual requirements.

Sole trader A business the identify of which is indistinguishable from that of its owner.

Stakeholder Any person with an interest in the activities of an organization (e.g. customers, employees, government agencies, and local communities).

Value chain The sequence of activities and organizations involved in transforming a product from one which is of low value to one that is of high value.

Vertical integration   The extension of a firm's activities to prior or subsequent points in a value chain.

Visible trade   Overseas trade in manufactured goods.

AUTHOR INDEX

SUBJECT INDEX